EASTERN EUROPE

Focusing on the post-war period, David Turnock sets the economic and political geography of Eastern Europe in the broad context of its history and its physical landscape. He looks at the position of 'problem regions' which have affected the stability of the countries concerned: these include Slovakia in Czechoslovakia and Macedonia in Bulgaria and Yugoslavia. He examines boundary changes, which have long been a part of the political culture of the region, paying particular attention to the case of Berlin. The main demographic features are covered, notably living standards, natural increase, migration, and ethnicity.

The economic section includes a review of living standards, a discussion of central planning, and accounts of industrial planning and regional development, the agricultural sector, and the burgeoning tourist industry.

Together with the author's *The Human Geography of Eastern Europe*, this book forms a comprehensive study of the human geography of this region. It also complements Turnock's previous books: *Eastern Europe: An Historical Geography 1815–1945* and *The Making of Eastern Europe: From the Earliest Times to 1815*.

David Turnock is Reader in Geography at the University of Leicester.

EASTERN EUROPE

AN ECONOMIC AND POLITICAL GEOGRAPHY

DAVID TURNOCK

ROUTLEDGE
London and New York

First published 1989
by Routledge
11 New Fetter Lane, London EC4P 4EE
29 West 35th Street, New York, NY 10001

British Library Cataloguing in Publication Data

Turnock, David, *1938–*
　Eastern Europe: an economic and political
　geography.
　1. Eastern Europe. Social conditions
　I. Title
　947

　0-415-03740-9

Library of Congress Cataloging-in-Publication Data

Turnock, David.
　Eastern Europe: an economic and political geography / David
Turnock.
　　p. cm.
　Bibliography: p.
　Includes index.
　ISBN 0-415-03740-9
　1. Europe, Eastern – Economic conditions – 1945– 2. Europe,
Eastern – Politics and government – 1945– 3. Communism – Europe,
Eastern. I. Title.
HC244.T823　1989
330.947'0854-dc19　　　　　　　　　　　　　　　　　88-30333
　　　　　　　　　　　　　　　　　　　　　　　　　　　CIP

CONTENTS

v

LIST OF FIGURES

Figures

LIST OF TABLES

LIST OF ABBREVIATIONS

AIC	Agricultural-Industrial Complex
FAO	Food and Agriculture Organization
FRG	Federal Republic of (West) Germany
GDR	German Democratic Republic (East Germany)
GNP	Gross national product
IAC	Industrial-Agricultural Complex
LPG	Local collective farm (GDR)
NATO	North Atlantic Treaty Organization
NEM	New Economic Mechanism
VEG	State farm (GDR)

ACKNOWLEDGEMENTS

Eastern Europe is already well served by geography texts in the English language. Although the number of books is not great in comparison with other regions of the world, there is useful complementarity and the reader can choose between books which provide detailed information on individual countries with only limited coverage of general themes relevant to the region as a whole (Osborne 1967; Pounds 1969) and works which concentrate on the broader issues to the partial or complete exclusion of individual national profiles (Mellor 1975; Turnock, 1978). However, all the books available are now several years out of date and cannot offer much guidance on the important preoccupations of the present and the immediate future. Equally, the literature available in the journals for the 1980s cannot be summarized and referenced for the reader's convenience. It is the purpose of the present work to provide an up-date, concentrating on the themes relevant to the late 1980s, with general outlines supplemented by examples and case studies wherever possible. The work complements the author's previous books on The Historical Geography of Eastern Europe published by Routledge in 1988.

It was originally intended that the whole work should be published in one volume but it has proved necessary to divide the material into two separate publications. This books covers the political geography and the 'core' elements of the economic geography, while coverage of what can be broadly termed the infrastructure (trade, transport, energy, settlement patterns, and conservation) will be found in a companion volume entitled The Human Geography of Eastern Europe. Each book is divided into two sections with four chapters in each. The first chapter in each section provides a general review and a contextual essay for the more specialized studies which follow. A good many of the examples and illustrations are drawn from the author's own research on Romania. At the risk of over-emphasizing one country, this does allow for the elaboration of many aspects of central planning without excessive copying of the work of other writers.

Because there are other textbooks available to provide basic groundwork and to give detailed coverage of the events of the early post-war period, the referencing of articles is generally restricted to work which has appeared since 1970 (although in the case of books the more valuable items of the 1945-70 period are mentioned). It is often necessary to refer to particular parts of certain countries and the word 'region' is reserved for the official administrative regions (to avoid the complexities of using the various national labels like the Bezirke in the GDR, judet in Romania, or wojewodztwo in Poland).

Thanks are due to all the authors whose research is acknowledged in the pages that follow: without such analyses and commentaries works of synthesis would be virtually impossible. It is also a pleasure to thank Peter Sowden and Alan Jarvis at Routledge for their encouragement over the project and forebearance over the delays in delivering the typescript.

David Turnock
Leicester
July 1988

INTRODUCTION

Eastern Europe has never been prominent in the minds of English speakers, and westerners generally for that matter, but the rise of Russia to superpower status in the context of a Marxist ideology has converted the heart of Europe into a geopolitical watershed and given a new significance to the states lying immediately to the east of this divide. A substantial part of what used to be called 'Central Europe' has emerged as 'Eastern Europe', with coherence arising from government by Communist Parties conforming closely to the Soviet model. The fundamental characteristics of a socialist system of government are difficult to identify beyond appreciation of the Marxist inspiration of radical action by elites seeking to overcome the perceived evils of capitalism. The Soviet model of 'rapid industrialization, centrally planned within a system of state ownership of the means of production', and limited respect for consumption benefits and other human rights have been the strategies widely adopted by Communist Parties which have voluntarily selected elements of the system, or by others which have experienced Soviet coercion. (1) The visitor will certainly be impressed by the ability of monopoly parties to project themselves through propaganda and architecture; by the direct control exerted over the economy through state-owned industry and through the organization of most of the agriculture and services on a co-operative basis; and by the control of the individual through restrictions on international travel and a preference for investment in communal facilities rather than enhanced allocation of resources to individual families through higher wages and welfare benefits.

1

Figure I.1 Eastern Europe: the physical background

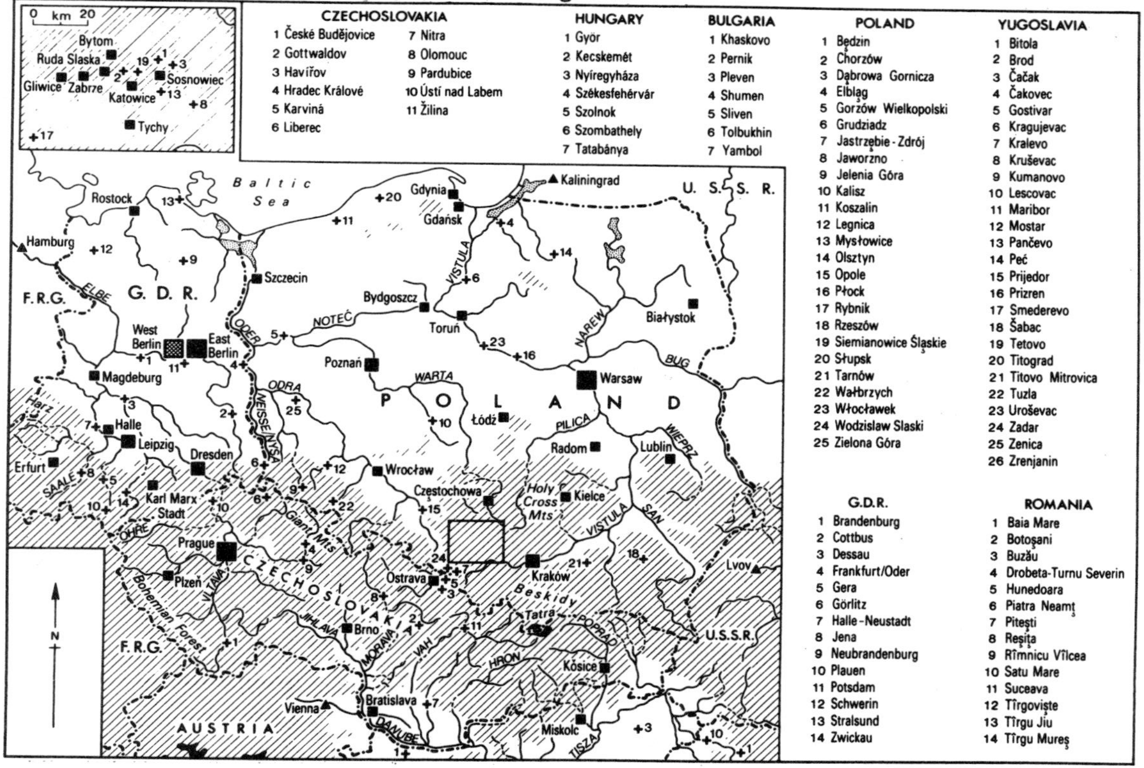

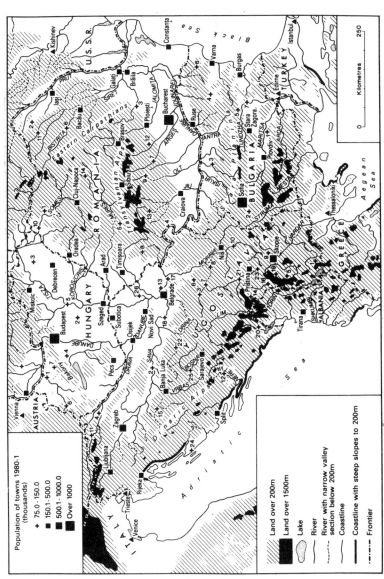

Source: World Atlases.

Writers are often preoccupied with the socialist character of Eastern Europe. It probably follows, in part, from an interest in regional geography and the responsibility of portraying an area as significantly, if not uniquely, distinct from others. It may also follow from the reaction to modelling in geography with its underlying assumption of uniformity: socialist Eastern Europe could be portrayed as being fundamentally different from the capitalist west. Differences can however be overstated and it is important to look beyond the simplistic formula that all modern developments are distinctly socialist because they are conditioned by socialist governments. 'Certainly the idea of a socialist landscape is intriguing but its establishment will rest on continued research on specific forms, their origin and change through time. (2) Equally, assertions about the inherent superiority of the socialist system should be subject to scrutiny. Revolutionary commitment by ruling groups should not conceal the possibility of more sustained development by governments which do not claim any emotive ideological commitment. Excessive copying of the Soviet model by small nation-states which cannot isolate themselves from the wider world market indefinitely has resulted in a cumbersome decision-making system which has difficulty in working towards international specialization with the requirement of constant adaptation to changing world-market trends. However, such shortcomings may be regarded primarily as a Soviet responsibility since the Soviets have imposed constraints on economic reform without being prepared to offer financial concessions in compensation. Autarky has certainly been broken down since the Khrushchev era when Comecon began to work for greater specialization, and closer contacts with the non-communist world have, on the whole, satisfied an important precondition for further progress. Realizing the potential is an issue which lies at the root of Eastern Europe's economic crisis today. With the Gorbachev era in the Soviet Union it seems that greater realism will prevail in the years ahead.

It cannot be overlooked that socialist policies have been applied to a terrain with its own specific characteristics (Figure I.1). With an area of 1.27 million square kilometres Eastern Europe is only 5.7 per cent the size of the Soviet Union (13.6 per cent of the USA) but is four times larger than the British Isles. In terms of north-south distances the maximum and minimum figures are 1.65 and 1.05 thousand kilometres respectively. Comparable figures for east-west distances are 1.25 and 0.65 respectively. Some parts of the region are as much as 600 kilometres from the sea, although navigable rivers, to say nothing of modern infrastucture, have reduced the significance of this apparent isolation. Contrasts in relief are spectacular; with Alpine-type fold mountain chains (most notably the Carpathian and Dinaric systems) and Hercynian plateau country of Bohemia and adjacent areas contrasting with the North European Plain and other extensive lowlands in Lower and Middle Danubia. Some 23.2 per cent of the land of Eastern Europe lies above 500 metres but the proportion is much higher in the south (37.1 per cent) than in the north (11.6); and it is in the south where the alignment of mountain chains achieves particular significance for cultural development through the influence exerted on the thrust of Prehistoric and Dark Age migration (Table I.1). The survival of a Romanized Dacian population in Transylvania, the base of the modern Romanian state, must be seen in the context of the encircling Carpathians and the availability of easier lines of advance to the north and south-east to Pannonia and the Black Sea coastlands respectively. Furthermore, given the lower latitudes and higher sunshine levels in the south, much of the mountain zone has a significant agricultural potential. The four Balkan countries and the southern half of Hungary have mean July temperatures in excess of 20°C; and with the exception of Baragan, Dobrogea, and Moldavia, rainfall exceeds 50 cm/20 inches. The mountains in the southern part of Eastern Europe offer a substantial mineral endowment including fuels (coal, gas, and oil) and ores (ferrous and non-ferrous). The North European Plain has for long been the scene of coal-mining (hard coal in Upper Silesia and lignite in Lusatia and Saxony) and further reserves have recently been discovered, but other minerals are not prominent apart from copper in Lower Silesia and sulphur in Tarnobrzeg.

Equally it cannot be overlooked that the eight nations of Eastern Europe have their own interests arising from ethnic origin and historical experience as well as the territorial base already referred to. Complexity is only too clearly evident in both cases with a process of migration extending from Prehistory to the resettlement programmes carried out after the Second World War and a turbulent history involving not only the fluctuating relations between nation states but the conflicting economic and territorial interests of city states and empires as well. Each state in

Table I.1 Relief and land use

	Area distributed according to altitudinal zones 000 square kilometres							Land use, 000 square kilometres: Agriculture			
	Below 200m	200-499m	500-999m	1,000-1,499m	1,500-1,999m	Above 1,999m	Total	Arable	Pasture	Forest	Other
Czechoslovakia	15.1	68.4	40.9	3.0	0.4	*	127.9	51.7	16.9	45.4	13.9
GDR	74.6	22.8	10.8	-	-	-	108.2	50.2	12.3	29.4	16.3
Hungary	77.6	14.8	0.6	*	-	-	93.0	53.3	12.9	15.9	10.9
Poland	234.2	69.1	9.1	0.3	-	-	312.7	149.2	40.3	86.9	36.3
NORTH	401.5	175.1	61.4	3.4	0.4	*	641.8	304.4	82.4	177.6	77.4
Albania	7.2	6.2	7.5	5.6	1.9	0.4	28.7	6.0	6.2	13.5	3.0
Bulgaria	35.2	38.5	23.2	9.6	3.5	1.2	110.9	43.8	18.1	38.4	10.6
Rumania	103.8	63.9	45.9	17.8	5.1	1.0	237.5	105.0	44.6	63.4	24.5
Yugoslavia	71.8	72.0	70.1	34.0	6.9	1.0	255.8	78.8	63.4	92.6	21.0
SOUTH	218.0	180.6	146.7	67.0	17.4	3.6	632.9	233.6	132.3	207.9	59.1
EASTERN EUROPE	619.5	355.7	208.1	70.4	17.8	3.6	1,274.7	538.0	214.7	385.5	136.5

Sources: J. Breu (1970) Atlas der Donauländer, Vienna: Osterreichisches Ost- und Sudosteuropa Institut), and statistical yearbooks.

Note: * denotes a total less than 0.1.

Eastern Europe can turn for inspiration to great achievements in the past but none can look back on a history of continuous existence extending even through modern times. In every country, therefore, there is the reality of a complex inheritance expressed in terms of ethnic minorities, variations in levels of economic development, and acute sensitivity over issues of sovereignty. All too easily it is overlooked that there are specific national characteristics in Eastern Europe, many of them relating to the pre-socialist period, and that the modernization process began long before the communists took power after 1945. It is often pointed out that communist regimes are essentially conservative, proudly inheriting much of the bureaucracy and protocol constructed by previous regimes. Equally, it could be argued that there is a large measure of continuity in economic development with the accelerated pace of modernization arising not so much from a new ideology of 'socialism' as from an extension of older strategies, making full use of new technology (such as electrification) and mobilizing the population without many of the human rights and financial rewards which westerners would normally expect in return for their labour.

The landscape of Eastern Europe reflects all these factors very clearly. (3) The growth of settlements and industrial complexes, integrated by a modern infrastructure (including transport, power supply, water, and drainage) is everywhere apparent and the patterns are broadly comparable with those found in other parts of the developed world. However, the relatively low levels of personal prosperity can be seen in the emphasis on apartment blocks in the towns, the overwhelming importance of public transport, the limited supply of shopping facilities and other services, and the low priority afforded to ecological problems. The complex cultural legacy emerges through settlement patterns, architectural styles, and local customs which have been only partially modified since 1945. Further, the attitudes of people in Eastern Europe are inevitably conditioned by awareness of earlier regimes, although increasingly such awareness arises through the education process. Particularly important here is the political geography of the inter-war period when the dismantling of the great empires of Central Europe provided for a degree of national self-expression unprecedented in modern times (Figure I.2). While the communist governments characteristically regard their predecessors as economically

Figure I.2 The political geography of Eastern Europe, 1918–39

Source: National atlases

conservative and socially reactionary the achievement of independence within specific frontiers is fundamental and any failure to maintain these frontiers remains a matter of great significance. The first half of the book therefore concentrates on the political geography, focusing initially on the emergence of Eastern Europe from the Second World War and the modifications of the frontiers.

Part One

POLITICAL GEOGRAPHY

Chapter One

COMMUNIST POWER IN EASTERN EUROPE

This section deals with several related political themes. The first chapter traces the success of Communist Parties in Eastern Europe in gaining power in the immediate aftermath of the Second World War. In the majority of cases the active involvement of the Soviet Union was an essential factor, with the uninhibited exercise of influence conditioned by the absence of western troops from the ground operations which cleared the German army from Eastern Europe. Then the impact of communist revolution on the peoples of Eastern Europe needs consideration, leading to questions about the legitimacy and reform of the system. There must also be recognition of the special circumstances arising in the three Balkan countries (Albania, Bulgaria, and Yugoslavia) lacking a common frontier with the USSR (Figure 1.1). The second chapter demonstrates that while some communist governments operate within frontiers already clearly established, a number of important territorial changes were made. Special attention is given to the occupation zones in Berlin and the legacy of this regime in the divided city. The third chapter in the section deals with the efforts made since 1945 to create greater homogeneity within each country and reduce contrasts between regions and peoples. While the broad theme of economic development is considered in the second section there is consideration here of perceived regional antagonisms which have attracted special aid programmes: the former Ottoman lands of Yugoslavia and the 'recovered territories' in Poland are two prominent examples but greatest emphasis is given to the easternmost region of Czechoslovakia - Slovakia. The final chapter in the section

Figure 1.1 The Countries of Eastern Europe today

Source: World atlases.

then deals with demographic matters including the problem of ethnic minorities and the gypsies in particular.

LIBERATION FROM THE AXIS

With the benefit of hindsight communism may be seen as a latent political force in Eastern Europe in 1945, generated by dissatisfaction with western-inspired strategies of economic development and interest in at least certain elements of the Soviet system. However, it would be wrong to suppose that the economic problems created an inevitable communist takeover. The war situation was crucial. German (and allied) forces were retreating from the area of occupation in the USSR after Stalingrad (1943) but within Eastern Europe the war effort was sustained by an enlarged German state (Grossdeutschland), incorporating much former Czechoslovak and Polish territory, and by allied governments in Hungary, Slovakia, and the Balkans. The prevailing political geography was a transformation of the pattern that had been created in 1918 in terms of both state frontiers and the ideologies of ruling groups (Figure 1.2). It was obvious that the framework would crumble on both counts in the event of an Axis defeat and that the transition would lead to an equally radical alternative, given the all-pervasive Soviet influence.

As R.L. Wolff argues for the Balkans,

> one of the chief reasons for the communist successes was obviously military: it was the Soviet Union whose armies defeated and invaded Romania and Bulgaria and completed the expulsion of Germans from Yugoslavia. There were no British or American troops in southeast Europe. (1)

The same applied in Hungary, Poland, and in most of Czechoslovakia. Developments might have followed a very different course had there been a landing by the western allies in the Balkans and much regret had been expressed that no operation comparable with the advance from Thessaloniki in the First World War was mounted. The issue has been widely debated on account of the supposition that Churchill was in favour of such a strategy (being keenly aware of Soviet intentions) but was pressed by the Americans to agree to landings in France and Italy instead.

15

Figure 1.2 Eastern Europe during the Second World War

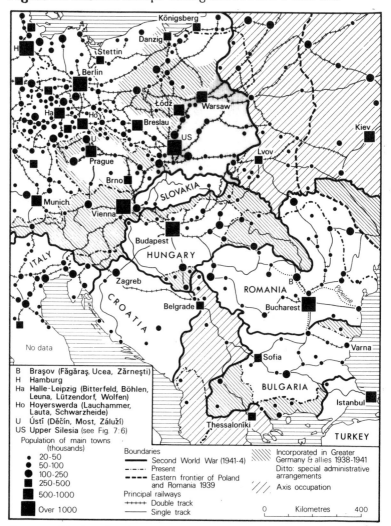

Source: National atlases.

In fact, Churchill's interest in the Balkans was not so direct. He favoured an operation to capture the Dodecanese Islands with a view to bringing Turkey into the war. This in turn would open the Straits and Black Sea to allied shipping, thereby extending to the Soviet Union a 'right hand along the Danube'. (2) In addition, he envisaged an advance from the head of the Adriatic through the Ljubljana Gap which might bring the western allies into Vienna ahead of the Soviets. However, it was not anticipated that forces would operate east of Vienna (for material assistance to the Partisans would help clear Yugoslavia) and intervention on the Balkan mainland would go no further than assisting in the liberation of Greece.

In the event, even these limited operations could not proceed, for there were insufficient resources committed to the campaign for the Aegean Islands in 1943 (so that Turkey stayed right out of the war) and resistance to the allied advance through Italy, the essential prelude to any campaign through the Ljubljana Gap, meant that they 'did not reach the take-off point for any hypothetical operation against Vienna until long after the Russians had forced the Romanian surrender and begun to sweep into Central Europe'. (3) Diplomatic events also tended to assist the communist cause. In 1942 it was agreed by the western allies and the Soviet Union that there would be no territorial changes that might hamper proceedings at a post-war peace conference: it was not even conceded that the USSR should enjoy a restoration of her 1941 frontiers. However, Soviet intrigues with Communist Parties in Axis-occupied territory led Churchill to propose the dubious 'percentage agreement' during discussions with Stalin in Moscow in 1944. Balancing a predominant Soviet interest in Bulgaria and Romania with an overriding British interest in Greece (leaving Hungary and Yugoslavia at 50:50) was not meant to justify a rigid system of spheres of influence: it was to be 'no more than a guide' in approaching the problems of occupation that would eventually arise. However, the subtlety of Churchill's proposal was lost on Stalin, who immediately accepted and subsequently reciprocated the resolute British action in Greece against the attempted communist takeover there. It was too late to reconsider at Yalta. The result was a conspicuous western failure to prevent communist takeovers in countries where they might have reasonably expected a different outcome. Although willing Soviet military collaboration had to be rewarded it is difficult to resist the view that Soviet influence could have been more effectively contained. Even if wartime strategy could not reasonably have been different, the failure to understand Soviet intentions immediately after hostilities ceased compounded the difficulties of non-communist political parties struggling for survival. (4) Certainly the arrangement was bitterly resented in Romania, where it seemed that the future of the country was being settled without proper consultation and discussion. It is still widely believed in the country that Soviet influence could have been moderated and that the elite need not have been left so vulnerable to destruction.

An immediate consequence of Soviet influence was the growth of Communist Parties dedicated to socialist policies. In Eastern Europe socialism has involved an economic programme contrasting with capitalism in that free-market forces are suppressed in the interests of central planning which could theoretically provide 'fair shares' for all and, by eliminating the waste of resources by the capitalist class (especially the foreign element) accelerate the growth of the economy: hence, rapid growth combined with prosperity for all and an end to the old regime of slow growth allied with discrimination between regions and classes. Idealists were prominent among the ranks of the national Communist Parties in 1945: like the visionaries in western countries they looked ahead to a period of reconstruction that would rebuild the socio-economic system along more progressive lines after the horrors of war. However, many of them knew from years of indoctrination that a total monopoly of political power was a precondition for effective action and that perceived enemies of the revolution would have to be eliminated. The political struggle might well involve serious economic dislocations in the short term. For the Soviets whose prime concern was a stable western frontier with friendly governments in power in neighbouring countries and unfettered access to the economies of Eastern Europe to facilitate reconstruction in the Soviet Union, the political priority was particularly pressing.

Within a few years Communist Parties were fully in control in all East European countries where the Soviets were able to set up an overwhelming military and political presence: the Soviet Occupation Zone (Sowjetische Besatzungszone - SBZ) of Germany and four neighbouring countries joined to the USSR by a common frontier. It is not clear whether or not Stalin had a timetable in mind because there was a transitional period of co-operation with coalition governments. Communist Parties needed time to develop, for they did not enjoy large memberships in 1945, and Stalin did not wish to alarm the western allies who had extracted certain undertakings from him regarding the maintenance of democracy. It is conceivable that coalitions might have been envisaged as a long-term arrangement but it seems that an increase in east-west tension over offers of Marshall Aid to some East European countries, and subsequently over hostilities in Korea, undermined such a conception, as did the increasing strains within coalitions between pro-Soviet sympathizers, nationally minded communists, and representatives of democratic parties. (5)

COMMUNIST POWER

Stalin was of course in a powerful position to manipulate political developments in Eastern Europe given the growth of Soviet influence during the later stages of the Second World War. In the majority of countries there was an important Red Army presence and economic penetration was facilitated by the armistice teams dictated by the Soviet Union. Naturally all the East European Communist Parties recognized Moscow as the leading centre of communism. Organizations like the Cominterm (dissolved in 1943) and the Cominform (dissolved in 1956) sought to create a socialist commonwealth. Later on the Soviet Union was to be less successful in claiming primacy in the communist world and the succession of conferences geared to unity under Soviet leadership extended only from 1957 through 1960 to 1969, but in the late 1940s Stalin's power in Eastern Europe was overwhelming. (6) His influence was of course significant in Eastern Europe even during the war years. As early as 1943 the exiled Czechoslovak government signed a treaty of friendship with the USSR and this later blossomed into a close economic liaison after 1945 with deliveries of raw materials to Czechoslovakia balanced by substantial Soviet orders for manufactures, especially in the engineering industry.

Collapse of the German military position in Eastern Europe began in August 1944 when King Mihai of Romania decided to take his country out of the war to prevent it becoming a battleground in the Axis-Soviet struggle. (7) German air raids gave Romania the pretext to re-enter the war on the allied side and her army subsequently assisted in the liberation of much of Hungary and Czechoslovakia. Communist penetration increased behind a façade of coalition government which lasted until the end of 1947 when increasing strain between the King and the left-wing parties led to Mihai's abdication and the declaration of the People's Republic with power concentrated in the hands of the Romanian Workers Party. (8) Meanwhile, in Hungary, where interest in an armistice had precipitated a German takeover and the installation of Hungarian facists in power, the Russians moved from the east and negotiated with a provisional government at Debrecen. The whole country was freed during the winter of 1944-5 and coalition governments were then sponsored by the Soviets until a People's Republic was inaugurated in 1949. (9) The entry of Soviet troops into Poland led to the installation of a provisional government at Lublin in July 1944. Although there was a broadly based Polish government in exile in London the Soviets decided to break off relations with it in 1943. The key issue was the discovery by the Germans of mass graves near Smolensk and the possible connection with Polish officers captured by the Soviets in 1939. In turning its back on the London government the Soviet Union was doubtless aware of the inevitable difficulty of dealing with such a regime in peacetime, not least over the troubled question of Poland's eastern frontier: by contrast, the friendly Lublin government was happy to accept the Curzon Line which the Soviets favoured. Further political advantage was gained in Poland by the failure to advance on Warsaw to support the Polish underground: the elimination of the Home Army by the Germans (along with the destruction of much of the city) removed a force which might well have challenged Soviet supremacy. Although it was agreed that the Lublin government should be broadened by the inclusion of members of the London government, the one man who took advantage of the arrangement (Mikolajczyk) had to flee the country in 1947. Left-wing elements gained ground and a People's Republic was declared in 1952. (10)

In Czechoslovakia a rising in Slovakia in the summer of 1944 was a failure and the liberation of the country did not begin until the autumn when the Soviets entered the Dukla Pass. The process was completed by May 1945 without excessive destruction, except in Prague where there was a popular rising and a German counter-attack. Western influence was relatively strong because American forces freed the Plzen area and the government exiled in the west was able to take power, albeit with the collaboration of leading communists who attracted a considerable measure of popular support (40 per cent in the elections of 1946). The socialist programme launched at Kosice in 1945 was put into effect, including nationalization of many large businesses. However, Soviet influence was very strong: the government was prevailed upon to refuse Marshall Aid in 1947 and the resignation of most non-Communist ministers in 1948 as a protest against Communist infiltration of the police enabled left-wing elements to extend their influence and so gain overwhelming success in the election held later in that year. (11)

In the case of the GDR post-war events converted the Soviet Occupation Zone (SBZ) of Germany into a satellite state, conflicting with the earlier (wartime) thinking of the Allies that Germany (albeit with somewhat reduced frontiers) should be kept together as one economic unit under a Control Council set up by the Potsdam Conference of July-August 1945. However, controls on movements between the four occupation zones (allegedly more difficult to circumvent than barriers normally existing between independent states) eventually stimulated a US proposal to integrate the occupation zones more effectively. However, while integration eventually brought the three western zones together, the frontier of the SBZ became increasingly divisive. Behind it the Soviet Union was systematically despoiling German industry in the name of reparations and was using German agriculture to supply the deficiencies at home. (12) Inability to achieve economic unity then prevented any progress on a new constitution for Germany in 1947. Instead there were arrangements made for the three western zones beginning with the formation of an American-British 'bizone' in 1947, and these developments led to the establishment of the FRG as an independent sovereign state in 1955. The Soviet Union rebuffed all subsequent attempts to bring its occupation zone into the system evolving in the west and chose instead to reinforce the separation and set up a separate state.

In 1945 the Soviet Military Administration blocked all bank accounts, expropriated estates larger than 100 ha and dismantled numerous industrial plants and transport installations. Then in 1949 a People's Council (<u>Volksrat</u>), the equivalent in the Soviet Zone for the <u>Landtäge</u> established for the western provinces, produced a constitution acceptable to the USSR. It promoted itself to parliamentary status as a Peoples Chamber or Legislature (Volkskammer) and declared the SBZ to be the GDR in 1949 with W. Pieck as the first president and O. Grotewohl the leader of the provisional government. The Soviets also engineered a political monopoly for the Communist Party. The Socialist Unity Party (SED) emerged out of a union of communist and socialist parties in 1946 and it remains the spearhead of the political movement, although other elements were absorbed into a National Union of Democratic Germany to which many organizations are related. In 1952 the SED declared that the building of socialism would be the chief task of the government, always relying on the experience and help of the USSR. The interzonal border was protected by a police cordon five kilometres wide and Berlin became the only place where it was a relatively simple matter to leave communist-controlled territory. Diplomatic relations were established with all other East European countries in 1949 except Yugoslavia (1957). The year 1950 saw the GDR accepting the Oder-Neisse frontier with Poland (Treaty of Zgorzelec) and becoming a member of Comecon. The Soviets signalled their approval by cutting reparation demands by half in 1950 and relaxing them altogether in 1954, following the wave of strikes and workers' demonstrations against austerity in 1953. In 1955 after recognition by the Soviet Union as a sovereign state, the GDR was accepted as a founder member of the Warsaw Pact. Two years later treaties of friendship and co-operation were signed with all the GDR's Warsaw Pact partners in Eastern Europe. For many years recognition of the GDR by western governments was withheld on the grounds that the Potsdam Agreement (on a future united Germany) was being violated and the Hallstein Doctrine required the severance of diplomatic relations by the FRG with any country recognizing the GDR. However, both camps have now recognized the reality of the two German states.

Evidently, the ability of the USSR to influence events in Eastern Europe is by no means uniform throughout the area. It is strongest where the country has a common frontier with its allies - Czechoslovakia, Hungary, Poland, and Romania. It is also strong in the GDR where the Soviet Union maintains the bulk of its forces in Eastern Europe, following the establishment of an occupation system in Germany at the end of the war. In addition, despite the GDR government's attempts to project itself in the world as a legitimate one it is still heavily dependent on the USSR for support, given the ambivalence of its own citizens. (13) However, in the Balkans, with the exception of Romania, the USSR has neither a common frontier nor a substantial Red Army presence. Albania, Bulgaria, and Yugoslavia were in a strong position to remain independent of Moscow. Yet Bulgaria chose close alignment with the Soviet Union while the other two countries examined in detail at the end of the chapter chose the opposite course.

The case of Bulgaria

In Bulgaria historic ties with Russia backed up by strong Soviet economic and political support have given rise to a close and stable association. (14) Communism arose out of developments in social democracy in the late nineteenth century. The split in the Social Democratic Party in 1891 resulted in a separate party for the radical tesni, who became alienated from non-working class elements, and it was this party that adopted the title of Bulgarian Communist Party in 1919. After some dubious decisions in the 1920s (including failure to support A. Stamboliski in 1923 and the instigation of terrorism, including a bomb outrage in Sofia cathedral in 1925), the party gained support in the 1930s through a Popular Front with Agrarians and Social Democrats. They may have benefited from a national affection for the USSR and from the prestige of certain leading figures like Dimitrov and Kolarov in international communism. During the war Bulgaria did not fight against the Soviet Union, for no government could ignore the traditional pro-Russian sentiment in the country, but an alliance with the Axis was seen as a means of gaining territory and so there was economic assistance for Germany and the ports of Burgas and Varna were made available.

The policy continued after the death of King Boris since Bulgaria did not wish to provoke a German occupation, although war with the UK and USA resulted in air raids in Sofia in 1943-4. Romania's dramatic change of loyalties in August 1944 in the face of the Red Army's advance towards the Carpathians made the Bulgarian government uneasy and feelers were put out to ascertain the Soviet attitude to Bulgaria's wartime territorial gains. The following month a Soviet declaration of war on Bulgaria was complemented by a coup by the communist-backed anti-German Fatherland

(<u>Otechestvan</u>) Front. Communists held key ministries in the new cabinet and after settling political scores with their enemies under the guise of war-crimes trials (though there were few genuine collaborators), this organization was well-placed to win the 1945 election. Wartime territorial gains in Macedonia were readily given up in a spirit of reconciliation with Tito's Partisans which seemed promising for the ideal of a Balkan Federation, but Bulgaria held on to South Dobrogea, gained by treaty in 1940. There were consequently genuine radical undercurrents for the communists to exploit, given the presence of Soviet occupation troops, and they were able to secure majority support for a republic (the young King Simeon and his mother Princess Ioanna went into exile after the plebiscite in 1946).

In a subsequent election the opposition won little more than one fifth of the vote and the struggles of the opposition leader N. Petkov to maintain a normal political activity were tolerated only until the Bulgarian peace treaty had been ratified. Radical economic measures were taken although there was at first no massive drive to collectivize agriculture. Some co-operatives were established after 1945 and under the Two Year Plan of 1947-8 the scheme was enlarged to cover 50,000 members and 0.19 million ha of land. Machine stations were supplied with Soviet equipment. Marshland was drained and increased areas were allocated to cotton. Electricity output was boosted by the Kazanlik dam and power station in the Tundzha Valley, and a new industrial city of Dimitrovgrad in the Maritsa Valley was underpinned by the establishment of chemical and cement industries. Throughout, Bulgaria has remained a staunch ally of the Soviet Union and close co-operation can be seen in economic matters (with Bulgaria a strong supporter of Comecon), in defence (through the Warsaw Pact), and in foreign policy (with Bulgaria assisting Soviet penetration through arms shipments to anti-colonial liberation groups and left-wing opposition forces, as well as training facilities for PLO terrorist activity).

COMMUNIST POLICIES

Various radical measures were taken before the communists were able to command total power. Land reforms were implemented, some enterprises were nationalized and former political leaders were put on trial. Communists penetrated all branches of the civil service. Soviet economic control was facilitated by the armistice terms dictated by the Soviet Union, including heavy reparations and/or confiscation of industrial plant. However, revolution gained momentum once the People's Republics were declared. The authority of the communists was maximized by elimination of all forms of actual or potential opposition: former activists in political parties now disbanded, leading churchmen, intellectuals, and businessmen. Many were killed while others died during years of imprisonment and forced labour. Simultaneously, governments moved to control all aspects of economic and social life through nationalization of factories, banks, and insurance houses, and collectivization of agriculture. The entire population was affected by the revolution and even those not picked out for persecution because of their political, religious, or business interests were subject to forced collectivization, currency reform (exhausting private capital reserves), and housing norms (which obliged the more affluent householders to accept tenants the state chose to allocate). The education system was transformed to fit the communist imperative of total subordination to the needs of the state; and various movement orders were imposed, as in Romania where the Baragan steppe was used as a resettlement area for intellectuals forced out of their houses in Bucharest and for respected farming families cleared out of villages situated close to the Yugoslav frontier (a sensitive area after Yugoslavia's expulsion from the Cominform in 1948).

The total amount of suffering extorted in the name of socialism is difficult to comprehend. It was unprecedented for Eastern Europe in modern times with the sole exception of Hitlerite policies towards the Jews during the Second World War. (15) It was all the more grotesque because of its irrelevance to the tenets of Marx and Lenin alike. Some of the excesses were obviously perpetrated by genuinely national elements acting out a sense of misguided idealism or crude political calculation but it is undeniable that the regime of terror was imposed directly and indirectly by the Soviet Union, demanding absolute loyalty from the satellites and achieving this through propaganda sustaining Moscow as the centre of the communist world and through coercion in the form of the high-level political meetings, representations by Russian ambassadors in Eastern Europe, and instructions from Soviet advisers present in government ministries. The purging of national communist leaderships to remove unreliable elements also served to ensure conformity in the ranks. Thus, national communist aspirations, which were themselves recklessly optimistic in terms of the dedication of the new 'socialist man' to achieve planning goals with minimal economic incentives, were soon found to be in conflict with Moscow's requirements of self-denial in the interests of the bloc. The international dimension would have been assimilated more easily if there had been genuine agreement over goals, but in fact Moscow alone determined priorities in the interest of the Soviet Union.

Attitudes to religion

Most anomalous in retrospect was the persecution of the churches which might have been seen as upholders of values relevant to the creation of a fairer society. (16) However, the pragmatism which has become more evident in recent years was ruled out by preoccupations over alleged wartime collaboration, church-owned estates, and threats to a state monopoly in education and propaganda. The extent of the challenge to the churches during the period of confrontation varied according to the level of ideological commitment to the secularization of society, of government perception of its strength, and of the churches' ambivalence or outright opposition towards the new regime. Another factor was the extent to which the new political elites shared the national cultural values of the churches; and also important was the supranational dimension manifested by the subordination of the Roman Catholic churches to the Vatican. Vatican influence in world diplomacy has provided some protection for the Roman Catholic Church in Eastern Europe (although some repressive measures have arguably been provoked by this situation), whereas other Christian churches (Orthodox and Protestant), as well as the Moslem Church, have not enjoyed such protection in the face of heavy state pressure. Government tactics towards the churches have shown significant variations, as can be seen in a review of the fortunes of the Catholic Church in the Balkans. The situation is outlined in some detail for Romania with briefer references to Bulgaria (and for the sake of completeness Albania and Yugoslavia too).

The Catholic Church in the Balkans

In Romania the Catholic Church was small and barely one-sixth of the population owed allegiance to Rome in the late 1940s. There were 1.05 million Roman Catholics (almost all Germans and Hungarians) and 1.60 million Uniates (Romanians who followed the eastern rite but under papal authority). The Uniate Church was strong in Galicia and Ruthenia as well, all former Habsburg territories where efforts had previously been made (1699) to draw Orthodox Christians within the orbit of Rome. The policy in Romania, as elsewhere, was to suppress the Uniate Church altogether by persecuting the clergy and coercing the faithful to return to the Orthodox fold. A congress at Cluj in 1948 provided a façade of democratic decision-making to this effect. Priests who would not go along with this involuntary decision were then condemned to forced labour while various economic sanctions were taken against laymen who tried to retain their faith. The Catholics, who were an ethnic minority as well as a religious minority, were denied contact with the west and rendered politically impotent. A campaign to this end started in 1947, depriving the Church of its schools, hospitals, and orphanages, as well as landed property. Its publications were suppressed and the concordat with the Vatican was revoked. Resistance from the clergy was particularly tenacious and an estimated three-quarters of the 800 clerics in the Catholic Church of Romania were imprisoned by 1950. Many were put to work on the Danube-Black Sea Canal, while a number of German priests were sent off to work in the Soviet Union as part of the Russian plan of persecuting the German ethnic group after the Second World War. Because 'faith' was involved, torture tactics often took on a frustrated savagery that went right to the limits of bestiality.

Bishops were removed in 1948 and the two who survived at Alba Iulia and Iasi were arrested in 1949. The next phase of the struggle involved a new statute for the Church, awarding the state jurisdiction over all aspects of church life except for dogma and morals, for which authority could remain with the papacy. In addition, the idea of an autonomous Church subservient to the state was furthered through attempts to form an action committee in 1950 at Tirgu Mures. This promised to bring the Catholics into line with other faiths whose pliant representatives had already expressed 'satisfaction' with the government's treatment of the Churches. To improve the credibility of the new focus of power in the Catholic Church the government took the ingenious decision of reviving the Status Catholicus, an administrative council of priests and laymen who had first managed the Church in Transylvania in the seventeenth century, when there were no bishops in the province. The machinery survived, though not always with great enthusiasm from the Vatican or from state government, and now provided a respectable rubber stamp for the recommendations of the action committee. With its ranks suitably infiltrated by puppet priests and collaborationist laymen, and its jurisdiction extended from Transylvania to the whole of Romania, it duly met in 1951 to call for good relations with government and to provide salaries for co-operative clerics.

Meanwhile, in Yugoslavia the Church was the subject of particular controversy on account of its association with the Ustasa regime in Croatia, and while the government accepted that the faith of millions of Croats and Slovenes could not be broken (and resumed diplomatic relations with the Vatican), it nevertheless persecuted individual priests who were considered guilty of collaborationism and war crimes by assisting in anti-Orthodox and anti-Jewish atrocities. (17) The communists were particularly anxious to condemn the primate of Yugoslavia, Msgr. A. Stepinats, and he was duly imprisoned in 1946 for his inevitable association with the wartime Croatian authorities, although there was no evidence to suggest that he approved of Ustasa excesses and failed to protect potential victims when he was able to do so. The action was unpopular in Croatia and since the imprisonment of Stepinats became an embarrassment to Yugoslavia in its foreign relations after 1948 he was eventually released in 1951, but confined to his native village and not allowed to resume his post as Archbishop of Zagreb. Nevertheless, the government remained distinctly ambivalent towards the Church, especially when Stepinats was elevated to the rank of cardinal in 1952: relations with the Vatican were severed for a time.

It was evident that if the clergy were subservient to the regime they would evidently be tolerated and the republics of Croatia and Slovenia provided funds to maintain the Church and included the clergy in social security arrangements. On the other hand, the power of the Church was reduced by anti-Catholic (as well as general anti-religious) propaganda, confiscation of monastic property, and imprisonment of priests who were over-zealous in performing their duties. At the same time the government set up its own 'associations' of Catholic priests and during 1952 and 1953 such groups were established in Bosnia-Hercegovina and Serbia as well as Croatia and Slovenia. The carrot of financial and social benefits and greater personal security helped the government to gain a measure of control, bringing the clergy round to accepting social reforms that might reduce the Church's authority. Of particular importance here was the legislation dealing with religious communities which deprived the Church of its own schools. However, the need to consider public opinion in western countries, which was not a factor in the calculations of other communist governments until the 1960s and 1970s, meant that pressure was restrained. The churches remained open and monastic life continued to flourish, even in Istria where the flight of Italian monks was followed by resettlement of Yugoslavs.

In Albania by contrast there has been a policy of total suppression of all Churches completed in 1967. None of the country's three faiths (Catholic, Orthodox, and Moslem) had identified closely with Albanian nationalism, and the religious divisions, on top of the tribal division between northern Gegs and southern Tosks, may have contributed to the government's assertion that 'our religion is Albanianism'. However, the Catholics were singled out for persecution immediately after the war. Since there had been a Catholic member of the wartime German-sponsored regency, charges of collaboration against the two hundred or so priests and monks were effective weapons. Arrests of the clergy began in 1946 and by the middle of 1951 virtually all bishops (Durres, Lesh, and Shkoder), priests, Franciscans, and Jesuits had been accounted for through death, imprisonment with forced labour, or exile. The handful who remained at liberty were presented at Shkoder to approve a new statute, followed up by a decree from the People's Assembly establishing a national Catholic Church. Government would support the Church but priests would only be allowed to celebrate mass and perform religious rites. Communications abroad would be restricted to religious questions only: they would pass through government officials and would imply no jurisdictional dependence on the Vatican.

In Bulgaria the Catholic population was the smallest in Eastern Europe, both absolutely (60,000 people) and proportionately (less than 1 per cent of the population). A regime-sponsored 'national' Church was therefore inappropriate and indeed action of any kind was delayed until 1952 when a quarter of the hierarchy was taken out of circulation and the Church's activities compromised by the closure of schools in Sofia and the college in Plovdiv. Conditions for imprisoned clerics were again harsh, with the forced labour camp on Persin Island, on the Danube near Belene, being particularly notorious. The picture of significant variations in individual countries, in the context of general mistrust and suspicion of the Churches, extends to the northern countries as well. Thus, the Uniate or Greek Catholic Church was forced into a 'reunion' with the Orthodox Church in Czechoslovakia (as in Romania), though not in Hungary and Poland. (18) Broadly speaking, the Churches have survived despite numerous restrictions and frustrations. Some attempt has been made to influence the Roman Catholic clergy through pro-regime organizations, like Pax in Poland and Pacem in Terris in Czechoslovakia, and church administration has been gravely weakened by difficulties in appointing high officials, notably bishops in Czechoslovakia.

THE WARSAW PACT

This is an essential base for Soviet control over much of Eastern Europe: an enduring alliance, formed in 1955 and confirmed for another thirty years in 1985. It has enormous military significance quite apart from its political and administrative functions. It was formed just after the FRG joined the North Atlantic Treaty Organization (NATO) (initially set up in 1950) and immediately before the signing of the Austrian State Treaty. (19) The treaty setting up the alliance was signed by all the East European countries with the exception of Yugoslavia. However, Albania formally left the Pact in 1968 after the invasion of Czechoslovakia, although effective withdrawal dated from 1961 (when the USSR broke off diplomatic relations). The treaty contained provisions for joint consultation, mutual defence, and military co-operation, but in reality it added little to the various political and economic ties which already existed, following the web of bilateral treaties of friendship, co-operation, and mutual assistance signed in the late 1940s. Furthermore, Soviet troops were in place in Eastern Europe long before 1955 and East European armed forces (although remaining strictly under national control) were nevertheless thoroughly Sovietized in terms of organization, training, and weaponry. Its significance in the early years was mainly symbolic, representing an effort on the part of the new Khrushchev leadership in the USSR to replace the discredited Stalinist control system with one that was more flexible and less obtrusive.

After the troubles in Hungary and Poland in 1956 a somewhat lower profile was given to Soviet hegemony in Eastern Europe through formal status-of-forces agreements (sanctioning the presence of Soviet troops on East European territory) and a joint command was constituted. However, it was only in the 1960s that the Warsaw Pact was given any real military and political content: on the military front East European armed forces were re-equipped and joint military exercises became common practice. Political activity was more evident through greater co-ordination of foreign policy. However, significant strains appeared during the decade, culminating in the Soviet-led invasion of Czechoslovakia which included contingents from Bulgaria, Hungary, Poland, and the GDR. Although the action was in clear violation of the Warsaw Treaty and condemned by one of the signatories (Romania), the Soviet leadership defended the action through the 'Brezhnev Doctrine' of limited sovereignty: national sovereignty was to be compromised in the general interests of the whole socialist community as assessed by the Soviet Union. The Albanians took the opportunity to withdraw from the Pact at this time, while the Romanians, who had previously broken the united policy towards the FRG by establishing diplomatic relations in 1967, persevered with a more autonomous foreign policy and reduced their military involvement (still refusing to allow foreign troops to enter the country for joint exercises and calling for the dissolution of all military blocs). Yet despite military intervention and continual political indoctrination, the commitment of the other East European armies cannot be taken for granted by the Soviet Union. (20) 'Only the GDR exhibits consistently a high level of systemic integration, a developed and productive economy, political control and military preparation to serve as an adjunct to Soviet interests were hostilities to occur in Europe.' (21)

Since 1968 there has been an intensive drive by the Soviet leadership to consolidate unity. The Political Consultative Committee of the alliance has been used increasingly as a forum for the announcement of major

Table 1.1 The armed forces and military expenditure

Country	Armed forces personnel				Military expenditure as a percentage of GNP	
	1970		1980		1970	1980
	A	B	A	B		
Bulgaria	175	20.6	162	18.2	7.7	7.4
Czechoslovakia	222	15.5	212	13.9	5.3	5.8
GDR	202	11.8	231	13.8	5.8	4.4
Hungary	146	14.2	119	11.1	5.8	5.4
Poland	314	9.7	421	11.8	6.0	4.3
Romania	211	10.4	215	9.7	5.6	4.3
Yugoslavia	257	12.6	258	11.6	3.0	4.7

Source: United States statistical yearbooks.

Notes: A - Totals in thousands; B - Armed forces as a percentage of total population.

foreign policy initiatives, and, to facilitate co-ordination, meetings of the foreign ministers have been convened regularly since 1969. The joint command has been reorganized but significantly, trends towards genuine collaboration in military matters have not matched the progress made in the Pact's political role. The Warsaw Pact provided a forum for discussion leading to agreements with western countries at Helsinki over a range of political, cultural, and human-rights issues and it continues to co-ordinate approaches to be adopted at review conferences. There appears to be scope for genuine disagreement during these meetings although the USSR has been able to insist on a united front once major policy decisions are reached, a convention which gives the Pact a distinct tactical advantage in dealing with NATO, whose internal disputes are widely publicized. Troop and equipment levels among the East European armies have changed little over the last fifteen years (apart from an increase in the number of tanks), and although selected units are equipped with modern Soviet weaponry the bulk of the allied forces use obsolete equipment (see Table 1.1). However, this is because the Soviet forces in Eastern Europe form the backbone of the so-called 'first strategic echelon', covering the northern countries, with control asserted by the Soviet Union as if Eastern Europe were just another military district of the USSR.

At present there are twenty divisions in the GDR, five in Czechoslovakia, four in Hungary, and two in Poland. Along with direct support forces along the western borders of the Soviet Union, this gives a total of 0.78 million ground troops backed by four tactical air armies. For despite tension in Asia, Soviet military strategy continues to be oriented towards a European theatre of operations. The Red Army divisions cast what has been described as a 'psychological shadow' over the entire region. It does not go unnoticed that the only occasions since 1945 in which shots have been fired in anger by Soviet soldiers in Europe have been in action against political developments in Eastern Europe itself: clearly the military might of the Soviet Union is the ultimate guardian of the political status quo of the region. Meanwhile, development of effective national defence policies among the East European countries is highly restricted because the entanglement of the national armies in the Soviet strategic web results in commitments to maintain large ground forces which absorb funds that could otherwise be allocated to the modernization of national defence. (22) A further constraint arises from the USSR's near monopoly over the manufacture of weapon systems and military equipment. Since almost all the weaponry is standardized and only certain types of military hardware are produced in East Europe (under licence from the Soviet Union), no East European country currently possesses a national manufacturing capacity sufficient to produce a full range of essential military equipment. Nevertheless, given the Soviet Union's preoccupation with Europe there is general acceptance among the allies of the continued function of the Pact as an 'entangling alliance' or as 'an iron corset to hold together the communist bloc'. (23) Limited accommodations to national interests will doubtless be made, as pragmatism requires, in political and economic matters. However, there is no compromise over the realities of Soviet military strength. Thus, Romanian actions are carefully controlled to restrict defiance to tolerable levels and other member states are unlikely to offer any open challenge to Soviet authority unless there is any gross provocation such as might arise through pressure to send combat troops into Africa or Asia. (24)

PRESSURES FOR REFORM

In spite of the institutions and vested interests making for stability, Eastern Europe has experienced strong pressures for reform. Economic development, quite apart from the foreign policy requirements of the Soviet Union, has necessitated greater integration with the world economy and economic problems have inevitably arisen from changing prices and market demands. Economic strains have combined with civil rights grievances to stimulate dissent, and in containing opposition governments have been ready to test the limits of Soviet toleration of political experiments. For, despite the legacy of multinational empires, like the Habsburg Empire which stimulated considerable idealism in the inter-war and early post-war years on the desirability of federation, nationalist feelings have developed very strongly and the prime objective for Eastern Europe involves political advancement to a genuinely semi-independent status for each individual state.

Pressure for reform has steadily mounted since Stalin's death. Many political prisoners were released during the late 1950s and 1960s and some of the leading figures who died in prison (like the Romanian historian and politician Gheorghe Bratianu at Sighetul Marmatiei in 1953) were rehabilitated. However, liberalization has always been a matter for the greatest caution. On the one hand, the Soviet leadership has sought to maintain its influence over the East European parties to ensure that developments do not create unacceptable difficulties for the USSR while Khrushchev's own brand of personal politics secured the acquiescence of Eastern Europe, his less charismatic successors have been much more difficult to assess and there has been a reluctance to contemplate radical decisions. On the other hand, the communist governments in Eastern Europe have tried to introduce limited reforms to meet popular aspirations and stimulate the economy while seeking to contain dissent and maintain the authority and leadership of the Party. Essentially, therefore, the order remains the same: communist regimes have not changed fundamentally and they are unlikely to do so as long as the Soviet Union has the power and motivation to maintain a cordon sanitaire along its western frontier. 'Eastern European leaders and part of the population were persuaded that while some change was necessary, a complete reversal of the existing order would be very dangerous indeed.' (25) Yet the uneasy compromises have brought some progress in terms of human rights and material prosperity (themes examined in detail in later chapters). Given the emphasis placed by western governments on human rights in Eastern Europe, it is becoming increasingly common for governments to remove political opponents by allowing them to emigrate and then destroying their credibility at home by propaganda. The solution raises questions about a government's image abroad and legitimacy at home but the tactic can certainly claim a subtlety which was hardly present in the methods of crude repression previously utilized.

Rewriting history in the GDR

Official loyalty to Moscow and a theoretical commitment to socialist internationalism must be combined with a cultivation of national pride so that governments can better project themselves as legitimate holders of power. History must often be rewritten to convey the impression of the younger generation that communist parties came to power by the triumph of progressive forces rather than by Russian pressure. Indeed, 'the prescriptive rather than descriptive writing of history, serving political expediency, has become standard practice for East European regimes looking for legitimacy.' (26) Yet a rigid Marxist interpretation is often inadequate to deal with the wealth of historical developments. The problem of combining nationalism with communism have been greatest in the GDR, which now considers itself to be the legitimate heir of the best historical traditions of the German people. Rehistorisierung has brought such individuals as Albert Einstein, Martin Luther, Richard Wagner, and even Frederick the Great back into circulation. It has given rise to a degree of self-confidence that allows the GDR to compete with its larger and more powerful rival as the true guardian of the Germanic past. (27)

Official references to German history may easily become counter-productive and stimulate a stronger desire for reunification, rather than further the conception of the GDR as a separate German nation. Difficulties have been increased by the conception of the Third Reich as the culmination of a linear historical process that called for apology rather than salutation: it was considered appropriate to leave official consideration of this embarrassing history to the FRG, which could then be portrayed as the natural heir of this dubious inheritance. In the past, therefore, the GDR leadership tended to shy away from any open competition with the FRG over German historical traditions and tried to legitimize its rule through the Soviet-centred theory of a proletarian (or socialist) internationalism with some inspiration from Germany's Weimarian socialist past. Socialist internationalism served as a form of ersatz patriotism, but it did not give rise to any strong sense of separate nationhood for East Germans: hence a reappraisal following the 1976 party congress which placed emphasis on the better use of Heimatgeschichte for building socialist consciousness in the GDR and called on the social sciences to develop a broader historical perspective.

While there is an element of continuity in policy, in so far as the GDR claims to inherit all that is good in German history, the separation of the 'good' from the 'reactionary' has now proceded from the identification of discrete periods of history (notably the Weimer Republic) and select individuals (progressive thinkers like Goethe and Schiller and 'enlightened' generals like Scharnhorst and Gneisenau who helped the Russian Army during the Napoleonic Wars) to a broader view that recognizes certain progressive elements in all periods of German history. These elements are, understandably, revealed through the medium of the class struggle, for a simple black-and-white cultural dichotomy distinguishes the exploited masses, whose living conditions inevitably given rise to the ideology of democracy and socialism from the bougeois-aristocratic elite. The same model allows a democratic and socialist GDR to be contrasted with an undemocratic and non-socialist FRG! Yet despite the naivety of the philosophical underpinning, some quite remarkable developments have followed. Although it was the driving force behind German imperialism it is now conceded that the Prussian elite also contributed to progressive societal development. For although government policies served the interests of the Junkers, they also supported industrial development which was a critical precondition for the evolution of the German working class.

A further step was taken in 1981 with the opening of a permanent exhibition in East Berlin about the history of the German people from prehistoric times to 1945. It is on display in the Museum of German History accommodated in a building dating back to 1706 and originally used by Frederick I of Prussia as his armoury. Basic tenets of the

Geschichtspolitik were restated at the opening ceremony: rooted in history, the GDR stood as the embodiment of the continuity of progressive ideas as well as the irrevocable break with reactionary forces. Yet it is hard to see how the new policy can succeed when the majority of GDR citizens (80 per cent, according to one authority) apparently see themselves as members of an all-German nation and are unimpressed by the subtle distinction the government tries to make about two German nations within a single German nationality. No doubt historians in the FRG and elsewhere will point out that the GDR did not emerge from some inexorable historical process in which 'good' and 'evil' crystallized out on a territorial basis but from the failure of Soviet diplomacy to forge an alliance between the two states (emerging out of the post-war occupation zones) into an independent and non-aligned confederation, a plan apparently favoured by the Soviets as late as 1957. However, there is, nevertheless, an interesting change in official attitudes which suggests a more positive approach to the realities of post-war Europe.

The new self-confidence in the GDR has given momentum to developing relations between the two Germanies. For years the FRG has been discreetly buying the freedom of East Germans arrested for trying to leave the country illegally, but in 1984 the GDR accepted a large FRG loan in return for relaxation of travel restrictions imposed on its own citizens. FRG television can be picked up throughout the GDR (apart from the area south-east of the Frankfurt/Oder - Karl Marx Stadt line). (28) Moscow is obviously sensitive over the rapprochement and dissuaded the GDR leader, E. Honecker, from going ahead with a proposed visit to the FRG in 1984. It is hardly likely that the GDR would sell out to the FRG after struggling for years to gain international recognition, but the regime is dependent on the Soviet Union for its survival, and this makes it more difficult to obtain economic or political concessions.

Pressures for reform: crises in Czechoslovakia, Poland, and Romania

In recent years most of the Soviet Union's East European allies have been able to make peaceful progress, although it should not be overlooked that both the GDR and Hungary experienced traumatic upheavals in 1953 and 1956 respectively, while the outstanding events in recent years have been the crises in Czechoslovakia (1968) and Poland (1981). (29) However, there have been severe economic problems in Romania, a country where a highly authoritarian party has been able to make effective nationalist gestures. In Czechoslovakia, economic difficulties in the early 1960s stimulated reformist thought, to allow greater market influence and further autonomy for Slovakia. (30) The Soviets initially went along with the 'New Course' set by the Dubcek leadership (consoled by the fact that former leader, Novotny, had become dispensable after a close colleague escaped abroad and gained political asylum in the USA), but subsequently moved to restore the status quo once the scope of the reforms became clear. It seems that Dubcek wanted to move slowly along a new course, pragmatically trying new strategies where old ones had failed. He sought to allay Soviet fears over the non-proletarian nature of the reforms by increasing the scope for worker involvement in decision-making by individual enterprises but failed to appreciate Soviet perception of this approach as 'self-management' of a kind denounced in Yugoslavia. Equally, Dubcek's plan to call a party congress in September 1968 to demonstrate rank-and-file support for reform alarmed the Russians because it threatened to turn the Party into a revisionist agency. The eleventh hour meeting at Cerna nad Tisou on the Czechoslovak-Soviet frontier merely re-emphasized the problem of mutual incomprehension and the Soviets felt obliged to intervene immediately to stop the reform movement dead in its tracks. Although the leadership insisted that socialism was safe, Moscow feared that, as momentum built up, change would be difficult to contain, with the result that irresistible pressures might build up elsewhere in the bloc and lead ultimately to a change in the balance of power in Europe. The invasion began at 2300 hours on 20 August 1968 with 170,000 Soviet troops (coming from the GDR and USSR) plus more than 50,000 troops from the other Warsaw Pact countries (Romania excepted). Although the government retained the support of the Party and the population at large the Soviets were able to insist on a reconstituted Dubcek administration and later, in April 1969, to install an even more submissive and dogmatic regime under Gustav Husak. (31)

Eastern Europe as a whole faced economic problems in the early 1980s as a result of world economic recession, but only Poland experienced a crisis with serious political repercussions. (32) This may have arisen from an ambivalent attitude towards a relatively weak regime, fortified by the ethnic coherence of Polish society, the position of the Catholic Church as an 'alternative' institution, and the experience of successful struggle exemplified by the rise of Solidarity as an independent trade union. Unfortunately, the union was unable to agree an economic programme with the communist government to stave off the worsening crisis and the collapse in the Party's authority led to a radical rebuilding operation under military leadership obliged to sacrifice western goodwill by disbanding the free trade union. The country remains heavily in debt: after a sharp rise from one billion dollars in 1971 to 24 billion in 1980 there has been a further increase to 27 billion in 1985 and 39 billion in 1987, aggravated by fluctuations in the values of different currencies and by arrears in interest payments.

Romania has experienced severe economic problems through drastic government action to reduce foreign debts yet the country has remained stable: there have been some organized protests but generally the people have greeted adversity with resignation rather than demonstrations and strikes. (33) However, the independent stance adopted by the Romanian government has helped to minimize alienation in a country where there is no alternative centre of power and where ethnic and occupational divisions are quite fundamental. The Romanian Party's thinly veiled references to the Soviet Union's seizure of Bessarabia and northern Bucovina (in 1940 and again in 1945) and its keen interest in the disarmament process in the Balkans are among the more remarkable demonstrations of national interest. (34) Moreover, informal networks involving family and friends have been very effective so that difficulties over provisioning have not developed into a politically volatile food crisis. (35) However, at the time of writing the situation is becoming more serious as the regime appears to be moving further out of touch with the population as a whole. There were serious disturbances in Brasov during the winter of 1987-8 and large numbers of people (not only members of the Hungarian minority) have crossed into Hungary. In what appears to be an unprecedented development between two Warsaw Pact member states, Romanians who arrive without visas are being allowed to stay and express their opposition to the Bucharest government.

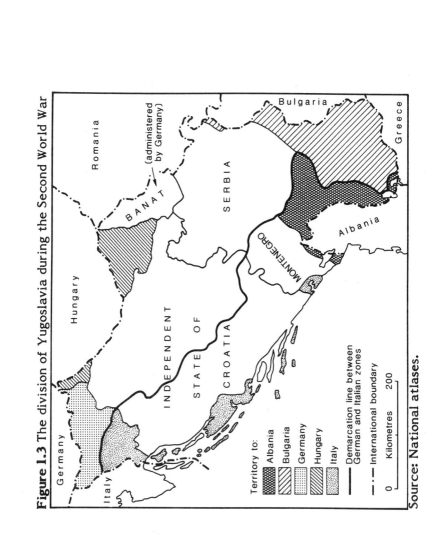

Figure 1.3 The division of Yugoslavia during the Second World War

Source: National atlases.

NON-ALIGNED COMMUNIST REGIMES: YUGOSLAVIA

Albania and Yugoslavia have been fiercely independent and Moscow's attempts at hegemony have been rebuffed by governments and peoples alike. These exceptional cases are remarkable enough to justify fairly detailed examination of the post-war developments, and all the more so in view of the frequently troubled relations between the two countries. In Yugoslavia the communists achieved power with relatively little difficulty. Tito's 'Partisans' enjoyed high regard for their solid offensive against the German occupation and against the Axis-aligned state of Croatia (Figure 1.3). They also made the fullest use of their military strength to gain political power and apply many aspects of the Soviet communist system to Yugoslavia. The Yugoslavs were 'the first communist party in eastern Europe to eliminate all competitors, to take over the state, to organise a political machine and an economy on the soviet model, (and) to start the process of collectivisation on the land'. (36) Despite the problems of a war-torn economy which was heavily dependent on United Nations' assistance (Yugoslavia received some $425 million or 14 per cent of the total relief budget between 1945 and 1947), there was an immediate effort to impose a socialist system. A currency reform in 1945 confiscated the fortunes of the rich without any discrimination between pre-war and wartime incomes.

A radical land reform was also implemented with expropriation of all holdings larger than 45 ha (or larger than 25-30 ha of arable land), though church and monastic holdings up to 200 ha were respected. A total of 1.64 million ha were made available to the peasantry, with priority given to Partisans and landless families. However, since not enough land could be made available in areas of greatest pressure there was some resettlement, and Montenegrans moved to take up expropriated land in Vojvodina, much of it previously owned by Germans and Hungarians. Some of the land was used to sustain an immediate collectivization drive: here, Yugoslavia led the way in the Balkans in 1948 with 60,000 peasant families organized into collectives responsible for some 300,000 hectares. These 'labour co-operative farms' offered returns to members (in proportion to the amount of land contributed) and the privilege of withdrawal after a trial period was conceded. The government did not resort to forcible collectivization but there were means whereby local officials could use the

41

system of compulsory deliveries and land taxes to intimidate private farmers:

> the local communists could use the system as a means to bring pressure on the more prosperous peasant, thus softening up the kulak for the future blows the regime would deal him. Indeed the local agents of the regime could and often did impose arbitrary additional property taxes which they might even make retroactive if they found themselves dealing with an 'enemy' of the regime. (37)

By their zealousness in extending nationalization from a number of key mining ventures (like the foreign-owned Bor copper and Trepca zinc mines which the Germans had taken over) to all parts of the country's industry it was possible to introduce a Five Year Plan in 1948. This was very ambitious with a new iron and steel complex envisaged for Doboj in Bosnia, and an extension to the aluminium industry with the enlargement of the Lozovac plant and a new electrolytic smelter at Strnisce. Oil output in Croatia, which had reached 150,000 tons per annum production by the end of the war, was to rise to 450,000! Agriculture was represented through irrigation in Croatia and drainage for Lake Scutari. The transport system was to be modernized and a new Belgrade was to rise on a site across the Danube 'where endless quantities of building materials and machinery were tied up in a difficult and unrewarding construction job'. (38) On the other hand, the Yugoslavs resisted Soviet overtures for the formation of joint companies in banking, metallurgy, mining, and oil: only transport companies (Juspad for river shipping and Justa for air transport) were approved.

Expulsion from the Cominform

Yet paradoxically, perhaps, because Tito was a powerful supporter of the USSR without being dependent on the Soviets for his political position (as were most other communist leaders in Eastern Europe), he quickly came to resent Soviet interference. Yugoslavia was seen as a sort of 'geopolitical advance guard of Soviet power' because borders were shared with three countries where communists might yet achieve power (Austria, Greece, and Italy. (39) The exuberant and perhaps arrogant self-confidence of Tito at this time knew no bounds and it was with a bad grace that he accepted Stalin's reservations over Yugoslav political ambitions in the Balkans and the failure of the Soviets to win the whole of Trieste for Yugoslavia. Offence was also taken over Soviet espionage and demands to establish joint companies, to say nothing of the cultural pressures and the bad behaviour of the Red Army immediately after the war. However, it was not Tito who contemplated, let alone sought, a break with Moscow and the reasons for this must be found in Soviet disenchantment with Yugoslav actions, particularly Tito's ambitious foreign policies. The break was formalized through Yugoslavia's expulsion from the communist club which, paradoxically, she had done much to create: for in 1946 Tito proposed to Stalin that an agency might be formed to co-ordinate views among Communist Parties and the idea blossomed a year later with the formation of the Information Bureau of Communist Parties (Cominform). The Soviet Union believed that Yugoslavs would respond to their country's expulsion with a demonstration of loyalty to Moscow, but popular support for Tito was strong enough to sustain his regime. Strong economic pressure was applied through cancellation of agreements and abandonment of further projects under negotiation. One casualty was the international project with Albania to drain Lake Scutari; another was the integrated iron and steel works planned for Doboj. Territorial ambitions were severely jolted, for the unsatisfactory compromise over Trieste was now followed by withdrawal of Soviet support for the Yugoslav claim to Austrian territory in Carinthia. Support for the communists in Greece had to end and the three-year Greek rebellion was defeated in 1949 after Yugoslavia closed its frontier in Macedonia. Then there were implications elsewhere in Eastern Europe, both economically through reorganization of industrial projects, like the Hungarian iron and steel works located at Dunaujvaros rather than Pecs with the shift from Yugoslav to Soviet iron ore supplies, and politically through the removal of communist leaders like W. Gomulka in Poland and L. Rajk in Hungary, who were thought likely to harbour 'independent' leanings: not that a break from Moscow was likely in many cases because of the presence of Soviet troops and the existence of common frontiers with the Soviet Union across which reinforcements could quickly be sent.

However, despite being 'alone in the world and naked to

a terrifying blast', Tito retained both his nerve and his deep mistrust of capitalist countries. (40) He had to steer a middle course between those who wanted greater freedom (including freedom to exacerbate tension between Serbs and Croats) and a small minority of communists who remained fanatically loyal to Moscow. The security police was strengthened and efforts were made to prevent armed bands hiding out in the mountains (as remnants of civil war factions) from becoming focal points for counter-revolution. The familiar purge tactics were employed to eliminate those in powerful positions whose loyalty to Tito was in doubt, and political trials were staged through 1948 and 1949. Tito was obliged to take drastic measures against pro-Soviet Yugoslavs and those who avoided execution spent much of the following decade enduring degrading treatment in 'Tito's Gulag' on Goli Otok (Naked Island) in the Adriatic. Yugoslavia could not manage without political prisoners, the number of whom has again increased since the Kosovo riots of 1981. However, the western powers showed considerable sensitivity over Tito's predicament. Greece was restrained from invading southern Albania and this avoided any dilemma for the Yugoslavs over their friendship treaty obligations: intervention would have been difficult in view of Albania's full support for Cominform sanctions (despite the fact that she was not a member), yet abstention would have left Yugoslavia exposed to criticism that she was in effect helping Greece. A delicate accommodation of Tito was also offered by economic and political support that did not undermine his credibility as a radical socialist.

Considerable progress was made in 1950 when drought increased the economic problems besetting the country. After a respectable period of ideological contemplation diplomatic relations with Greece were resumed and discussions with Italy over financial matters (including reparations) led to agreement over a formal partition of the 'Free Territory of Trieste' in 1954. This had implications for Yugoslav security by virtue of NATO, with which Yugoslav association was agreed at Bled in 1954. At home the call of Tito's old Partisan colleague M. Djilas for a 'withering away' of the Communist League (in favour of a multi-party system) was resisted, but collectivization made no further headway after 1951 and the establishment of workers' councils to allow for the self-management of enterprises was a significant democratic gesture: their impact was unfortunately blunted by failure to develop the system adequately before 1965 and then

> when the imperatives of efficiency began to call for
> integration into large units and for global economic
> decisions it became difficult for workers councils to be
> sources of real decisions especially in view of the
> general level of education among Yugoslavia's industrial
> labour. (41)

There was reconciliation with the east as well, first of all
over Danube shipping. In 1953 a Yugoslav-Romanian
commission began to meet alternatively at Orsova and
Tekija (on the opposite bank) and Yugoslavia agreed to make
the locomotive-powered tugging service on the Sip Canal
available to Romanian vessels. Later in the year Yugoslavia
was reconciled with other members of the Danube
Commission at Galati and diplomatic relations were
resumed in 1954. However, for ideological companionship
the Yugoslav leadership supported the neutralist stance
adopted in parts of the Third World, especially in Africa,
and a close relationship developed between Tito and
Ethiopia's Haile Selassie. This was by no means an
embarrassment to the western nations who have seen in
recent Yugoslav history 'a reassuring example of a country
which the west had helped but had not tried to dominate.'
(42)

Regional problems

It is perhaps rather paradoxical that Yugoslavia's initially
powerful political ambitions in south-eastern Europe should
be complemented by considerable domestic instability.
Ethnic conflict may have been contained by the Communist
government but it has certainly not been eliminated.
Indeed, authoritarian government, however well-meaning,
may have exacerbated tension: 'the less political freedom
there is to discuss the country's important problems,
including that of its national identity, the more the question
of national identity, because of its outstandingly emotional
nature, tends to permeate all others'. (43) To further the
Yugoslav ideal, national groups must understand each other's
sectional history and a wider role for the intellectuals may
be preferable to heavy concentration of power in
government hands: 'if the young were taught how to think

Yugoslavia could perhaps be exorcised of its demons'. (44) Even the federal system introduced in 1949 may be called in question for the way in which national interests are linked with discrete territories. Bosnia-Hercegovina and Montenegro prevent undue dominance by the larger Croatian and Serbian republics while creating a centre for the Moslems on the one hand and retaining an identity for one of the most durable states of Eastern Europe on the other. Yet each individual republic is plagued at the regional level by the same stresses as debilitated the earlier centralized state at the national level, with a particular ethnic interest being maintained over a somewhat arbitrarily defined area which is multinational in character. Hence the value of the Turkish idea of the millet as a national interest group, but one divorced from a specific national territory. (45) The regional theme is developed further in Chapter 3.

NON-ALIGNED COMMUNIST REGIMES: ALBANIA

Albania's profile has been even more remarkable, marked by hostility to Moscow and deep suspicion of Yugoslav intentions (given historic Serb ambitions and unequivocal advice from Stalin to Tito to 'swallow up Albania'). The post-war period began with a close accord between the two communist leaders Hoxha and Tito. Partiality for the Soviet Union was underlined by provocative acts against the western allies since ideological conflict became more relevant than recognition of wartime assistance: the US mission withdrew in 1946 after accusations of American sabotage of the Lake Maliq drainage project, while relations with the British literally blew up when deliberate withholding of information led to British destroyers striking mines in Albanian waters. Yugoslavia provided valuable economic assistance under a treaty of friendship and mutual co-operation signed in 1946. Joint companies were active in the major sectors of the economy: banking, electricity, metallic ores, oil, railways, and trade. The results were considerable, with the Velika Selita (Lenin) hydro-power station near Tirana, oil production from Kuchovo and Patos, food processing at Elbasan (marmalade), Korce (sugar) and Vlore (fish canning) and railway construction inland from Durres for just over forty kilometres to Peqin. Meanwhile, agriculture was being reorganized. Holdings over 20 ha were expropriated (40 ha if advanced methods were being used) and allotted in units of 5 ha to the peasants. By the end of 1948 some 6,000 peasants had received a total of 0.32 million ha. To modernize farming, an agricultural school was founded with United Nations' assistance on a former Italian model farm and aid was also directed to the Lake Maliq drainage project.

However, it was not long before the traditional emnity between Albania and Yugoslavia was reasserted. Yugoslavia's desire to station two army divisions was resisted. Yet Albania was beholden to Tito for military help in consolidating the Tosk authority over the Geg tribes, and stripping their leaders (bajraktars) of their traditional authority, and Kosovo territory had to be returned. Again, it did not escape the notice of the Albanian leadership that the Albanian Party was the only one in Eastern Europe not invited by the Soviet Union to join the Cominform in 1947. At best this was a humiliating indication of Albania's insignificance and at worst a signal of Soviet anticipation of Yugoslav absorption of the whole country. Understandably, therefore, the expulsion of Yugoslavia from the Cominform allowed Hoxha and his hard-line deputy M. Shehu to rid the Party of all Yugoslav elements.

Close links with Moscow continued for some years, and brought important economic benefits. The joint company formula was continued, with Alsovpetrol a conspicuous example: the 1950-5 Five Year Plan provided for a refinery at Cerrik (started in 1952) and a pipeline to Tirana. Electricity output from hydro stations was to be increased sixfold to 121 million kwh through the Enver dam on the Mati River and associated 20 MW capacity Uj power station. Further development of infrastructure arose through the extension of the Durres-Peqin railway to Elbasan and the construction of another line from Durres to Tirana (and ultimately to Vlore). A further railway from Shkoder to Kukes was also planned. Manufacturing extended to textiles with cotton mills a further sugar mill appeared at Maliq: overall in the consumer industries' sector output was expected to increase more than three times between 1950 and 1955. Cement production was to be boosted by a new factory at Vlore. However, Stalin's death in 1953 and Krushchev's progress in healing the breach with Tito in 1955 placed Hoxha in peril since he could not survive any reintroduction of Yugoslav influence. He reacted by opening up links with China and purging the Party's ranks over the period 1955-7, tactics that were initially successful in consolidating his regime and attracting capital from both China and the USSR to develop the oil industry and improve education and health standards. However, open conflict between the Soviet Union and China in 1960, along with Soviet sympathy for Greek territorial claims on south Albania and continued cordiality towards the Yugoslavs (which implied a partition threat in the eyes of the xenophobic Albanians), brought a clear shift to China.

The Chinese connection

Diplomatic relations with the USSR were broken off in 1961 and thenceforth Albania supported the Chinese in the deepening Sino-Soviet rift. Meanwhile, Soviet aid fell off from very high levels in 1957-9 to virtual cessation in 1960-1. This coincided with a severe drought in Albania and the desperate situation was relieved only by grain from France, paid for by the Chinese. Trade was switched dramatically, with a decline in turnover with the Soviet Union (from 3.50 billion leks to less than 0.01) balanced by growth in Chinese trade (0.45 to 2.70) between 1960 and 1962 when Albania left Comecon. (46) China provided military/technical equipment, skilled workers, and more grain, the latter purchased from Australia and Canada. Chinese-built factories were opened in the principal towns but considerable emphasis was also placed on the greater self-sufficiency in food, with Chinese help in the supply of fertilizers and agricultural machinery and over drainage of coastal marshes, which made an extra 0.2 million ha of land available for cultivation. The sown area was reported as 0.22 million ha in 1938 but 0.36 in 1953 and 0.62 in 1980. Land is used primarily for cereals (with self-sufficiency achieved in 1975-6), but also for increasing amounts of cotton, sugar beet, oil-seeds, tobacco, and rice, backed up by investment in textile and food-processing industries.

The Cultural Revolution in China gave Hoxha the opportunity to launch a new attack on traditional Albanian attitudes. (47) There was a shake-up in the bureaucracy and women gained greater equality through erosion of the custom of arranged marriages (linked with dowry payments) which had kept them in a subservient role and reduced their availability for employment. Most radical, however, was the abandonment of religion, for with the closure of some 2,200 churches, mosques, and monasteries in 1967, Albania became the first atheistic state in the world. This brought to a conclusion the offensive against the Churches which had begun as early as 1944 with the takeover of Catholic schools and kindergartens in the north of the country and the confiscation of Church publications. Further measures were taken against the Catholic Church, as already described, and meanwhile, the small and already autonomous Orthodox Church was brought under government control. The head of the Church was arrested in 1948 and deposed the following year, to be replaced by the more pliable Bishop of Korce. By contrast the Muslim majority was treated sympathetically, for the Sunni and Bektashi hoxhas (the latter particularly tolerant and nationalistic) were seen as a minor threat to the regime in contrast with the Catholic and Orthodox priests. Yet the rival religious establishments starkly illustrated continuing divisions in society, most dramatically reflected in the blood feuds that continued to isolate Christian and Muslim clans in the early post-war years.

Atheism has the merit of eliminating any formal expression of religious division among Albanians and consolidating the nation (komb) in the eyes of the leadership; for the leadership argued that 'the faith of an Albanian is Albanianism': national identity was to be preserved at all costs. (48) The notion was current at the turn of the century but without the present radical expression. The Christians were the main target because of the strong cultural ties with Greece (Orthodox) and Italy (Catholic). Yet it is ironic that the state should have moved against the northern (Geg) Catholics for whom religion has traditionally been associated with nationality (distinguishing the Albanian community from Muslims and Slavs) and also against the Orthodox Church which played an important role in the creation of the state. People can still practice their religion by 'adjusting' to the conditions. Nevertheless, the vigilance of the authorities which extends to the collection of information about family activities from schoolchildren, may well have harmful cultural repercussions (despite superficial logic justifying liberation from a creed imposed through imperialism), and must leave a sobering impression in Kosovo among Albanians who had tended to look to their mother country for guidance in the past. The Muslims have perhaps been least emphatically obliterated and various religious survivals are still evident, notably in the observance of Muslim holidays in the Greek frontier area.

Self-reliance

Chinese aid continued to be important in building up industrial areas in the Tosk dominated parts of the country: the central region of Durres-Elbasan-Tirana with a degree of heavy industry and outlying centres of Vlore and Korce with considerable light industry. These economic achievements were threatened by the upheavals in the country during the years 1973-6 which precipitated a breakdown of contacts with China in 1978, following the latter's abandonment of its Cultural Revolution. The Albanians were upset by the decline in China's interest in its Balkan ally and offended by Chinese overtures to the USA, NATO, and the EEC. Criticisms were made through confidential channels at first but statements were published in 1977. (49) The Party is now giving more prominence to people with professional qualifications and also to women; and while the Tosk leadership is still asserted, much thought is being given to the regional background of Party members, with some people from poorer regions brought in to represent areas which have not benefited from the industrial-location policies to date. It is perhaps curious that in such a small country as Albania decentralization should be regarded with the greatest misgiving. Paradoxically, it was relaxation of centralization in Yugoslavia in 1966, through the dismissal of A. Rankovic and subsequent curbs on the secret police, that worried Tirana. Because of their greater powers of expression the Albanians of Kosovo were seen as a threat and the utmost vigilance was called for against the infiltration of subversive ideas. Yet the fragmentation of the country through the mountain topography is only very slowly overcome by modern infrastructure. The isolation and backwardness of the northern (Geg) people remains although their capital, Shkoder, has become an industrial centre, and connection by rail with Tirana is being followed by construction of the country's first international railway connection, between Shkoder and Titograd in Yugoslavia. Yet there is also potential for separatism in the Tosk areas close to the Greek border.

> Should strong regional feelings emerge in the major economic regions of the country it would seem that the Tosk districts between Lake Prespa and Gjirokaster might again show strong centrifugal tendencies,

especially if and when Tosk intellectuals no longer dominate the party hierarchy. (50)

At the time of writing Albanian politics remain typically enigmatic. The break with China in 1978 has been followed by a determination to get by in future without foreign assistance. Self-reliance was therefore the keynote for the 1981-5 Five Year Plan. The country now has the benefit of a substantial production of oil (some 5.0 million tonnes per annum) and also chromium (for which Albania is the world's third largest producer). The break with China left the Albanians with 0.4 million tonnes of chromite which had been earmarked for the Chinese market each year. Alternative markets can readily be found in the west since chrome is a strategic material essential for the manufacture of stainless steel. With its hydroelectric resources, Albanian chromite is relatively cheap, all the more so in view of the nickel and cobalt available as by-products. Electricity is also in surplus and deliveries are made not only to Yugoslavia (as agreed in 1980) but also to Italy. A large hydro station on the Drin started with Chinese aid was due for completion early in the 1980s and another is being built with equipment imported 'self-reliantly' from Austria and Yugoslavia. With self-sufficiency in cereals and a deficiency of only some 15 per cent in other foodstuffs, Albania could, with customary inattention to consumer goods, earmark large amounts of foreign exchange for imports of machinery. Trade contacts have improved with various European countries, both communist and non-communist (though emphatically not the Soviet Union). Italy is once again coming to the fore, with trade exchanges amounting to $70 million in 1980, backed up by cultural ties between the universities of Tirana, Rome, and Venice. Commercial contacts with France, Japan, and the UK are also developing while border demarcation with Greece has been started.

Relations with Yugoslavia were also improving, with plans for $720 million worth of trade for 1981-5, until the sharp deterioration of 1981 due to disturbances in Kosovo, where the rapid growth of population has placed considerable strain on the authorities through the provision of education and employment in what is clearly the most backward part of Yugoslavia. Trouble flared up among dissatisfied students at the University of Pristina. Poor accommodation at the university found an outlet in Greater Albanian nationalism, organized by an illegal 'National

51

Movement for the Liberation of Kosovo', seeking republican status for the province or outright transfer to Albanian sovereignty. Trouble also arose in the towns of Kosovska Mitrovica, Obilic, and Podujevo, and in various villages where conflict between Albanian and Yugoslav (Serbian and Montenegran) people caused the latter to leave the province altogether. While it is questionable how far Albania was involved in fermenting the trouble, there is no doubt that she has made use of the conflict to generate a new round of polemics; and there is acute embarrassment in Yugoslavia after years of moderation towards Albania with Kosovo as the bridge between the two nations. In the propaganda war local broadcasts are important. Kosovo's radio in Pristina competes not only with Tirana but with a new station in Kukes close to the border: from this new town (a symbol of socialist Albania by virtue of its origin as a resettlement scheme related to hydroelectric works) the television transmitter can reach out to virtually the whole of Kosovo. Nationalism of course is all-important in Albania, as witnessed by the recent completion of the National History Museum in Skanderbeg Square in Tirana, the Skanderbeg conservation museum complex in Kruja (famous for Albanian resistance to the Ottomans), and the Skanderbeg mausoleum in Lesh. However, with the strains of the policy of 'total self-reliance' the leadership may be anxious to demonstrate that the conditions in Kosovo (where there is freedom to migrate to other parts of Yugoslavia and even abroad) are much less than satisfactory. That the row over Kosovo is symptomatic of Albanian insecurity is borne out by the mysterious death of M. Shehu in 1981, Hoxha's hard-line prime minister, who appears to have been responsible for the particularly strident nature of Albanian polemics.

The death in 1985 of Enver Hoxha (who led the Albanian party since its foundation in 1941) has provided further opportunity for change. However, while it is possible that Albania will seek somewhat closer trade relations with Europe, both east and west, any thought of substantial internal reform seems highly speculative at this stage. (51) The economy would certainly benefit from smaller state farms, more investment in fishing, new technology in industry, and some foreign involvement in mining but all these changes would require major departures from orthodox policies. Even less likely is an Albanian association with one of major military blocs and substantial internal liberalization: both moves would incidentally create strategic problems for Yugoslavia through the Vlore naval base and a stronger secessionist movement in Kosovo and could precipitate some form of Yugoslav intervention, but with its attendant risks of an Albanian appeal for great power protection.

Chapter Two

POST-WAR CHANGES IN STATE BOUNDARIES

This chapter surveys the changes in state boundaries which have occurred as a result of the Second World War and comments on how the important decisions were made. The focus then shifts to two cities which have been drastically affected by the creation of a new political geography - first Trieste and then Berlin, with a detailed investigation of the reorganization of the latter city and the search for political and economic stability. The new boundaries of 1945 were to a large extent dictated by the Soviet Union seeking a more acceptable western frontier. Strategic motives concerned with defence in depth, access to harbours, and control over non-Soviet peoples, not to mention the Tsarist precedent of imperial frontiers extending well into Polish and Romanian territory, underpinned the urge for substantial frontier revisions. The alignments were however not entirely new. In the north the line suggested by Lord Curzon as an appropriate Russo-Polish frontier in the aftermath of the First World War was adopted and in the south the frontier line imposed on Romania in 1940 (following the old tsarist frontier along the River Prut) was reasserted. These gains were then rounded off by the annexation of Konigsberg (renamed Kaliningrad) and its hinterland in the northern part of East Prussia and by the annexation of Ruthenia, previously administered by Czechoslovakia. Both these areas were important in their own right: Konigsberg because of its port on the relatively warm waters of the southern Baltic, and Ruthenia because it provided the USSR with a common frontier with Hungary and control of virtually the entire Ukrainian population. These various changes were accepted by the Soviet Union's wartime allies and generated no opposition except among the provisional governments and non-communist political parties in the relevant East European states.

THE DIVISION OF GERMANY

Much more difficult however were the decisions over Germany. (1) It was generally accepted among the allies that Poland would be compensated for the loss of her eastern territories to Russia by gains from Germany in East Prussia, Pomerania, and Silesia. However, where should the new frontier be drawn and how should the remainder of Germany be divided up for the purposes of military occupation by the victorious armies? Serious thought began in 1942-3 when Germany's defeat became inevitable. At that time Soviet forces were poised to move west after the epic battle of Stalingrad. Since no allied landing in France had then been launched it was thought appropriate that the UK and USA should lay claim to two-thirds of German territory and thereby provide a legal basis for their presence should the Soviet advance prove to be particularly rapid. For there was even a possibility that Germany might collapse before the Red Army during the winter of 1943-4. On the other hand the heavy dependence of the western allies on the co-operation of the Soviet Union to achieve Germany's unconditional surrender made a generous Soviet occupation zone essential. Furthermore, once a western front was opened it was of course imperative that there should be sufficient pressure in the east to prevent German forces being transferred to deal with the new threat. In the event, however, the Soviets did not waver in their commitment, while considerable allied successes in the west (coupled with Soviet diversions to gain advantage in the Balkans and Poland) enabled the partners to compete meaningfully in a 'Race for Berlin'.

Curiously, perhaps the greatest disagreements were between the UK and USA in the north-western and southern parts of Germany. The limits of the Soviet zone were settled quite amicably once it was agreed that there would be national occupational zones, that both Austria and Berlin would be divided separately, and that East Prussia would probably be ceded to Poland. Working on the basis of equality in population between the three zones and respect for the boundaries of the historic provinces of Germany the

Soviet zone would extend as far west as Mecklenburg and Thuringia. Late in 1943 the Americans envisaged a Soviet zone that would extend no further west than a line from Stettin (now Szczecin) to the western edge of Bohemia (and so prevent Berlin being surrounded by a single national occupation zone) but that view could not be sustained and the Zonal Protocol of 1944 settled the matter. In the end the Soviets might appear to have been generously treated for Soviet withdrawal from parts of Berlin (captured in 1945) was amply reciprocated in areas east of the zonal boundary into which the British and especially American forces had initially advanced. Perhaps at least Thuringia might have been retained in one of the western zones (as part of the readjustments made in the west to provide for a French occupation zone). However, it was decided that modification of the 1944 protocol would create a dangerous precedent. The western powers could at least console themselves with their earlier resistance to the idea of Soviet occupation right up to the lower Elbe with Schleswig-Holstein a base for a possible Soviet advance in Denmark. The divisions within Berlin are also of interest, although once again the greatest amount of discussion was between the western allies (especially over the location of the French sector) rather than between these allies and the Soviets. Respect for the existing boroughs was a fundamental principle and the initial division into three sectors involved approximate parity of population with allocation taking place geographically according to the location of the occupation zones. There was of course no strong perception of the western boundary of the Soviet zone as the closely guarded frontier that it has become. Still less was there a view of the Soviet sector of Berlin walled off from other parts of the city.

GERMANY AND POLAND: THE ODER-NEISSE LINE

The Oder-Neisse (Odra-Nysa) frontier also emerged out of discussions in the closing stages of the war. The Poles were anxious to make certain that future German aggression should be avoided and this seemed to require not only closer co-operation with Czechoslovakia but a straightening of the German frontier and Polish control of the entire Upper Silesian coalfield. When General Sikorski visited President Roosevelt in 1942 he argued in a memorandum that 'the

Oder with the Stettin estuary and its tributaries down to the Czech frontier constitutes for Poland a natural line of security against Germany'. (2) This implied a frontier very much like the present Oder-Neisse line, although this would almost certainly have been Sikorski's most extreme demand: his basic aim was to gain part of the Pomeranian coast, to Kolberg (Kolobrzeg). It is also important to remember that the Poles were not then ready to agree to any modification of their eastern frontier and this brought them into conflict with the Soviets, who insisted on an advance to the River Bug. At Teheran in 1943 the western allies accepted Soviet claims for Konigsberg and for a revised western frontier to conform to the Curzon Line, with the Poles compensated by German territory, certainly in East Prussia and perhaps also in Pomerania and Silesia. The Oder was then seen as a reasonable western boundary for Poland. However, the proposal to use the Neisse tributary threw the allies into confusion over the eastern and western Neisse rivers. The present frontier follows the western (Gorlitzer or Lausitzer) Neisse and provides a straight frontier line from the Oder estuary to the northern edge of the Bohemian 'diamond', thus modifying the German encirclement of Czechoslovakia and providing Czechslovakia and Poland with a lengthy common frontier. However, the British were thinking of the eastern (Glatzer) Neisse, which would involve transfer of the German section of the Silesian coalfield but not the Liegnitz (Legnica) and Waldenburg (Walbrzych) areas. It seems doubtful if the Polish government in exile would have wanted these essentially German territories because of the ethnic problems that would have arisen; but refusal to accept the Curzon Line as the eastern frontier resulted in a rift with the Soviets, who set up a number of their own Polish proteges as the 'Lublin Committee', and it was this body which approved of both the Curzon Line and the western Neisse. The latter proposal implied expulsion of the German population from the ceded territories, a move which the western allies had not contemplated at Teheran (or at Yalta in 1945 when the western Neisse was clearly opposed by the UK and USA), but which was now attainable because the Soviet Union had gained the initiative in the east. Possibly the Germans themselves contributed to the decision by fleeing in the face of the Soviet advance, thus creating frightful confusion in the hard winter of 1944-5, especially when very large numbers of German refugees were stranded in utter distress not only at Gorlitz but also at Cottbus,

Figure 2.1 Trieste: boundary proposals, 1947

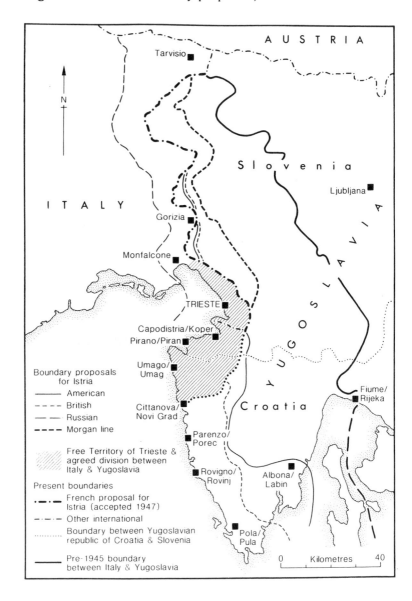

Source: R.L. Wolff 1974: 308.

Frankfurt, Kustrin, and Stettin. Of course, the Germans had good reason to fear assaults by Soviets as well as recruitment for forced labour in the east and it cannot be argued that if the Germans had waited the outcome would have been different.

DIVIDED CITIES: TRIESTE

Outside the area of effective Soviet control a number of territorial adjustments have either been made or contemplated, and Yugoslavia has inevitably been at the centre of these matters. Italian withdrawal from the Zara (Zadar) enclave was not particularly controversial, but the Istrian Peninsula (the Italian province of Venezia-Giulia), including Trieste, was a bone of bitter contention (Figure 2.1). The Yugoslav Partisans declared the annexation of this province at their Jajce meeting in 1943, but the Allies would not accept this. As Axis forces withdrew from the head of Adriatic, Partisan infiltration of Istria (up to the Morgan Line agreed with the British) was balanced by the presence of New Zealand troops in Trieste itself. In discussions over a permanent frontier Soviet backing for the exaggerated Yugoslav claim that the Partisans had 'conquered' the whole of Venezia-Giulia was countered by the opinion of the other allies that the Germans had withdrawn in the face of the overall military situation and that territorial adjustments should be based on ethnic considerations, so as to leave the minimum number of people under alien rule. At a foreign ministers' conference in 1945 it was agreed that experts should suggest possible frontier lines, and the result was a set of proposals advanced in 1946. There were considerable discrepancies, however, with the Soviet proposal most favourable and the American proposal least favourable to the Yugoslavs. The French proposal was the most evenly balanced ethnically, leaving 115,000 Yugoslavs in Italy and 130,000 Italians in Yugoslavia. It left Trieste itself to Italy but, by taking the frontier along the Quieto river, ceded the southern Istrian towns of Albona (Labin), Parenzo (Porec), and Pola (Pula) to Yugoslavia. Acceptance of the French proposal as a compromise was strongly resented by the Yugoslav government, thinking that the Soviets should have applied greater pressure. Yugoslav belligerence was brought to a critical level by the shooting down of an American plane which had strayed into Yugoslav airspace on a flight

59

from Rome to Vienna. However, some territory on the western side of the agreed boundary was to compose a 'Free Territory of Trieste' with the northern half occupied by the Americans and British and the southern by Yugoslavia. (3)

In 1947 the UN Security Council accepted responsibility for governing Trieste and an Italian peace treaty, including the Trieste settlement, was then signed. However, because of disagreement between the Soviet Union and the western allies, no governor for Trieste was ever appointed and administration remained in the hands of the occupying forces. A new situation emerged in 1948, however, when a violent election campaign in Italy called for some western concessions over Trieste to head off a communist victory, while the rupture in relations between the Soviet Union and Yugoslavia produced a less intransigent attitude from both Moscow and Belgrade (the latter now dependent on western economic assistance). The idea of a 'Free Territory of Trieste' was eventually dropped, therefore, and the two sections were handed over to the governments of the adjacent countries: Zone B to the Yugoslavs (who had illegally treated the area as part of their own country since 1945) and Zone A to the Italians. This happened in 1954, when relations between Yugoslavia and the USSR were cool and while contacts with the west were growing. Yugoslavia was happy to settle for a partition of the 'Free Zone' (with a small section of Zone A - Lazaretto - going to Yugoslavia) since it gave her more territory than any other power except the Soviet Union had demanded. It is also worth noting that Yugoslavia advanced a territorial claim against Austria in respect of the Slovene-inhabited area of Carinthia, despite the plebiscite of 1920 which had revealed a majority preference for Austria in the Klagenfurt area. However, this made little headway and no progress was made after the withdrawal of Soviet support in 1948 through Yugoslavia's expulsion from the Cominform. Yugoslavia renounced her claims in 1950 and the Austrian State Treaty's guarantee of the pre-Anschluss frontiers effectively ruled out any possibility of change. (4)

BERLIN (5)

The division of Berlin was never envisaged by the wartime allies and the four occupation zones were to be significant only for some local administration. The city was to be governed as a unit by the commandants of the four occupation powers without any separation from the surrounding Soviet occupation zone of Germany or the rest of the country. However, the withdrawal of the Soviet representative from the control council in 1948 signalled the beginning of a process of division between the Soviet and western zones of the city. The Soviets hoped to gain control of the whole city and tested the resolve of the western powers to remain in Berlin by closing all surface access routes to the city in June 1948 after the introduction of a currency reform in West Berlin. The key test of allied resolve came in June 1948 when the Russians halted all canal, rail, and road traffic to West Berlin and cut off supplies of coal and milk. The city was to acknowledge Soviet rule or starve. This was the Soviet response to the decision by western powers to run their occupation zones of Germany as a single economic unit, thereby achieving the currency reform which the Soviets· had previously frustrated. The initial strategy of an airlift (Luftbrucke) was not seriously regarded as an effective solution to the problems of feeding the city and maintaining the industries in operation, but with a substantial stockpile of food already in place there was a basis for negotiations. The airports were not well situated for a major increase in traffic (Tempelhof was situated in the very heart of the city and a steep-angled approach was necessary) and insufficient aircraft were available. With additional aircraft, landing facilities at a new airfield at Tegel in addition to Tempelhof and Gatow, and close co-ordination between American and British forces so that flights were made in the same direction from Rhein-Main near Frankfurt (American Zone) to Berlin and from Berlin to Fassberg near Hannover (British Zone), it was possible to increase the daily load from just 80 tonnes on the first day of the airlift to 3.8 thousand tonnes in August 1948 and 7.5 in February 1949; and this despite some very bad flying conditions (including dense fog) and Soviet harrassment. Altogether, 2.3 million tonnes of cargo were flown to Berlin until the blockade was removed in May 1949: this figure included 1.4 million tonnes of coal. Because of further problems the airlift continued until September 1949 when a working agreement was reached involving separate administration for the two parts of the city in terms of civilian government as well as military occupation. (6)

Construction of the Berlin Wall

The Berlin Wall of 1961 has now become the starkest symbol of the division of Germany and, more generally, the east-west conflict. Some 45 kilometres of wall separate the two halves of Berlin while a further 120 kilometres separate West Berlin from the GDR. There was no legal impediment constraining frontier controls at state boundaries, including the occupation zones of Germany, but the four-power agreement over Berlin reached at Potsdam in 1945 provided for free movement between the various sectors of the city. While travel from the Soviet occupation zone into East Berlin might be controlled, people in East Berlin could move freely into the western sectors. Indeed, before 1961 it was common for residents living in one part of the city to work in another. However, the higher living standards in the FRG and the more stimulating cultural environment there, led to a massive exodus of GDR citizens who used Berlin's special status to flee to the west. The closed border between the two Germanies was ineffective as long as a potential escape route via Berlin remained open. It is estimated that up to four million people left the Soviet zone in the period up to 1961, leading to an absolute drop in the population of the country (including East Berlin) from 18.4 to 17.3 million. The flow increased after 1959 with the completion of collectivization. A disproportionately large number of those leaving were professionals and young people, with the result that the economy was burdened by a loss of skilled manpower and a falling rate of natural increase. The problem was acutely embarrassing in the political sense for the USSR and GDR governments, as western observers ironically quoted Lenin's words about a people 'voting with their feet'. However, there was also the important matter of a final German peace treaty which the USSR wanted its former wartime allies to sign, so as to recognize the FRG and GDR as sovereign states and confirm the transfers of German territory east of the Oder-Neisse to Poland and the USSR. Unilateral action by the USSR to solve the Berlin problem was therefore postponed to avoid antagonizing the wartime allies, while there appears to have been some complacency in western circles as to the likelihood of a wall, in contrast to other action such as controls between East Berlin and the GDR. Unprecedently high levels of migration, reaching a thousand people per day in July 1961, precipitated the decision to build the wall, a task which was carried through with remarkable speed and skill.

Sealing off West Berlin has been described as 'a model of concealment, deception and surprise'. (7) Some 50,000 men went into action at 0230 hours on 13 August 1961, dividing the city by a cordon of barbed wire and other crude barriers, replaced after a few weeks by more solid structures. Escape was still possible in the early days by tunnelling and evacuation from buildings standing on the frontier line. However, the defences have been strengthened by removing buildings adjacent to the wall to create a broad fortified strip virtually impossible to cross except at checkpoints. A correspondent standing in Spandau Forest in West Berlin describes how he was faced by

> a ten foot barrier of concrete slabs; beyond it was a strip of raked sand 50 yards wide: the free-fire zone. Beyond that was a row of arc-lights mounted high on pylons. Beneath them black shaggy alsations tethered to running wires lay palpitating in the afternoon heat. Behind the dogs was a tarmaced road and an anti-vehicle ditch. Beyond these ran a fence of twenty-four electrified wires which, when touched, remain mute at the site but give audible and visible warning to the nearest guards. Behind that was yet another fence, of razor-edged metal sheeting, designed to keep game animals away from the warning systems. And to our right, invigilating over the whole dreadful death-trap, two guards in their concrete watchtower with Kalashnikov automatics slung over their shoulders, watched and photographed our every movement through binoculars and zoom lenses (Sunday Telegraph, 10 August 1986).

Small wonder that more than seventy GDR citizens have been killed trying to cross the wall since 1971 alone. Most of these deaths have arisen through shooting by border guards, though some guards have been shot by their fleeing comrades when trying to prevent escapes. More than a hundred people have been wounded and some 3,000 have been arrested for attempting to flee (though the true figures may be higher). On the other hand some 5,000 people have been successful, with relatively large numbers in the early years when the fortifications were not so formidable in contrast with the modest level of about a hundred per annum at present. Simpler routes are available to GDR citizens through Bulgaria and Romania, where holidays can be taken with relatively few formalities and where the frontiers with other Balkan countries (Greece and Yugoslavia) are not quite so carefully controlled. The 1.39 thousand kilometre-long inter-zonal frontier is equally well defended although the fortifications are older, dating back to 1952: mines and self-firing shrapnel guns have been installed. Some 30,000 soldiers are involved with border duties.

Officially the GDR government sees the wall as a positive achievement and its citizens have been brainwashed by the Schutzwall propaganda: the wall is an anti-fascist defence to preserve socialism from subversive western pressure. In reality, however, the wall is of course an extremely emotive issue and may be regarded as simultaneously a defeat for its builders (who could not compete freely with the west for the loyalty of GDR citizens) and for its western detractors (who lacked the means and the will to force Soviet compliance with the Potsdam agreement with its provision for free movement so flagrantly violated). It is interesting to speculate that the wall might never have been necessary had there not been a dogmatic imposition of communism in the GDR under the leadership of W. Ulbricht, provoking a stronger desire in the FRG for reunification, rather than constructive dialogue between two German states. However, it is hard to see how the Soviet Union under any post-war leadership could have accepted a regime in the GDR liberal enough to remove the incentive for migration to the west and to attract willing recognition from Bonn. Equally, it is difficult to deny that the wall was a precondition for detente in Europe. As long as Berlin was undivided by any continuous barrier there was instability because of unrealistic expectations on both sides. The GDR anticipated taking control of the entire city while the FRG held out real hopes of reunification of the whole of Germany. Hints in the summer of 1961 that American interests were tied up with West Berlin rather than with Berlin as a whole may have been taken by the Soviets as a signal to build a wall which would at least imply acceptance of western interests in one part of the city. The wall thus contributed to an atmosphere of realism from which the Ostpolitik of the former FRG Chancellor, W. Brandt, was born.

Any tacit acknowledgement by the GDR government of its insecurity has been followed by some growth of confidence and a cautious programme of reform. (8) In 1962 the legal system placed a new emphasis on leniency and rehabilitation instead of punitive measures and a year later the introduction of the New Economic System began a period of substantial economic growth. On the other hand the demonstration of Soviet determination to defend its European interests and permit limited reform when appropriate in the context of long-term stability has brought about a new appraisal of the communist bloc by the western powers, most clearly seen in the Ostpolitik of the FRG government. The underlying proposition is that while the communist system is unacceptable its forcible overthrow is impossible and therefore the best approach to the objective of a freer environment is a reduction of tension to the point where the USSR sees an interest in further liberalization. The policy is fraught with difficulty, particularly since any slackening of controls may encourage a rise of popular expectations which can then only be contained through a renewed clamp-down.

Uncertainty over the frontiers has largely been removed by the treaties signed by the FRG in 1970, implying acceptance of the reality of two German states. (9) GDR frontiers are described as 'inviolable' (and equally the frontiers of the GDR's socialist neighbours) so that any western pretences about the achievement of radical political change in Eastern Europe are now destroyed. The admission of the two German states to the United Nations was delayed until 1973 but the GDR government gained considerably in confidence: the stability of the state was assured and the right to a diplomatic presence in the FRG (with a large mission in Bonn) facilitated further espionage which (notwithstanding any domestic 'German' dimension) served to increase the prestige of the state in the eyes of the Soviets, who were obviously far less well able to penetrate NATO's crucial forward area themselves. The developing barter trade in human beings, exchanging spies in the FRG for political prisoners in the GDR maintains a high morale among GDR agents in the Federal Republic.

The Four-Power Agreement on Berlin

Such concessions by the FRG paved the way for the 1971 Four-Power Agreement on Berlin which came into force in June 1972 after the signing of the FRG's treaties with the

USSR and Poland in 1970. (10) Although the contemporary euphoria over détente may have led to some popular overstatement of the value of the new arrangement, no vital western interests in Berlin were abandoned and a written undertaking was obtained from the Soviet government that 'transit traffic by road, rail and waterways through the territory of the GDR of civilian persons and goods between the western sectors of Berlin and the FRG will be facilitated and unimpeded.' Moreover, practical arrangements were spelt out. On the other hand the Russians have gained a Consulate General and a trade mission in West Berlin and they have secured a reduced 'Federal presence' (specifically, activities related to the Federal Parliament). Moreover, the agreement has not changed basic geographical realities: West Berlin is a vulnerable enclave and while there appears to be a continuing determination to defend the city, with the power of nuclear deterrence in the background, there must be some lingering uncertainty in West Berlin over the disposition of American public opinion in the event of a new crisis which the USSR and GDR between them can create whenever it suits them. However, at present Berlin is experiencing a considerable easing of tension, and the exchanges of prisoners across the Glienicke bridge, between the Spandau area of West Berlin and Potsdam in the GDR, reflect the improving relations between the superpowers.

Since the 1971 agreement Berlin has enjoyed more than a decade of relative stability and prosperity: the 1970s were certainly the most tranquil post-war decade. There remain ambiguities over the status of East Berlin (as opposed to other parts of the GDR) and over the relationship between West Berlin and the FRG. The western powers insist that East Berlin is subject to Four-Power Agreements, yet although the city was demilitarized in 1945 the Soviet Union has allowed the GDR National People's Army to hold annual May Day parades in East Berlin since 1956. The GDR has extended conscription to East Berlin and has removed the check-points between East Berlin and the GDR (in 1977). All GDR legislation has been extended to East Berlin and East Berliners have participated directly in the elections to the GDR People's Chamber since 1979. Visa and currency exchange regulations have been applied to visits to East Berlin. On the other hand, despite some prevarication, the FRG has been generally successful in signing agreements with Warsaw Pact states in which West Berlin is specifically included. Moreover, FRG embassies in Eastern Europe represent the residents of West Berlin.

It was unfortunate that visits across the wall by Berliners were so slow to be properly organized. Only in December 1963 was a pass system introduced allowing West Berliners to visit relatives in the east for Christmas. Movement in the other direction was only possible for pensioners in 1964 and for younger people in 1972 (given pressing family circumstances). Financial assistance from the FRG has induced some concessions over currency exchanges for West German visitors to the east (and the defences along the inter-zonal frontier where some automatic shooting-devices have been removed). People living in West Berlin can go into East Berlin for a day at a time and may stay until midnight. Some thirty million visits were made in 1980 alone. Citizens of the FRG may travel anywhere in the GDR, entering from West Berlin, but must state the regions (Bezirken) to which they wish to travel and must complete their return journey by 0200 hours the following day. Such visits, along with others made by citizens from non-socialist countries, totalled some ten million in 1980. However, visits to East Berlin have been adversely affected by increases in the currency exchange requirement in 1973 and 1980. The present requirement is DM25 per day. Although there have been concessions for young children and for pensioners, the economic pressure remains controversial and explains why the number of visits to East Berlin and the GDR by West Berliners was only 2.10 millions in 1985-6 compared with 3.72 in 1972-3. Movement from the east has always been comparatively modest. Apart from a number of special cases involving attendance at conferences, cultural exchanges, and sporting engagements, the 1.3 million GDR citizens travelling to the west (and primarily the FRG) in 1980 were pensioners (women over sixty years of age and men over sixty-five).

Since the transit agreement was signed in 1972, travel links between West Berlin and the FRG have been greatly improved. Transit fees are no longer payable and delays have been greatly reduced. Goods are conveyed in sealed containers and the GDR authorities have no right to search travellers or vehicles unless they suspect a serious breach of the law. Road links by autobahn are available to Hamburg, Hannover, Frankfurt am Main, and Nurnberg, crossing the GDR/FRG frontier at Gudow, Helmstedt, Herleshausen, and Rudolphstein respectively. The access routes leave West

Table 2.1 Population trends in Berlin, 1905–84

Year	Berlin			East Berlin			West Berlin			
	A	B	C	A	B	C	A	B	C	D
1905	2,034	3.35	48.8			35.9			35.8	
1919	3,804	6.36	66.9			53.4			47.4	
1939	4,332	5.44	58.9			55.0			39.6	
1946	3,134	4.90	50.9	1,175	6.50	49.0	1,969	4.29	35.4	59.7
1950	3,328	4.87	49.3	1,189	6.47	45.2	2,139	4.28	33.0	55.6
1955	3,345	4.76	43.4	1,150	6.41	43.5	2,195	4.19	28.9	52.4
1960	3,281	4.51	39.7	1,077	6.25	41.4	2,204	3.97	26.9	48.9
1965	3,276	4.43	38.9	1,074	6.31	40.4	2,202	3.87	26.2	48.8
1970	3,206	4.19	38.5	1,084	6.35	40.9	2,122	3.57	25.6	51.1
1975	3,078	3.91	36.2	1,094	6.49	41.0	1,984	3.21	23.6	55.1
1980	3,042	3.89	37.6	1,146	6.83	41.8	1,896	3.08	23.4	60.4
1984	3,044	3.91	38.6	1,189	7.13	43.0	1,855	3.03	23.5	64.1

Source: Census returns and estimates in statistical yearbooks.

Notes: A – Total population (thousands);

B – Population as a percentage of the total population of GDR/FRG (Reich for 1905-39);

C – Population as a percentage of the total population of the ten largest provincial cities in GDR/FRG (if the whole Reich is taken for 1905-39 Breslau would come into the reckoning and the figures would read 46.3, 65.0, and 57.7). Figures for East and West Berlin for 1905-39 assume the same proportions of the Berlin population as in 194...

Berlin in Wannsee, with the exception of the Hamburg route, a relatively new facility (1982), which runs from Spandau. The same links are available by railway. The line from Hannover (which runs through the GDR from Helmstedt to Babelsberg) is part of the west-east trunk route which runs on from the Zoologische Garten station in West Berlin to Friedrichstrasse and Ostbahnhof in the East. Lines running from West Berlin to Frankfurt and Nurnberg also leave the city at Wannsee/Babelsberg but cross into the FRG at Bebra, Ludwigsstadt, or Hof, while the Hamburg service leaves West Berlin at Spandau/Falkensee and arrives in the FRG at Buchen. Over twenty connections are provided each day with various cities in the FRG. Over a hundred flights operate daily from Tegel airport to cities in the FRG and beyond, although only American, British, and French airlines can use the corridors across the GDR. Improvements continue with the resurfacing of the autobahn from Helmstedt in 1979. Direct access from the west to the Teltow Canal was provided in 1981 and the rail link between Helmstedt and West Berlin is now double-tracked throughout (an improvement completed in 1983). Future plans include a new high-speed railway from West Berlin, bifurcating at Stendal to reach Hamburg and the Puttgarden ferry (for Denmark) via Uelzen and Luneburg; and to reach Hannover and Gottingen via Wolfsburg.

Berlin: post-war changes in its urban geography

The outstanding feature is the much reduced importance of Berlin in the context of the two German states. In 1946 Berlin accounted for 4.90 per cent of the population of Germany (1945 frontiers), but since then the share has fallen continuously to 3.89 in 1980 (with a slight revival to 3.91 in 1984). West Berlin has lost ground in relation to the FRG (4.29 per cent of the population in 1946 and 3.03 in 1984), whereas East Berlin has gained in relation to the GDR since 1960 (Table 2.1). The same divergence appears when the population of Berlin is related to the top ten other cities: a decline from 50.9 per cent (1946) to 38.6 (1984) for Berlin as a whole, a steeper decline from 35.2 per cent to 23.5 for West Berlin and a relatively modest loss from 49.0 to 43.0 in East Berlin (with a gain from the lowest level of 40.4 reached in 1965). It is surprising that as the GDR's capital (Haupstadt) East Berlin has not grown more rapidly: if the new city of Halle-Neustadt were to be included in the population of Halle then East Berlin even now would not be keeping pace with the main provincial cities of the country. In absolute terms the population of Berlin increased up to 1955 and then declined continuously to 1980 since when there has been a slight revival. In West Berlin the growth continued up to 1960 but the decline has since been continuous whereas growth in East Berlin resumed after 1965 following fifteen years of decline.

Demographically, the situation is clearly most serious in West Berlin. The age structure is becoming more unbalanced, with 38,000 deaths each year but only 18,000 births. Migration patterns have changed quite radically. Traditional source areas of migrants (east of the Oder-Neisse) were cut off after the Second World War and most newcomers during the 1950s were refugees from East Berlin and the GDR. This immediate hinterland was then cut off by the Berlin Wall in 1961, and migrants have been attracted from the FRG, especially the northern parts (Bremen, Hamburg, Lower Saxony, and Schleswig-Holstein). Many young people left the city, primarily because of the decline in manufacturing: a quarter of West Berlin's industrial employment (70,000 jobs) was lost between 1970 and 1977 alone. High operating costs, including the burden of transport to EEC markets, wrought havoc with the electrical engineering industry. All the major firms have cut jobs, including Siemens, and the clearance of AEG factories in the Gesundbrunnen area has been particularly spectacular. Elsewhere, at Wilhelmsruh for example, old factories have been converted into warehouses. Electrical engineering is still the city's largest industry with a total employment of 57,000, followed by food processing (17,000), mechanical engineering (16,000), and chemicals (12,000). However, these traditional industries have been far less stable in West Berlin than in the East.

Ever since 1952 the West Berlin economy has been supported by subsidies from the FRG and at the present time a rebate scheme operates in the FRG whereby tax allowances are made against purchases from West Berlin. This helps to stimulate the market for manufacturers in West Berlin. Also important is the legislation allowing tax concessions to West Berlin firms in relation to the value added in the city. Some 2,300 industrial companies operate in West Berlin, including over thirty American firms (such as Ford, IBM, ITT, and Westinghouse). So there has been some worthwhile consolidation of West Berlin industry, while at the same time there has been growth in the tertiary sector. Efforts have been made to boost the conference business (witness the new international conference centre) and to maximize the city's potential as a commercial centre in the context of east-west trade. The demographic situation has improved recently, with migration stimulated by the payment of travel and removal expenses as well as the tax-free bonuses and higher child allowances paid to all employees in West Berlin. These incentives have brought about an increase in the number of people of working age (as well as a net growth of population) in 1985 and 1986. Reference should also be made to the influx of guest workers (Gastarbeiter), especially from Turkey, but also from Greece, Italy, Spain, and Yugoslavia. There has also been a considerable movement of refugees from the GDR and many have chosen to live in West Berlin.

There are now about 115,000 Turks living in West Berlin (along with 31,000 Yugoslavs, 12,000 Poles, 8,000 Italians, and 7,000 Greeks). They are to be found principally in Kreuzberg (where 28 per cent of the population consists of foreign residents), Tiergarten, and Wedding. More than a quarter of all births in West Berlin relate to these immigrant communities. Shortage of space for single-family houses means that West Berlin is a city of tenants. The high cost of housing is also a problem, especially in the environmentally attractive areas with ample provision of forests, lakes, and parks. Emphasis in the 1960s on new housing projects in the outer suburbs (such as Markisches Viertel in Reinickendorf) has given way to slum clearance and modernization in the inner city. Old tenements are being improved as the middle is ripped out of each square block and replaced by low-density flats and gardens. There are also areas where comprehensive redevelopment has taken place.

The division of the city is very clearly apparent in the spheres of transport and energy. (11) Since the war the development of ring railways and roads has been modified to ensure that transit through West Berlin is never necessary for domestic GDR traffic (Figure 2.2). A canal system bypassing West Berlin is also available. The transport system of West Berlin is largely isolated and most railways and roads are now blocked on all sides. However, since 1928 there has been co-ordination between different modes through the formation of the municipal transport

71

Figure 2.2 Berlin's transport network

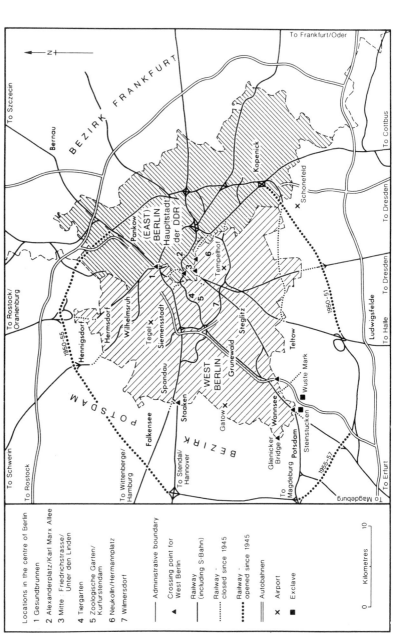

Locations in the centre of Berlin

1 Gesundbrunnen
2 Alexanderplatz/Karl Marx Allee
3 Mitte   Friedrichstrasse/
         Unter den Linden
4 Tiergarten
5 Zoologische Garten/
  Kurfurstendam
6 Neukolln/Hermannplatz
7 Wilmersdorf

— Administrative boundary

▲ Crossing point for
  West Berlin

── Railway
   (including S-Bahn)

········· Railway -
          closed since 1945

•••••••• Railway -
         opened since 1945

═══ Autobahnen

✕ Airport

■ Exclave

0   10
└──────────────────────┘
     Kilometres

department <u>Berliner Verkehrs-Betriebe</u> (BVG). Bus services are integrated with the U-Bahn (underground railway), the first section of which opened in 1902. The network has been developed very considerably in West Berlin since 1945. Some 90 kilometres of route length were in use by 1976 with a further 35 kilometres under construction or planned (including a direct line from Steglitz into the centre of West Berlin, connecting with various lines <u>en route</u>). Disruption arising from the division of the city is minimized by the arrangement whereby the main north-south route operates on a transit basis under the East Berlin Mitte with a stop only at the Friedrichstrasse. The BVG has recently taken over the surface suburban railway (S-Bahn) which dates back to the nineteenth century (with electrification from 1924). The network was severed in 1961 when the wall was built and, since it was then operated by the GDR railway company (<u>Deutsche Reichsbahn</u>), it was boycotted in protest by the citizens of West Berlin. Following the complete closure of the system in West Berlin (following a strike by West Berlin S-Bahn staff in 1980), the system has been partially modernized under new management. Since 1984 a magnetically driven train has been in service: this M-Bahn operates between Gleisdreieck U-Bahn station and the Kulturforum in Tiergarten. West Berlin maintains its own electricity supply without any grid system to fall back on: coal and oil are brought in by land and water with stockpiling to ensure ample reserves in the event of a crisis. The total installed capacity of eight power stations was 2233 MW in 1986. Town gas is produced by cracking light fuel-oil and methanol, but West Berlin is now linked to the pipeline bringing gas from Siberia to Western Europe and town gas supplies will gradually be replaced. To prevent any risk of political dependence a year's supply of natural gas will be stored underground.

The planning of housing, offices, and shops has also involved separate strategies highlighted by ideological differences. (12) In East Berlin the post-war period has, of course, seen a sharp decline in the functions of the old Mitte. Many businesses were destroyed and other enterprises migrated to the FRG. However, the historic street network is retained and certain functions have been re-established: ministries, embassies (including the Soviet embassy) and trade union buildings in the former government zone (west of the Friedrichstrasse), banks in the old finance zone (Behrenstrasse), printing and publishing establishments in the pre-war newspaper district, and cultural-scientific institutions on Unter den Linden when several historic buildings, including the Opera and University have been refurbished. This continuity was sustained by the lack of resources for any radical replanning in the early post-war period (both in respect of building materials and planning concepts), together with the importance of national culture and history for the new socialist state. However, following legislation in 1950 which paved the way for expropriation of privately owned buildings and land, a plan was implemented to create a central square, surrounded by prestigious buildings with cultural and political functions and linked with other parts of the city by broad avenues. This gave rise to Stalinallee (Frankfurter Allee and Karl-Marx-Allee since 1961) and Marx-Engels-Platz, which lead through to Unter den Linden and the Brandenburg Gate: the Soviet-style flats of 1952 were followed, after 1959, by another residential complex using prefabricated units. A building plan for the whole city centre did not appear until 1961: it has been responsible for buildings around Marx-Engels-Platz including those for the Council of State and Ministry of Foreign Affairs. Then, a further plan for the city centre in 1964 introduced a television tower as the dominant 'high-altitude' feature.

Not until the General Master Plan of 1968 (part of a strategy of 'fundamental renewal' for cities in the GDR intitiated by the Party in 1967) was there a comprehensive plan for the whole of East Berlin, concentrating new housing and services into four axes (Tangenten), each intersecting with the main radial roads of the city at progressively greater distances from the centre. Industry was to be accommodated between the two outer axes, convenient for both travel to work and the transport of raw materials and finished products. On the other hand, the development of the innermost axis involved substantial improvements to the Mitte: new building in the Alexanderplatz area including the Stadt Berlin hotel and the headquarters of the city's electrical engineering industry; a complex close to the television tower including a new 'Palace of the Republic' and historic buildings such as the Marienkirche and Town Hall; commercial and cultural developments on Friedrichstrasse to occupy spaces which have remained empty since the clearance of war debris (despite some previous developments for banking and hotel/catering services) and residential complexes involving high-rise flats on Leipziger

Strasse (a former shopping street) at densities exceeding 500 persons per ha. However, despite all the redevelopment the provision of services is conspicuously sparse, certainly by comparison with the pre-communist era: retail establishments, medical practices, travel agencies, and catering establishments are all reduced in number to a greater extent than the increase in average size would justify; and the entire insurance system of the GDR is concentrated on just three sites on the eastern side of the city centre. Lack of competition creates a situation where, for example, there is just one photographic shop in the centre, belonging to the industrial enterprise Carl Zeiss Jena. It is also the result of planning which seeks to reduce city centre (and city-district) shopping to specialized shops and department stores offering goods in occasional demand, while third- and fourth-order centres provide goods subject to frequent or daily demand.

In West Berlin there has been a spontaneous process of development to bring out local centres in locations with good accessibility and only limited bomb damage. Examples include Charlottenburg (Wilmersdorfer Strasse) and Neukolln (Karl-Marx-Strasse/Hermannplatz), but the outstanding case is Steglitz's Schlosstrasse where shopping comprises rebuilt specialized stores, several department stores, and the integrated shopping centre of 'Forum Steglitz' opened in 1974. Steglitz also accommodates many other types of business including a considerable number of restaurants and medical practices. Services for West Berlin as a whole are provided in a new <u>Stadtmitte</u> which has emerged in what used to be the business and entertainment area for the West End of the unified city. The main focus for commercial functions is the Kurfurstendamm/Breitscheidplatz with shops, (including the Europa Centre at Breitscheidplatz - 1965) hotels, various professional services, and clothing industries; but banking and administration of the electrical industry dominate Ernst-Reuter-Platz and Hardenberg-strasse. There is a cultural complex nearby in the south of Tiergarten Park including the Congress Hall (1957), Philharmonic Hall (1963), National Gallery (1968), and State Library (1972), but the administration of West Berlin is based largely at the old town hall of Schoneberg and to a lesser extent at Charlottenburg and Wilmersdorf. This reflects West Berlin's perception of the divided city as a temporary abberation. Certainly, there has been encouragement of West Berlin's commercial growth through the European Recovery Programme and by laws passed by the FRG Bundestag, but long-term planning anticipates reunification.

> West Berlin city planners have tried to preserve from other uses the larger reserved spaces to the east and south of Tiergarten Park for the projected location of government buildings and foreign embassies in the event of future reunion of the two parts of Berlin and of both Germanies. (13)

There is a considerable amount of open space in West Berlin immediately adjacent to the wall which may be needed one day for buildings and infrastructure, such as an autobahn link which could easily connect the links with the orbital motorway which at present terminate in Wedding in West Berlin and Pankow in the East.

CONCLUSION

Although the divided nature of Berlin is still all too obvious, there have been a number of significant improvements. The isolation of West Berlin has been eased not only by improvements on the access routes from the FRG but by various local arrangements. The enclave of Steinstucken (part of Zehlendorf), can now be reached without checks by GDR border guards (though negotiations on the possible exchange of territory have not yet succeeded). The disposal of West Berlin's garbage is now effected in the GDR with a special border crossing-point opened for the purpose between Neukolln and Gross Zeithen; and pollution of the Havel Lakes in West Berlin has been reduced by the construction of sewage treatment works in the GDR. Church administration has been made easier. Thus, for example, permission has been given to the Roman Catholic bishop, whose diocese covers the whole of Berlin and part of the GDR as well, to spend up to thirty days each quarter on visits to parishes in West Berlin where a more highly autonomous administration was previously necessary.

It is evident that several improvements have been made in the quality of life in East Berlin. Although cultural life in Berlin is limited, it is now vastly superior to other cities in the GDR: Deutsche Staatsoper, Komische Oper, and Berliner Ensemble were joined in 1983 by a reopened Deutsches

Theater. There has also been a significant conservation effort in East Berlin: for although the Schloss (the city palace of the Prussian monarchy) was demolished in 1950 and ultimately replaced in 1976 by the Palace of the Republic, the new outlook on German and Prussian history has resulted in some important initiatives. The equestrian statue of Frederick the Great has been returned to its vantage point on Unter den Linden, the boulevard laid out by the Great Elector in 1647 to connect the Schloss with Tiergarten. Historic buildings along this street have been restored, including the Altes Palace, the Prinzessinnen-palais, St Hedwig's cathedral, the Zeughaus, and the old Royal Library. The Nikolaiviertel district has been restored and the Ephraim Palace, built after the Thirty Years War by Frederick the Great's mintmaster (V.H. Ephraim) but demolished to make way for street widening in 1935, is being reconstructed. This is an interesting development, part of the celebrations marking the 750th anniversary of the city (1988), because it was agreed that segments of the original façade, which had been stored in the western part of the city, should be handed over. On the other hand serious difficulties remain, especially with regard to travel for East Berliners.

Chapter Three

THE REGIONAL DIMENSION

East European governments can implement regional policies very effectively through their near monopoly over investment so that the required discrimination can be imposed on appropriate branches of the economy: agriculture, manufacturing, transport, and other services. People can be positively stimulated by such allocations (migration may be induced by new jobs and apartments in certain towns) and they can also be constrained by shortages, administrative controls, and in the last resort by coercion. In all cases propaganda plays an important supportive role. However, the authorities must also decide between sectoral and regional priorities, and generally speaking it seems that planning has given priority to the expansion of industries the national economy requires rather than the development of regions: the latter have advanced through harmonizing their resources with sectoral plans which have been determined centrally. However, most industries are now 'footloose' and provided that infrastructure is up to the national standard, any individual region can be assisted on the basis of an appropriate share of the total investment, whatever the sectoral priorities. (1)

Governments are concerned about equity, defined in the case of Hungary in 1971, as optimum use of resources and convergence in standards of living. (2) It is usual to find that the poorer regions have made progress in catching up with the more advanced areas, although significant differences still exist between regions and between countries. (3) The progress made by backward areas in general will be examined in the next section. The purpose of this chapter is to look at the ways in which regional inequalities have been perceived apart from the general question of equity related to homogeneity across the nation (Figure 3.1). (4) First, there are historic imbalances which threaten the stability of the state: hence the problem of Slovakia (Czechoslovakia). Second, the assimilation of new territories in order to demonstrate effective occupation and forestall claims for further frontier changes: the case of Poland's recovered territories. The third category comprises regions where ethnic conflicts create instability and bring the adequacy of the present frontiers into question. The issues are often complicated by the historical legacy and by the events of the early post-war years. Discussion concentrates on the Macedonian question but there are also references to Kosovo, another part of Yugoslavia wrested from the Ottoman Empire between 1833 and 1913; also Transylvania (Romania), where the continued presence of a large Hungarian minority adds to the government's sensitivity over a province annexed in 1918 after a long period of Hungarian/Habsburg administration. Finally, there are the special problems of small frontier districts where isolation is emphasized by the very low level of cross-border activity. Various examples are mentioned: northern Albania, where there has been conscious discrimination for many years; northern Czechoslovakia, where problems arose through the expulsion of the German population; southern Bulgaria, here potentials have been neglected through the departure of many Turkish people; and Hungary, where the government has worked for co-operation with neighbouring states in all border areas.

BACKWARD REGIONS: SLOVAKIA

Ever since the formation of the state in 1918 Czechoslovakia has had to cope with the contrast between the relatively well-developed lands of Bohemia and Moravia and the more backward Slovakia. Some progress was made in the 1920s and 1930s but Slovaks remained dissatisfied with their living standards and employment opportunities. The wartime Slovak Republic, although a satellite of Nazi Germany, strengthened Slovak national awareness but neither Czechoslovakia's exiled government in London nor the Communist Party leadership in Moscow were prepared to countenance a federal arrangement after the war. However, Slovakia was granted a large measure of autonomy

79

Figure 3.1 Regional problems in Eastern Europe

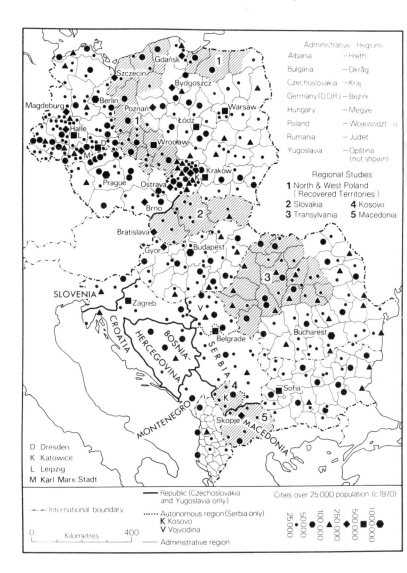

Source: Compiled from administrative maps.

within a Czechoslovak Republic and a pledge to this effect was made in the Kosice Programme of 1945: 'the Slovaks should be masters in their Slovak land', with legislative and executive bodies in Bratislava. However, autonomy was then whittled away, initially by three successive Prague Agreements and later by the communist coup of 1948, followed by the 1960 constitution which eliminated the executive arm of Slovak self-government. Subsequent pressure for devolution was first dismissed as 'nationalistic', but the federal principle was accepted during the 'Prague Spring' of 1968 and implemented in January 1969, despite the Soviet occupation in force at that time. However, by the end of 1970 the only areas of government resting exclusively in the hands of the provincial governments were culture, education, health, and justice. Since then, all legislative measures have been designed to strengthen the functions and integrating role of federal bodies and to solidify the management of a unified Czechoslovak economy. Ideas of federalism within the Czechoslovak Community Party have been strongly rebuffed since 1970.

Although Slovakia has had to settle more for the form than the substance of federalism, its inhabitants have nevertheless taken a surprising amount of satisfaction from this modest gesture towards their national self-identity. Bratislava is now officially a capital city, a matter of no small pride to the Slovaks who relish the increase in prestige and material resources that this has brought with it (Table 3.1). In addition,the Slovak intelligentsia has benefited from the career opportunities offered by the considerable expansion of Slovakia's governmental apparatus, where key executives are ministers, on a par with their Czech counterparts. Perhaps autonomy is most effective in the cultural sphere. Even before 1969 Slovak culture showed a capacity for separate development, especially since the Party overseers of cultural matters in Slovakia did not exercise such a firm control as their Czech counterparts. As for religious life the Catholic Church has played an important role in the history of the Slovak nation; 'moreover Slovak Catholicism is of a peasant variety', closely connected with the lives of believers and therefore more difficult to root out'. (5)

Slovakia is by no means an industrial desert when considered in historical perspective. Metallurgy has been important in the past, along with chemicals (especially glass), wood processing (especially paper), and textiles (flax

Table 3.1 Settlement structure of the Czech Lands and Slovakia, 1930-70

| Region | Year | Population (millions) | | | | |
		A	B	C	D	E
Czech lands	1930	10.67	5.43	2.52	1.37	1.35
	1970	9.82	3.47	2.04	2.47	1.84
Slovakia	1930	3.33	1.94	0.90	0.37	0.12
	1970	4.54	1.94	1.30	0.87	0.43
Czechoslovakia	1930	14.00	7.37	3.41	1.74	1.48
	1970	14.36	5.41	3.34	3.34	2.27

Source: Statistical yearbooks.
Notes: A - Total population;
        B - Population in settlements with fewer than 2,000 inhabitants;
        C - Ditto, 2,000-9,999;
        D - Ditto, 10,000-99,999;
        E - Ditto, over 100,000.

and hemp). However, the factory system developed relatively late and the autonomous industrial development of the Hungarian section of the Habsburg Empire, although closely geared to resources in Slovakia, failed to bring activity up to the level reached in the Czech Lands as regards both employment rates and efficiency. After the First World War much was done to improve the infrastructure so that Slovakia would have good rail links with the Czech Lands, but manufacturing did not make immediate advances since Slovak industries had difficulty in competing with their Czech counterparts. In 1937 the Slovak population represented 24.6 per cent of the total population of Czechoslovakia but the province received only 15 per cent of the total national income and provided only 7.3 per cent of the total industrial output. Again, Slovakia comprised 35.6 per cent of the country's total area but the share of agricultural production was only 22.9 per cent. Among the developments of the period may be mentioned the hosiery factory opened at Svit in 1933. This has now developed into the largest knitwear enterprise in the region, employing 8,000 people in Kosice, Levoca, Nova Ves, Roznava, and Spisska Stara Ves, as well as the parent factory at Svit. Bata built a shoe factory at Batavany (now Partizanske, commemorating the town's involvement in the Slovak National Uprising) in 1939. It stimulated a complex of related industries in the northern part of the Nitra valley, including rubber production (Dolne Vestenice), tanning (Boscany), and wood processing. Along with others in Slovakia the factory now comprises the August 29 enterprise, with substantial exports and collaboration with footwear industries in several developing countries.

Progress has been more pronounced since the Second World War on account of investments and subsidies, coupled with locational advantages for Slovakia in the context of close economic links with the Soviet Union. The USSR supplies crude oil and iron ore to the Bratislava and Kosice complexes respectively, while orders for ships have been all-important in maintaining the shipbuilding industry at Komarno. Under such conditions the labour resources and hydro-power potentials of Slovakia have been fully utilized. More than 300 plants were transferred to Slovakia from the Czech border areas between 1945 and 1948 after the expulsion of the Germans. Young people assisted with railway and hydroelectric works. Then the economic development plan for 1947-8 formalized the programme of assistance to Slovakia, gradually enabling Slovakia to 'catch up' with the Czech Lands. Industrialization was the key and in 1947-8 Slovakia's industrial output increased by 96 per cent compared with just 8 per cent in the Czech Lands. Agricultural targets were not met, however, due to serious drought in 1947. The first Five Year Plan (1949-53) emphasized the need for heavy industry in Slovakia, and a growth of industrial production of 128 per cent was achieved, raising the Slovak share of total industrial output from 13.2 per cent in 1948 to 15.6 in 1953. Agriculture registered an increase of 17.5 per cent, but this was below the plan target. During the 1956-60 Five Year Plan industrial output rose by 90 per cent and the share of national output rose from 16.1 to 18.6 per cent. The number of workers in industry in Slovakia advanced to 412,000, compared with 311,000 in 1953 and 218,000 in 1948. However, the increase in agricultural output of 16.9 per cent was well below the target of 23.5. The 1961-5 Five Year Plan envisaged a growth in industrial output of 84 per cent, but only 44 per cent was actually achieved: in both Slovakia and the Czech Lands the economy failed to sustain the 'intensive' development expected. Agriculture again failed to come up to expectations: production increased by 6.9 per cent compared with the planned rate of 22.5 per cent. The consolidation plan for 1966-70 set modest growth targets: 56.5 per cent for industry and 18.3 per cent for agriculture in Slovakia. In the event industrial production increased by 59.7 per cent and agricultural output by 35.4!

Although the economic path is being charted in Prague, Slovakia has continued to develop more rapidly than the Czech Lands. By 1975 Slovakia accounted for 27.6 per cent of industrial production, 32.5 per cent of agricultural production, and 33.6 per cent of all construction work. National income per capita reached 94 per cent of the Czech level, (industrial output 87 per cent), despite the relatively rapid growth of the labour force (150,000 or 3.6 times the growth in the Czech Lands in the early 1970s). This is possible because Slovakia has been taking increasing shares of investment: 29.8 per cent in 1948 but 31.8 by 1970 and 34.6 by 1980. The average annual growth of national income in Slovakia was 8.5 per cent in the 1950s (6.1 in the Czech Lands), 7.8 in the 1960s (6.0) and 5.3 in the 1970s (4.0); while productivity increased by 8.9 (5.3), 6.0 (5.6), and 4.1 (4.0) respectively. However, the case for subsidies to Slovakia has recently come under close scrutiny, on the grounds that capital earmarked for Slovakia would be better invested in the more efficient economy of the Czech Lands. For the Slovak economy is no more efficient than the Czech counterpart despite having more modern equipment: only 34.9 per cent of the machinery is obsolete compared with 46.4 in the Czech Lands, and on average, every Slovak worker handles equipment worth 0.32 million crowns compared with 0.30 in the Czech Lands (although the figures for agriculture are the other way round: 0.18 and 0.24, respectively). It is possible that the subsidy scheme is being scrutinized at this time because of the priority attaching to domestic sources of energy and in particular to lignite in north and north-west Bohemia where heavy investments will be needed: hence, the politically appropriate conclusion that Slovakia has now virtually 'caught up' with Czech Lands and that the transfer of resources to Slovakia is no longer a stimulus to increased economic efficiency. However, Slovakia continues to receive rather more than its fair share of capital investment and price subsidies to industry.

Slovakia now has a well-developed industry with a share of total production much more closely in line with population (28 and 33 per cent respectively) in 1980 compared with 1938 (8 and 25). There is particular strength in chemicals, metallurgy, and wood processing, whereas the Czech Lands are more prominent in engineering and fuels. In metallurgy the iron and steel complex at Kosice is complemented by the aluminium works at Ziar nad Hronom and the nickel smelter at Sered (with raw materials supplied largely by the Soviet Union, Hungary, and Albania respectively). The supply of metal supports local engineering and some steel from Ostrava in Moravia has been used to sustain engineering industries in adjacent areas of Slovakia like the Vah valley where there are factories producing machinery (Martin), ball bearings (Kysucke Nove Mesto), and spare parts (Banovce nad Bebravou). The main chemical complex is located at Bratislava. Slovnaft dates back to the kerosene and candle factory of 1895 which grew into a substantial oil refinery, producing various propellants and lubricants for IG Farben during the Second World War. The plant was renamed 'Slovnaft' in 1947 and plans for a new refinery, drawn up in 1950, were implemented between 1956 and 1962 when the first oil began flowing through the Friendship Pipeline. Diversification into petrochemicals was achieved after 1965. During the 1970s the plant was equipped for ethylene and propylene production with downstream production of polyethylene, polypropylene, and ethylene glycol. New petrochemical capacities should raise ethylene output to half a million tonnes by 1990. There are also smaller chemical capacities at several other locations including Hlohovec (Slovakofarma medicines), Humenne (Kapron synthetic fibres), Michalany (veterinary medicines), Novaky (fertilizers, flooring, and plastics from the Pieck factory), Sala nad Vlahom (fertilizer), and Slovenska Lupca near Kaliste (penicillin). Wood processing has expanded beyond the inherited factories (Banska Bystrica, Ruzomberok, and Zvolen) and others built by independent Slovakia during the Second World War (like the veneers factory at Zarnovica): for example, cellulose at Sturovo. The cement works at Banska Bystrica and Bystre supplement older units at Horni Srnie, Ladce, Lietavska Lucka, and Stupava. Food processing is represented by chains of bakeries, breweries, dairies, and freezing plants.

Table 3.2 Resettlement of Poland's recovered territories, 1945-7

Area	Migrants (thousands) arriving in:							
	1945		1946		1947		1945-7	
	A	B	A	B	A	B	A	B
Bialystok	25.4	8.9	8.7	4.2	4.8	3.8	38.9	16.9
Gdansk	19.0	19.9	49.3	65.1	31.5	184.4	99.8	269.4
Olsztyn	78.5	69.7	89.8	61.7	104.4	16.7	272.7	148.1
Poznan	119.5	76.7	86.6	60.0	12.9	25.2	219.0	161.9
Silesia	158.7	115.7	22.9	93.3	0.0	68.9	180.6	277.9
Szczecin	124.4	84.3	245.7	274.3	84.7	19.8	454.8	378.4
Wroclaw	394.5	157.1	272.7	513.1	121.3	121.6	788.5	791.8
Total	920.0	532.3	775.7	1,071.7	359.6	440.4	2,054.3	2,044.4

Source: S. Banasiak (1965) 'Resettlement of the Polish western territories', Polish Western Affairs 6: 121-49.

Notes: A - From other parts of Poland;
B - From territories annexed by the USSR.

TERRITORIAL ASSIMILATION: NORTHERN AND WESTERN POLAND

Poland has been particularly anxious to demonstrate her capacity to settle the recovered northern and western territories and integrate them fully into the national economy. (6) Population has risen steadily since the war: 5.02 million in 1946 but 5.85 in 1950 (despite the transfers), 7.62 in 1960 and 8.50 in 1968. The resettlement programme assumed quite heroic proportions in the immediate post-war years (Table 3.2). There was a flood of migrants moving westwards from territories occupied by the Soviet Union: 1.5 million between 1944 and 1947, while the movement from Germany and lands occupied by the Axis was exactly twice that figure. Of the total 4.5 million, slightly more than 4.0 million were settled in the 'recovered territories' (Ziem Odzyskanych) in the west and north. About 150,000 Poles from the Lublin and Rzeszow areas were resettled in the new lands while some 550,000 refugees were settled in 'Old Poland'. Initially the process seems to have been quite spontaneous as people decided to settle in places where they happened to pause, either to rest or to await further transport: for in the summer of 1945 families could move straight into empty farms and attend to the harvest, while arrivals in 1946 could immediately re-sow (while coping with a much reduced livestock population.) However, with the establishment of a scientific council the programme became more closely controlled, with settlers directed to areas where there were still empty lands. In 1947, for example, rural Silesia was saturated, as were parts in the Poznan, Olsztyn, and Wroclaw provinces. Thus, settlement in that year was modest compared with the previous two years. Farms of up to 15 ha were allocated to individual families, but two families were to work units up to 10 ha larger. Any excess called for additional families on the basis of one for each 25 ha.

The situation has now stabilized but in the difficult hill country, attachment to farm land has been relatively tenuous. Many of the settlers from the east have left their holdings in the Sudety, especially in the industrialized area of Walbrzych, and a special programme of economic development has now been launched. The state has acquired much of the land vacated by young migrants heading for the towns, and development of this large estate is being handled by Agrokompleks Sudety. Agriculture is being assisted by the provision of machines (along with repair workshops), seeds, and breeding animals, and private farmers are being drawn into the co-operative system without, however, giving up their titles. The organization is also looking after food processing, forestry, and tourism (including game hunting, which is a lucrative business attracting many foreign tourists).

Recovery in the northern and western territories has involved the rebuilding of the industrial base. This includes the shipyards in Gdansk and Szczecin; and engineering in Wroclaw where new complexes have emerged on sites formerly occupied by German factories (Pafawag, producing railway rolling-stock on the site of Linke-Hoffman Werke and electrical engineering where the Famo tractor company was once located). Regarding the chemical industry, fertilizers and other products are now produced at Brzeg Dolny, Kedzierzyn, and Oswiecim, where poison gas and other war materials were previously manufactured. Knitwear is now produced at the old flax works of Lubawka. However, the industrial recovery has been assisted by the exploitation of newly discovered resources: the copper of Legnica/Glogow and the lignite of Turoszow. (7) Urban growth has resumed in all the northern and western territories. The level of urbanization fell from 47.6 per cent in 1939 to 39.0 in 1946 due to the fact that war damage was less serious in the countryside but the situation was almost normal in 1950 (47.2 per cent) and by 1958 the urbanization rate was well above the 1939 level (54.3 per cent). This pattern applied in all constituent areas although in Koszalin, Olsztyn, Opole, and Zielona Gora urbanization rates in 1958 were only slightly above the 1939 levels. Conservation of historic townscapes has been given priority, especially in Gdansk where old buildings (the town hall, many burghers' houses, and various gates and towers forming part of the city walls) and quays have been preserved.

Assimilation of the recovered territories is thus well advanced. There is still some perception of differences within the present Katowice region between former Prussian, Russian, and Austrian territory (with the Prussian sector, around Katowice itself, attracting the highest status). Nevertheless there is an increasing tendency to equate Upper Silesia and the Katowice region although this is manifestly inaccurate in historical terms. (8) The only significant revisionist threat (apart from the delay in granting full western - and especially FRG - recognition, which resulted in ambivalent map references placing the western and northern territories rather enigmatically under 'Polish administration') has been focused on Szczecin and the Polish bridgehead west of the Oder. It is reported that in 1963 the GDR sought the return of Szczecin from Poland along with some adjacent territory and it appears that the then Soviet leader, N.S. Khrushchev, was sympathetic, even tempting the Poles with the return of the Drohobycz-Boryslaw oil basin as compensation. The Polish leader W. Gomulka declined this proposal, however, and also rejected a modified GDR proposal of 1965 for joint administration of Szczecin. It may be that it was in response to this 'threat' that the Poles went ahead with the chemical complex of Police to emphasize the Polish presence on the Odra-Nysa Rivers and establish in the words of the Foreign Minister 'a Polish bridgehead west of Oder'. The requirements of this new complex, along with further coal exports, triggered the investment at Swinoujscie. The Swinoport project extended from the first (1961-4), second (1965-8), and third (1969-71) phases to a grandiose conception in the early 1970s for an extended trans-shipment port integrated with the improvement of the Oder and new canal schemes to link through Silesia with the Vistula and by a projected Raciborz reservoir to an Oder-Danube Canal drawing cargoes from Czechoslovakia and the Danubian countries. This prospect upset the GDR and in 1973 the Soviets persuaded the Poles to delay this investment in favour of improvements at Gdansk, where the development of the Northern Port had been going on since 1971. The tug-of-war over Szczecin only came to an end in 1974 when the Interport organization was set up to co-ordinate developments at the Baltic ports of both the GDR and Poland. (9) The latest development concerns a duty-free zone at Szczecin to stimulate further interest in the port, especially from Austria and Czechoslovakia. The development of warehousing could be followed by more substantial enterprises involving a considerable influx of foreign capital.

ETHNIC COMPLICATIONS: MACEDONIA

While Yugoslavia has been preoccupied with the development of several backward areas, there are two cases with a particular political significance. The territorial extent of Macedonia and the ethnic status of its people has

Figure 3.2 Historical background to the Macedonian problem

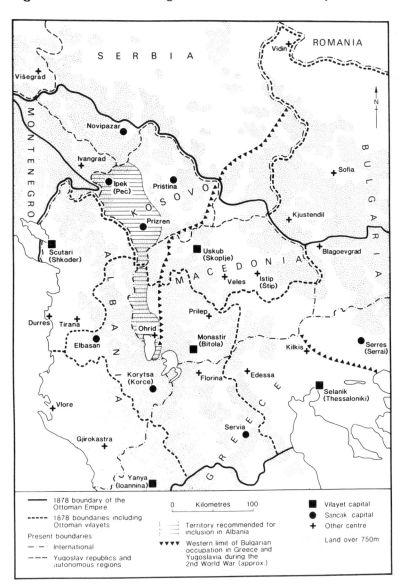

Source: Pribichevich 1982 (note 10).

generated controversy between Yugoslavia and the neighbouring states of Bulgaria and Greece (Figure 3.2). While there are some linguistic and cultural characteristics distinguishing the Macedonians from other Slav groups in the Balkans, these have never assumed such a coherence among the Macedonians as a whole to sustain a deep sense of national consciousness. (10) However, after the Second World War Tito regarded the division of the Macedonian people as unsatisfactory; he hoped to annex Greek Macedonia and cultivated the grand idea of a Balkan Federation which would include Bulgaria and thereby unite all Macedonians within one state. During the war years the Bulgarians had occupied Yugoslav Macedonia (1941) and incorporated Greek territory, evicting some 200,000 Greeks to German or Italian-occupied territory in the process. However, there appears to have been some ambivalence over the Macedonian question on the Bulgarian side, for although their army went far into Greek territory in 1943, west of the Strymon River, they did not enter Thessaloniki and withdrew from all Greek land by the end of 1944. It would appear that they had little real desire to sponsor a large Macedonia which they may have seen as potentially damaging to the integrity of an ethnically compact nation state. Western Thrace was seen as a much more important territorial acquisition and unsuccessful claims were made accordingly at the Paris peace conference. In Yugoslav Macedonia, the Bulgarians failed to make much headway in transferring the loyalties of the local population to a Bulgarian-sponsored Macedonian state: people became disillusioned with the occupation authorities and initiative passed to Tito's Partisans.

Balkan federation

Policy emanating from the Anti-Fascist (AVNOJ) Conferences at Bihac and Jajce favoured a federal structure for Yugoslavia with the whole of Macedonia as one of the constituent republics. However, it says much for Tito's stature and self-confidence in 1945 that the federal system for the Slavic population of the Balkans as a whole could be seriously contemplated. Greece bitterly opposed the plan (even the Greek communists, despite their dependence on Yugoslavia) because the 40,000 Slavs of Greek Macedonia were imbued with a Greek national consciousness. The

Bulgarians showed sympathy for a federation which would allow for a united Macedonia but could hardly accept a Tito-dominated federation with Belgrade as its capital. In 1946, however, the tenth plenum of the Bulgarian Communist Party passed a resolution providing for union between Pirin Macedonia and the Macedonian Peoples Republic of Yugoslavia, though the resolution went unpublished and was balanced by another which enabled the Pirin Macedonia population to opt for Bulgarian citizenship. The following year a meeting between Tito and the Bulgarian leader Dimitrov at Bled in Slovenia provided for a customs union and removal of travel barriers as well as movement towards unity in Macedonia: Pirin Macedonia gained rights of free cultural development and teachers from Yugoslavia were allowed to operate across the frontier, but the formal union of the Bulgarian and Yugoslav Macedonian territories was to await completion of the arrangements for a federation. It was followed up by a further meeting between the two leaders later in 1947 in Sofia which yielded a friendship treaty enabling co-operation to be so close that federation would be a mere formality. In the name of communist internationalism, Bulgaria seemed to be modifying its traditionally aggressive nationalism, a move made in an apparent spirit of idealism which is difficult to explain: for there must have been some resentment of the superiority complex of the Yugoslav communists and misgivings over Yugoslav infilitration of Pirin Macedonia. On the other hand, the Bulgarian stance may well have been a balancing act, with Dimitrov keeping options open for the time being: perhaps an even wider union could be cemented embracing other Balkan countries under communist rule for, significantly, in 1948 Dimitrov proposed (in Bucharest) a Danubian customs union as a first stage in the formation of a Balkan federation.

By this time the Soviets were becoming quite alarmed at the turn of events in the Balkans. At the beginning of 1948 tension in Europe was rising and each superpower was becoming reconciled to the essentially aggressive designs of the other. The last four-power conference at the end of 1947 had conspicuously failed to find any settlement for the German question and conflict over Berlin now seemed a distinct possibility. In such a situation it was important that the Soviets should be able to control foreign policy for the communist bloc as a whole, but the Soviet will could hardly prevail if a powerful Balkan state emerged. Such a state might well be a communist bastion and fundamentally loyal to the Soviet Union but with Tito's apparently uncontrollable illusions of grandeur there could be no guarantee that his aspirations would be realistic. The Soviet Union was not opposed to a union between Bulgaria and Yugoslavia (with Albania too) but anxious that the federation plan should be drawn up with close consultation with Moscow. Having in mind Yugoslav involvements in Albania and Greece, there may have been a desire to control the Yugoslavs through the Bulgarians (although there are conflicting views on the nature of any disagreements over Yugoslav actions in these two neighbouring states). Consequently, at a Kremlin meeting early in 1948 Stalin tried to get the Balkan communists to accommodate Soviet interests without actually opposing the idea of a union. In fact, an immediate federation between Bulgaria and Yugoslavia was advocated and it was now the Yugoslavs who dragged their feet in order to resist Soviet pressure. In March 1948 they informed the Bulgarians that they would not pursue the federation plan any longer, though they did wish to proceed immediately with the incorporation of some Bulgarian territory into the Yugoslav republic of Macedonia. The Bulgarians naturally opposed this and in the immediate aftermath of Yugoslavia's expulsion from the Cominform tried to eradicate Yugoslav propaganda from Pirin Macedonia altogether. The attitude hardened in 1949 with deportations of pro-Yugoslav Macedonians to other parts of Bulgaria and political trials to find scapegoats for the earlier policy of collaboration with Yugoslavia (though Dimitrov himself managed to survive by shifting responsibility on to the shoulders of subordinates). Yugoslavia also reciprocated with trials of some people who had collaborated with the Bulgarian occupation during the Second World War.

Meanwhile, the expulsion of Yugoslavia from the Cominform was having a decisive effect on the civil war in Greece, for Yugoslavia ceased supporting the Greek communists and the rebellion came to an end. The war had been damaging to Greece, with some 70,000 deaths and a million people displaced from their homes. However, some 35,000 Macedonians resettled in Bulgaria or Yugoslavia, leaving behind only about 40,000 Slav speakers who preferred Greek citizenship. Greece was therefore relieved of an embarrassing minority problem and claims to Greek territory by both Bulgaria and Yugoslavia have now been dropped. Yugoslavia did try and create difficulty in 1962 through raising the issue of the Macedonian minority and the frontier was closed for some months. A modus vivendi was re-established by the end of the year, but Bulgarian-Yugoslav relations continued to be complicated by the Macedonian issue. Between 1948 and 1954 Bulgaria sought a Macedonian state under Bulgarian tutelage: Macedonians were now Bulgarians! However, there followed a reconciliation between the two neighbours during the years 1954-6 and Bulgaria once more seemed prepared to make territorial concessions. The people of Pirin Macedonia were not now Bulgarians and were instead related to the state of Yugoslav Macedonia which they might eventually join. It is widely believed that this gesture was made after Soviet prompting in order to try and bring Tito into the Soviet camp, but after a visit to Moscow in 1956 relations again deteriorated as Tito failed to endorse the Soviet Union's intervention in Hungary in 1956 and opposed plans for a Cominform-type organization in 1957. This brought a further feud between Bulgaria and Yugoslavia: Macedonians were again regarded as Bulgarians and the notion of Macedonian nationality was suppressed.

Recognition of a Macedonian nation

The Bulgarian government still refuses to recognize the population of Pirin Macedonia as an ethnic minority. By contrast the Yugoslav government has given due recognition to its own piece of Macedonian territory so that it comprises one of the republics of the federal state. Both countries have vested interests in their stand, however. In Yugoslavia the federal system is best sustained by a judicious blend of ethnic/cultural self-consciousness within each constituent republic and loyalty to a wider Yugoslav ideal. Any cultural programme in Yugoslav Macedonia is bound to draw attention to Macedonian people living beyond the frontiers of the federation but, additionally, the aggressive foreign policy of communist Yugoslavia envisaged frontier modifications in its favour related to the territorial extent of the Macedonian nation. In its turn the Bulgarian government, with an eye on the Bulgarian empires of the Middle Ages, finds it convenient to treat the Bulgarian and Macedonian populations as one. Rightly or wrongly Yugoslavia sees this stance as an aggressive design by the Bulgarian government which has been accused of trying to wash its hands in the Adriatic Sea, its legs in the Black Sea, and its head in the Aegean! Given the complicated historical background, academic activities are inevitably placed on the political platform with Bulgarians refusing to co-operate in international Slavic projects if these give any recognition to Macedonia as a distinct language or nation. Yugoslavs in their turn issue criticisms of Bulgarian disregard of historical realities and exchanges are all the more brisk in view of the commitment of Skopje University to the study of Macedonian culture, history, and language. Equally, economic development has accelerated in Yugoslav Macedonia under the regional programme and reference can be made to a number of new industries, including steel (Skopje), copper flotation (Radovis), electro-metallurgy (Jegunovce), chemicals (Skopje), woollen textiles (Tetovo), clothing (Stip), footwear (Kumanovo), and furniture (Skopje).

ETHNIC COMPLICATIONS: KOSOVO

Kosovo has already been identified as a largely Albanian speaking province, recognized as an autonomous region (Kosovo-Metohija or Kosmet) in 1945. In 1963 the higher status of 'autonomous province' was granted and the name was subsequently changed to Kosovo: this followed a difficult period when Tito's expulsion from the Cominform led to Soviet encouragement of Tirana in the propaganda war, with incitement of Albanians in Yugoslavia to riot and secede. Under the circumstances Albanian autonomy was strictly controlled by the Serbs and especially by A. Rankovic, whose rule in Kosovo was equated with 'Greater Serb' hegemony. Liberalization followed the purge of Rankovic in 1966 and the growing assertiveness of the Albanians then resulted in discrimination against Serbs and Montenegrans, many of whom were obliged to leave the province. The number of Serbs and Montenegrans fell from 264,000 in 1961 to 261,000 in 1971 and 236,000 in 1981 (in percentage terms a decline from 27.2 to 20.5 and 14.4), and more have left since. Meanwhile, the populations of Albanians and Moslems increased from 654,000 in 1961 (67.4 per cent) to 942,000 in 1971 (74.1) and 1.29 million in 1981 (78.3). Comparable figures for Turks and Others are 53,000 (5.5), 69,000 (5.4), and 121,000 (7.4). Disturbances in April

Table 3.3 Regional variations in Yugoslavia in the 1970s

Region	A	B	Criterion C	D	E	F
Bosnia-Hercegovina	64.2	−18.7	70.9	123.8	80.8	87.3
Croatia	124.3	+17.1	116.5	178.6	128.1	105.4
Kosovo	32.2	−20.4	43.4	47.6	44.2	78.0
Macedonia	68.1	+6.1	85.2	83.3	84.8	80.4
Montenegro	70.3	−0.5	75.8	123.8	84.8	80.2
Serbia proper	98.3	+2.7	100.5	54.8	92.0	100.3
Slovenia	201.7	+26.4	169.8	83.3	153.6	115.6
Vojvodina	116.6	+7.8	113.2	78.6	106.7	99.7

Sources: Statistical yearbooks, and F.B. Singleton (1979) 'Regional economic inequalities', Bradford Studies on Yugoslavia 1.

Notes: A - Income per capita, 1976;
          B - Change since 1947;
          C - Employment in Yugoslavia;
          D - Employment abroad;
          E - All employment;
          F - Labour productivity in industry.

All figures are related to the national average = 100

1981 (and further demonstrations a year later) indicated a desire for radical change: full republican status for the province and, for the extremists, unification with Albania. However, neither demand can seriously be contemplated since Kosovo comprises the historic heartland of Serbia.

The state has tried to make progress through economic development. The programme of assistance to poorer regions began in the 1950s when it was envisaged that levels of development would be equalized in little more than ten years. (11) Investment was initially organized through the federal budget but after 1954 by investment funds controlled by the Yugoslav Investment Bank, and after 1965 an independent 'Federal Investment Fund' was founded. Kosovo has been receiving about 30 per cent of the money distributed by the Federal Development Board in the form of fifteen-year loans at 3 per cent per annum interest. Resources have been pumped into labour training, basic industries, and infrastructure. Before the Second World War the only industry of any size was Trepca with its lead-zinc mines (Stari Trg), and smelter (Zvecan) near Kosovska Mitrovica. Trepca remains an important complex with a diversified chemical industry but there is now a Kosovo complex at Obilic with lignite mining, electricity generation (1,470 MW capacity), and chemicals. There are various new light industries: food processing in Kosovo Polje, Pec, Prizren, Urosevac, and Zrza; leather and footwear at Pec, Prizren, and Titova Mitrovica; textiles and clothing at Djakovica, Gnjilane, and Prizren. There are also heavier industries: engineering at Gnjilane, Pec, Pristina, and Prizren; chemicals at Orahovac and Suva Reka; building materials at Djeneral Jankovic and Kacanik, and wood processing at Pec, Pristina, and Urosevac.

However, employment opportunities have not kept pace with the rapid growth of the Albanian population from 0.41 million in 1921 to 1.70 in 1980. The 1971 Census indicated that each Kosovo woman bore 6.6 children on average, compared with 2.7 in other parts of the Serbian Republic. Thus, economic development, together with a significant amount of migration, has not prevented rising unemployment: 68,000 in 1981. Only 11.5 per cent of the population of Kosovo has regular employment, compared with 26 per cent in the country as a whole (Table 3.3). Moreover, average incomes are low, at hardly one-third of the Yugoslav level and less than one-sixth of the level prevailing in the most prosperous region (Slovenia).

Figure 3.3 Ethnicity and literacy in mountain villages near Cluj-Napoca, Transylvania, 1930

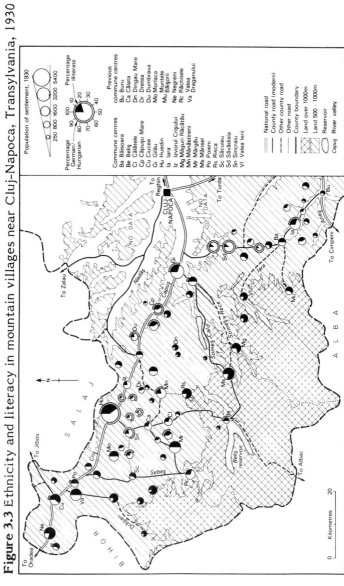

Source: Census

Moreover, the position has deteriorated significantly between 1947 and 1976. (12) With 7 per cent of the country's population the contribution to GNP is only 2.9 per cent and to foreign trade just 2.4 per cent. Such is the economic context of the Kosovo riots of 1981. (13) The unrest focused on the university at Pristina. Overcrowding was excessive because the premises were built for some 15,000 students, in contrast with the 47,000 enrolled at the present time. Even more serious, however, was the lack of jobs for the graduates. Considerable distance now separates the young radical unemployed from the Albanian elite with secure well-paid jobs in administration. Although the situation is complicated by Tirana, whose television transmitters are able to cover some 60 per cent of the autonomous region, it is unfortunate that substantial funds injected into the province are absorbed by an administrative apparatus of disproportionate size.

ETHNIC COMPLICATIONS: TRANSYLVANIA

Hungarians are reluctant to accept the permanent loss of territories once embraced by the crown of St Stephen, especially when these lands contain significant Hungarian minorities. Sensitivities over certain Austrian (Burgenland), Czechoslovak (Slovakia), and Yugoslav (Croatia and Vojvodina) territories are mild by comparison with the tension generated by the Transylvanian problem which has coloured relations between Hungarians and Romanians for centuries. Under Hungarian administration, Romanians suffered discrimination and there were great differences in cultural standards. Statistical data for 1930 shows, with respect to the mountain district south-west of Cluj-Napoca, how illiteracy was a much greater problem in Romanian communities than in villages with a large proportion of Hungarian and German residents (Figure 3.3). Transylvania was transferred to Romanian administration after the First World War, and the partition of 1940 (which saw the return of North Transylvania to Hungary) was followed by restoration of Romanian control over the entire region in 1945. (14) Despite real autonomy in cultural matters and vigorous efforts to develop the economy in the more backward parts of the region Hungarians in the mother country are convinced that there is discrimination against the Hungarians in Transylvania. The issues are complex and emotions must play a part because Transylvania is prominent in the history of Hungary as the homeland of the famous King Matthias Corvinus (the son of J. Hunyadi who forced the Turks back from Belgrade in 1440) and of various writers and poets. On the other hand the Romanians regard Transylvania as the cradle of the nation and so there are conflicting historical accounts of the province which extend right up to the controversial Vienna Award of 1940 which was cancelled informally in 1944 and formally, the Paris Conference in 1946-7. (15) The administration of the territory by Romanians, once despised by the cultured Magyars, is a reality which is hard to accept, especially when the regime in Bucharest shows rather less sensitivity over human rights than its counterpart in Budapest.

The issue is complicated, however, by the developments which have occurred since 1945. During the early years of communist government it seems that the Hungarians enjoyed a privileged position, being over-represented in the Party and government at the instigation of the Soviet Union, which was anxious to strengthen the Party in Romania where little support was forthcoming from ethnic Romanians. It is no coincidence that the establishment of a government under Petru Groza, acceptable to both the Soviets and the Hungarians of Transylvania was followed by the return of North Transylvania to Romanian administration. Hungarians remained prominent during the last years of Stalin's life: there were allegedly no Hungarians among the prison population assigned to work on the Danube-Black Sea Canal but many Hungarian guards! It was the Hungarian uprising in Budapest in 1956 (for which much sympathy was expressed among Hungarians in Transylvania) that brought a change in attitude in Moscow since ethnic Romanians in power in Bucharest gained considerable prestige in the eyes of the Soviets for helping to restore the authority of the party in Hungary. The Hungarians have been resentful of what they see as a loss of autonomy since 1956: the withdrawal of the status of 'autonomous region' for eastern Transylvania (1969), and the consolidation of the administration of the Babes-Bolyai University in Cluj where there had previously been Hungarian and Romanian sections. Also, some measures affecting all Romanian citizens have affected the Hungarians disproportionately. Most recently, the regulations which prevent any Romanian citizen from accommodating foreign visitors in their homes (unless they are very close relatives) has been seen as a particular irritation to the Hungarian minority since they often receive visitors from the mother country. Rural settlement planning is another sensitive issue.

The Romanian government for its part is bitterly indignant · about charges of discrimination and the authorities are known to have overlooked Hungarian nationalist manifestations that would not normally be tolerated. In the economic sphere the programme of aid for backward regions, greatly extended in 1968, has brought considerable benefit to the Hungarians. In 1978 the Hungarian chairman of the Council of Working People of Magyar Nationality declared that the

> party policy of rational distribution of productive forces all over the country is the only one able to secure the bridging of gaps among areas and localities, gaps inherited from the past, to create the most favourable conditions for the equality in rights and the unhindered assertion of all working people, irrespective of nationality, in all domains of life. (16)

Other speakers at the same conference mentioned specific local developments like the knitwear factories of Hunedoara and Petrosani, the clothing factory of Vulcan, and the silk weaving mill of Lupeni 'where many Hungarian women will find work'. However, it was also pointed out that 'even nowadays there are prejudiced people with backward views in whose conscience there are still reminiscences of the policy of national feud and dissension'. (17) Thus, although the Hungarian government has shown restraint towards Romania it has been under pressure from its citizens to campaign more strongly for greater privileges. In addition to equal career opportunities, which Romania would argue are already available, Hungarians in Transylvania might have their cultural autonomy institutionalized (to a greater extent than is permitted by the Council of Working People of Magyar Nationality), enabling ties with Hungary to be cultivated on both an organized and a personal basis. There might also be greater administrative autonomy, co-equal status for the Hungarian language and greater priority for the preservation of the environment relating to the history of the Hungarian minority. In addition, it is argued that an impartial international committee could examine the situation and settle all contentious questions such as the education tax (imposed on all emigrants) which is a serious impediment to Hungarians wishing to leave Romania.

FRONTIER ZONES

In the past such areas have often been neglected partly because of remoteness and partly because of a reluctance to provide infrastructure which could be useful to an invader. In modern times, however, the formation of new nation states has sometimes resulted in policies to favour the newly recognized capital over powerful provincial interests. (18) In the post-war period there is evidence of discrimination against the north of Albania by the communist leadership, drawn predominantly from the south; notably by the delay in extending rail communications with Shkoder which, as the Turkish administrative centre of Scutari, was by far the largest urban centre on present Albanian territory through the nineteenth century and also in the early years of Albanian independence. Its position near the northern frontier made it inappropriate as the Albanian capital but even so its neglect is surprising and the railway arrived only in 1981. Priority had meanwhile been given to the links from Durres to the Elbasan metallurgical works and its resource area to the east (Pishkash, Pogradec, and Prrenjas); also, the oil producing area of Ballsh, Cerrik, and Fier, as well as the superphosphate complex at Lac. (19)

However, there are many more examples of positive assistance to border areas. Following the expulsion of the German population, the resettlement of the border areas of Bohemia (Czechoslovakia) was carried out in three main stages. Until 1954 resettlement was poorly organized with ad hoc sales of former German properties to people who were willing to join and co-operate with the Party. There were almost certainly many irregularities and the remoter settlements, with few opportunities other than agriculture, were neglected. Between 1954 and 1958 agriculture was given more assistance to prevent former farm land degenerating into waste; and finally from 1958 to 1963 attention was given to local industry in places where it had not previously existed. Several new plants were built, along with housing and services. Since then government aid has been aimed at places where living conditions are well below the average for the country: since 1966-70 subsidies have been granted for programmes involving manufacturing and services and a decree of 1972 provided for subsidies of up to 70 per cent. Recently, agriculture has been given greater priority, notably in the context of the national drive for self-sufficiency in cereal production.

In Bulgaria the departure of many Turkish-speaking people has created serious depopulation problems in the south. A decree issued in 1982 gave particular attention to settlement systems in border areas, and especially the Strandzha-Sakar area in the south-east, adjacent to the Turkish frontier. In these areas greater emphasis is to be given to forestry, livestock breeding (especially sheep) and small industrial enterprises (including branch plants). Tourism is to be encouraged by the conversion of small hamlet settlements into vacation sites. Cash incentives are on offer to encourage migration into the border regions and these will cover movement costs, housing construction, and the breaking in of personal plots. Particular emphasis is given to families and individuals with higher education and professional qualifications. The communist youth organization (Komsomol) has been instructed to recruit 4,000 young workers and specialists with families: 2,000 to work in Strandzha-Sakar and 2,000 in other border regions. Such recruits will be entitled to free travel twice a year to their place of birth. People benefiting from state and local authority assistance will be required to work in the border areas for at least ten years.

Hungary has shown considerable interest in frontier planning: it involves economic development in areas near the international borders in co-operation with neighbouring countries since the 1960s. Local border traffic has developed in the frontier zones with Czechoslovakia and Yugoslavia. The scheme has since been extended to Austria, Romania, and the Soviet Union, resulting in a general increase in commerce and improvements in the supply of goods which were previously very scarce. Various frontier crossing points are required specially for this local commerce. A committee to look after the Yugoslav frontier districts was set up in Belgrade in 1970: there will be joint construction of industrial plants and waterworks as well as joint measures for environmental protection. A similar organization was set up in Bratislava in 1971 and co-operation is developing in such areas as drinking water supplies, supplies for co-operative farms, and building materials (components manufactured in Hungary will be used to build houses in Czechoslovakia). Hungary has also provided labour to work the border railway station of Agcsernyo and to build a workers' hostel in the same location. Future possibilities include closer collaboration by metallurgical works in the Kosice and Miskolc areas, the opening of another border crossing point at Aggtelek-Domica (suitable for journeys between Budapest and the Tatra Mountains) and the supply of gas by the Slovakian system for the Hungarian settlements of Hollohaz and Satoraljaujhely.

Hungarian officials have been in touch with Austrian planners in Vienna since 1967; plans for the frontier include joint development of railways and industrial co-operation. There has also been a joint project for Lake Ferto and for the Pinka and Sed streams which flow through the border area, while Austrians have been allowed to use a road which crosses Hungarian territory between the villages of Morbisch and Siegendorf in Burgenland. Austrians frequently go shopping in Sopron since the currency exchange-rate is favourable and goods are plentiful. Even beauty parlours and dressmaking establishments are crowded with foreigners, sometimes to the annoyance of local inhabitants who have to wait a long time for service. Special cross-border train services give Austrians the option of leaving their cars at home and spending more money in restaurants and wine bars. Then, the magazine Pannonia, published in Eisenstadt in the Austrian Burgenland, has become in effect a joint Austro-Hungarian venture with authors drawn from the two countries and with an editorial office in Budapest.

Hungary's interest in frontier planning finds an echo in the Soviet Union through closer links between Hungary and the Transcarpathian Oblast of the USSR. Some 180,000 Hungarians live in the vicinity of Uzhgorod, supported by various educational and cultural facilities. A bus service now runs between Budapest and Uzhgorod, Hungarian fruit is sent into the district, and there is a cross-border trade in consumer goods. Hungarian workers have been active in hotel building in Uzhgorod and in construction of the Khust section of the Orenburg gas pipeline. It is not known if similar collaboration is maintained with Romania but some local arrangements are in force whereby Romanians can cross the frontier for farm work, and Romanian natural gas is exported to supply the chemical industry in Hungary. Individual local authorities in Hungary are encouraged to develop contacts with similar organizations abroad. Vas county (a region based on Szombathely) has links with

Razgrad in Bulgaria and the Mari ASSR in the Soviet Union, but is particularly active in dealing across the frontier with Austria (Burgenland and Styria) and Yugoslavia (Croatia and Slovenia). There are cultural and sporting programmes and co-operation with regional planning initiatives, such as Alps-Adriatic regional co-operation. Economic benefits arise from the purchase of manufactured goods from factories situated in close proximity in neighbouring countries, or from the processing of sugar beet. Austrian and Swiss companies are being consulted over the construction of a sanatorium in Szombathely and an associated resort village.

Chapter Four

POPULATION PROBLEMS

This final chapter in a selection of political themes deals with various aspects of population geography. Since these are among the basic realities with which East European governments must come to terms it follows that policy-making by Communist Parties with pretensions of comprehensive leadership in society must have a strong bearing on population. However, there is no clear thread running through the policies of all Parties for the whole period of communist rule. On population growth the current interest in stimulating the birth rate follows a period of ambivalence when the flow of workers from agriculture to industry was great enough to meet all demands: hence the widespread availability of abortion facilities which kept women at work and reduced pressure on health services. With respect to the quality of life there is a vested interest in greater prosperity and cultural advancement to increase legitimacy at home and abroad, yet there has always been a preference, inherent in the system of central planning, to concentrate on increases in output which do not necessarily result in higher real wages for the individual; while development in terms of pluralism in society has always been resisted.

The movement of people is always regulated through registration formalities but migration may well be positively stimulated or constrained. Population movement is encouraged when it is necessary, to fulfil the policies of governments, but discouraged when conflicts arise. Rural-urban movement has been stimulated by collectivization of agriculture (removing incentives for many farmers who previously took a pride in their own land) and priority investment in industry, although housing shortages in the towns and provision of private plots on co-operative farms make daily commuting an acceptable option for many country dwellers. However, concern over the viability of agriculture and the urban development pressures have resulted in the prohibition (with certain exceptions) of migration into the larger towns. (1) Persecution of certain families by compulsory evacuation from the cities in the early post-war years finds an echo in draconian proposals contemplated in Romania to clear the pensioners out into the countryside to relieve pressure on urban services. Movement across international frontiers is very strictly controlled through careful scrutiny of applications for passports, exit visas and foreign currency, as well as strict security at the frontiers: only in the case of Yugoslavia is there a significant level of international movement not expressly provided for by the authorities in the context of group tourism, repatriation of ethnic minorities, and work for the state on cultural, diplomatic, and industrial assignments. Ethnic minorities are still prominent in Eastern Europe and they have been granted constitutional rights. Yet the policies of homogenization have weakened the minorities, while discouragement of spontaneous developments in cultural and economic matters limits the scope for effective organization. Migration to the mother country may be tolerated - even encouraged - in certain cases (such as the Jews who lost their economic interests with nationalization), but discouraged in other instances when would-be migrants are valued as key workers. Overall there is an impression of inconsistency but this should not be seen as indifference. The young women pressurized by the authorities to have more children, the priest frustrated in the discharge of his pastoral duties, the pensioner discouraged from moving to join his children in the city, and the ethnic denied the right to emigrate are all acutely aware that the state has definite population policies which go beyond the normal requirements of state bureaucracies.

POPULATION GROWTH

There has been a substantial growth of population in Eastern Europe during the post-war period, but striking variations arise with the extremes marked by Albania, where population has doubled during the 35-year period 1950-85,

Table 4.1 Area and population

| Country | A | 1985 Area/Population | | | |
		B	C	D	E
Albania	11.1	28.7	267	103	2.96
Bulgaria	42.8	110.9	210	81	8.97
Czechoslovakia	49.4	127.9	314	121	15.50
GDR	41.8	107.8	399	155	16.69
Hungary	35.9	93.0	296	114	10.64
Poland	120.7	312.7	308	119	37.23
Romania	91.7	237.5	248	96	22.73
Yugoslavia	98.8	255.8	234	90	23.12
Eastern Europe	492.2	1,274.2	280	108	137.84

Table 4.1 continued

	Population (millions) and change over the previous decade (per cent)										
	1950		1960		1970		1980		1990		2000*
	1.22	12.0	1.61	32.0	2.14	32.9	2.59	21.0	3.4	31.3	4.1	20.6
	7.27	8.8	7.87	8.3	8.49	7.9	8.88	4.6	9.4	5.9	9.7	13.2
	13.09	-15.8	13.65	4.3	14.33	5.0	15.28	6.6	16.0	10.5	16.8	5.0
	17.94	9.5	17.24	-3.9	17.06	-1.0	16.74	-1.9	16.6	-0.8	16.6	0.0
	9.80	0.6	10.00	2.0	10.34	3.4	10.71	3.6	10.8	0.8	10.9	0.9
	24.82	-23.3	29.70	19.7	32.53	9.5	35.73	9.8	39.0	9.2	41.4	6.2
	16.31	1.3	18.40	12.8	20.35	10.6	22.20	9.1	23.9	7.7	25.6	7.1
	16.35	-0.5	18.54	13.4	20.37	9.9	22.30	9.5	23.9	7.2	25.2	5.4
	106.80	-7.2	117.01	10.0	125.61	7.3	134.43	7.1	143.0	6.4	150.3	5.1

Source: statistical yearbooks.

Notes: A – square miles (thousands);
        B – square kilometres (thousands);
        C – persons per square mile;
        D – persons per square kilometre;
        E – total population (millions);
        * – US forecasts.

and the GDR, where a net decline has been experienced (Table 4.1). More generally, the Balkan countries exhibit much more demographic strength than the northern group, with a 40.4 per cent growth compared with 23.3, and their share of the East Europe population as a whole has risen from 38.8 per cent to 41.9. These trends seem likely to continue for the foreseeable future and projections for the year 2000 suggest the Balkan countries will advance their share to 43.0 per cent. These figures arise primarily out of the balance between births and deaths because migration across international frontiers is very limited in Eastern Europe. Death-rates have fallen due to improved diet, hygiene and medical care, but birth-rates have declined even more rapidly. (2) Natural increase rates have fallen to zero in the GDR and Hungary as there are fewer women in the fertile age-group. Economic growth and the urban environment have induced attitudes favouring small families and low marital fertility. Furthermore, abortion was readily available to women in most countries in 1956 (Czechoslovakia 1958) but the short-sighted nature of this step, reducing the birth-rate and constraining the growth of the work-force over the long term, led to restrictions which came first in the Balkans (Romania in 1966 and Bulgaria in 1967) and later in the north (Czechoslovakia 1973, Hungary 1974, and Poland in 1981). (3) Abortion is now strictly controlled and unless there are very pressing medical or domestic reasons it is not possible for a young woman to get an abortion until she has given birth to at least three living children. This situation contrasts with the extremely liberal approach taken until c. 1970 when the service was freely available to women on account of the state's priority to keep women at work.

Falling birth-rates should not be a great problem from an economic point of view, given the increasing importance of high technology: only in parts of the Balkans is there still a mentality which favours a labour-intensive approach to future modernization, and even in such limited cases there is often a political motive to boost the numerical strength of a particular nationality vis-à-vis minority groups. (4) However, while governments concede that technical progress will eventually reduce the demand for labour to meet the needs of society, they claim that it is difficult to decide at just which point in time a pronatalist approach can be abandoned (Table 4.2). Even if productivity increases in industry, there may be greater labour demands in education,

Table 4.2 Annual average growth rates (%) of the population of working age, 1971-90

Country	1971-5	1976-80	1981-5	1986-90
Bulgaria	0.7	0.3	-0.2	-0.1
Czechoslovakia	0.8	0.5	0.1	0.4
GDR	0.3	1.2	n.a.	n.a.
Hungary	0.6	-0.1	-0.1	0.1
Poland	1.8	1.4	0.6	0.3
Romania	0.8	1.1	0.7	0.7

Source: Radio Free Europe Background Report 202 (1978)

Note: n.a. - not available.

medical services, research, and conservation, to say nothing of strategic matters involving recruits for the armed services and the threat of increasing numerical inferiority for the less-fertile populations. Concern has been expressed in Hungary because half the families with a background of high school or university education have only one child or none at all. Thus, the higher cultural standards of these families will be carried on by comparatively fewer people. At a time of rapid advance in science and technology, Hungary seems to be losing some of its intellectual force every year: educational standards have apparently fallen at all levels from primary school to the university.

Pronatalist policies at their simplest involve curbs on abortion, coupled with greater accommodation in maternity hospitals and an appropriate propaganda effort. In Romania, where the average number of children born to each family fell from 2.9 in 1956 to 1.9 in 1966, such measures led to a growth in the birth-rate from 6.0 per thousand in 1966 to 18.1 the following year. However, the figure gradually fell back to 7.6 in 1980 (the equivalent of 2.5 children per family compared with 3.7 in 1967) as doctors started to perform illegal abortions despite the risk of between one and three years imprisonment. The inevitability of a shortfall on the planned 1985 population figure of 23.4-23.7 million led to a decision in 1983 requiring the local authorities to exercise even closer scrutiny over abortion and 'stimulate' families to

produce more children. (5) The rate of natural increase rose
from 3.9 per thousand in 1983 to 5.2 in 1984 and 4.9 in 1985,
but the 1985 total of 22.7 million was still well below the
planned target. More might be done to reduce the levels of
infant mortality in Romania: 31.2 per thousand live births
in 1977 compared with 21.0 in Bulgaria, 19.6 in Czechoslovakia, 13.1 in the GDR, and even lower in the west.
However, the economic crisis and especially the drive for
fuel economy has exacerbated the problem, although the
official rates (23.4 in 1984) may be artificially low on
account of the current practice of registering births only
when the child is one month old. Meanwhile, the position of
old people leaves a lot to be desired, especially in rural
areas. Some of them receive only symbolic pensions and are
not always given the basic foodstuffs to which they are
entitled. Illness may be a particularly severe burden when
overstretched medical services give priority to working
people.

However, it is increasingly common for the cruder
pronatalist methods to be supplemented by economic
incentives. In Czechoslovakia a social policy was worked out
in 1971 and as a result the birth-rate, which had fallen from
22.0 per thousand in the 1950s to 15.9 in 1970 rose towards
20.0 by the middle 1970s. Close scrutiny of abortion and
'parenthood education' (geared to raising the social esteem
of families with children) are complemented by income tax
rebates, family allowances, concessions over rents and
transport charges, as well as crèche and nursery-school
facilities and low rates of turnover tax on childrens'
clothing. At birth a cash allowance is payable and the
mother has the right to twenty-six weeks maternity leave
(thirty-five weeks in the case of the single-parent family)
with normal salary payable at the rate of 90 per cent.
Loans of 75 per cent help families to build their own homes
and repayment obligations are moderated as children arrive.
This is a generous incentive and particularly helpful if
building materials are readily available locally. Similar
measures were taken in the GDR in 1972. Married couples
receive interest-free loans for up to 10,000 marks with
deductions then made from repayment obligations in
increasing amounts for each successive child: 1,000 marks
for the first, 1,500 for the second and 2,500 for the third.
During the first nine years of the scheme, 4,000 million
marks were loaned with a fifth of the total written off on
account of the 'baby boom' of the 1975-80 period. The

subsequent decline in the birth-rate has led to some further concessions, widening the scope of the loan scheme, but it is doubtful if they will have much effect since the birth-rate seems to be largely a function of the number of women of child-bearing age. Most couples want only two children and the state's financial incentives have only a marginal effect, especially when the financial inducements have to be set against inadequate day-care facilities for small children. However, further economic incentives were announced in 1986: mothers will be granted twelve months' paid leave for child care after the birth of the first baby while working mothers with two children could take paid leave to care for their offspring in the case of sickness. Loans for young married couples have been made more generous and age limits have been revised upwards. Child allowances are also to increase in 1987 as part of the plan to reduce differences in prosperity between households with and without children.

SOCIETAL PROBLEMS

Governments may be worried about the rates of population growth but people in general are rather more concerned about the quality of life. Here, the post-war record is a mixed one. Real wages have increased for most people, although the recent economic difficulties have meant comparative stagnation against expectations of significant improvement (Table 4.3). Many more goods are available although, at the same time, most people are aware that costs (related to average salaries) are far lower in the west and that choice and quality are superior. Improvements in education and health are undeniable, although many drugs, manufactured only in the west, are difficult or impossible to obtain. In the past, people have judged shortages and shortcomings in Eastern Europe in relation to historical experiences like the depression years in the 1930s or the Second World War, but as more people are drawn into the towns, the stabilizing factor of the rural reference point loses its importance and progress is critically evaluated over shorter periods. The intelligentsia in particular poses as a potentially strong destabilizing force, expecting social prosperity to follow automatically from economic growth. The recession has had serious implications, increasing perceptions of income differentials: surprisingly, perhaps, in view of the elimination of large private property holdings

Table 4.3 Wages and labour productivity in industry, 1961-84

| Country | Average annual growth (per cent) of: | | | | | | | | | | Wages as a ratio of labour productivity | | | | |
| | Wages | | | | | Labour productivity | | | | | | | | | |
	A	B	C	D	E	A	B	C	D	E	A	B	C	D	E
Bulgaria	3.5	5.4	3.9	5.4	3.6	7.0	6.7	6.7	5.9	4.5	2.0	1.2	1.7	1.1	1.2
Czechoslovakia	1.8	4.6	5.3	3.3	2.3	3.2	3.5	5.2	4.9	1.6	1.8	1.2	1.5	1.5	0.7
GDR	2.6	3.2	3.1	3.4	1.9	5.7	5.8	5.1	4.3	2.7	2.6	1.8	1.6	1.3	1.4
Hungary	1.8	3.6	3.2	7.9	9.5	4.6	3.5	5.9	4.7	4.3	2.6	1.0	0.9	0.6	0.5
Poland	3.4	3.4	9.3	11.1	n.a.	5.3	4.9	7.4	4.3	-0.7	1.6	1.4	0.8	0.4	n.a.
Romania	5.5	4.3	4.9	8.8	4.5	7.5	7.3	6.2	5.8	1.5	1.8	1.7	1.3	0.7	0.3

Sources: Comecon yearbooks (A, B, and C), United Nations Yearbooks (Labour Statistics), and national yearbooks (D and E).

Notes: A – 1961-5; B – 1966-70; C – 1971-5; D – 1976-80; E – 1981-4; n.a. - not available. Figures for the last two periods are estimates based on wage figures in the United Nations yearbooks of labour statistics and Comecon yearbooks on employment. Figures for Bulgaria since 1976 do not take account of changes in employment.

and the state's dedication to equality, the differences in wealth are still considerable. (6) There are also contrasting lifestyles when the intelligentsia (especially the factions recruited into party membership) is compared with the work-force in agriculture and industry. Such contrasts are of course felt more acutely by families with low incomes. (7)

Attitudes do, however, vary between regions, for Yugoslavs differ significantly in their attitudes towards private property. (8) There are also differences between age-groups and between countries. Although evidence is inevitably limited, it seems that young people in socialist countries are not very materialistic and that 'they value a happy family life and successful marriage substantially more than material or occupational success'. (9) Materialistic values are perhaps found most prominently in the GDR and Hungary, where 'petty bourgeois' attitudes relating to car ownership and modern apartments have been clearly noted. (10) However, survey results in other countries create problems when behaviour fails to reflect all the moral standards claimed by the population! Despite strident propaganda, 'it seems reasonable to characterize public postures toward ideology and politics in Eastern Europe in terms such as passivity, withdrawal and uncertainty'. (11) On the other hand, people seem to be mildly positive about socialism and recognize the improvements made in education and health since the Second World War, although industrial development per se is not greatly appreciated. But there is an inevitable tendency, encouraged by the media, to compare socialism and capitalism on the basis of standards applying at quite different times (the post-war and inter-war periods), and few people in Eastern Europe have the perspective to contemplate a capitalist alternative for the present period.

The authorities maintain their responsibility for educating the new generation in the values of socialist realism and avoiding the pitfalls of 'moral pollution' from western sources. Reports of conflict between ideological and economic objectives provide insights into the workings of communist society which are not without their amusement value. Official concern in Romania over the proliferation of western-style garments stands in contrast with the commercial instincts of certain clothing co-operatives which have tried to produce the goods that people want to buy. A producer from Satu Mare got into trouble with the local authorities in Zalau for selling shirts with a picture of a cowboy smoking <u>Marlboro</u> cigarettes. In this case it seems there was a happy outcome since ideological sensitivities were calmed by a switch from the offending American brand of cigarettes to the Romanian product (<u>Snagov</u>) and assurances that the cowboy hats were in fact meant to resemble the traditional Romanian headgear from the Oas district! Thus, even the local authorities are not unaware of the need for commercial enterprise.

Societal problems in Eastern Europe go beyond the trivialities of clothing fashions. Crime is a growing problem, aggravated by a generally ambivalent attitude to public property and a tendency towards passivity in the face of hooliganism. Alcoholism and housing shortages also cause concern, all the more so because they have some bearing on crime rates. Suicide is a problem in Hungary, and in Czechoslovakia there is widespread concern over the deterioration of the environment. (12) Perhaps the greatest concern arises over human rights since many thinking people are not only aware of restrictions but are indignant and resentful about them. Freedoms which are guaranteed under the Constitution and safeguarded through international treaties are easily infringed where there are few democratic institutions to check intimidation and abuses of power. Freedom to travel is seriously restricted in some countries while access to literature and entertainment is constrained by state censorship which exercises political as well as moral judgement. Eastern Europe has certainly benefited from the slow growth in international acceptance of universal human rights marked by the 1948 Universal Declaration of Human Rights, the 1966 International Convenant on Civil and Political Rights, and most recently the Helsinki Final Act of 1975 with its mechanism of periodic review conferences. The latter has legitimized the monitoring of East European compliance with the Helsinki human rights provisions, among which the right to religious freedom has been particularly clearly defined. Monitoring groups have even appeared within Eastern Europe and the Charter 77 group in Czechoslovakia has become very well known: although harrassed by the authorities there are obvious reasons why the membership cannot now be summarily liquidated. In east-west negotiations it has become conventional for economic concessions to Eastern Europe to be conditional on respect for human rights. Such arrangements make it more difficult for governments to contemplate any return to the crude repressive measures of the Stalin Era. (13)

The Churches: a case study

Most problematic, perhaps, is the state's relationship with the Churches since people continue to be harrassed and frustrated in their attempts to participate in organized religious activity. This is curious because the comfort and moral guidance derived from religious observance would appear to harmonize with the state's interest in a contented and disciplined society. Religion remains very important, but especially for the older and less well educated people living in rural areas. Also, many people who do not profess a religion nevertheless believe that religious instruction strengthens morality in young people. However, as already noted, the Churches were persecuted for various reasons in the early years of communist rule. In all countries except Albania and Yugoslavia the Churches were adversely affected by early land reform programmes and thus followed a phase of confrontation everywhere as communist parties consolidated their control and started to settle accounts with their opponents.

A series of sweeping legislative and administrative measures on religion (particularly severe in Albania, Bulgaria, Czechoslovakia, Hungary and Romania) deprived the churches of economic security and institutional autonomy. At the same time anti-constitutional police and judicial mechanisms were employed to intimidate, divide and disorganize the hierarchy and the clergy, thus compelling the church to submit to far-reaching control and political manipulation by state organs. (14)

Recently a stage of accommodation has been reached between Church and state, reflecting the reduction in Soviet influence. (15) The process did not begin at the same time in all countries and it has not been free from reversion back to confrontationalist stances. However, there has been substantial improvement and momentum has been gained by east-west détente and by the Vatican's Ostpolitik following the election of Pope John. (16) Other arguments called for a change in tactics. The desire for better relations with the

117

non-communist world required the presentation of a façade of religious normality, a façade which could have positive political results through membership of the World Council of Churches and the development of the Peace Movement. Furthermore, as nationalism was rediscovered, in some countries the Church was seen as an ally of the government and toleration of the Church within limits was a 'safe' means whereby the state could win a measure of popular support and understanding. It is now commonplace to find churches and monasteries preserved as national monuments (as well as places of worship) by state funds and with major projects like the Benedictine Monastery of Pannonhalma in Hungary state funds have supplemented other resources collected through an international appeal. Fundamental to the current attitude is the realization that political ideology has not really inspired the people and that the Churches can contribute to a new national identity. (17) Better material conditions do not automatically create human beings: rather, they may give rise to moral problems.

However, there is little sign that the Churches are being accepted as associates in building up a real socialist society to the point where aggressive atheistic propaganda can be abandoned. Religious activities are still closely scrutinized and Church-state relations are usually entrusted to a special government like the State Office for Church Affairs set up in Hungary in 1951. Religious sects are licensed by the state and their places of worship are 'approved'. This means that all places of worship are under party surveillance: the faithful are known to the authorities and the more zealous priests can be identified and moved on if their influence is considered undesirable. The secret police infiltrate congregations, giving rise to the joke that such people are the keenest Christians because they never miss a meeting! There is a particularly tight rein on evangelistic organizations which try and maintain a profile: hence the discrimination in licensing sects and the control on bibles. This results in an underground church with furtive meetings in private houses, perhaps under the guise of birthday celebrations.

P. Ramet points out the divergent trends in the various countries. (18) In Poland the Roman Catholic Church has great strength at the grass roots and has therefore been effective in dealing with government (Table 4.4). Despite some intimidation the population remains deeply religious and candidates for the priesthood are plentiful. In addition to the allegiance of the people, there is recognition of the deep roots of the Church in national culture and tradition. So the Catholic Church in Poland is hardly an oppressed institution for it is accepted by the state as an important stabilizing force. (19) The Church certainly worked for reform in Poland but in a highly controlled manner and the radical approach of Cardinal Wojtyla of Krakow adopted during the 1970s was not reciprocated by the then Primate, Cardinal Wyszynski. Indeed, the rise of the Solidarity trade union must be seen against a background of Vatican support (Wojtyla having been elected Pope in 1978) and episcopal ambivalence. Since the imposition of martial law, the Catholic hierarchy in Poland has struggled to control the reform movement and guide it along relatively peaceful channels which will ensure stability and maintain the Church as an integral part of the normalization strategy of the Jaruzelski regime. Although the Vatican can afford to stand aloof from the political maneouvrings inside Poland and maintain support for the ideals of Solidarity, the union activists are under pressure to accept the authority of the Church or face an increasingly uncertain future as a largely underground movement. The Church has the resources, through its own infrastructure in Poland and through international contacts, to contemplate major initiatives in the economy. It was reported in 1983 that $5 billion might be raised from the Catholic Church outside Poland and from philanthropic institutions, as well as western governments, to provide private farmers with essential equipment which could be paid for in Polish currency. However, the state is obviously going to be reluctant to tolerate independent action by the Church dealing with foreign governments and extending, on a permanent basis, the internal distribution system established to deal with foreign charity gifts in the early 1980s.

In Hungary the Catholic Church enjoys the protection of the state. It is no longer subject to harrassment and continues to run a number of schools and hospitals. In recognition of this relatively liberal policy, the Church adopts a generally supportive attitude towards the government. The role of the Church is also quite significant in the GDR where the leaderships of the various evangelical Churches have been supporting an unofficial peace movement. This is not meant to constitute an open challenge to the regime, especially since the government has been highly supportive of the same movement in the

119

Table 4.4 Religious affiliations

Country	Year	Catholic	Jew	Percentage distribution Moslem	Orthodox	Protestant	Others(a)
Albania	1930	11.0		68.0	21.0		
Bulgaria	1946	0.8	0.6	13.4	83.8		1.4
Czechoslovakia	1950	76.3	0.2		2.6	16.0	0.7
GDR	1964	8.1				59.4	
Hungary	1949	70.5	1.5		0.4	27.4	0.2
Poland	1971	93.4			1.4	0.4	
Romania	1948	17.2	2.6	1.0	70.2	6.1	1.2
Yugoslavia	1953	31.8		12.3	41.5	0.9	

Source: Bociurkiw 1985 (note 14): 29.

Note: a. This category does not include the non-religious element amounting to 4.3 per cent in Bulgaria, 31.8 in the GDR, 4.6 in Poland, and 12.3 in Yugoslavia west. However, any movement not inspired directly by the ruling party causes concern, especially when it advocates progressive reforms like the introduction of 'social peace service' as an alternative to conscription into the armed services. (20) However, in Czechoslovakia the Catholic Church is going through a difficult time. (21) It continues to attract widespread support in Slovakia, but since training is strictly controlled there is a very serious shortage of priests (leading to excessive grouping of parishes), and several bishoprics are empty. For the government has always resented the influence of the Vatican and hints have been dropped to suggest that a separation from the Vatican may be a precondition for a normalization of Church-state relations. Nevertheless, there is evidence of a modest revival of religious observance, related to a perception of moral laxity in society against which many parents wish to protect their children. This increasing involvement by young people in Church life has increased the sensitivity of the government towards the influence of the Church in Poland and resulted in some return to coercive measures. Priests have been imprisoned for such minor transgressions as organizing processions or celebrating mass without permission, while the ability of others to perform their pastoral duties has been reduced by compulsory retirement, suspension of driving licences, and other obstructionist tactics.

MIGRATION

Population movements have been very numerous and in the domestic context they have been dominated by transfers from backward to advanced regions and from country to town. In Romania there has been a substantial export of population from Moldavia (amounting to 47 per cent of the natural increase between 1966 and 1983), and to a lesser extent from Oltenia (20 per cent), with most of the migrants heading for Muntenia and especially the city of Bucharest, where the growth was five times greater than the natural increase (Table 4.5). Almost 150,000 went abroad, largely German and Jewish emigrants but a significant number of Romanians who left the country illegally. However, the international dimension was much more important in Yugoslavia because during the 1970s it is estimated that there was a net outward movement of 225,000 people from

Table 4.5 Population growth and migration in Romania, 1966-83

Region	A	B	C	D	E
Banat	1,107	141	14.5	52	+88
Bucharest	2,192	740	51.0	146	+594
Crisana-Maramures	2,097	246	13.3	252	-6
Dobrogea	946	244	34.8	166	+78
Moldavia	4,615	653	16.5	1,157	-504
Muntenia	4,512	413	10.0	778	-366
Oltenia	2,416	274	12.8	343	-69
Transylvania	4,643	750	19.3	713	+36
Romania	22,528	3,461	18.1	3,608	-149

Source: V. Trebici and I. Hristache (1986) Demografia teritoriala a Romaniei, Bucharest: Ed. Academiei R.S.R.

Notes:
    A   - Population (thousands), 1983;
    B   - Growth since 1966;
    C   - Ditto, per cent;
    D   - Natural increase;
    E   - Net Migration.

Bosnia-Hercegovina, Kosovo, Macedonia, and Monetenegro, compared with a net inflow of 80,000 into Vojvodina, Serbia, and Slovenia - a net emigration of 145,000. This left Croatia in balance, with arrivals from the south and return migrants from Western Europe equalling the number of Croats leaving for work abroad. Exporting regions tend to be not only the more economically backward areas, with insufficient employment to retain the young people, but also the most demographically fertile, with high rates of natural increase, and the most culturally traditional. (22) Thus, in Kosovo (Yugoslavia) population growth has been rapid, despite losses by migration, and while the average size of each family in Yugoslavia has been decreasing, especially in the rural areas (from 4.5 members to 4.1), the trend in Kosovo is the reverse (from 7.0 to 7.9 in the rural areas and from 4.6 to 5.5 in the towns). Underpinning these trends is the immobility and traditional organization (the extended family) of the Albanian population of the area. (23)

Migration within the countries of Eastern Europe has to a large extent gone hand in hand with national development policies and will be dealt with more fully in the next section of the book. Here the emphasis will be placed on the international dimension. This is less important than in other developed countries in view of strict controls which are imposed, but in view of the attitude of official discouragement, the significant numbers involved merit some scrutiny. The historical dimension is important in understanding why a country like Hungary has lost so many people over the years: emigration has become part of history. There was a considerable peasant emigration to the New World in the late nineteenth century and again in the inter-war period when the emigré population has been estimated at 0.40 million. Some 1.20 million stayed abroad after the Second World War and a further 0.64 million escaped from the country between 1946 and 1957 (most of them leaving in the immediate aftermath of the 1956 uprising). Since then a further 0.09 million people have been lost through escapes as well as legal emigration. The losses are quite remarkable for a country with a population today of just 10.6 million, even allowing for the fact that significant losses arise from immediate post-war deportations of Germans (including some to the Soviet Union) and from more recent departures by young people who seek greater political freedom and scope for work where there are good economic opportunities.

Post-war international migration figures are shown in Table 4.6. The information is produced from various sources and should be treated with caution, although the contrasts between countries are probably accurate. The great majority of the recent migrants are members of ethnic and religious groups whose departure has been tolerated and in some cases expedited by governments in Eastern Europe. (24) There is, however, a steady flow of migrants who are allowed to leave in connection with marriages and family reunions or who manage to leave without the blessing of the authorities by crossing frontiers illegally, jumping ship, or seeking asylum while abroad on tourist itineraries or on cultural and sporting engagements. It is perhaps over emigration that the greatest range of official attitudes is encountered, extending from mass expulsion at the one extreme to total rejection of applications (sometimes with

Table 4.6 International migration, 1950-84

Country	1950-70			1965-74			1975-84			1950-84
	A	B	C	A	B	C	A	B	C	D
Albania	75.4	75.4	0.00	29.4	29.4	0.00	23.4	23.4	0.00	0.0
Bulgaria	19.3	16.8	0.18	6.4	5.9	0.01	3.9	3.1	0.10	11.4
Czechoslovakia	17.0	15.7	0.17	4.8	3.7	0.16	5.5	5.0	0.07	12.2
GDR	6.3	-7.2	2.49	0.1	-0.5	0.11	0.6	-2.1	0.28	112.6
Hungary	12.5	10.8	0.16	3.2	3.1	*	1.8	1.0	0.06	8.8
Poland	33.2	31.1	0.53	8.4	7.0	0.45	10.4	9.5	0.28	39.6
Romania	25.7	24.2	0.25	11.1	10.5	0.11	8.2	7.6	0.13	17.0
Yugoslavia	32.4	24.6	1.28	9.6	8.9	0.13	8.6	8.2	0.10	57.3
Eastern Europe	23.1	18.3	5.06	7.2	6.3	1.03	6.9	5.5	1.02	259.0

Sources: For 1950-70. The Population Debate: Dimensions and Perspectives, New York: United Nations Department of Economic & Social Affairs, I, 237-48; for 1965-84, United Nations demographic yearbooks.

Notes: A - Percentage growth based on natural increase;
       B - Actual percentage growth;
       C - Inferred out-migration (millions);
       D - Estimated annual average out-migration (thousands);
       * - denotes a total less than 0.01.

subsequent persecution of the people concerned) at the other. The differences arise from variation in perception of the value of potential emigrants as workers at home and as pawns in international relations.

Many people leaving Eastern Europe immediately after the war were Jews who survived Nazi extermination and were allowed to go to Israel until Soviet-Israeli relations deteriorated by the late 1940s. However, the outstanding case is that of the Germans, many of whom were expelled after the war partly as a punitive measure and partly to create room for the resettlement of displaced nationals like the Poles from the eastern provinces lost to the Soviet Union. The greatest number of German refugees came from the recovered territories of Poland. In the case of Czechoslovakia up to 0.8 million left voluntarily before the end of hostilities and all but 0.3 million of the 2.7 million then remaining were expelled in 1945-6. Other German minorities were subjected to discrimination but with a notable exception in Romania where a strong German minority remains. Germans suffered expropriation and forced labour, many of them working in the Soviet Union whose demands on Romania for labour reparations were met by departing Germans of working age (younger than 45 for men and 30 for women). Some of the deportees chose eventually to return from the Soviet Union to Germany and many others emigrated from Romania to the FRG (some of them moving out with the German army before the end of the war), but there was never any specific expulsion policy. The relatively small numbers of Germans who survived in Eastern Europe (outside the GDR) are appreciated as skilled workers to the point where protracted negotiations have been set up by the FRG to expediate the emigration of those who wish to leave. (25) Economic incentives have been important and the Romanian government has tried to exploit this type of barter by levying education taxes on would-be emigrants.

The Turkish minority in Bulgaria was also subject to expulsion in the 1950s (26) when it would have numbered some 0.75 million (about 10 per cet of the total population). The Bulgarian government was initially opposed to emigration although the minority suffered through collectivization and the takeover of the Moslem schools. Then suddenly, in 1950, after mysterious bomb outrages on both the Bulgarian consulate in Istanbul and the Turkish consulate in Plovdiv, policy was reversed and Turkey was deluged with applications for entry visas from people who were now able to leave Bulgaria. Clearly Turkey could not process these applications immediately without relaxing its checks for communist agents. The Bulgarians, however, escalated the conflict by driving out Turks who had received exit visas from Bulgaria but no entry visas for Turkey: on being refused entry to Turkey they crossed into Greece and broadened the dispute to involve a third government. It would appear that the uncivilized behaviour of the Bulgarians arose from Soviet plans for Dobrogea which required the displacement of both Turks and Gypsies (a number of whom the Bulgarians tried to foist on the Turkish government as genuine Turks). It required a firm Turkish reaction, closing the frontier and threatening an approach to the United Nations, to force the Soviets to call their satellite to order. The Bulgarians then agreed (late in 1950) to delay the issue of exit visas until entry visas for Turkey were granted, and to respect the provisions of the Ankara treaty over property rights: for they had previously been stripping the deportees of all their property, including ox-carts, and leaving them waiting helplessly without shelter on a closed frontier. There was a temporary improvement which expedited the transfer of Turks from Bulgaria (bringing the total to about 155,000 for the period since 1944). Before the end of 1951, however, the frontier was again closed because Bulgarians tried to smuggle Gypsies out of the country. Turkish membership of NATO also contributed to tension at this time. Relations became more relaxed in the 1970s. Some 60,000 Turks emigrated in the early 1970s under the ten-year Bulgarian-Turkish agreement of 1968. The impact of this was particularly strong in the districts of Kardzhali, Razgrad, and Targovishte.

Travel to countries outside the Soviet bloc is extremely difficult, even on a temporary basis. Citizens of socialist countries may return infected with ideological contagion or, worse still, may not come back at all. Furthermore, the trade deficits in hard currency mean that the authorities are extremely reluctant to grant generous allowances. People therefore wishing to travel to the west have had to follow a complicated administrative process and, in the event of success, have had to pay heavily for a passport and convertible currency. The Conference on Security and Co-operation which ended in August 1975 helped to ease travel restrictions because the participating states agreed to facilitate freer movement for people wishing to travel, whether individually or collectively and whether on private or official business. However, the controls are still heavy. The granting of a passport is not a right and if applicants have not received an invitation from a family in the west with an assurance of the financial means for travel and subsistence, the lack of hard currency may make a journey impossible. Apart from Yugoslavia the most liberal regime is in Hungary where any citizen is normally allowed to make a visit to the west, supported by a reasonable allocation of hard currency, once every three years. If invitations are forthcoming then more frequent visits are possible and pensioners may spend up to three months each year living with relatives in the west. Yugoslavs are quite free to travel abroad and the discretionary powers of the security service are exercised in the case of well under 1 per cent of all applications for passports and exit visas. In 1983, however, the Yugoslav authorities demanded a deposit of 5,000 dinars for each trip abroad and the number of travellers has declined sharply as a result.

International migration of labour

Travel to communist countries, especially on a group basis, is relatively easy and there is now a considerable amount of temporary migration for work purposes arising out of the more pragmatic attitude of the post-Stalin era (and especially the 1960s). While the international migration of labour is unacceptable, in principle it can be tolerated in the short term. However, migration does not take place on an individual basis in response to ad hoc demands: exchanges of labour are carefully organized, usually with a fixed term in mind. (27) There are some perceived political benefits through contact between workers from different socialist countries but the main justification is economic: balancing labour shortages in one country with the surplus in another so that both governments gain financially as well as the guest workers (Gastarbeiter) themselves. Czechoslovakia and the GDR are the main importing countries in Eastern Europe and only small numbers move in the opposite direction. However, Czechoslovakia has shipping and harbour interests in Szczecin and some local cross-border commuting takes place along the Hungarian frontier, while the GDR makes a gesture to Hungary by allowing some reciprocity in the bilateral arrangements for labour exchanges. Both countries have modest numbers of workers in the Soviet Union while the GDR makes a major effort in military training outside the bloc.

Polish Gastarbeiter first moved into the GDR in 1963 to work on construction projects. Two years later an agreement was reached for the supply of Polish workers to factories in the GDR close to the frontier and the numbers of commuters climbed to around 30,000 by 1975. Some 400 Poles were commuting daily across the frontier to the synthetic fibre works at Guben, while 500 were living and working at the Schwarze Pumpe complex. Up to 25,000 Poles were employed in a dozen factory building sites, including those at Limenau (china), Leuna and Magdeburg (chemicals), and Weisendorf (paper). Under an agreement reached in 1967 up to 10,000 young Hungarians find training and work experience in the GDR. Several of them have married girls from the GDR and have stayed in the country semi-permanently. The expression 'professional training' is of course a euphemism which disguises the fact that such workers are primarily Gastarbeiter in a country with a chronic labour shortage. Most are employed in oil refinery at Schwedt, the shipyards at Rostock, and important enterprises in Dresden, Erfurt, Halle, Karl Marx Stadt, and Leipzig. The arrangement has a bilateral character but the first young people from the GDR arrived in Hungary only in 1974 and the numbers are relatively small at around 200.

There were agreements in 1945 and 1946 which formalized the flow of workers to Czechoslovakia from Poland and Bulgaria respectively, but the numbers involved remained small until the late 1960s. The number of Bulgarians is still small (about 500) but there were around 30,000 Polish workers in the early 1970s. Numbers fell during the Solidarity crisis in Poland when there were fears that Polish workers might extend the unrest to Czechoslovakia, but the situation has now been normalized. Women workers have been recruited by the textile, clothing and leather industries, while the men have been employed on building work in connection with projects in the chemical industry, power (Tusemice power station) and transport. Shortage of labour is very serious in the border regions, arising out of the expulsion of Germans and leading to the employment of Poles living just across the frontier. The Nachod area registered the highest relative influx with Polish workers accounting for up to an eighth of the total workforce in certain enterprises. Commuting is organized on a daily or weekly basis. Yugoslav workers have been engaged on building sites in Czechoslovakia since 1966. They have constructed new housing units and various factories including the glass works at Novy Bor and extensions to the Skoda motor factory at Mlada Boleslav. The economy can evidently absorb more Bulgarian, Polish, and Yugoslav workers, particularly in the building and textile industries, but further recruitment has been difficult and in recent years the Vietnamese have been the largest foreign worker contingent in Czechoslovakia. Numbers increased from approximately 3,000 in 1979 to 26,000 by the end of 1982. Most of them are expected to stay for four years and undertake training and factory work but some difficulties have been reported, involving cultural incompatibility and alleged discrimination over wages and working conditions. By the end of 1983 there were also 4,600 Cubans in Czechoslovakia.

Up to 8,000 Poles work in Hungary each year in manufacturing and construction, along with small numbers from Austria, Czechoslovakia, and the GDR, as well as China and Cuba. Naturally there are few labour exchanges within the Balkans but Yugoslavs have been reported in Bulgaria working on building contracts negotiated by firms in Nis and Skopje, while some Romanians from the Banat have undertaken harvest work in the adjacent parts of Yugoslavia where labour shortages have arisen through migration to non-agricultural work in the cities of Yugoslavia or Western Europe. A local arrangement operates between the border villages of Mali Zam and Jamul Mare. Migrants from Romania work for several days and then return home with various consumer goods normally difficult to find. Some branches of Yugoslav industry cannot find all the workers they need. Several hundred cooks and waiters have been recruited for the summer tourist season from various East European countries (Bulgaria, Czechoslovakia, and Poland), and in 1978 skilled workers were recruited in Western Europe (actually Naples in Italy) to work in the shipyards at Rijeka.

It was estimated in 1975 that some 50,000 East Europeans were working in the Soviet Union, at least 20,000 of them on the Orenburg gas project. (28) The great majority of the East European workers (as many as 40,000) are Bulgarians. A major consideration here has been the woodcutting project in Komi based on an agreement of 1967: this is virtually a Bulgarian enterprise operating on Soviet soil. More than 5,000 Bulgarians have been reported at the

Kursk Magnetic Anomaly, based at the towns of Stari Oskol and Zheleznogorsk with work at mining and ore dressing plants. Another 5,000 are based at metallurgical combine in Zhdanov and some 2,500 work at the paper and cellulose combine of Arkhangelsk. Other Bulgarians are involved with various Comecon joint projects in the Soviet Union. Some 300 Hungarians went to help build the Ust Ilimsk cellulose complex in 1976, after brigades of young construction workers were solicited from the countries participating in the scheme. However, surprisingly Romania has not become deeply involved in labour exchanges and only modest numbers have been reported in the Soviet Union on joint projects.

The GDR's active military involvement in the Third World began in 1973 when a military agreement was signed with Congo-Brazzaville. Since then it is estimated that about 15,000 'advisers and experts' have been dispatched to cover communications, espionage, and security. Ethiopia's police force was trained by the GDR and training camps for Palestinian commandos are maintained in South Yemen. East Europeans have frequently worked abroad on other projects undertaken in the context of international trade. The construction of the 3.1 million tonne capacity oil refinery at Basra involved 1,300 workers from various factories in Czechoslovakia and 4,000 Iraqis. Three years were taken to complete the complex extending over an area of some 2 square kilometres in a semi-desert environment close to the confluence of the Euphrates and Tigris. The Czechs were confronted with an unfamiliar environment, poor working, and living conditions and local firms unaccustomed to work on large construction projects. Yugoslav building firms have been very active abroad, working on factories, hotels, houses, and offices. Thus, for example, the Sheraton hotel and congress hall complex in Harare (Zimbabwe), a similar complex including reception and concert halls in Libreville (Gabon), and the international trading fair in Lagos (Nigeria). Total earnings between 1978 and 1983 inclusive amounted to $11.27 billion, 76.9 per cent from the Third World, 13.3 per cent from capitalist countries, and 9.8 per cent from socialist countries. Looking at individual countries, the most important customers were Iraq with 41.7 per cent, Libya with 13.6, and the FRG with 11.1, followed by the USSR (3.7), Czechoslovakia (3.3), Nigeria (3.1), Algeria (2.8), GDR (2.6), and Gabon and Kuwait (both 2.4).

The case of Yugoslavia

Yugoslavia is exceptional in allowing people to work abroad on an individual basis and in western countries too. Small numbers have gone to Australasia and North America (c. 150,000 in 1975) but many have gone to Western Europe: nearly 750,000 to the FRG, Austria and Switzerland, and about 100,000 to France, Benelux, and Scandinavia. Thus, the tradition of Yugoslavs working for German industry in Yugoslavia is now maintained through work for German industry in German-speaking countries! Many young people speak German and remain abroad for several years in most cases, returning when their financial objectives have been met or when residence permits are revoked due to unemployment. The migration of young workers to Western Europe arose out of Yugoslavia's policy of open borders during an era of reform (post-1965) seeking much greater efficiency in domestic industry which had previously been excessively labour-intensive. Domestic non-agricultural employment absorbed 140,000 new workers annually between 1948 and 1964, but only 29,000 per annum during the rest of the decade (when 115,000 young people were reaching working age each year). By 1970 unemployment was becoming a serious issue, to say nothing of the problems of underemployment on small family farms unable to improve their efficiency because of lack of capital and the state's ambivalent attitude to private enterprise. However, not all migrants have been rural dwellers unable to find work in Yugoslav cities, for the 1971 Census revealed that the flow of migrant workers originated in urban areas of the country among skilled workers of middle age. The main source areas were the northern republics where people were relatively well informed about foreign employment prospects and less apprehensive about facing a strange environment. The main incentive was a higher salary. However, emigration has now spread to rural areas and to the less-developed republics, encouraged to some extent by the government's information machine. Migrant workers constitute a relatively high proportion of the labour forces of the backward republics, although in absolute terms the more advanced areas retain their prominence.

Because of the relatively high wages paid in Western Europe the earning capacity of the migrants has been estimated at equivalent to half the total domestic wage bill. The migrants have a relatively high saving ratio and cash remittances back to Yugoslavia have been equivalent to a third of foreign exchange earnings from commodity exports (and far in excess of total receipts from the tourist industry). The remittances add to the purchasing power of individuals rather than government bodies and so in contrast to government expenditure much of the money is invested in housing and in vehicles (including farm equipment) which is nevertheless relevant to economic growth through improved farm efficiency and employment generated locally in the construction industry. Some new houses have been built in remote locations lacking an adequate infrastructure, contrary to the provisions of local plans. Benefits also accrue through work experience and increased interregional labour movement to maintain the growth of domestic employment and moderate the problems of relatively high unemployment in the more backward areas.

On the other hand remittances have added to inflationary pressures and the country has become vulnerable to economic fluctuations in the labour-importing countries: periods of cyclical slack abroad may induce flows of returning emigrant workers too great for the domestic economy to absorb in an orderly way. Again, the migrant worker phenomenon may be seen as socially disruptive because of the separation of husbands and fathers from wives and children, tangibly expressed in such ways as a reduced rate of natural increase. Social costs also include poor educational performances by children whose fathers are abroad and psychic strains on individuals isolated from their normal social environment. Then there are political problems such as a reduced military potential, a lower commitment to socialism on the part of workers' 'resocialized' by their years in the west, and increased nationalism within the Yugoslav republics especially Croatia. (29) By 1973 efforts were being made to control the outflow. Official Yugoslav statistics place 0.63 million Yugoslavs working abroad in 1981, together with another 0.24 million family members. These figures should be related to an economically active population within Yugoslavia of 9.36 million and a total resident population of 21.55. Apart from the Yugoslavs the numbers of East European workers in Western Europe are small, consisting mainly of specialists (including professional and sports people) who can make special arrangements to work or participate in cultural exchanges. Some skilled Hungarian workers have been reported in Austria, however.

Table 4.7 Ethnic minorities, 1950-84

Country	Large minorities (population above 400,000)									Small minorities								
	c.1935			c.1960			c.1985			c.1935			c.1960			c.1985		
	A	B	C	A	B	C	A	B	C	A	B	C	A	B	C	A	B	C
Albania										3	0.08	7.5	3	0.06	3.6		n.a.	
Bulgaria	1	0.62	10.2	1	0.68	8.6	1	0.72	8.0		n.a.		3	0.44	5.5		n.a.	
Czechoslovakia	3	4.61	31.3	1	0.53	3.9	1	0.58	3.8	2	0.12	0.8	4	0.31	2.3	4	0.22	1.4
GDR	1	0.44	0.7							2	0.06	*	1	0.10	0.6	1	0.07	0.4
Hungary	1	0.48	5.5							7	0.80	2.1	4	0.32	3.2	4	0.36	3.4
Poland	3	6.88	21.6							2	0.18	0.6	5	0.34	1.1		n.a.	
Romania	4	3.41	18.9	2	2.10	11.3	2	2.10	9.3	7	0.80	4.4	9	0.27	1.5	9	0.23	1.0
Yugoslavia	3	1.68	12.1	2	1.42	7.6	2	2.16	9.6	8	0.76	5.5	8	0.62	3.3	8	0.41	1.8
Eastern Europe		18.12	11.3		4.73	4.0		5.56	4.1		2.80a	1.8		2.46	2.1		n.a.	

Sources: King 1973; Mellor 1975: 121-2; Statesman's Yearbook.

Notes: A - Number of minorities (excluding gypsies and Jews, and combining ethnic groups as follows: Czechs and Slovaks; Serbs, Croats, Macedonians, Montenegrans and Slovenes; Romanians and Vlachs; Turks and Tatars);

B - Total population;

C - Ditto as percentage of the population of the state;

* - denotes a total less than 0.1.

a - excludes Bulgaria

Figure 4.1 Ethnic minorities in Eastern Europe, 1930–70

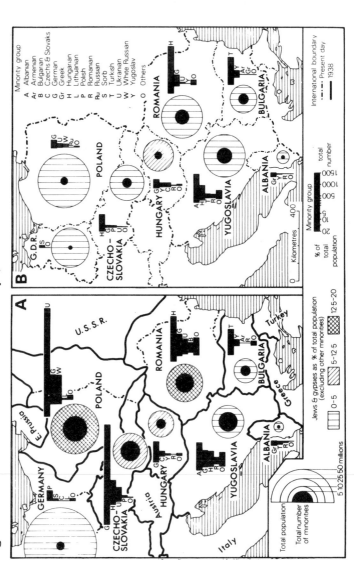

Source: Compiled from census returns and estimates.

ETHNIC MINORITIES

Reliable statistics on ethic minorities throughout Eastern Europe are very difficult to come by. For the early post-war years the largest minorities were the Hungarian (2.62 million), Albanian (0.91), Turkish-Tartar (0.88), German (0.58), Ukrainian (0.29), and Yugoslav (0.27). Some are restricted to one country (for example, the entire Albanian minority is to be found in Yugoslavia) while others are distributed across as many as three or four countries: Germans in Czechoslovakia, Hungary, Poland, and Romania; and Yugoslavs in Albania, Bulgaria, Hungary, and Romania. This of course is the picture in Eastern Europe only: Hungarians and Yugoslavs are to be found in parts of Austria and all ethnic groups are well represented in Western Europe and North America. As for the overall significance of minorities within individual countries, a clear distinction may be made between Bulgaria, Romania, and Yugoslavia on the one hand, with minorities comprising between 10 and 15 per cent of the total population, and Albania, GDR, Hungary, and Poland on the other, with minorities representing 5 per cent or less of the total population. Czechoslovakia is intermediate between the two groups. By and large, however, the population of Eastern Europe is ethnically much more homogeneous now than it was fifty years ago, thanks to international transfers, frontier changes, and continuing assimilation (Table 4.7). (30) The frontier changes in Poland, along with the resettlement of Poles from the east within the new frontiers and expulsions and transfers of Germans westwards and Byelorussians, Lithuanians, and Ukrainians eastwards has made the population of Poland much more homogeneous: 98 per cent now speak Polish compared with 69 per cent in 1931. Some 77,000 Germans remain in Czechoslovakia (1975) but only a small number are actively seeking permission to emigrate. It seems that the assimilation process is well advanced, for unlike the Hungarian, Polish, and Ukranian minorities which form cohesive groups, the Germans are dispersed among the Czech population. In the north-western parts of Romania, the relatively rapid growth of the Romanian population and some emigration by members of ethnic minorities has produced a transformation during this century (Table 4.8).

In the GDR it is remarkable that there are some 70,000 Slavs (the Sorbs of Lusatia) who have survived centuries of German political domination and cultural pressure and still

135

Table 4.8 Ethnic structure of the Centre, North, and West of Romania, 1891-1948

Nationality	Centre			North			West			Total		
	1891	1930	1948	1891	1930	1948	1891	1930	1948	1891	1930	1948
Germans	14.3	14.1	8.8	2.8	2.9	0.6	11.7	13.2	7.9	9.4	9.8	5.8
Hungarians	19.8	22.5	17.3	34.5	32.1	39.4	28.1	18.7	20.6	28.2	24.4	25.7
Jews	1.6	1.1	0.4	4.7	4.9	0.6	3.9	3.1	0.5	3.6	3.2	0.5
Romanians	62.4	62.1	72.6	47.3	54.3	57.2	48.8	58.1	66.1	51.6	57.8	65.1
Total	1,151	1,427	1,698	1,560	1,953	1,873	2,080	2,170	2,190	4,790	5,549	5,761

Source: Census.

.Figures show the percentage distribution and the total population in thousands.

live their own national life. However, although there is genuine encouragement of the language by the authorities there are inevitable social factors which encourage Germanization, even in the absence of any explicit Germanizing policy, and the Sorb population is almost totally bilingual. (31) Tartar enclaves in Poland still remain, although the people were thoroughly Polonised centuries ago and actively participated in Polish freedom fights from the late eighteenth century. Some 7,000 Tartars were present in inter-war Poland, enjoying considerable social and cultural liberties and after the shift in Poland's eastern frontier to the Curzon Line, some 3,000 Tartars were able to secure resettlement. Some 1,800 Tartars are Muslim believers with the strongest group, numbering some 800, in Bialystok. However, the scattered community is no longer a well-organized ethnic group (for the Communist government abolished the Tartar Association established in 1925) and it remains significant only as an exotic oriental element in Polish folklore. Among the more unusual minorities may be cited the Greek community in Hungary, a legacy of the civil war of 1949 when asylum was offered to several thousand refugees, including many orphan children. The children were placed in hostels and a Greek colony was established in the Dunaujvar district of Fejer County and named Gorogfalva (Greek Village) but later Beloiannisz. There were some 1,600 people in the village in 1972: 1,300 Greeks and 300 Hungarians, but altogether the Greek exiles in various parts of Hungary number 5,000.

Ethnic minorities create problems in several ways. They are inevitably seem by governments as potential sources of instability, especially when their life-style is particularly distinct and when their main area of settlement is so situated as to nourish aspirations of boundary changes which could place the minority under the authority of the government of its mother country. On the whole, however, it must be said that ethnic problems have been contained in the post-war period: governments have worked for integration while at the same time allowing each minority plenty of scope for cultural expression through education facilities in minority languages, special publishing and media programmes, and cultural establishments. Soviet-style cultural autonomy policies, providing lectures in Turkish at Sofia University for the Turkish minority in Bulgaria, have become the norm throughout Eastern Europe and have contributed to stability. At the same time mother-country governments have been diplomatic in their efforts to support the claims of minorities in other countries and no explicit territorial claims have been made. Yugoslavia has been restrained in its support for the Croat and Slovene minorities in Austria though some strains have arisen over the failure to honour an undertaking made in 1972 to erect bilingual topographic signs in various parts of Carinthia, a move strongly opposed by the German population of the province. However, conflicts do arise under certain circumstances. Differences in behavioural norms between governments can result in perceived discrimination even when the minority concerned (for example, Hungarians in Romania) is being treated no differently from the population of the relevant nation as a whole. Again, differences of policy in the recognition of minorities (for example, Macedonians in Bulgaria) can cause considerable international irritation.

In Yugoslavia there is a delicate balance to be struck between self-expression by the minorities and loyalty to the Yugoslav idea. (32) In the 1980s there has been concern about 'Pan-Islamic nationalism', especially in the Bosnia-Hercegovina where there are 1.63 million ethnic Moslems (out of a total of 2.00 million in Yugoslavia as a whole). There are fears that the Bosnian Moslems, many of whom have become fervent advocates of Islam as a result of visits to centres like Cairo and Mecca, wish to create a Moslem republic in Yugoslavia. Moslem academics in Yugoslavia have argued that greater self-awareness is a purely religious manifestation. It is unlikely to generate enthusiasm to the point where a Bosnian ayatollah is cast on to the political stage, since many of the Moslems are not particularly devout (having broken basic Koranic laws on alcohol and adultery for centuries) and have no racial ties with the Middle East. However, official anxiety is deepened by the link with Kosovo where national consciousness on the part of the Albanian minority could be enhanced by a renaissance in spiritual life. The perceived assertiveness of the Albanian Moslems in Yugoslavia is most worrying for the Serbs, many of whom have been forced to leave Kosovo. Further, it is evident from newspaper articles that there is also some concern over alleged Albanian expansionism in Macedonia. However, while the Moslems in Kosovo are numerous (1.1 million), they are not very active politically: groups initiating the riots in 1981 comprised atheistically educated youths motivated by Albanian nationalism and Marxist ideology, looking to Tirana as a new Mecca. However, the authorities remain worried and various tactics have been used to contain the situation. One of these is greater support for the Turkish minority as a narodnost (nation) in Kosovo as part of an attempt to emphasize the multinational character of this region. (33) The gypsies are also important in a policy which may well serve Yugoslav as well as individual national interests by differentiating the Yugoslav Albanians from the Albanians of the Albanian state.

There appears to be the greatest contentment where minorities are small and where they are well-integrated into national life. Under such conditions the minorities pose no threat to the state, socially or strategically; they make limited demands and receive the support of the authorities interested to develop good relations and to maintain a rich cultural heritage. Apart from certain irritations, like the attempt by the authorities to eliminate 'foreign' Christian names between 1963 and 1968, Hungarian policy towards the minorities has been liberal. Hungary's minorities (Germans 200,000, Slovaks 110,000, South Slavs 80,000, and Romanians 25,000) are concentrated in certain areas (for example, Germans in Komarom, Slovaks in Bekescsaba, and Romanians in Gyula), but, broadly speaking, they are scattered through the country and have intermingled to a large degree with the Hungarians. The south-eastern part of Hungary is the most ethnically mixed, with non-Hungarian majorities in some villages (Romanians in Mehkerek, for example). There is a substantial education programme with special schools for the minorities offering 3,750 nursery places, 22,260 primary places, and 710 secondary school places, notably the high schools at Baja, Bekescsaba, and Gyula for Germans, Slovaks and Romanians respectively. The minorities have their newspapers and radio stations, as well as cultural associations and libraries. On the whole it seems that many members of minority communities are tending to discard active identification with their own ethnic group. Many non-Hungarians who choose not to send their children to schools which offer instruction in native languages, presumably because the main consideration is now the social mobility of the children. Evidence however is limited and it is clear that some groups, like the gypsies, frequently cling to traditional values and lifestyles. (34)

The atmosphere of détente has made it possible for various East European governments to open contacts with emigré communities in the west since the maintenance of national consciousness can bring dividends to the mother country in both the short and long term. Hungary is a case in point because the 1980 Census in the USA revealed that 1.78 million people were of Hungarian origin (although only some 0.50 million can still speak the language). In addition, there are some 250,000 of Hungarian descent in Western Europe (including some 50,000 in both the FRG and France) and some 200,000 in other parts of the world, chiefly Australia and Israel. In the short term there is a boost to the Hungarian tourist industry through visits related to cultural events like the summer camps (at Balaton) and summer schools (organized by the teacher training college at Debrecen) to encourage the use of the Hungarian language. Such events have gathered momentum since the first 'Mother Tongue Conference' was held in 1970. Over the longer term a heightened national consciousness among Hungarian emigrés can work for the benefit of the mother country through economic assistance, offered directly or indirectly through governments. Similar to the World Federation of Hungarians is the Polonia Society which encourages visits to Poland for family or cultural reasons; and despite some difficulties for Jewish minorities many people now in Israel maintain links with their former homelands. (35) Of course, where East European governments implement policies which attract strong criticisms from emigrés, such liaison is heavily circumscribed: in particular, many Romanian emigrés are strongly critical of the Bucharest government (notably with respect to official emigration policy) and close relations with the emigré communities are therefore impossible.

The gypsies: a case study

The number of gypsies in Eastern Europe is very difficult to ascertain. Official figures of 0.33 million in Eastern Europe as a whole, with the main groups in Bulgaria (0.20 million), Hungary (0.03), and Romania (0.10), would appear to be far too low, and the World Association of Gypsies (established in London in 1961) has estimated a total gypsy population in Eastern Europe of 2.61 million, distributed as follows: Bulgaria 0.40 million, Czechoslovakia 0.32, Hungary 0.36, Poland, 0.30, Romania 0.60, and Yugoslavia 0.70. (36) In Eastern Europe as a whole it is probably the gypsy community which creates most public disquiet. Despite great efforts to accelerate integration there is considerable feeling against the gypsies because they do not all share the values of the rest of the population. The gypsies' vigorous sense of their own identity makes it hard for them to adapt to a new lifestyle. Public animosity towards gypsies is increased by their perceived involvement in crime and in various anti-social activities (such as non-payment of rents and other financial obligations and abuse of state property). Gypsies are often indifferent to the fact that outsiders consider their behaviour erratic: they take advantage of almost any occasion to arrange a celebration and it is especially on such occasions that their loud voices and general exuberance create controversy with neighbours. Efforts to improve housing conditions for gypsy families has been constrained not only by limited investment but also by gross neglect of new apartments, which has sometimes resulted in entire blocks being abandoned as uninhabitable.

Part of the problem arises from the limited scope for gypsies in their traditional employments. These include fortune telling; violin making and entertaining; horse dealing; and metal work. The great majority of gypsies with regular employment are working in manual jobs and only 1 or 2 per cent can be classified among the intelligentsia. Unemployment is a problem among both adults and children, although slow progress is being made and larger numbers of young people are now taking up jobs or apprentice training courses after completing their compulsory education. Again, while illiteracy has been virtually eliminated among other groups it remains a problem among gypsies, affecting over 10 per cent of the adult population. It is difficult for adult gypsies to change their life-style but progress with gypsy children is by no means easy. Relatively small numbers attend kindergartens and so most gypsy children enter primary school knowing only a few hundred words in the official language of the country (compared with a few thousand in the case of children from kindergartens). School attendance tends to be irregular: on average, gypsy children in Czechoslovakia miss about 100 hours of education each year. Again, in Czechoslovakia only 4 per cent of gypsy children proceed beyond elementary education and less than 2 per cent go to university. At the same time the growth of the gypsy population generally exceeds the national average: in Slovakia, where two-thirds of Czechoslovakia's gypsies are living, the gypsy population grew by 23.8 per cent in the

1970s compared with 10.5 per cent for Slovakia as a whole.

During the Second World War, there were some attempts to solve the gypsy problem by genocide and since 1945 there has been some deportation. Many gypsies left Yugoslavia for the Netherlands in the 1970s, and it was claimed in 1985 that some 20,000 gypsies had been forced out of Poland, victims of a latter-day pogrom, eventually to find refuge in the Netherlands. Some governments are reluctant to recognize the gypsies as national minorities and policies towards them reflect an uneasy blend of despotism and paternalism. In Czechoslovakia the traditional nomadic gypsy life has been made a criminal offence and the settlement of the gypsies has been particularly noticeable in the border regions where many houses were left empty when the German population was expelled. (37) Whole streets were allocated to gypsy families in Ceske Budejovice but the property was badly treated by the new occupants. On the other hand, there has been some success in Slovakia, where standardized housing has replaced gypsy camp-sites, with schools and other urban facilities provided in the vicinity. Such projects brought about an increase in living standards while enabling the gypsies to preserve some of their customs. Yet Czechoslovakia has been denounced in international gypsy circles for encouraging the sterilization of gypsy women and for impeding migration of gypsies from Slovakia to Bohemia and Moravia where there is a large demand for unskilled labour.

The gypsies in Hungary

Policy is relatively enlightened in Hungary, where there is a gypsy population of some 400,000. A national gypsy council has been set up and this provides a formal line of communication between the government and the minority group. Some 40 per cent of gypsies are well-integrated, with regular employment and normal housing conditions. However, while this group comprises a gypsy intelligentsia dedicated to the survival of a distinct sub-culture, covering language, customs, and musical heritage, the majority is less committed and often fails to declare its ethnic/cultural origins. About half of Hungary's gypsies are not integrated and maintain a traditional, though non-nomadic, way of life in gypsy colonies or slum accommodation. A small minority of some 10 per cent still maintains a nomadic life, wandering from village to village and drawing some income from sporadic commercial activities. Prejudice against gypsies therefore continues, although most Hungarians believe that the crime problem is not really a gypsy problem so much as an expression of deprivation, the proportion of uneducated and disadvantaged people being relatively high among the gypsy communities.

Gypsy women bear twice as many children as other Hungarian women (thirty-two compared with fifteen per thousand in 1971). In general, they have been slow to take advantage of improved medical facilities but now over 90 per cent of gypsy women in Hungary have their babies in hospital and there has been a sharp drop in infant mortality rates as a result. However, family planning is still a concept which seems alien to the gypsies: gypsy women usually step straight from childhood to motherhood and continue to bear children from the age of fifteen until their forties. Between eight and ten children in a family is normal, with some having as many as twelve to fifteen. For the gypsy population as a whole, life expectancy is 10-15 years below the average for the rest of the population, reflecting the relatively harsh living conditions which result in lessened sensitivity to heat, cold, and hunger.

While the gypsies constitute a distinct ethnic group, it is highly stratified socially, for some gypsies lead a successful professional life while others remain nomadic. Family ties are very strong and mixed marriages are difficult to maintain on account of the steady flood of relatives who invade the homes of newly-weds and in the process upset all endeavours at neatness and a higher standard of living. However, government efforts to improve the conditions for gypsies have shown commitment and sensitivity. The clearance of gypsy slums was tackled by a decree in 1964 and an amendment in 1967 offering loans for the building of simple new houses. By 1975 18,000 out of 55,000 gypsy families had improved their housing conditions. Present policies aim at the settlement of gypsies within towns and villages instead of the outskirts. They have opportunities to obtain council flats in the same way as other citizens and they can participate in co-operative schemes to build blocks of flats. Also, like others suffering from bad housing conditions they are eligible for a plot of land, free of charge, with interest-free credits (repayable over thirty-five years) to help with building costs; however, one year's permanent employment and 10 per cent down-payment are conditions for obtaining such credits which many gypsy families cannot meet. Unfortunately, the older generation is particularly reluctant to leave the traditional hovels. It is claimed that less than 30,000 gypsies still reside in shanty villages compared with 70,000 ten years ago. Employment rates are stated to be 85 per cent for gypsy men and 60 per cent for women.

Substantial progress has also been made in education and illiteracy levels, which exceeded 90 per cent at the beginning of the century, are now well below a third. It seems particularly necessary to find more kindergarten places for gypsy children, because as long as places are given to children whose parents are working the young gypsies are at a disadvantage. Without any kindergarten experience gypsy children begin their primary education still speaking their Romany language (certainly in the case of children still living in slums), and they have only half the Hungarian vocabulary of other children. Gypsy language kindergartens and schools have been tried but they tend to foster isolation and prevent further assimilation. A further problem in education concerns the low level of teacher-parent co-operation where the latter has little education: no help can be given with homework, and inadequate supervision often results in the appropriation and destruction of books and writing utensils by smaller children in the household. On the positive side in education, many gypsy children are particularly adept at artistic subjects. At Bekes, where the culture centre was opened in 1949, the first in the country, there is now a club (known as 'Pista Danko' after a nineteenth-century gypsy song-writer) which caters for adult gypsies who wish to catch up on their formal education and indulge in cultural pursuits. Gypsy orchestras boast a total membership of some 8,000 and they offer a wide repertoire ranging from folk songs to concert pieces.

Conclusion

At the time of writing, ethnic problems continue to loom large in Eastern Europe as governments become ever more sensitive over any lack of homogeneity. There is particular sensitivity in the Balkans, where Romania, for example, will not tolerate any internationalization of ethnic questions: the problems of the Hungarian minority in Transylvania will be solved only by the Romanian Communist Party in Bucharest. Nevertheless, the Hungarians are extremely discontented and considerable numbers of many have been given entry visas for Hungary where a resistance movement is gathering momentum. Of course there is little dialogue with the Hungarian authorities since the government cannot assume responsibility openly for Romanian citizens, but the development is nevertheless remarkable. In Yugoslavia, meanwhile, there is increased awareness of national identity among Serbs, a reaction to the unrest in Kosovo which has forced many Serbs to leave the area in the face of extreme assertiveness by Albanian Moslems. (38) However, perhaps the greatest tensions have been generated in Bulgaria, where the authorities are anxious to realize the state of 'ethnic homogeneity' first asserted in 1977. Official census enumeration of the minorities (principally Macedonians and Turks) has been highly inconsistent and it is extremely difficult to establish the position accurately. The Turkish minority has been assessed by the state at only 450,000, while some foreign estimates would put the figure as high as 1.5 million: 10 per cent of the total population seems a reasonable compromise. It seems that a powerful assimilation campaign was carried out between 1984 and 1986, involving coercion to change names and abandon certain social and religious practices (like Ramadan). There are reports of violence, involving a number of deaths, and it is evident that the pressure has been applied to ethnic Turks as well as Pomaks (Bulgarian Moslems). Evidently the state does not wish to allow further emigration to Turkey because of the adverse effect this might have on agricultural labour in certain parts of the country. On the other hand, however, it does not want to see the Turkish minority expanding (through relatively high rates of natural increase) to the point where it might press for far-reaching minority rights and become, potentially, a fifth column: hence the claim of 1985 that 'no part of the Bulgarian population belongs to any other nation'. Thus, the ethnic scenario continues to unfold in Eastern Europe, compromising closer relations between the states of the region and dissipating any possibility that the Soviet Union might be faced by pressures from a united East European lobby.

Part Two

ECONOMIC GEOGRAPHY

Chapter Five

ECONOMIC GROWTH AND CENTRAL PLANNING

Existing textbooks on Eastern Europe provide detailed information on the economy with particular reference to the planned development of industry and agriculture, bearing in mind the natural resources (supplemented increasingly by imported raw materials and fuels) and the tenets of socialism. The aim here is to provide some complementary perspectives. Industry, making increased use of improved technology, is examined in the context of regional development; while agriculture, which is the subject of a continuing debate over organization, involves consideration of policies aiming at greater self-sufficiency in food production. The tertiary sector, which has often been accorded a relatively low priority by planners, is dealt with in the companion volume (with particular emphasis on transport and housing), but the final case study in this section covers tourism and recreation, a growth industry which hitherto has not featured prominently in the literature. However, an essential context for these studies is the planning system and the economic reform movement, the critical component of the decision-making environment.

Impressive rates of growth have been registered in Eastern Europe and it is interesting to note the gross national product (GNP) calculations made by Bairoch (Table 5.1). (1) The survey covered the whole of Europe and so it is possible to see that the Eastern Europe (excluding Albania) increased its share of the European total from 12.3 per cent in 1950 to 14.4 in 1970, while the total itself increased by exactly three times. All individual countries increased GNP more rapidly than did Europe as a whole but the margin was small in Czechoslovakia and Hungary. The improvement was

Table 5.1 Gross national product, 1950-70

	1950				1970			
	A	B	C	D	A	B	C	D
Bulgaria	5.2	1.2	0.4	56.5	21.2	1.6	1.5	79.9
Czechoslovakia	9.7	2.3	0.8	104.8	31.0	2.4	2.2	118.3
GDR	10.5	2.4	0.6	76.2	36.1	2.8	2.1	115.7
Hungary	5.2	1.2	0.6	74.8	16.3	1.3	1.6	86.2
Poland	13.8	2.4	0.6	74.2	47.3	2.8	1.5	79.5
Romania	5.2	1.2	0.3	42.6	21.2	1.6	1.0	57.4
Yugoslavia	5.7	1.3	0.3	45.5	20.7	1.6	1.0	55.7

Source: P. Bairoch 1976 (see note 1).

Notes: A – Total GNP (thousand million US dollars);
  B – A as a percentage of the total GNP of Europe;
  C – GNP per capita (thousand US dollars);
  D – C as a percentage of the European average.

noticeably better in the three Balkan countries (3.9 times) than in the four northern countries (3.3 times). The improvements also apply on a per capita basis: in Europe as a whole the increase has been 2.4 times while Eastern Europe has advanced by amounts ranging from 2.6 times (Poland) to 4.5 times (Czechoslovakia). The three Balkan countries performed better than Hungary and Poland but less well than Czechoslovakia and the GDR. These economic successes deserve considerable recognition, for they have been achieved through sustained effort to maximize investment and harness new technology to the exploitation of natural resources.

CENTRAL PLANNING

It is not clear, however, how far the communist system would be regarded as a precondition for such rapid progress. State ownership of the means of production, brought about by sweeping nationalization, leads naturally to central planning and the co-ordinated investment of capital through medium-term plans (usually five years). However, the potential efficiency of this complex arrangement may not necessarily be realized while the tight controls over price levels and foreign trade protect industries from the discipline of market forces. (2) In the early years the planning operation was relatively crude. (3) Until Stalin's death medium-term plans were bundles of directives drawn up largely on the strength of Soviet orders conveyed through meetings of Party leaders. Plans for the early 1950s were then altered to increase production of consumer goods under the new course adopted in 1953, while several subsequent plans were upset by political upheavals in Hungary and Poland and by the first moves towards economic reform in the 1960s. Comecon co-ordination, discussed more fully in the companion volume, has only slowly brought the plans of member states into phase (Figure 5.1). However, some member states, especially Romania, have misgivings about collaboration, and in any case efficiency has been compromised by a heavy concentration in the 1960s and 1970s on long-maturing industrial projects, with investment tied up over lengthy gestation periods in advance of production. Inevitably it has taken time to build up expertise in planning but it is equally inevitable that central planning should result in economic efficiency criteria being

Figure 5.1 Medium-term planning in Eastern Europe

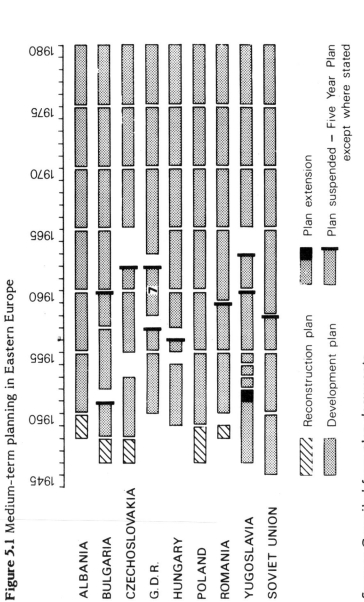

Source: Compiled from plan documents.

compromised by political considerations and there are still reported cases of crude decision-making based on the instincts of Party leaders. Albania and Yugoslavia are not altogether removed from the environment of political constraint within which the economic planners of the permanent Comecon member states are obliged to operate. Albania's record is particularly bizarre; for the first medium-term plan was substantially modified in 1953 to eliminate impressions of excessive imitation of projects favoured by Stalin, while the second and third plans were changed at mid term because the Soviet Union respectively increased and withdrew development assistance. The fourth plan, drafted with belated inspiration from China's 'Great Leap Forward', overtaken by the Cultural Revolution, was then adjusted during its course to cope with the eclipse of both concepts.

Self-management in Yugoslavia

In the case of Yugoslavia the 1948 rift with Stalin rapidly propelled the country towards a model of market socialism with autonomy and democracy for each enterprise assured through the principle of self-management by elected workers' councils. The state has set various limits, especially during the inflationary decade of the 1970s, through price controls and social contracts which moderated the trend to prefer wage increases to the ploughing-back of profits, but decentralization has never lost its momentum. A significant amount of private enterprise is also tolerated and the conspicuous affluence of a small minority of successful operators has created public disquiet regarding the ethics of excessive enrichment in a socialist society. However, while prosecuting those who have traded illegally or evaded taxation, the state has nevertheless defended the legitimacy of private property earned through honest labour. An outstanding success for the Yugoslav approach is demonstrated by the Slovenian Gorenje company, producing household appliances. The enterprise has set up a production and sales network across the country, growing from a small workshop with a dozen engineers and technicians (opened at Velenje in 1953) into a national leader with a dozen factories which can respond effectively to market opportunities. Co-operation with electronics companies in Austria and the FRG has brought in western technology and some guaranteed export outlets. In 1978 Gorenje acquired the Koerting Radio Werke of Grassau in the FRG to provide a base for expansion into West European markets. The company also operates in Greece (with a factory in Thessaloniki for household appliances, radios, and television sets) and now has a world-wide network of interests. This is a remarkable success for private enterprise in Slovenia but it is by no means an isolated example. (4)

However, the formula has not spared the country from a sharply deteriorating economic situation, with rising prices, falling production, and an increasing burden of indebtedness to foreign creditors. Indeed, the Yugoslav system may be contributing to the crisis: for decentralization has not weakened the authority of the Party and so could be considered as a rather superficial ideological improvization to challenge Soviet political and ideological supremacy and make some accommodation for the critics of central planning in the immediate aftermath of Yugoslavia's expulsion from the Cominform. Despite the large managerial prerogatives of factory workers, the Party's unwillingness to allow trade unions to become truly independent organizations prevents effective worker participation in decision-making. Such is the problem in harmonizing economics and politics. If self-management is the hallmark of socialist society (in Yugoslavia at any rate), then the notion of autonomy and independence should extend from the enterprise to each individual in society. However, self-management in politics is not well developed and idealists would argue that, despite the abandonment of some of the Party's initial pretensions in 1960, the government has been too anxious to 'extinguish fires' rather than play a truly leading role in society. However, enterprise in the economy is strongest in the north, in Croatia and Slovenia, where there are close contacts with Austria and the FRG, and the removal of further governmental controls would appear tantamount to the reintroduction of capitalism (at least to those Yugoslavs from the conservatively minded and economically backward southern republics). The authorities in Belgrade therefore have to be pragmatic, trying to avoid destruction of the state by maintaining the command structure of the Party hierarchy throughout national life, even though it must obviously conflict with the self-management principle and prevent local enterprises from exercising their full strength outside the sphere of Party activity. (5)

THE REFORM MOVEMENT

Yugoslavia has set the pace in economic reform in Eastern Europe, for change elsewhere has been slow and tentative. Workers' councils were formed spontaneously in Poland in 1956-7 but, though legalized, their powers were curtailed in 1958 and 'associations' now serve only as administrative links between enterprise and ministry. The 1960s saw a series of initiatives in various parts of Eastern Europe after discussions, beginning in the Soviet media in 1962, made for some flexibility. Autarky and arbitrary pricing could be moderated by greater emphasis on international trade and price-fixing which paid more attention to world values. Centrally determined plan targets might be reduced and limited autonomy granted to enterprises which, reorganized into a pattern of large companies, could be left to allocate investments and production requirements at individual factories. A common trend was the grouping of enterprises into large organizations, thereby reducing quite drastically the number of enterprises which had to enter into the calculations of the various ministries. Czechoslovakia set up 'industrial associations' (VJH) while the GDR came up with its 'associations of nationalized enterprises' (VVB) and the basic production unit in Romania became the 'central' (centrala). (6) Basic production units thus became very large, capable of achieving economies of scale and of linking research and development with production. In Hungary the number of state industrial enterprises fell from 1,368 in 1960 to 812 in 1970 and 702 in 1980. In the process, levels of employment per enterprise increased, respectively, from 839 to 1,836 and 2,035, while fixed capital increased from 105 million forints to 369 and 852. The same trend is evident for industrial co-operatives, which declined in number from 1,251 to 821 and 670, but increased in average size from 128 to 290 and 344 as regards employment, and from 0.7 million forints to 5.0 and 21.0 for fixed capital. Horizontal integration is the rule although there is an element of vertical integration in the GDR where a mechanical engineering combine may control its own foundries or a shoe-making enterprise may produce its own leather. However, while the reforms have been blessed with an impressive nomenclature like the GDR's new economic system of 1963, it is evident that the control of the ministries remains very tight. Enterprise autonomy is closely circumscribed and workers' associations and

Table 5.2 Annual average growth rates, 1961-9 to 1981-3

Country	Net material product/national income							Gross industrial production						
	1961-9	1971-5		1976-80		1981-3		1961-9	1971-5		1976-80		1981-3	
	A	A	B	A	B	A	B	A	A	B	A	B	A	B
Bulgaria	10.7	7.9	8.3	6.2	7.8	4.1	5.0	11.5	8.9	9.2	6.0	9.1	4.5	6.8
Czechoslovakia	5.4	5.6	5.1	3.7	4.9	0.8	2.8	5.7	6.7	6.2	4.6	5.8	2.0	3.5
GDR	5.0	5.5	4.9	4.2	5.1	3.9	5.2	6.1	6.3	6.0	4.9	6.1	3.8	5.2
Hungary	6.2	6.3	5.8	3.2	5.1	1.8	2.9	6.9	6.5	5.9	3.4	6.0	2.0	3.8
Poland	7.9	9.8	8.0	1.7	7.1	4.2	n.a.	8.4	10.6	8.5	4.5	8.3	2.4	n.a.
Romania	12.1	11.3	10.8	7.2	10.5	2.9	7.1	12.9	13.2	11.5	9.5	10.7	2.9	7.6

Source: Statistical yearbooks.

Notes: A – Actual growth;
B – Planned growth (the middle value is taken where official figures quote a range);
n.a. – not available.

committees have little effective power even though they may be forums for genuine discussion. It has been stated that the 'unions' which were established in the GDR achieved some decentralization of offices from East Berlin to various towns and cities in the provinces selected as the administrative centres (usually the chief town in the region where the manufacturing carried out by the horizontally organized corporation was most strongly represented), but this resulted in minimal devolution of authority to the grass-roots.

The need for reform is becoming more urgent because growth rates are falling (Table 5.2) and it is generally agreed that the phase of extensive growth has come to an end. (7) In future, development will involve modernization and extension of existing factories rather than a proliferation of labour-intensive projects at new locations. There is also the record of increasing prosperity in advanced capitalist countries which the socialist countries were quite unable to match, given flagging growth rates and modest gains in labour productivity. Eastern Europe had to face the challenge of higher energy and raw material prices during the 1970s, with a more serious crisis at the end of the decade as foreign credit, the last source of extensive economic growth, began to dry up. These developments definitely marked the end of an era and imposed the imperative of careful management to avoid the wasteful use of labour and resources. However, abandonment of central planning and state ownership of the means of production is out of the question on account of the vested interests in the status quo and the Soviet-inspired imperative of government powers of 'command' over the economy. More emphasis could be placed on stimulation through incentives rather than ideologically motivated propaganda and decision-making could be approached on a more rigorous scientific basis with the employment of modern data-processing systems to ensure an adequate supply of information, implying that a professional approach was needed and that crude decision-making by politically reliable functionaries was no longer acceptable. The orthodox argument, still advanced in the GDR, is that collective ownership of the means of production is unthinkable without centralized economic management. On the other hand, in Hungary and also to some extent in Bulgaria, there is readiness to differentiate between the owner (the state) and the managers who may be work teams or local communities. (8)

Hungary's new economic mechanism

Greatest progress has been made in Hungary. (9) The reform movement grew out of the 1956 revolution for Janos Kadar, who was put in charge by Soviet tanks, steered a delicate middle course, saving the revolution without a return to the regime of the Stalinist Matyas Rakosi (1945 to 1953). The economic reform committees of 1957 led on the New Economic Mechanism (NEM) as a repressive phase in the late 1950s (when Kadar's opponents threatened a coup in sympathy with a more authoritarian approach in Moscow under Malenkov and Molotov) gave way in the early 1960s to an end to internment and internal exile. Kadar was able to strike a careful balance. The control maintained by the Party is not so stifling as to inhibit genuine discussion (through restrained censorship) and foreign travel. There is respect for human rights even though there is no effective machinery which citizens can use to call the authorities to account; and, in the economy, central planning and state ownership of all key industries is combined with sensitivity to market trends and acceptance of private enterprise, especially in the tertiary sector. In 1968 the NEM started to use the market to determine more efficiently the dis-aggregated details of resource allocation. In addition a further round of reform in 1980 reasserted the market mechanism and need for close links between domestic and world market prices.

The Hungarian NEM is remarkable for its comprehensive nature, involving all the themes explored by the theorists, and for the genuine interest in decentral-ization. Factory managers set their targets with regard to both short- and long-term profit motives; a premium is placed on skilled workers and professional managers; international trade is encouraged by simplified procedures and more realistic pricing; and the drive for incentives is underpinned by efforts to increase food supply by encouraging co-operation between socialist agricultural units and individual gardeners and smallholders, thus ensuring that higher real wages are translated into higher living standards. Removal of restrictions on second-home ownership and on private enterprise in the building trade and other tertiary activities also contributed to this objective. Of course there are difficulties. Quite apart from basic ideological objections to economic reform there have been problems arising out of the vested interests of different groups involved. Managers and workers may feel less secure in their jobs while ministers and party activists have lost some of their authority to professionals who try to respond to market trends. However, even genuine pragmatism requires compromises. Sensitivity over inflation and unemployment has instilled a fear of full-blown market pressure. Brakes are therefore built into the system with some stabilization of prices (to control inflation) which means that pricing cannot exactly reflect world market conditions. Again, control on wage growth has made it difficult for higher salaries to be paid to skilled technical and managerial staff without the need to alter the balance between skilled and unskilled workers. Also, from the worker's point of view disappointment over wages forces them further into the second economy which must have negative implications for the enterprise. (10)

Despite these difficulties the Hungarian reform movement is gaining momentum for it is almost universally accepted that the old highly centralized system cannot cope with the needs of Hungary today. There have been radical changes in the Party hierarchy with the removal of those (like the former Party leader Janos Kadar) who cannot come to terms with a genuine market economy. The scope for private enterprise is increasing with the removal of restrictions and provisions of finance through state loans. Successful private businesses, in computer software for example, are emerging and people have the incentive to make profits through wider investment opportunities: dealings on the small Budapest stock market, currently confined to institutions, will be opened to the individual and a unit trust scheme is being considered. The service sector is being exposed to more foreign competition through joint ventures. Marks & Spencer operate in the border town of Sopron and McDonalds are developing a chain of fast-food shops in Budapest in co-operation with the Hungarian state farm of Babolna. More Hungarians currently living abroad are now interested in returning home and more foreigners (particularly Austrians and Scandinavians) are keen to acquire the small holiday and retirement homes which can now be secured in Hungary.

Reform in other countries

Reforms in other Comecon states have achieved some

modernization through a reorganization of enterprises and more efficient information-gathering but they have left the command structure intact. The GDR has slowly come to accept the need for increases in some consumer prices while maintaining stability for basic necessities, but in both Czechoslovakia and Poland, limited changes have arisen through conservative reaction to more ambitious reform plans. (11) Czechoslovak planners repudiated the market-oriented reformism of the 'Prague Spring' of 1968 and so undermined the capacity of enterprises to cope with the challenges of the late 1970s. An extensive investment policy was pursued for too long, with the additional difficulty of a proliferation of separate projects which meant a disproportionate amount of capital tied up in uncompleted developments. Greater selectivity in the context of higher raw material prices and more competitive export marketing is now becoming evident. Provisions for self-finance enable enterprises to modify their production quickly, in line with their progress in world market penetration. They also facilitate foreign travel which is so important in assimilating new technology. Successful businesses like the Crystalex glassworks at Novy Bor in North Bohemia maintain their own foreign currency account, retaining almost one-sixth of the proceeds of foreign trade for raw materials and development costs.

There is also a clear hint of dilemma in Poland. Before the crisis of 1981 interesting moves were being contemplated and even now it is suggested that radical changes may eventually be carried out under conducive economic and political circumstances. (12) For the present, however, caution and orthodoxy are much in evidence, although such a reaction may be counter-productive. Drastic reductions in the import of western machinery may reduce the efficiency of industry, limiting the scope for the export of manufactures while increasing problems of compatibility. Further, a sharp cut-back in cereal imports may result in long-term damage to agriculture by forcing increased grain deliveries from farmers whose enterprises are geared to the use of grain for livestock feed. Polish farmers are involved principally in meat production and they have resisted demands from the government to put more of their grain on the market. However, reforms are now moving forward despite resistance in the Party and considerable scepticism about the leadership's intentions in the leading economic enterprises (which suffer sporadic outbreaks of labour unrest) and in the country at large where the Catholic Church is a focus for disaffection. However, the country is better supplied than it was at the time of the Solidarity crisis and the atmosphere is less oppressive. It is now established that the economy comprises state, co-operative, and private sectors, with economic performance the sole criterion of evaluation: in setting the ground rules for the economy, the state may discriminate according to the nature of production but not according to the character of ownership. The private sector has grown between 1980 and 1986, especially in non-agricultural activities. Employment in the private sector increased from 28.0 per cent in 1980 (including 3.5 per cent employed outside agriculture) to 30.5 in 1986 (5.8) and the share of national income generated rose from 15.7 to 19.8 per cent. With only 3.2 per cent of industrial output in 1986 and 2.5 per cent of retail trade turnover, the private sector is still very weak, but the trend is clearly upwards (2.0 and 1.7 per cent respectively in 1980).

There are again contrasts in the Balkans where, generally speaking, the problems are less severe than those in the northern countries. Bulgaria has followed an orthodox route within Comecon. In a country without a strong industrial tradition (with the attendant dangers of inherited antagonisms between advanced and backward regions), good dividends have come from the reliance placed on Soviet assistance through technological inputs, fuel and raw material deliveries, and orders for Bulgarian agricultural and industrial products. The Bulgarian economy has performed relatively well over the past decade and has maintained a hard currency surplus in trading. The system remains highly centralized but does encourage some competition between enterprises and flexibility in price-fixing and priority has been given to improving the export performance of engineering products. (13) Romania, on the other hand, has a recent history as perhaps the most highly industrialized Balkan state. Close western trading links have been restored during the last two decades but this exposure to the world economy has been traumatic: the Party retains firm control of the economy, yet 'greater efficiency requires more flexibility, which in turn implies a greater freedom of initiative at the lower economic levels than the Party has been prepared to grant so far'. (14) Local authorities have greater powers to collect taxes and devise their own economic plans, a reform which has led to the

161

Table 5.3 Romania's economic performance, 1951-85

Criterion	1951-85 B	1966-70 B	Average annual growth (per cent) 1971-5 A	1971-5 B	1976-80 A	1976-80 B	1981-5 A	1981-5 B	1986-90 A
Investment	10.5	10.9	12.1	11.5	12.8	8.5	5.8	-0.1	3.6
National income	8.6	7.7	12.5	11.3	11.0	7.2	7.0	4.4	10.2
Industrial production	11.1	11.9	12.1	12.9	11.5	9.5	8.5	4.0	7.9
Agricultural production	4.1	1.9	7.0	6.5	8.0	4.2	4.8	3.5	6.4
Social product	8.4	8.7	9.6	10.5	8.5	7.0	6.3	3.3	6.7
Foreign trade	11.0	11.8	11.0	18.4	15.9	16.3	9.0	-0.5	8.8
Manpower	0.7	0.6	1.8	0.6	3.5	0.4	2.2	0.5	0.7

Source: Statistical yearbooks and planning reports.

Notes: A - Plan target; B - Actual performance.

growth of small industries (in places where the officials have good contacts and management skills) and greater self-sufficiency in foodstuffs. For the larger enterprises, however, the workers councils formed in 1971 were seen by many as symbolic gatherings and although self-management (autoconducerea) was given greater emphasis from 1977 there are clear guidelines to limit its scope.

Dissatisfaction in Romania over wages and working conditions has hardly been relieved by the new self-financing mechanism which provides for compulsory contributions from employees to boost capital investment with the prospect of very limited rewards in proportion to output above planned target levels. (15) Table 5.3 indicates how an impressive economic performance in the early 1970s has given way to serious difficulty in the early 1980s. Failure to meet plan targets has been particularly evident in the energy sector since 1978 and there continue to be serious shortfalls on coal and oil production and in the generation of electricity (Table 5.4). This inevitably affects performance in manufacturing with persistent failures in steel, fertilizers, cement, and other basic commodities. Essentially, therefore, the command structure is retained in Romania while across Eastern Europe as a whole the transition from an extensive to an efficient economy has been marked by tinkering. Bold initiatives are needed but they can only come from the Soviet Union or gain momentum from Soviet encouragement. However, any Soviet leader is reluctant to abandon continuity and the Gorbachev regime is no exception. (16)

THE WORKER DIMENSION

For many years the authorities have been able to depend on a largely co-operative work-force. There has been a large-scale recruitment of young peasants for whom the move to urban employment has been seen as upward social mobility. Thus, 'the inundation of working-class ranks by these poorly educated and organizationally inexperienced urban migrants helps to account for the success of the communist regimes in maintaining working-class conformism despite dis-orienting change and often severe material deprivations'. (17) Workers often enjoy relatively good access to medical services and recreation facilities. Thus, the employees at the Ziar nad Hronom aluminium works have the benefit of a

Table 5.4 Romania: Planned and actual production for leading commodities

Commodity	1978 A	1978 B	1979 A	1979 B	1980 A	1980 B	1981 A	1981 B	1982 A	1982 B	1983 A	1983 B	1984 A	1984 B	1985 A	1985 B
Electricity	64.5	64.2	70.2	64.9	72.0	67.5	72.7	70.0	74.1	68.9	76.8	70.3	77.0	71.6	76.7	71.8
Coal	36.4	29.3	45.2	32.8	54.1	37.8	50.8	37.0	44.0	41.4	52.2	44.5	61.7	47.8	64.3	46.6
Crude oil	15.1	13.7	14.8	12.3	15.0	11.5	12.6	11.6	12.5	11.7	13.5	11.6	13.0	11.5	12.6	10.7
Methane gas	26.8	29.0	27.1	27.2	27.1	28.2	29.6	29.3	33.0	28.6	33.0	27.6	33.5	28.1	32.8	27.2
Steel	12.1	11.8	13.7	12.9	15.6	13.2	14.7	13.0	14.2	13.1	15.2	12.6	14.3	14.4	16.0	13.8
Cement	16.2	14.7	17.6	15.6	18.3	15.6	15.9	14.7	15.8	15.0	15.8	14.0	16.2	14.0	16.5	12.2
Fertilizers	3.1	2.5	3.5	2.5	3.8	2.5	3.6	2.6	3.5	2.7	3.6	2.1	3.6	3.1	3.9	3.1
Sugar	0.8	0.6	0.9	0.5	0.8	0.5	0.7	0.6	0.8	0.6	0.9	0.6	0.9	0.8	0.9	0.6
Syn. fibres	n.a.	197	222	196	254	206	253	205	266	222	327	235	346	281	372	257
Syn. rubber	n.a.	147	219	149	250	150	167	146	207	137	185	147	210	159	211	156

Source: Statistical yearbooks and planning reports.

Notes: A – Plan target; B – Actual production; All figures in million tons except electricity (million Kwh), methane gas (billion cubic metres), synthetic fibres and synthetic rubber (both in thousand tons).

sanatorium at Sklene Teplice (13 kilometres from the factory), which can be used for evening treatment, and recreational facilities in the Donovaly district are available for skiing, swimming, and walking according to seasonal conditions. People have benefited from good training facilities. Thus, the Vodni stavni construction and engineering enterprise in Prague maintains a training centre (450 places) of secondary school status which generates workers with a range of skills for its Vltava complex.

Encouragement of young people has been a striking feature of socialist planning. Although there has been an element of exploitation through the emphasis on volunteer or conscript labour for harvest and construction work, there has also been ample provision of industrial training programmes with scope for rapid promotion. Some examples may be drawn from Bulgaria where young people have been prominent in construction projects like the extension of the oil refinery and petrochemical complex at Burgas and the Debelt metallurgical scheme in the same area. Young people have also contributed to certain power projects like the Kozlodoui atomic power station, the Belmeken-Sestrimo hydro scheme, and the Maritsa-Iztok thermal complex at Dimitrovgrad. The Bulgarian government also provides incentives for young people to settle in the heavily depopulated Strandja-Sakar area of south-east Bulgaria and the new residents are now helping with the modernization of this so-called 'Republic of Youth'. Dedicated agricultural work by young people in Bulgaria has become a matter of honour. Every winter young front-rankers from the country's agriculture assembly at the Zlatni Pyassatsi resort for a 'Rally of Fertility' where awards are made for outstanding performances and experiences can be shared. Various technological achievements have been made in Bulgarian industry by young people: repairing dams with a special caisson allowed for work to proceed at the Georgi Traikov reservoir near Devnya without the need to empty it, while substantial economies were also made through a new control system for the electric arc furnaces at the Kremikovtsi iron and steel works.

There are indications that workers are becoming more assertive because protest can no longer be blunted by upward social mobility, given the switch from extensive to intensive development, or by better living standards, in view of the economic problems of the 1980s. (18) With greater emphasis on skills the less-educated people become vulnerable, as the promise of full employment becomes less reliable. Unemployment is now a serious problem in Yugoslavia. In 1984 the official rate was 13.5 per cent, with slightly higher rates in Vojvodina (13.7) and Serbia (14.6) and substantially poorer performances in Bosnia-Hercegovina (18.8), Montenegro (19.1), Macedonia (21.1), and Kosovo (33.3). The best ratings were registered by Croatia (7.2) and Slovenia (1.9). Overall the numbers of unemployed have increased by 28 per cent from 0.76 million in 1979 and 0.97 in 1984. Elsewhere, unemployment is not so highly publicized but it is clearly implied by statistics dealing with transfers of employment with gaps of various periods (often more than six months) between one job and another. Also, state propaganda against the evils of parasitism indicates the considerable scale of unemployment among young people. Moreover, underemployment is frequently encount- ered in the factories and, taking the year as a whole, in agriculture. Strike action thus becomes more likely, certainly in countries with a history of successful civil protest and a government which is reluctant to countenance immediate suppression of strikes at any cost. Another possible trend is the transfer of interest from factory work to the service industries, especially if there are possibilities for self-employment as artisans in the latter case. An interesting study of changing attitudes relates to the shoe factory at Novy Targ near Krakow in Poland. When the factory opened in the 1950s, it was considered highly beneficial for the population of a densely settled region of hill and mountain country. However, when confronted with the technological regime of conveyor belt production, resistance became strong and the factory suffered from a very high labour turnover. This has become more marked with the growth of opportunity in the tourist industry which offers employment more congenial to the individualistic outlook of the local peasantry and the situation has also been complicated by the actions of management on the occasions of 1976 strike and the 1979 papal visit. (19)

Variations in policy are well exemplified by the tertiary sector where private artisans are now widely tolerated in contrast with co-operative organizations. (20) Figures for 1978 put their numbers at only 27,500 in Bulgaria, 9,900 in Czechoslovakia, and 39,900 in Romania (less than 0.1 per cent of the total work-force in all cases), but numbers are much larger in the GDR (247,900 and 3.0 per cent of the work-force), Hungary (106,200 and 2.0), and Poland (232,500 and 1.3), and in all three cases the employment of non-family labour is permitted up to a maximum of ten, three, and fifty respectively. Bulgarian artisans can, however, employ disabled relatives and Romanians may train apprentices. It seems that after presiding over a reduction in the numbers of private artisans and craftsmen from 0.86 million in 1950 to 0.43 in 1960 and 0.35 in 1970, the GDR leadership reversed its policy in 1976 due to increasing difficulties over the provision of services at a time when the purchase of consumer durables was reaching record levels. Many new enterprises were set up (nearly 300 in East Berlin alone within a year of the new regulations coming into force) and more apprentices are being trained although the average age of the artistans is high and government encouragement seems too guarded to ensure that all the population's requirements for services will be met. In Hungary there are lower limits on the employment of non-family labour than in the GDR and Poland, but the maximum of three non-family employees or cottage workers is additional to the right to employ up to six family members, so quite significant enterprises can emerge. Moreover, there are stimulative income tax and social insurance schemes so that by 1981 there were 100,000 artisans each employing on average 1.5 workers. They are especially prominent in the villages dealing with hairdressing, tailoring, and shoe repairs, but there is also some building and transport work. (21) Some artisans operate illegally and charge relatively low prices but they cannot be held responsible for poor work. Loans for workshop modernization would be helpful in increasing the effectiveness of the private sector.

The 'second economy'

Private tradesmen are just one feature of what is known in Hungary as maszek, the 'second economy' which is developing alongside the 'first' centrally controlled state and co-operative sector. It involves not so much the legalized private enterprise prominent in agriculture and the service sector as a substantial amount of part-time work by people who combine 'full-time' work in the first economy (with its various welfare benefits) with secondary employment (in effect moonlighting) which attracts additional untaxed income. The strong prejudice against private enterprise restricted the secondary economy during the 1950s but a

more pragmatic approach has been taken in the reform era.
(22) The second economy provides services which are badly
needed but which the central planning system is unable to
provide. The production from small gardens and plots
provides more than half the total output of potatoes and
vegetables, fruit, grapes, and pigs in Hungary; and the
contribution of the second economy to house building and
repair is equally significant. However, the second economy
creates problems for the state. At the ideological level
there is the embarrassing reality of the state's inability to
control an entire economy in the sense that an independent
private sector undermines the government's legitimation as
a 'socialist' regime. It threatens the integrity of the
communist elite by obliging its members to pay lip-service
to the fundamentals of central planning and state control of
the means of production while tolerating (and sometimes
corruptly profiting from) the wealth which successful
operators in the second economy can create. Further,
economically it is disturbing that workers who retain their
employment in the first economy because of the security
and welfare benefits it provides nevertheless reserve their
best efforts for the second economy where success may
depend in part in pilfering and other irregularities at their
main place of work (as private commercial transactions may
be made in the state's time involving the use of state-owned
materials or space in state-owned vehicles). Unfortunately
the compromises involved in economic reform create the
need for a second economy and the more it succeeds in
meeting the demand for goods and services triggered by
rising urban wage levels, the more it expands at the expense
of the first economy which in turn bears the brunt of its
corrupting effect.

The second economy has therefore become a vital
necessity in Eastern Europe. Although not part of any state
plan it nevertheless offers some stability for the state,
providing services which are in demand and guiding social
discontent into consumer competition which is less
dangerous than direct political activity: small dissident
groups may be harrassed while affluence and even
corruption is tolerated. Thus new houses in rural Hungary
seem to 'show off' as a result of superfluous decoration as
accessories like iron railings become objects of keen
competition. More generally there are the various informal
channels which corrupt part of the system while enabling it
to go on 'muddling through'. Informal networks can be a

valuable means of communication for politicians when the official media is not trusted. Local politicians who normally receive no official media coverage can project themselves effectively through informal channels and establish the desired reputations by rumour. People will continue to maintain close personal relations rather than throw their entire allegiance into the hands of the formal apparatus of Party and government. Indeed, in Romania it is frequently noted that the letters PCR indicate not only the Party (Partidul Comunist Roman) but also the informal equivalent of 'pile, cunostiinta si relatii' (fixers, acquaintances, and contacts). At the same time the political élites will depend on the second economy to help them achieve their economic objectives and thereby retain some popular support, while seeking to neutralize its most corruptive effects. Such is the society which has developed spontaneously to survive in the ideological era of central planning.

THE ENVIRONMENTAL DIMENSION

It is worth remembering that economic efficiency is constrained by various environmental difficulties which are not always appreciated outside Eastern Europe. There are certain hazards which are constantly evident. Mountainous country implies relatively costly infrastructure but the acute instability of slopes in plateau lands, developed on clays, sands, and shales, has resulted in serious erosion once the forest cover was stripped away. Land is lost to agriculture by gullying and roads are frequently blocked by landslides. In several cases, schemes to extend railway communication across the Carpathians have been abandoned because of difficult terrain. Meanwhile, in the lowlands, loess deposits give rise to erosion hazards than can threaten settlements situated in river banks. Thus, along the Hungarian section of the Danube, with the river contained by a loess bluff which extends for some 180 kilometres south of Budapest, landslides and other mass movements occur periodically. A notable landslide occurred at Dunafoldvar and this has attracted considerable research into the lithological and strength properties of the loess beds. Trouble has also occurred at Dunaujvaros where a slide along a 3-kilometre section of the river bank threatened some of the water supply installations. It seems that substantial bank protection work will be needed: grading,

Figure 5.2 The site of the Romanian village of Patirlagele

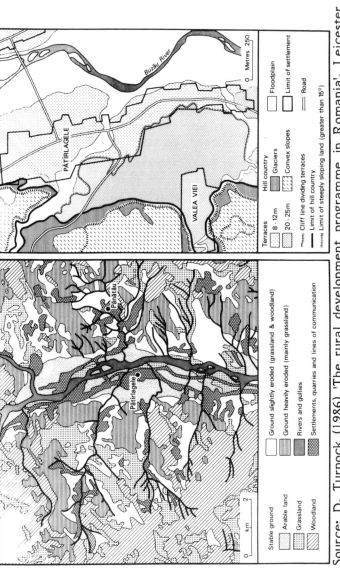

A. LAND CLASSIFICATION

B. SITE OF PĂTÎRLAGELE

PĂTÎRLAGELE

VALEA VIEI

Buzău River

0 — Metres — 250

Stable ground

Arable land

Grassland

Woodland

0 — km — 2

Ground slightly eroded (grassland & woodland)

Ground heavily eroded (mainly grassland)

Rivers and gullies

Settlements, quarries and lines of communication

Terraces

8 - 12m

20 - 25m

Hill country

Glaciers

Convex slopes

Cliff line dividing terraces

Limit of hill country

Limit of steeply sloping land (greater than 15°)

Floodplain

Limit of settlement

Road

Source: D. Turnock (1986) 'The rural development programme in Romania', Leicester University, Geography Department Occasional Paper 13.

reinforcing, and planting the bluffs and draining water from sandy acquifers within them. Work was carried out extensively during the 1970s, with encouraging results to date. (23)

With regard to climate the dangers for agriculture arising out of summer drought are well known, although they are becoming less serious as a result of irrigation in the Balkans. Less well appreciated are the problems of severe winter weather. A cold winter with a light snow cover can mean serious damage for the winter wheat crop, especially if a dry spring follows. The economy is also disrupted through the difficulty in maintaining power output. Coal production can be seriously disrupted by severe winter weather. Opencast mines may alternately be inundated with rain or frozen solid. In either case machinery will not function efficiently and with very low temperatures there is the additional problem of coal being frozen into railway wagons. Frozen lignite may have to be thawed out in heating halls before it can be used in power stations. The maintenance of power stations is also difficult when spare parts are not immediately available. Overland transport may be disrupted by deep snow, or by heavy rain on unsurfaced roads, while severe frosts can result in the closure of ports on the Baltic and navigable rivers like the Danube, where coal shipments from Reni to Ruse power station were disrupted in 1984-5, necessitating the costly diversion of coal to Varna for forwarding to Ruse by rail. There are also serious social problems since the old people suffer acutely in especially cold weather. A hard winter can bring back death-rates characteristic of the early post-war years because of severe outbreaks of influenza and similar diseases for which winter stockpiles of drugs may be inadequate.

The case of Romania

Romania suffers acutely from the erosion of valley slopes in the Subcarpathians and plateau land such as the Moldavian tableland. The problem relates to centuries of forest clearance but it has become more serious with the commercial exploitation of the woodlands and the development of a modern transport system involving not only high costs for construction and maintenance but also heavy losses when circulation is interrupted by damage.

Railway building in the Subcarpathians has often proved difficult. The link between Deva and Brad was planned in the 1930s but the central section had to remain incomplete until the project was eventually finished in 1987. In the Buzau valley a railway was driven for 4.4 kilometres through the Teliu tunnel (the longest in Romania) to connect Brasov with Intorsura Buzaului, but because of the difficult terrain the line could not be extended to Nehoiu and Buzau to provide a new route to the ports of Galati and Braila. A line intended for heavy international traffic carries only a sparse branch line service. Similar problems arise where settlements are vulnerable to landslides (and in some cases by mudflows). With threats to factories and distribution systems (electricity, gas, and water) as well as private houses, it is essential that new developments are carefully sited and adequately protected. Thus, land surveys have been carried out in the area around Patirlagele in the Buzau valley (Figure 5.2). The village is destined to graduate to urban status with a much broader economic base and a larger population.

There are also the occasional natural disasters, which can be enormously costly in terms of both life and property. Romania has been very adversely affected by floods and earthquakes, and while both hazards are traditional, the impact of such calamities is all the greater given the concentration of population in cities, the dependence on a modern system of communications, and the well-developed forest economy which has resulted in more rapid run-off from the mountains following heavy rain. There was serious flooding in the south-east of Romania in 1972 during an exceptionally wet autumn and further floods in the Mures basin in 1975, but the risks were most fully exposed by the disastrous floods of 1970, with rainfall well above the average in all parts of the country for the first four months of the year, combined with a record rainfall in May when intense depressions deposited a third of the annual rainfall in northern Transylvania in just two days. (24) With saturated ground and a high drainage density (developed on Miocene/Pliocene formations) water was rapidly transferred along numerous short and steeply graded water courses, producing high discharges in main and tributary streams simultaneously. There was a very rapid onset of flood conditions along the Somes which devastated the towns of Dej and Satu Mare as well as many rural localities in the valley and also in the Tur and Crasna valleys (into which

Somes water was diverted through an old abandoned channel). The Mures was also affected severely: Arad was saved serious damage but towns further upstream were badly hit. Tirgu Mures was the largest town affected, but the biggest proportional damage was suffered by Medias on the Tirnava Mare and Alba Iulia, near the confluence of the Mures and Tirnava. Continued heavy rainfall in southern and eastern districts of the Carpathians brought serious flooding to the Siret, Prut, and above all the Olt (including the towns of Fagaras and Rimnicu Vilcea). Further damage was caused in loessic areas through rising ground-water levels and by landslides in the hill country. Finally in late May and early June the Danube valley was threatened with discharges approaching the 1895 record levels. It is of course an unfortunate result of Romania's position that she is threatened twice over by flooding in the Carpathians since the high water immediately encountered in the mountains is eventually fed to the Danube. Although the river marks the southern frontier of the country, much Romanian territory is vulnerable because of the extensive dyked lands and the low terraces on the northern side. There is ample flood warning, up to a fortnight for the Tulcea section, so that threatened towns can be evacuated; but the heavy investments made in agriculture in recent years increase the risk of serious economic damage. The total area flooded in 1970 was 1.06 million ha (0.56 being arable land) and damage was estimated at $500 million. Such losses make it particularly appropriate to persevere with a programme of environmental protection involving the damming of rivers (providing hydroelectricity and industrial/irrigation water as well as flood relief) and stabilizing hill slopes (Figure 5.3).

Romania has also experienced serious earthquakes during this century (1908 and 1940) and minor tremors (as in 1986) but the greatest such disaster occurred on 4 March 1977 when the south-eastern part of Romania was devastated by a severe earthquake measuring 7.2 on the Richter scale. (25) The tremors were felt most acutely on an axis running south-westwards from the Vrancea mountains through Bucharest to the Danube. It was still winter and so many animals were killed as concrete buildings collapsed, while the loss of silos and hothouses increased the damage to agriculture. However, the greatest damage occurred in multi-storey buildings in the towns where building standards were often inadequate. The small Danube town of Zimnicea was almost completely destroyed while the cities of

Figure 5.3 Aspects of water management in Romania

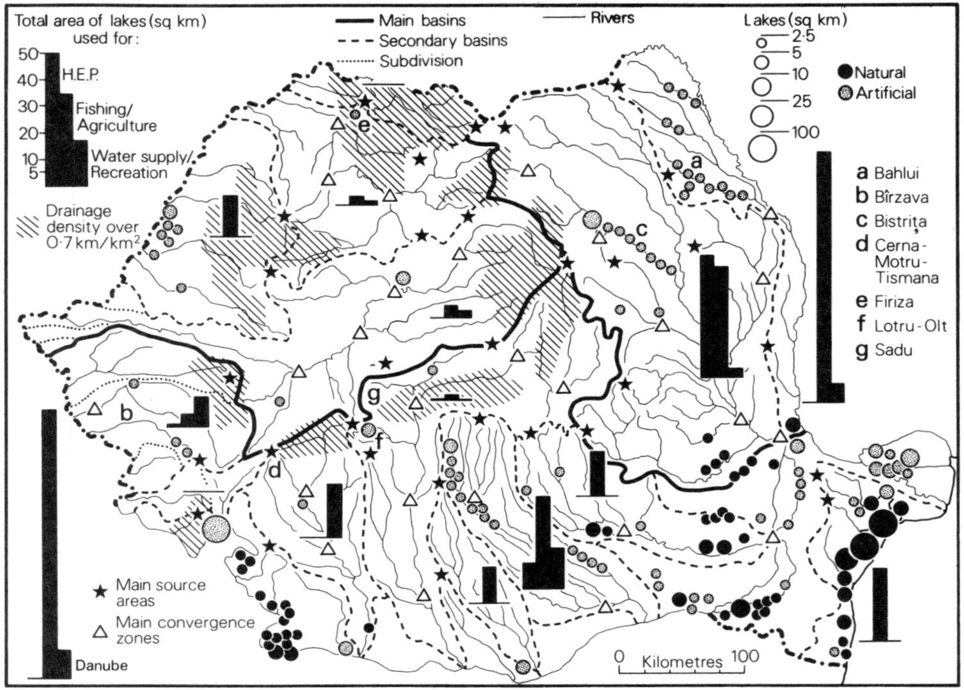

Source: Turnock (1979) (note 24).

Craiova, Pitesti, and Ploiesti incurred heavy losses in residential and industrial buildings. However, the losses were greatest in Bucharest. Several towns in Bulgaria were affected, including the capital, Sofia, but the worst damage occurred on the Danube at Ruse, Silistra and Svishtov. In the latter case the synthetic-fibre factory was severely damaged but the atomic power station of Kozlodoui was allegedly not affected. There was heavy loss of life - officially declared to be 1,575 (and another 124 in Bulgaria) - but the scale of the human tragedy was also brought out by the initial plight of some 35,000 families who were left homeless. There are also longer-term problems of a psychological nature and also in financial terms because there is no comprehensive insurance cover and state grants for repairs and rebuilding have met only a fraction of the actual costs. The earthquake was a major economic disaster for the Romanian state and was one of the events contributing to the onset of the economic crisis at the end of the decade. (26) Major industries were seriously affected: chemical industries in Pitesti, Ploiesti and Turnu Magurele and engineering/metallurgical industries in Bucharest, Craiova, and Tirgoviste. The disruption of trade meant further deterioration in the balance of payments, although damage to hotels was only modest and the tourist industry was not gravely affected. Once again the planning process must allow for the risks with appropriate zoning policies and suitable building regulations in the most vulnerable areas.

Chapter Six

INDUSTRY: PLANNING TECHNOLOGY AND REGIONAL DEVELOPMENT

Eastern Europe was by no means an industrial desert in 1945. Some activities - like printing at Vimperk (Czechoslovakia) mentioned in 1485 - date back to Medieval times. Modernization was pronounced in the Habsburg and Prussian Empires in the late eighteenth century and many new industries of strategic importance were established by the state. Private entrepreneurs were encouraged to start textile industries while the demand for luxury goods gave a fillip to the glass industry with a history dating back to the fourteenth century, and in the case of crystal to the sixteenth. The glass sand at Strelec provided a raw material base for Bohemian products which became world famous as a result of the expertise of glass workers like Kaspar Lehmann (seventeenth century) and Bedrich Egermann (nineteenth). Frantisek Kavalier built a reputation for technical and laboratory glass at his factory at Sazava near Prague, established in 1837. The good quality kaolin of Bohemia was used to build up the manufacture of fine porcelain at Karlovy Vary from 1792, with Duchov and Loket following in the nineteenth century. Industrialization in the Ottoman Empire was restrained, especially in the peripheral Balkan provinces, but there was a notable acceleration in the rate of growth when the nation states began to emerge in the late nineteenth century. Of course foreign capital was important and emphasis rested with the processing of fuels and minerals required by the more developed countries.

During the inter-war years there was further progress with import substitution. Heavy industries were most prominent in Czechoslovakia and Germany but progress was made elsewhere, stimulated by modest consumer demand and by the state's strategic interest in the production of armaments. Romania began to use natural gas as a raw material in the chemical industry (producing synthetic ammonia at Tirnaveni from 1936 and formaldehyde at Copsa Mica in 1941. Meanwhile, Hungary extended her capacities in pharmaceuticals, initiated before the war by the Richter, (1901) and Chinoin (1912) enterprises: Janos Kabay produced morphine from green poppies in 1924 and set up his Tiszavasvari (now Alkaloid) factory three years later while Albert Szent-Gyorgyi isolated vitamin C from paprika in 1928. Meanwhile, great effort went into the improvement of infrastructure and the modernization of agriculture because a prosperous peasantry would create a greater demand for manufactures.

THE SOVIET MODEL

This western model of industrialization was however superseded by the Soviet model, which gave priority to industry and especially to heavy industry (Table 6.1). Consumer demand could not justify this because living standards were kept down by low wages and by various fiscal measures which effectively eliminated all accumulated wealth. The demand came from construction (factories, mines, power stations, railways, and so on) and from rearmament (with particular pressure for higher steel production during the Korean War) related to both domestic and Soviet needs. It is a generally accepted principle that the rates of growth of total output and military power are positively correlated with the proportion of total resources devoted to heavy industry, and if Eastern Europe is to remain independent of outside influences these heavy industrial resources must be produced domestically and not imported. Of course the majority of East European economies were not meant to be independent, given the high level of Soviet penetration, but at a time when transport capacities were limited Stalin was anxious that each satellite state should operate as a self-contained unit (as far as possible) to meet his requirements. The result was pronounced structural change throughout each national economy (with the bias towards industry) and within industry (through the emphasis on heavy industry). Scarce capital was ploughed into heavy industry, with economically irrational

Table 6.1 Average annual growth rates in major industrial branches, 1950-70 (%)

| Country | Energy | Growth rate in branch where overall national industrial growth rate = 1.00 | | | | | | |
		Fuel	Metallurgy	Chemicals	Engineering	Building materials	Light industries	Food processing
Czechoslovakia	1.08	0.78	1.01	1.54	1.43	1.24	0.69	0.59
GDR	0.94	0.63	0.75	1.04	1.29	1.15	na	0.62
Hungary	1.06	0.59	0.90	1.61	1.21	0.93	0.87	0.78
Poland	1.16	0.54	0.88	1.51	1.78	1.00	0.88	0.59
Romania	1.43	0.72	1.10	1.84	1.49	1.20	0.83	0.68

Source: United Nations Economic Commission for Europe.

Table 6.2 Contributions of industry and agriculture to national income and employment, 1965-83

Country	National income 1965 A	B	National income 1975 A	B	National income 1983 A	B	Employment 1965 A	B	Employment 1975 A	B	Employment 1983 A	B
Bulgaria	45.0	1.3	51.0	2.3	58.1	3.4	0.95	0.5	1.44	1.2	2.12	2.2
Czechoslovakia	66.4	5.5	64.4	7.8	62.0	7.3	2.48	1.9	2.86	2.5	2.86	2.8
GDR	62.9	5.0	59.8	5.4	68.5	8.8	3.09	3.1	3.54	3.7	3.81	4.1
Hungary	42.1	1.7	47.0	2.9	45.3	2.5	1.60	1.1	1.82	1.6	1.58	1.4
Poland	51.1	2.5	59.1	3.9	50.0	2.7	3.86	0.7	5.40	1.0	5.24	1.0
Romania	48.9	1.7	56.2	3.4	60.2	3.8	1.86	0.3	3.11	0.8	3.84	1.3
Yugoslavia	42.9	1.5	43.1	2.4	40.9	2.4	1.58	0.4	1.61	0.4	2.95	1.2

Source: Statistical yearbooks.

Notes: A - Percentage contribution of industry to national income/employment in millions;
B - Percentage/employment level related to agriculture, where agriculture = 1.00.

emphasis on high-cost working of low-grade raw materials, while light industries were strictly contained, especially where capital requirements were high: labour-intensive sectors like textiles and clothing fared better. (1)

This highly simplistic approach to industrialization has been substantially modified over the years. Soviet dependence on East European production has declined so there is no longer an interest in direct control of resources and insistence on specific production demands. The interest of the USSR has shifted to the maintenance of cohesion in the bloc without the crude coercive measures previously employed: hence the concensus on the need for efficiency to reduce pressure on the now-scarce fuel resources and to maintain the upward movement in living standards. The priority for heavy industry is maintained but costs are more carefully taken into account and international trade in raw materials and semi-manufactures has become more prominent in both chemical and metallurgical industries. There is even a trend towards joint investment in manufacturing capacities in the Soviet Union in preference to separate ventures (each requiring imported raw materials) in the various East European countries. The belated interest in international specialization has come about for various reasons: better systems of transport and electricity distribution, more stable relations between ruling Communist Parties, more sophisticated central planning procedures and competition from capitalist countries on living standards. However, nationalism is strong throughout Eastern Europe and there is still a tendency to forego economies of scale in the interests of self-sufficiency. Thus, the growth of industry is still rapid but the structural changes within this sector is now moderate. Nevertheless taking the post-war period as a whole changes have been dramatic. (2) Industry accounts for more than half of the net material product in all countries except Hungary (and more than three-quarters of the GDR) while the share of light industry has fallen sharply (from 48 to 27 per cent in Poland between 1950 and 1978, reckoning on textiles, clothing, leather, and food processing) (Table 6.2).

High technology

There has been a substantial increase in output of basic products and a reduced emphasis on the northern countries

as the Balkan states have developed relatively quickly
(Table 6.3). However, Eastern Europe is still handicapped by
early post-war investment decisions involving high-cost
production because of poor machinery, excessive energy
consumption and wasteful use of raw materials. High fuel
costs are now stimulating more energy-efficient production
methods, while the collection and recycling of scrap is a big
business which is both economically and ecologically
desirable. In Czechoslovakia the Sberne Suroviny enterprise
employs some 1,500 people to collect scrap in all parts of
the country. The enterprise maintains nearly 150 workshops
and nearly 1,650 collection points. Wastepaper, scrap iron,
and textile waste could all be put to better use. Even more
significant is the modernization of existing enterprises to
permit more sophisticated production. In engineering there
have been considerable advances in microelectronics with
firms like Tesla (Czechoslovakia) famous throughout the
bloc for a range of products, including a central nervous
system simulator produced at the Valasske Meziricii factory
in Moravia. A programme for the development and
production of robots and electronic devices was launched in
Czechoslovakia in 1976 two years after the first equipment
of this kind had been imported. The effort, co-ordinated by
a research centre for industrial metallurgy in Presov, (a
Czechoslovak-Soviet scientific association) resulted in the
production of nearly 5,000 robots and manipulators by the
end of 1985. The equipment has been installed in various
engineering factories, including the Tatra lorry factory at
Koprivnice, and to a lesser extent in light industry. With
production capacities at Presov and Sabinov, co-operating
with the Soviet machine tool factory at Mukachevo.
Czecholsovakia is now poised to play a prominent role in the
Comecon Interrobot organization set up in 1985. The Balkan
states are also involved in such technological advances.
Bulgaria has entered the field of robotics with a factory at
Stara Zagora and instrument-making is also a promising new
industry. A state economic corporation for instrument-
making was set up in 1965 and subsequent developments
have included a research institute in Sofia (1966) and
factories at Blagoevgrad, Knezha, Mihailovgrad and Petrich
based on Soviet models. Most foreign orders are from the
Soviet Union and other Comecon states.

The accent on innovation can be seen throughout
industry with new machinery (like the pneumatic jet looms
produced for export by Zbrojovka at Vsetin in

Table 6.3 Production of basic commodities, 1953–83

Commodity/group	East European production excluding Albania (A), and percentage of total output from the northern countries (B)									
	1953		1965		1974		1980		1983	
	A	B	A	B	A	B	A	B	A	B
Metals/Energy										
Iron ore	2,130	74.0	4,343	48.5	4,474	22.0	3,257	20.2	3,208	19.2
Aluminium	48.8	94.3	225.4	79.0	606.2	44.9	747.3	40.6	785.2	32.8
Oil refinery capacity	13.5	32.4	37.2	52.5	95.8	54.6	144.0	57.4	144.2	57.8
Copper lead zinc	419	69.3	829	47.6	1,331	49.5	1,621	53.5	1,564	51.8
*Energy production	265	84.8	380	79.3	489	76.1	477	72.5	495	71.1
*Energy consumption	245	85.8	394	79.2	565	73.7	615	69.3	765	74.1
*Electricity cap.	14.6	84.8	39.4	76.7	76.9	66.9	103.4	62.9	118.3	60.7
*Hydro-electric cap.	2.2	41.5	5.8	40.1	11.7	27.0	15.5	28.4	18.5	35.4
*Nuclear elec. cap.			0.07	100.0	1.05	58.1	3.13	71.9	4.66	57.7
*Electricity output	62.9	87.3	185.7	76.9	358.2	68.9	479.0	66.2	511.4	65.1
Chemicals										
Caustic soda	418	89.5	1,130	69.0	1,716	64.6	2,566	60.2	2,655	60.0
Fertilizer	1.96	97.8	4.56	81.4	9.40	73.5	12.83	68.6	13.51	65.7
Hydrochloric acid	104	96.8	168	86.3	296	67.4	459	59.3	498	55.5
Plastics	125	92.7	655	74.8	1,980	69.9	3,853	68.7	4,278	68.2
Sulphuric acid	1,400	91.3	4,660	72.2	9,261	67.1	9,670	60.7	9,584	60.4
Synthetic fibres	193	98.9	335	88.1	507	67.7	689	63.4	762	59.7
Synthetic rubber	64.1	100.0	194.8	84.2	401.9	72.4	521.4	65.4	520.1	66.9
*Tyres	2.1	88.9	8.5	71.9	24.4	61.9	35.3	54.4	33.8	51.6

Food processing										
*Beer	28.3	91.4	52.0	85.8	80.5	75.0	94.9	71.7	96.2	71.1
*Wine	12.7	20.9	16.6	14.6	21.9	24.7	27.0	26.4	30.4	27.9
Butter-cheese	542	76.0	1,146	72.6	1,750	76.6	2,097	76.7	2,169	76.6
*Cigarettes	11,457	67.4	19,754	59.0	28,568	50.6	34,646	48.8	34,670	46.4
Fish	246	71.7	735	76.4	1,391	78.3	1,283	72.1	1,482	70.1
Meat	3,308	75.0	53.1	75.4	8,339	74.0	9,301	67.6	9,082	66.3
Flour	7.4	47.7	11.5	46.6	12.4	48.3	13.0	52.8	12.7	53.7
Sugar	3.48	88.5	4.34	76.0	4.42	72.4	4.67	67.7	5.68	75.0
Other industries										
*Cars	22	100.0	242	84.7	663	70.3	1,101	64.7	908	69.9
Cement	13.0	70.1	34.9	68.0	61.4	63.9	75.8	60.8	70.9	60.2
*Cloth	1,813	73.5	3,432	68.2	4,172	63.9	4,442	60.5	4,225	58.1
Paper	1,283	85.8	3,489	75.3	5,345	68.7	6,458	64.2	6,594	63.7
Radio-television	1,470	94.3	4,875	71.6	6,846	73.0	8,629	74.3	7,318	75.5
*Roundwood	89.2	51.0	86.2	53.2	91.3	55.9	91.9	61.4	104.4	58.6
*Sawn wood	20.9	67.7	22.4	58.6	26.0	59.9	26.4	60.8	26.2	59.2
Steel	12.9	90.3	30.3	80.9	51.7	73.2	62.7	70.7	59.4	71.3
Yarn	508	74.6	900	66.8	1,203	61.4	1,352	59.2	1,279	57.4

Source: United Nations statistical yearbooks.

All output figures are in thousand metric tonnes except where asterisked. Cars and radio/television sets are given in thousands; electricity, hydroelectricity, and nuclear capacities in thousand megawatts; tyres and cigarettes in millions; roundwood and sawn wood in million cubic metres; beer and wine in hectalitres; oil refinery capacity, flour, sugar, cement, and steel in million metric tonnes; cloth in million square metres; energy production/consumption in million metric tonnes coal equivalent.

For further analysis of the commodities and groups see D. Turnock (1989) The Human Geography of Eastern Europe, London: Routledge (Table 1.1).

Czechoslovakia) and new products, sometimes incorporating western components, like the cranes from the CKD factory at Slany in Czecholovakia which use Austrian Steyer undercarriages. Individual enterprises have become larger but they have also specialized. Thus, Skoda in Czechoslovakia operate nineteen factories with 42,000 employees but their once extensive product range has been drastically curtailed through various specialization agreements reached between 1958 and 1965: pumps, steel structures, and certain types of machinery and transport equipment (including lorries and ships) are no longer made. On the other hand the company has become stronger in the production of plant for the rubber and textile industries, for automatic control devices, and most notably, nuclear power station equipment, in connection with which the company has developed a special steel (resistant to steam) for turbine blades. The company can thus extend its market penetration on a world-wide basis with major orders recently secured from the engineering complexes of Pyongyang in North Korea and Ranchi in India. One GDR Party functionary has referred to high-technology industries in the way that Lenin regarded electrification in the 1920s: as 'our revolutionary barricade for the 1980s'. Yet progress will create awkward social problems for economies which have traditionally tended to be labour-intensive in order to minimize unemployment. How will redundancies be avoided and how will recalcitrant employees be dealt with (those unable or unwilling to accept the new technology)?

Technological progress: the case of wood processing

Timber remains a basic resource which, like other raw materials, is being subjected to more sophisticated processing in order to maximize its value to the economy. The initial emphasis on sawn timber is giving way to a more diverse range of products including furniture, chipboard, fibreboard, and paper. Some of these industries are long-established, especially in the northern countries. The first factories producing bent beechwood furniture were set up amid the woodlands of south Moravia at Korycany in 1857 and Bystrice pod Hostynem in 1859. Chairs, stools, settees, and coatstands were sent all over the world. The furniture combine TON still operates at Bystrice pod Hostynem and also at Uherske Hradiste. In the Balkans much of the furniture was made in small workshops, from which larger units were derived after nationalization. Various paper-mills also date back to the nineteenth century. In the countryside there were many craftsmen busy sawing timber, usually with the assistance of water power and producing a range of goods for local sale. Some of this activity still continues but nationalization of the forests and the concentration on the large electrically powered mills has limited the opportunities for the private operator who is also burdened by high taxes. Some co-operative farms may retain significant areas of woodland, and small water-powered mills, in order to be self-sufficient with regard to the production of boxes for packing fruit and grapes, but the number has been drastically reduced. Wood carving continues in the countryside with considerable opportunities for marketing (often informally) in the tourist industry and there are some small factories in the villages which are satellites of the large industrialization complexes. Thus, for example, the main factory at Cimpeni in Romania has outlying units at Girda de Sus and Avram Iancu concerned respectively with the production of staves and the assembly of barrels.

Since nationalization, saw-milling has been modified in a number of ways. Old factories, like the pulp and paper mill at Ruzomberok in Slovakia, have been extensively modernized and enlarged. They now draw on extensive supply areas thanks to improved transport arrangements and the electricity programme of the 1950s. In Romania 115 mills produced some 4.1 million cubic metres of sawn timber in 1966, whereas in 1938, 516 units turned out just 2.2 million cubic metres. The distribution of factories has also changed, with emphasis on the main towns adjacent to the forest zone rather than rural locations within the woodlands themselves. There has also been much greater use made of beechwood, which accounted for only 4.1 per cent of Romania's sawn timber output in 1938, but 15.6 in 1955, and 26.3 in 1966. This reflects a willingness to install new mills and transport systems, especially for the beech forests (a programme started in the 1930s) and also a reduced consumption of firewood which was traditionally the main commercial use for this type of wood. Further use of beechwood arises through the expanding furniture industry, and also the production of fibreboard and chipboard.

It is still common to find enterprises concerned with single products like furniture and paper but there is also a

Table 6.4 Production and trade in forest products, 1961-85

Country	Production											
	Panels/board			Paper/pulp (b)			Roundwood			Sawn timber		
	1960s	1970s	1980s	1960s	1970s	1980s	1960s	1970s	1980s	1960s	1970s	1980s
Albania	0.08	0.12	0.06	0.08	0.16	0.08	17.93	23.30	11.65	1.78	2.00	1.00
Bulgaria	3.65	5.74	2.94	2.30	5.14	3.45	53.82	46.03	24.27	16.58	16.30	7.30
Czechoslovakia	6.12	10.83	6.53	13.79	18.12	11.53	133.23	165.14	94.65	38.57	44.39	25.52
GDR	6.96	12.63	5.95	16.26	19.21	9.99	71.10	85.17	52.36	21.03	21.57	12.29
Hungary	1.97	3.58	1.91	2.66	4.34	2.82	42.46	55.76	31.81	8.67	10.71	6.17
Poland	11.26	22.89	9.70	13.67	19.55	9.84	172.51	207.06	114.31	71.22	79.31	33.20
Romania	7.44	16.39	8.07	6.39	13.00	7.44	218.35	208.56	113.18	51.04	49.04	23.52
Yugoslavia	5.68	10.86	6.47	8.28	13.25	9.74	174.30	146.15	74.74	28.54	37.43	22.16
Eastern Europe	43.16	83.05	41.63	63.43	92.77	54.89	883.71	937.18	516.97	237.42	260.76	131.16

Country	Panels/board			Paper/pulp (b)			Trade (a) Roundwood			Sawn timber			Total trade (c)		
	1960s	1970s	1980s	1960s	1970s	1980s	1960s	1970s	1980s	1960s	1970s	1980s	1960s	1970s	1980s
Albania	-0.04	-0.02	-0.10	+0.05	+0.06	+0.03							+0.04	+0.07	+0.08
Bulgaria	+0.11	-1.04	-0.29	+0.96	+1.83	+1.18	+1.49	+3.27	+1.74	+0.33	+1.42	+0.70	+1.12	+4.23	+3.25
Czecho-slovakia	+0.20	+1.16	+0.17	-0.12	+0.70	-0.75	-9.67	-22.53	-12.30	-5.43	-7.03	-5.08	-1.95	-5.16	-7.42
GDR	+1.63	+4.35	+1.69	+1.84	+3.63	+1.62	+9.27	+6.34	+2.97	+12.58	+13.44	+6.88	+6.08	+12.76	+8.98
Hungary	+0.35	+0.87	+0.41	+0.47	+3.24	+2.06	+15.96	+9.11	+1.75	+7.84	+8.34	+3.19	+4.71	+11.20	+5.01
Poland	-0.86	+1.45	+0.48	+1.44	+3.73	+1.11	-2.70	-7.75	-6.15	-6.04	-4.84	-1.79	-0.17	+3.41	+1.34
Romania	-2.03	-4.73	-1.65	-0.26	-0.39	-0.20	-11.63	-3.18	-0.21	-20.05	-14.15	-5.50	-6.11	-10.45	-8.35
Yugo-slavia	-0.47	-0.43	-0.63	-0.18	+0.82	+0.17	-6.60	+3.32	+3.77	-7.33	-8.55	-3.22	-2.55	-4.17	-3.29
Eastern Europe	-1.11	+1.61	+0.08	+4.20	+13.62	+5.22	-3.88	-11.42	-8.43	-18.10	-11.37	-4.82	+1.17	+11.89	-0.40

Source: FAO yearbooks.

Notes: a. + figures indicate net imports, - figures indicate net exports. All figures in million cubic metres except (b) million tonnes and (c) billion dollars. Information for the 1980s relates to a five-year period only and values should therefore be doubled to be directly comparable with those for the 1960s and 1970s.

trend towards the grouping of several industries in a processing complex, known in Romania as a Combinat pentru industrializarea lemnului (CIL). There are some forty such plants administered by a single authority: the centrala for wood processing based at Pipera, Bucharest. The idea of an integrated processing unit is sustained by very close linkages, as exemplified by furniture production which requires wooden components as well as melamine-coated hardboard and chipboard and in turn generates waste material which can be combined with waste from other departments to yield a volume sufficient for board production. The Smrecine complex in the Slovakian village of Polomka, an area rich in fir and spruce wood, includes a sawmill and a unit for the manufacture of blockboard suitable for the production of pianos and other musical instruments. All waste materials including chips and sawdust will be utilized in this process. Not all inputs can be generated within the complex from raw timber alone: paper and chemicals for the melamine coating must be brought in, along with upholstery and veneers. Factories are now distributed widely across each country. Most are close to the main forest zones but others are oriented towards markets, such as Romania's Bucharest factories, and ports like Constanta process imported timber needed for veneers and panels. Factories usually have their own raw material supply areas and their own hinterlands for the distribution of finished products.

The emphasis on better processing comes out dramatically in the foreign trade pattern. Exports of sawn timber from Romania involved only 16.2 per cent of production in 1980 compared with 39.5 per cent in 1965 (the change being particularly pronounced with resinous timber). (3) By contrast there are increases in exports in other lines of production like boards and panels. Over Eastern Europe as a whole there is a balance of importing and exporting, given the rising domestic requirements and the modest importance of forestry in countries like the GDR and Hungary (Table 6.4). But once again the limited role of roundwood and sawn timber is brought out.

Wood processing: maintaining the supply of raw material

Given the raw material limitations wood processing cannot now expand as rapidly as most other industries. In Romania

Figure 6.1 Woodlands in Romania

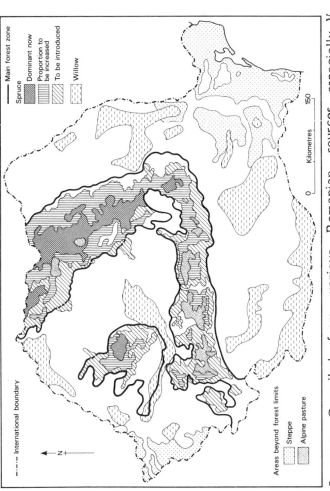

Sources: Compiled from various Romanian sources, especially V. Giurgiu and others (eds) (1968) *Contributii privind zonarea padurilor si a productiei forestiere in RPR*, Bucharest: Institutul de Cercetari Forestiere.

Note: for key to maps, see note 4 on page 314.

wood processing (including paper) accounted for only 5.5 per cent of total industrial output in 1980 compared with 9.8 in 1955, while the share of investment has fallen to 3.7 per cent in 1976-80 compared with 6.7 in 1951-5. Forestry in Romania is even losing ground in relation to agriculture, with 3.8 per cent of the total agriculture/forestry investment in 1976-80 compared with 8.1 in 1951-5 (though the share did fall as low as 2.8 between 1966 and 1975). Trees can grow in virtually all parts of Eastern Europe with only small areas of true steppe and alpine mountain environment ruled out. However, after centuries of cutting to make way for agriculture, forest is now largely restricted to the mountain zones (Figure 6.1).

The management system is now overwhelmingly geared to the felling of whole trees and their replacement by new growth arising from artificial planting or natural regeneration. Coppicing systems are retained only in some restricted areas for the production of bark and tanning materials. Cutting is done overwhelmingly with electric chain-saws. Branches are removed immediately and this results in masses of waste material strewn over the hillside. However, the need for conservation in the forests, balancing cutting with growth, has meant greater attention to the elimination of waste: hence the interest shown recently in whole-tree harvesting. This would mean that the branches, accounting for a quarter of the total volume of the tree, bark, and needles (presently left in the forest) would be processed. Coniferous branches may be processed for turpentine and paper while beech branches could furnish chips acceptable for chipboard production. Bark can be utilized by the chemical industry (also for tanning materials and fuel) while needles can be converted into powder and used in production of cattle feed. Transport of the whole tree would only be necessary as far as the pre-processing points, of which there would be several units for each major wood-industrialization complex, but even so special transport arrangements will be needed. Also, much care will be needed to ensure that the dragging out of whole trees does not damage the surrounding vegetation or retard natural regeneration.

With the development of a system of unsurfaced roads the transport of timber is now handled almost exclusively by lorries which have gradually increased in size in sympathy with road standards. In the past timber was floated or rafted along rivers but this method was wasteful, besides being inappropriate for heavy wood like beech. Moreover, water levels were often too low, necessitating dams to accumulate a reserve of water which could be used to generate a 'tide' on the crest of which a consignment of material could be dispatched down river. Narrow gauge railways were built from the late nineteenth century taking off along tributary valleys from standard gauge railheads. Construction continued until the 1950s in the Balkans but with the need for funiculars and inclines where steep gradients were encountered and heavy maintenance costs arising out of frequent flood damage, road transport was found to be cheaper and more flexible once suitable vehicles were available. However, there are some surviving railways, especially in Romania where the rising cost of oil led to a decision to maintain those lines still in existence in the late 1970s.

Careful records are kept so that cutting can be placed on a proper rational basis. Such management practices, to maintain a steady output, date back to the eighteenth century in some areas (the first management plan at Chynov estate in Bohemia dates back to 1739). Such caution was often abandoned in the 1950s when the volume of timber removed might exceed natural reproduction by more than half. Excessive cutting in Poland has reduced the proportion of fully mature trees (80 years old) from 27 per cent in 1945 to 18 in 1980 (and an estimated 15 per cent in 1990); and in spite of increased cutting of young trees, plan targets are not being reached. To maximize output, 'two-tier' forests have been evolved in Bulgaria, mixing species that can tolerate sunshine (or conversely, shade) to obtain increases of productivity per unit of area by about a third. It is also desirable to mix according to age. Young beech, fir, and oak trees need shelter and so a system of natural regeneration may be employed using the cover of mature trees. In each parcel of some 15 ha the mature trees may be cut in three stages at three to five year intervals, giving young trees the space and shelter to develop. There has been some emphasis on species change in Romania to replace beech with the more valuable fir or spruce. However, this is not ecologically desirable since soil and climate may not be suitable for the preferred species even if they are established artificially. It is therefore usual to seek only a modest change in the balance between different species by planting some fir and spruce in spaces where there is shelter from adjacent stands of beech. Interest is also shown in accessory products such as berries, fruits, mushrooms, and

Table 6.5 Land use 1984 and changes since 1950

Country	Land use 1984 (million ha)						Change 1950-84 (thousand ha)				
	A	B	C	D	E	F	A	B	C	D	E
Albania	1.04	0.59	0.12	0.40	0.59	2.74	-254	+237	+97	-421	+341
Bulgaria	3.86	3.81	0.33	2.04	1.02	11.06	-133	-539	+106	+878	-312
Czechoslovakia	4.58	5.03	0.13	1.66	1.14	12.54	+363	-282	+33	-431	+317
GDR	2.96	4.78	0.21	1.25	1.38	10.59	+66	-247	+14	-67	+234
Hungary	1.65	5.04	0.26	1.25	1.05	9.23	+482	-618	-53	-228	+417
Poland	8.72	14.53	0.26	4.08	2.85	30.45	+1,798	-1,348	-61	-110	-279
Romania	6.34	9.93	0.64	4.42	1.70	23.03	-108	+566	+230	-122	-566
Yugoslavia	9.29	7.04	0.71	6.38	2.11	25.54	+1,500	-192	+111	+419	-1,838
Eastern Europe	38.45	50.76	2.67	21.47	11.84	125.19	+3,714	-2,423	+477	-82	-1,686

	Change 1970-5				Change 1976-80				Change 1981-4			
	A	B	C	D	A	B	C	D	A	B	C	D
Albania	-162	+45	+23	-232	-66	+20	+16	-2	+24	+7	+4	-16
Bulgaria	+92	-146	-1	+197	+47	-171	-34	+326	+19	-20	-26	+33
Czechoslovakia	+42	-77	+10	-12	+80	-102	+3	-62	+4	-5	+1	-21
GDR	+3	+86	+29	-113	+4	+97	-5	-116	+10	-31	-12	+14
Hungary	+75	-70	-32	-1	+64	-95	-62	+14	+38	+9	-49	-48
Poland	+48	-287	+42	-85	+80	-149	-17	-93	+39	-86	-15	+30
Romania		-9	-16	+24	+22	+99	-98	+19	+1	+101	-24	-49
Yugoslavia	+176	-205	+35	-48	+222	-142	-9	+59	+44	-108	-18	-22
Eastern Europe	+274	-664	+90	-270	+453	-443	-206	+145	+179	-133	-139	-79

Source: FAO Yearbooks.

Notes: A – Forest; B – Arable; C – Permanent Crops; D – Pasture; E – Other uses; F – Total.

tanning materials. The domestic scale of operation is usual but some local fruit-processing industries have become viable. Expansion might require better roads and refrigerated vehicles. Other products such as juices and alcoholic drinks based on fruits and pine needles have been looked at experimentally. The Forestry Faculty at Brasov University (Romania) is interested in the production of brandy from fir needles and a small factory is planned. Bulgarian woodlands yield various oils suitable for the perfume industry. Juniper and various species of pine (Roumelian pine) and spruce (Norway spruce) are exploited for use in cosmetic creams, foam baths, shampoos, and soaps.

The forest area is tending to increase through shelterbelts in the lowlands and through the planting of grazing lands in the mountains (Table 6.5). The clearance of forest to create more grazing land was stopped in Yugoslavia in the 1950s, partly through government prohibitions and partly through a reduction of pressure (brought about by depopulation of mountain villages and the abandonment of farm land). The area of meadows and pastures averaged 6.60 million ha between 1936 and 1940 but declined to 6.40 in 1972-6 and 6.38 in 1982-4. This trend is likely to continue everywhere as the pressure from the pastoralists declines. Romanian foresters believe that much of the pastoral activity on the high ground is unnecessary and that adequate provision for animals could be made by more intensive use of the lower ground. Thus in 1983 the forest authorities took over the management of communal pastures from the local councils and stricter measures to protect woodlands are now being taken. Forests are rarely fenced on the high ground and animals can enter the woodlands on a controlled basis. People in Yugoslavia were forbidden to keep goats in the 1950s in order to conserve forests in karst areas, where there was excessive grazing pressure. The ban has since been revised and numbers of goats are again rising. This is due to relaxation of pressure as many farmers have left the mountains and the sheep flocks have declined (15.1 million animals in 1931 but 12.8 in 1954, 9.8 in 1964, 8.0 in 1974, and 7.7 in 1984). Transhumance has virtually disappeared and the mountain grazings are now under-utilized.

Conservation

Finally mention should be made of the other functions of woodland which have attracted greater concern: protection of river basins against erosion and rapid run-off and aesthetic/ecological value of certain woodlands which justifies the designation of forest reserves. Both considerations justify additional planting. In Bulgaria 0.20 million ha have been planted for protective purposes, against erosion, and a further 0.15 million ha has decorative and landscaping functions. It is becoming clear that forests stabilize run-off and also protect the environment by filtering smoke and gas, maintaining a varied flora and fauna and serving recreational and sporting purposes - hence the formulation of stringent measures to control cutting and the use of chemicals. Unfortunately, such measures are not always effective, except in the cases of special forests, with military significance or the most critical protective functions, where no commercial felling is permitted. It is also appreciated that forests contribute to the quality of life by maintaining a varied flora and fauna and by providing recreational and sporting facilities. At Bolovice in Moravia, for example, the forest contributes to the scenic quality of an area known as 'Moravian Switzerland'. Also, in Czechoslovakia the vegetation of the Velka Fatra is particularly interesting, with remnants of hornbeam and oak at the lower levels around Ruzomberok and beechwoods, mixed with fir and pine, extending to 1,200 metres. The beechwoods of the Bystricka and Lubochriarska valleys are particularly fine. The pine then extends to 1,400 metres and even to 1,500 metres on limestock rocks. Evergreen pine trees with reddish brown stems present a picturesque contrast to the grey rocky background. A speciality of the Velka Fatra is the presence of the near-extinct yew tree, with a particularly remarkable stand, in the Harmanescka valley, of some 120,000 trees, including some more than 200 years old (up to 18 metres high and 270 cm in diameter). Also of interest are the maple trees which extend to the summits above the Japen valley at altitudes of 1,200-1,300 metres.

In addition to informal recreation there is scope for organized hunting to exploit the large animal population. This is a lucrative business, attracting wealthy foreign visitors for whom special accommodation is available in chalets in the forest. However, forest management has to be modified by designation of sanctuaries and by planting programmes to allow a mixing of species conducive to animal feed. Small clearings could encourage shrub growth for food and so reduce damage to trees. The most important recreational functions apply in and around the big cities. In Prague several woods (Dablice, Hostivar, and Velka Chuchle) have been used for the establishment of health parks so that people may not only walk in the forest but can utilize gymnastic and other apparatus in pursuit of physical fitness. Poland's Pszczyna forest on the Rybnik Plateau is important for recreation for Upper Silesia. Such functions have to be safeguarded by the creation of forest reservations (the first date to the early nineteenth century, as in Bohemia where the Zofin forest was first protected in the 1840s). Also, recreational facilities are important in planning the reclamation of wasteland in Upper Silesia: Chorzow's 600 ha park of culture and recreation was established on wasteland, and sandpits have been flooded to provide scope for water sports.

INDUSTRIAL LOCATION AND REGIONAL DEVELOPMENT

From the geographical point of view the well-publicized achievements of the East European countries over industrial development and structural change are less interesting than the overall changes in location patterns. (5) Communists have repeatedly stated their intentions of overcoming inequalities inherited from the capitalist past. They believe that the operation of free-market forces creates inequalities between people and between regions: people who have little to offer by way of capital and skills cannot bargain for high wages, while regions which are remote from the main centres of commerce, with few raw materials and skilled workers, will have difficulty in attracting investment in manufacturing. If the market is replaced by the plan, then greater equality can be achieved. Opportunity may still vary between individuals and communities but without excessive discrimination. However, while it is comparatively easy for a powerful government to destroy the privileges of the élite (and indeed to destroy the élite altogether), it is less easy to improve conditions for the masses. Equally, factories may be dismantled and relocated in backward regions of the country, but difficulties over the supply of raw materials and the training of labour may depress output and profitability. In so far as socialism can claim legitimacy it does so on the grounds that it can modernize society more rapidly and more fairly than capitalism. Yet this challenge calls for rapid overall growth rates and automatically limits the amount of assistance which can be given to poorer people and poorer regions. Gross locational inefficiency cannot be tolerated. In practice, therefore, communist governments have been obliged to compromise on equity in order to maximize output: disparities between regions and income groups have been reduced only slowly and significant variations remain (especially when allowance is made for the whole regime of taxation and welfare benefits). So the superiority of socialism in Eastern Europe is therefore by no means proved by the experience of the last forty years. (6) Certainly, communist governments have succeeded in controlling the means of production (a political imperative that was important for its own sake as well as an essential precondition for efficient planning), but they have been less successful in maintaining a steady rate of growth of output and living standards in all countries and regions.

While there are strident propaganda claims about the importance of equity in location decisions it is not easy in practice to see any fundamental difference between socialist and capitalist systems with regard to the need for a pragmatic trade-off between equity and efficiency. (7) Western observers have identified a mismatch between generalized assertions that socialism seeks a new geography of human endeavour and individual decisions which reflect conventional western principles: least-cost location having in mind the movement of raw materials to the factory and finished goods to markets, with adjustments where necessary to expedite the supply of labour and adequate services (supplies of electricity and water, waste disposal, and so on). There are, however, problems of interpretation because the decision-making process cannot be observed in detail. It is easy to claim that a particular decision articulates the equity argument when purely economic considerations may be primarily responsible: low raw material collection costs, exploitation of newly discovered mineral resources, recruitment of underemployed rural labour, or loose trade linkages with the Soviet Union (for the latter have provided an economic rationale for several large industries in the relatively backward eastern regions of Eastern Europe). Again, a rural location (like Calbe in the GDR, where a blast furnace was built) could be inspired by the desire to provide jobs in rural areas and so reduce disparities in living standards between town and country before it became usual to seek the integration of town and country through city regions. Yet Calbe is convenient for canal and rail transport, needed to assemble the various inputs (ore from the Harz Mountains and coke from Lauchammer), and the location was economically acceptable. The closure of the furnace and the switch to aluminium products, using metal from Bitterfeld and Lauta, has arisen from the lack of economies of scale and the changed raw material supply arrangements.

Planning procedures

It is important to appreciate the context in which location decisions are taken in order to understand the difficulties in reaching the best solutions. Administrative regions are important to central planning as well as the traditional functions of local government. (8) State investments must be allocated to regions as well as sectors and within each region there must be co-ordination to ensure a reasonable balance of development projects in harmony with local potentials. Regions must be numerous enough for effective discrimination between alternative regional allocations but not too numerous for the central planning machinery to cope with, in the sense that too many regions in relation to the efficiency of the planning system and the scale of resources would make it impossible to develop a complex of industries in each case. With this last point in mind regions need to be delimited with regard to raw materials, ensuring an adequate range of resources, and infrastructure, to provide the possibility of an integrated settlement system focusing on a town selected as the regional centre. Given the limited resources available to the planners it is usually appropriate to select as regional centres towns with a good infrastructure and long administrative experience, although the demarcation of the hinterlands has frequently led to radical changes compared with traditional arrangements. Regions were usually large, and became even larger in the light of experience, before substantially increased resources in the 1970s allowed for a finer focus and the overhaul of the system to recognize a larger number of regional centres. Meanwhile, the difficulty of administering a large region usually led to a two- or three-tier structure, with the region split into districts and again into communes. Administrative regions therefore involve a whole series of compromises, and the changes in the patterns which are necessary to ensure an effective framework as economic development proceeds are the product of complex decision-making processes which can only be partially reconstructed. Although the regions may be regarded as objective realities this status follows from their significance in the planning process and does not mean that Communist Parties have found a solution to the age-old problem of regional delimitation.

All this is significant for location because of the proven tendency for regional Party leaders to encourage the growth of industrial complexes in the administrative centres, which thereby grow at a disproportionate rate. Where there are essential location criteria which the regional centre cannot satisfy, the search for a suitable site is based on the main centre and a complex of industries may then develop in the core of the region (Calbe, mentioned above, is close to Magdeburg, the regional centre). More sophisticated regional planning is only slowly overcoming the distortions inherited not from capitalism in this instance but from socialism. The industrial hierarchy now fits the settlement hierarchy more closely, although the hierarchy is itself a product of regionalization to a considerable extent. Bulgaria differentiates between the largest concentrations of Dimitrovgrad, Gabrovo-Veliko Turnovo, Plovdiv-Pazardjik, Sofia-Pernik, Stara Zagora, and Varna-Devnya, known as territorial industrial complexes; the smaller 'industrial units'; and finally the groupings in individual large towns (industrial centres) or small towns and villages (industrial points).

More fundamental than the regional allocation of investment, however, is the distribution between sectors. It is the ministries who must arrange a spatial allocation for the investments allocated under the plan and the ability of local authorities to plan the development of individual settlements and districts is constrained by the limited scope for independent initiative to create employment. Enterprises which might appear well suited to local resources can only be established if the national plan makes provision for them and if the relevant ministry approves of the location. The flexibility of the western situation where an enterprise may emerge spontaneously and compete for capital in the open market is not available in Eastern

Europe. However, close personal contacts between business people in town and country can sometimes result in the setting up of useful rural industries. At Szony near Komarom in Hungary an enterprise for the retreading of tyres was set up in 1980 within the framework of an agricultural co-operative responding to the shortage of new tyres for agricultural use. An organization concerned with the provision of services for agricultural co-operatives collaborated with a rubber repair enterprise to set up production facilities in various rural locations. Freedom for local authorities to borrow money for the setting up of local industries in Romania has drawn an encouraging response, especially from communes where the leadership has close connections with industry to the point where second-hand machinery can be purchased and sub-contracting undertaken.

Not only does Soviet-style central planning lack any sophisticated spatial content; the challenging nature of early five-year plans demanded a great deal of location decision-making for which inadequate information was available. It is clear that a good deal of subjectivism has been involved, in the judgements of Party leaders who have often tried to help their home towns or regions. A subjective decision may arise where there is a multiplicity of more or less equal choices when least-cost analysis (in so far as this is possible), security matters and regional needs are taken into account. However, there would appear to be cases where subjectivism has resulted in the selection of sub-optimal locations. 'In a planned economy state-owned industry decisions and economic activities are far from rational', being based on inadequate information and conditioned by the subjective approaches or ambitions of decision-makers at all levels. (9) Personal preferences are known to have played a part in the siting of Huta Katowice near Dabrowa Gornicza (Poland) since the then Party leader E. Gierek was determined it should be on the edge of the Upper Silesian conurbation (on a site selected from a helicopter) and not in a town close to the Soviet frontier, which would have meant a much shorter raw material haul. In Anina (Romania) the Party leader N. Ceausescu decided that the power station burning the bituminous schists should be sited adjacent to the quarries in the Anina Mountains and not on low ground close to cooling water at Oravita. Socialist decision-makers are therefore capable of irrational decisions which may result from the possession of adequate or inadequate information about the alternatives available, and this excessive subjectivism may be a distinguishing feature which has not been adequately recognized. In other cases irrationality has arisen through conflict between different enterprises. It has been shown that installations processing potatoes in the Poznan voivodship (Poland) have failed to draw all the raw material they require from the immediate locality. (10) This is because growers have been induced to sell to other outlets through higher prices or barter arrangements involving the supply of building materials, fertilizers, or the loan of agricultural machinery. It therefore becomes necessary for the processors to meet their plan targets by extending the supply areas to places like Lukow, Siedlce, and Sokolow Podlaski where producers do not have the benefit of local industrial outlets. However, such measures are irrational in terms of transport costs.

Suboptimal location is not in itself remarkable. Even if decisions were entirely rational in the first place (an unlikely event given the crude nature of many allocations and the compromises involved when relevant economic criteria are in conflict), changing circumstances would almost certainly introduce complications (perhaps in the context of labour shortages or changes in markets and raw material or component suppliers). The difficulties need emphasis only as a corrective to propaganda claims that state-directed central planning has an inherent rationality which eludes the decision-making of western capitalism. However, in spite of the inevitable shortcomings, remarkable progress has been made and the geography of industry seems to be much more even in countries like Bulgaria and Romania, which have witnessed particularly rapid growth under socialism, than in the northern countries of Czechoslovakia and the GDR which were already advanced in 1945. This contrast may well arise fundamentally because of the available technology with the electricity grid, in addition to rail and road transport, offering a wide choice of locations. Market towns in areas lacking local energy resources have become attractive locations for factory industry, while the optimum size of a single enterprise has been reduced by the ease with which intermediates (in the chemical industry for example) can be transported by rail, road, or pipeline. The huge complexes inherited by the GDR, based on the lignite deposits extending from Bitterfeld through Halle and Leipzig to Zeitz (Figure 6.2), have not been generated to the same

Figure 6.2 Industrial development in the Halle-Leipzig lignite field of the GDR

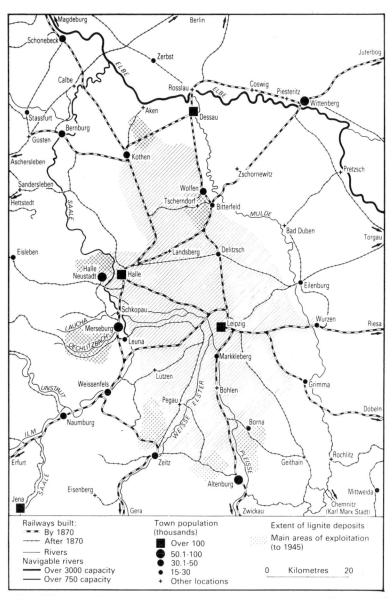

Source: Topographical maps.

Figure 6.3 Industrial development of the regions of Romania, 1965-75

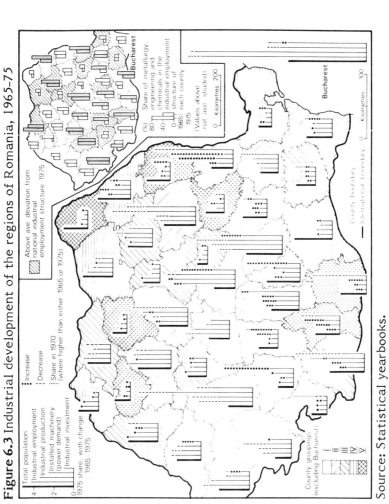

Source: Statistical yearbooks.

Figure 6.4 Regional trends in the number of wage earners in Romania, 1965–75

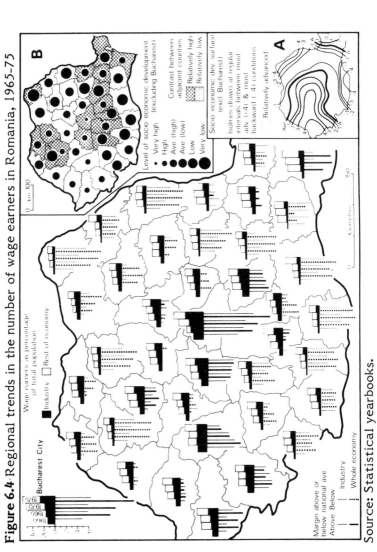

Source: Statistical yearbooks.

extent in the Balkans since 1945 because of the feasibility of dispersing the investment (and so exploiting suitable local labour catchments). However, in view of the need to plan an investment strategy over a long period of time and to build up both planning expertise and the country's infrastructure, it is evident that early post-war investment has been directed primarily towards the major cities and resource bases and that a wider spread of investment has been achieved only during the last two decades. Figure 6.3 shows the switch in emphasis in Romania with the backward areas (country groups four and five) attracting greater support during the 1970s (in the context of the administrative reform of 1968, which broke down the large planning regions built up around the major cities of the country). (11)

The backward areas of Romania are generating more wage earners (as a percentage of a total population) and their relatively weak position is being gradually modified in relation to the national average (Figure 6.4). However, strong contrasts remain between adjacent regions (inset (A) and more generally between the areas at the opposite ends of the socio-economic gradient running from the relatively advanced south-west to the more backward north-east (inset B). It is also evident that developments in the backward regions tend to be more labour-intensive in both industrial and non-industrial projects (Figure 6.5). Moreover, in considering the role of industry in regional development it is important to remember that the process is still at an early in comparison with western countries, and the limited number of developments in individual towns and regions means that there is often a high degree of specialization. This is again demonstrated in the Romanian context (Figure 6.6) where it is evident that specialization also varies according to sectors of manufacturing. Finally there are the increasing labour and raw material shortages which have constrained regional development strategies based on industry since the late 1970s. (12) The slowdown in the growth of employment in industry and the need for restructuring is having important implications for regional change, which may in future have to find a greater inspiration from non-industrial activities.

Figure 6.5 The relationship between investment and job creation in the regions of Romania, 1960-75 (A) industry (B) non-industrial sectors

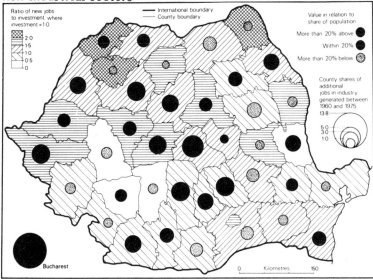

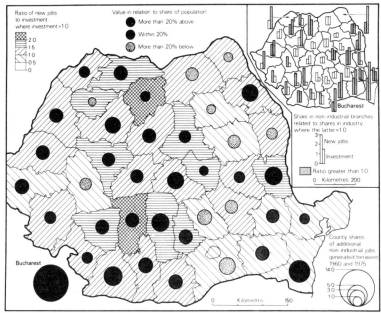

Source: Statistical yearbooks.

Figure 6.6 Employment and specialization in industry in the towns of Romania, 1977, and changing regional industrial structures, 1960–80

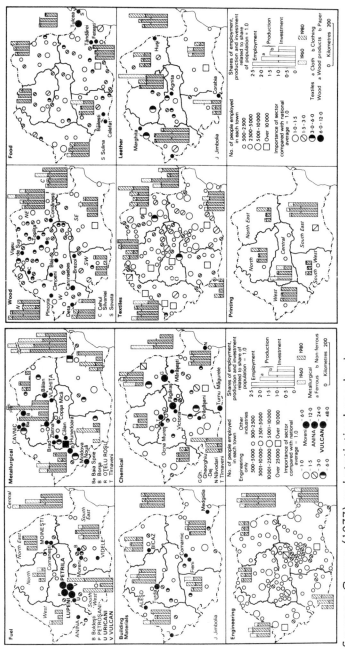

Sources: Census (1977) and statistical yearbooks.

Table 6.6 Metallurgical industries

(a) Iron ore (A) and steel (B) output (million metric tonnes), 1938–85

Country	1938 A	1938 B	1948 A	1948 B	1960 A	1960 B	1970 A	1970 B	1980 A	1980 B	1985 A	1985 B
Bulgaria	*	*	*	*	0.4	0.3	2.4	1.8	1.8	2.6	2.0	2.9
Czechoslovakia	0.5	1.9	0.4	2.6	3.1	6.8	1.6	11.5	1.9	15.2	1.8	15.3
GDR	*	1.2	*	0.2	1.6	3.7	0.4	5.1	*	7.3	*	6.7
Hungary	*	0.6	0.2	0.8	0.5	1.9	0.6	3.1	0.4	3.8	0.3	3.6
Poland	0.3	1.4	0.2	2.0	2.2	6.7	2.6	11.8	*	18.6	*	16.1
Romania	*	0.3	*	0.3	1.5	1.8	3.2	6.5	2.3	13.2	1.9	14.4
Yugoslavia	0.3	0.2	0.3	0.4	2.2	1.4	3.7	2.2	4.5	2.3	5.3	2.0

Note: * denotes totals less than 0.1.

(b) Production and trade, 1970-83

Country	1970								1983							
	A	B	C	D	E	F	G	H	A	B	C	D	E	F	G	H
Bulgaria	0.79	1.25	1.80	2.32	+0.52	0.22	222	63	0.47	1.62	2.58	3.01	+0.43	0.28	69	186
Czechoslovakia	0.45	7.65	11.48	8.84	-2.64	0.07	236	40	0.50	9.69	14.99	11.13	-3.66	0.09	233	34
GDR	0.11	2.09	5.05	9.08	+4.03	0.16	90	82	*	2.15	7.17	9.52	+2.35	0.17	102	61
Hungary	0.16	1.84	3.11	3.08	-0.03	0.09	90	76	0.10	2.19	3.62	3.69	+0.07	0.11	125	63
Poland	0.71	7.11	11.75	11.68	-0.07	0.39	105	102	0.01	8.36	14.14	14.43	+0.29	0.70	94	116
Romania	0.88	4.21	6.52	6.43	-0.09	0.17	94	73	0.55	8.64	10.94	11.61	+0.67	0.31	117	83
Yugoslavia	1.30	1.38	2.23	3.42	+1.19	0.34	32	142	1.68	2.92	2.02	5.22	+3.20	0.56	22	149

Source: Statistical yearbooks.

Notes: A – Iron ore (metal content); B – Pig iron production; C – Steel production; D – Steel consumption; E – Steel trade (+ indicates import); F – Aluminium, copper, lead, zinc production; G – Share of total steel output related to share of population (= 1.00); H – Ditto – aluminium, copper, lead, zinc.

Location patterns for metallurgical industries

The iron and steel industry has grown very rapidly indeed since 1945, being a major priority of central planning (Table 6.6). Despite modest domestic resources in some countries, the scale of demand anticipated by the projected expansion of the engineering industry and the ability to mobilize capital have justified the construction of new integrated plants, although severe difficulties were encountered in some cases. Given an outstanding economic aberration involving self-sufficiency compromised only by bilateral trade links with the USSR, each country set out to expand its iron and steel industry in order to secure the metal required for the engineering industry, which would in turn produce the equipment for light industry and for the electrification and transport programmes. Such complexes of heavy industry would stimulate mining and a whole range of jobs in 'downstream' manufacturing (quite apart from the employment in the combine itself) necessary for the formation of a large urban proletariat. Large metallurgical works would also serve as impressive monuments of socialist endeavour and would inspire confidence in a new value system, especially if they were located in backward areas. The exact order of priorities will probably never be fully established but it may be argued that a simplistic autarkic approach suited the conservatively minded communist leaderships in Eastern Europe and also the Soviet authorities who were anxious to avoid any move towards integration or federation in Eastern Europe which could threaten their authority. It is also likely that the Korean War increased Soviet interest in heavy industry in Eastern Europe as a means of increasing the capacity of armaments industries. Two countries have built up a steel industry virtually from scratch, selecting coalfield locations close to the capital city. Bulgaria opened the Lenin iron and steel works at Pernik in 1953 and followed this with another project close to the iron ore mine of Kremikovtsi in 1965. Albania has been operating a steel works at Elbasan during the 1980s and a capacity of some two million tonnes has been reported.

On the whole quite new locations have been sought for these major new investments because dependence on Soviet and other imported raw materials suggests proximity to the major transport routes (also rational in relation to distribution of finished products to the home market). At the same time the total number of works producing iron has tended to fall although most inherited works survive as integrated units (like Ostrava in Czechoslovakia, Hunedoara and Resita in Romania) or as producers of special steels. Thus, Unterwellenborn in the GDR still produces steel, using pig iron from the new complex of Eisenhuttenstadt, although its own blast furnaces have closed, while Czechoslovakia's inherited steelworks at Podbrezova (built originally to supply special steels to Hungary) has been modernized as the Sverma tube mill, with metal supplied by the new integrated works at Koscie, and the Trinec steelworks near Bohumin has also been modernized, given the easy linkage with the Ostrava complex. Locations selected for new complexes would appear to satisfy both efficiency and equity criteria. The Kosice project in Czechoslovakia, which appears a rational one in the light of imports of Soviet iron ore, was in fact conceived with domestic as well as Soviet ores in mind; and it was the great difficulty experienced with the Slovak ores as well as high construction costs that led to a lapse in building at Kosice between 1953 and 1958. Domestic ore output grew from 1.60 million tonnes in 1950 (1.19 from Slovakia) to 3.12 (1.85) in 1960, but fell back to 1.61 (1.52) in 1970. Meanwhile, ore imports rose sharply from 2.19 million tonnes in 1950 (1.05 from the USSR) to 7.21 (5.02) in 1960, and 12.72 (10.84) in 1970. Case studies presented later in the chapter will show that whereas Yugoslavia opted for dispersal of new plant, Poland kept her new capacities close to the inherited plant in Upper Silesia.

Non-ferrous metallurgy is again stimulated by the rising domestic demand for various metals (like copper for electrification) but also by the ample ore deposits which exist in some countries. However, post-war planning has not regarded non-ferrous metallurgy with the same degree of importance as iron and steel from the standpoint of autarky. Certainly, there has been a massive prospecting effort to locate the full range of ores, and this has been successful to the extent that many new ore bodies have been exploited (though at great expense in the case of low-grade material). But, given the relatively low level of demand for each of the commodities there has been a greater readiness to import refined metal rather than build up national industries on the basis of imported ores. Production is therefore much more closely tied to domestic raw materials than is the case with iron and steel and so there is more variation when production shares are placed against population than does iron and steel (Table 6.6b). Again, within each national economy the regional importance of the non-ferrous branches is largely fortuitous, with processing usually located close to the ores, as in the case of the large copper deposits developed in Lower Silesia in the 1960s or the complex ores of Kosovo and Macedonia which have been worked over a much longer period and processed at smelters like Trepca.

An exception is aluminium because the raw material (bauxite) is relatively easy to transport in bulk, especially if converted into aluminium oxide (alumina), while the heavy electricity demands for the reduction of alumina to aluminium make it unattractive for the bauxite producers to concentrate too heavily on processing beyond the requirements of their home markets. Hungary is the outstanding East European bauxite producer with mines at Ajka, developed during the 1920s. However, the lack of an adequate power supply kept the industry small during the inter-war years and even so reduction and rolling had to be located in Csepel, Budapest with production of alumina at Ajka and also on the Danube at Mosonmagyarovar. Since the war another smelter has been built at Inota using power derived from the local lignite (Varpalota), and this has recently been modernized and enlarged to 100,000 tonnes capacity. Even so, much of the output is exported as alumina and a small amount of bauxite is not processed at all. During the 1970s only about 0.15 million tonnes of the total alumina output of 0.80 was actually smelted inside Hungary: the rest was exported, half to the Soviet Union under the agreement first worked out in 1960. Hungary was able to export a substantial amount of aluminium ingots and products (from rolling mills in Szekesfehervar and Budapest) in advance of the Inota development thanks to arrangements made with the Soviet Union to have alumina smelted at Volgograd and returned to Hungary for further processing. However, even with Inota on stream and domestic electricty production (from lignite) increased, there is still a dependence on imported energy through the 750 Kv power line which now connects Hungary with the Soviet Union. In 1986 the Hungarian economy acquired 0.18 million tonnes of aluminium (of which 41 per cent was smelted within the country), but the depression in the world aluminium market has rendered this speculation in 'Hungarian silver' somewhat problematical. Romania and Yugoslavia have attempted to build up an aluminium export business on the strength of their own bauxite reserves but they do not have to use outside sources of power. Czechoslovakia, (with a smelter at Ziar nad Hronom), the GDR (Bitterfeld and Lauta), and Poland (Skawina and Konin) all import alumina, much of it from Hungary (Almasfuzito as well as the two older factories). Locations are tied to electricty generation but there are some opportunities to develop backward areas: Konin is based on the local lignite while Ziar nad Hronom is close to the hydroelectric power stations on the Hron and Romania's smelter at Slatina is close to the Oltenian lignite field.

Metallurgical industries and regional development: Poland (13)

Investment in industry was heavily concentrated initially but there has been a spread from the south and west to the north and east, aided not only improvements in infrastructure and demand for labour which have added an economic dimension to the welfare-based principle of equity, but also by the need for decongestion in old industrial areas (especially Upper Silesia) and the need to invest in new resource areas (hard coal near Lublin, lignite at Konin, and copper near Glogow and Lubin). (14) There has also been a shift from large towns to smaller settlements for the same reasons, but also because of labour shortages, inadequate space for the enlargement of enterprises, and problems over pollution and water supply. The situation is summarized, for regional groups, in Table 6.7, but the effectiveness of policy is also demonstrated by A. Wrobel who uses shift-share analysis related to total employment in industry, to bring out a strong shift during the 1950s and 1960s in favour of the underdeveloped regions (voivodships) against the highly developed region of Katowice. (15) Since then further gains have been registered in the poorer regions. If the regions are arranged into four groups according to industrial strength, then the top group (with 64.9 per cent of all industrial employment in 1965) lost 6.7 per cent over the following fourteen years, a proportion equally distributed among the three weaker groups with shares of 20.8, 9.5 and 4.8 in 1965. Disparities between individual voivodships also narrowed. In 1965, regions had employment rates for industry which deviated from the national average by more than a quarter, but by 1978 the number had declined to twenty-five, the change being

Table 6.7 Industrialization in Poland, 1939-75

Region	1939 A	B	C	1975 A	B	C
Centre	664.8	24.5	11.2	1,062.0	19.2	17.3
Centre-west	252.5	9.2	6.2	674.7	12.2	14.6
East-north	124.7	4.6	5.0	225.3	4.0	9.5
East-centre	112.8	4.1	4.1	240.5	4.3	9.7
East-south	246.9	9.1	4.9	743.8	13.4	14.1
North	231.0	8.5	7.7	457.6	8.2	13.8
South	575.4	21.1	12.3	1,414.7	25.3	23.7
South-west	518.9	19.0	13.0	746.6	13.4	18.7
Poland	2,727.0	100.0	8.5	5,565.1	100.0	16.3

Source: S. Misztal and W. Kaczorowski (1981) 'Spatial problems of Poland's post-war industrialization 1945-1975', Geographia Polonica 43:199-212.

Notes: A - Employment in industry, '000s;
B - Share of total industrial employment (per cent);
C - Jobs in industry per 100 population.

particularly noticeable among the weaker regions: only twenty had employment levels below 75 per cent of the national average in 1978 compared with 29 per cent in 1965.

The eastern regions of Poland have gained considerable ground during the post-war period. In 1950, with 51.3 per cent of the total population and 54.9 per cent of the active population, the share of employment in industry was only 37.7 per cent. Comparable figures for 1978 were 48.0, 50.1, and 43.6: the disparity between the last two criteria fell from 14.2 per cent to 6.5. However, the employment structure of the east is still relatively backward compared with the west, with a much higher proportion employed in

Industry

agriculture (34.3 per cent compared with 21.2) and lower proportions in both manufacturing (26.8 per cent compared with 34.8) and other activities (39.0 and 44.0). This is because half the increase in industrial employment between 1946 and 1981 has taken place in just eleven regions (Katowice with 13.9 per cent and Warsaw with 7.2, along with Kielce, Gdansk, Wroclaw, Opole, Krakow, Lodz, Bielsko-Biala, Bydogoszcz, and Poznan), leaving the other half distributed among the other thirty-eight regions thirteen of which attracted less than 1 per cent of the national increase. Significantly, before the communist takeover in Poland there were plans for large industrial developments in Stalowa Wola, Lomza/Ostroleka, Pila, and other towns, along with a regional pattern of agricultural specialization and a hierarchy of service centres. (16) However, the plans were abandoned, the central planning office was closed, and Soviet-style planning was adopted: 'The spatial element was largely absent' and the simplistic view that industry should be spread evenly across the country could not be implemented. (17) Regional problems seem to have been somewhat overlooked, particularly during the investment jump of the 1970s. (18)

The Poles have clearly recognized the essential importance of the Upper Silesian industrial region (Gornoslaskie okreg przemyslowy) and have done little to weaken its stake in the national economy (Figure 6.7). (19) The population of this 'core region' has grown from 2.8 million in 1946 to 4.3 in 1976, and may reach 4.9 in 1990. The 1.05 million industrial workers represent 24.5 per cent of the total population (as against 13.7 in Poland as a whole), and they contribute some 23 per cent of the country's industrial output. Investments have been high throughout the post-war period: 65 per cent of all industrial investment, 1946-9; 45 per cent, 1950-60; and 27 per cent, 1961-70. Development has tended to favour the fringe districts of East-Opole to the north-west, Czestochowa to the north-east, Bielsko Biala to the south-east and Rybnik to the south-west. Even so, considerable decentralization has been necessary to relieve the central axis (Zone A) from Gliwice to Chrzanow, with an area of 3,150 square kilometres and a population density of 856 per square kilometre. Movement has taken place into the adjacent Zone B with its new towns of Tarnowskie Gory and Tychy. The importance of the basic industries (coal, chemicals, engineering, metallurgy, and power) has declined slightly in

Figure 6.7 The Upper Silesian industrial region, 1914–75

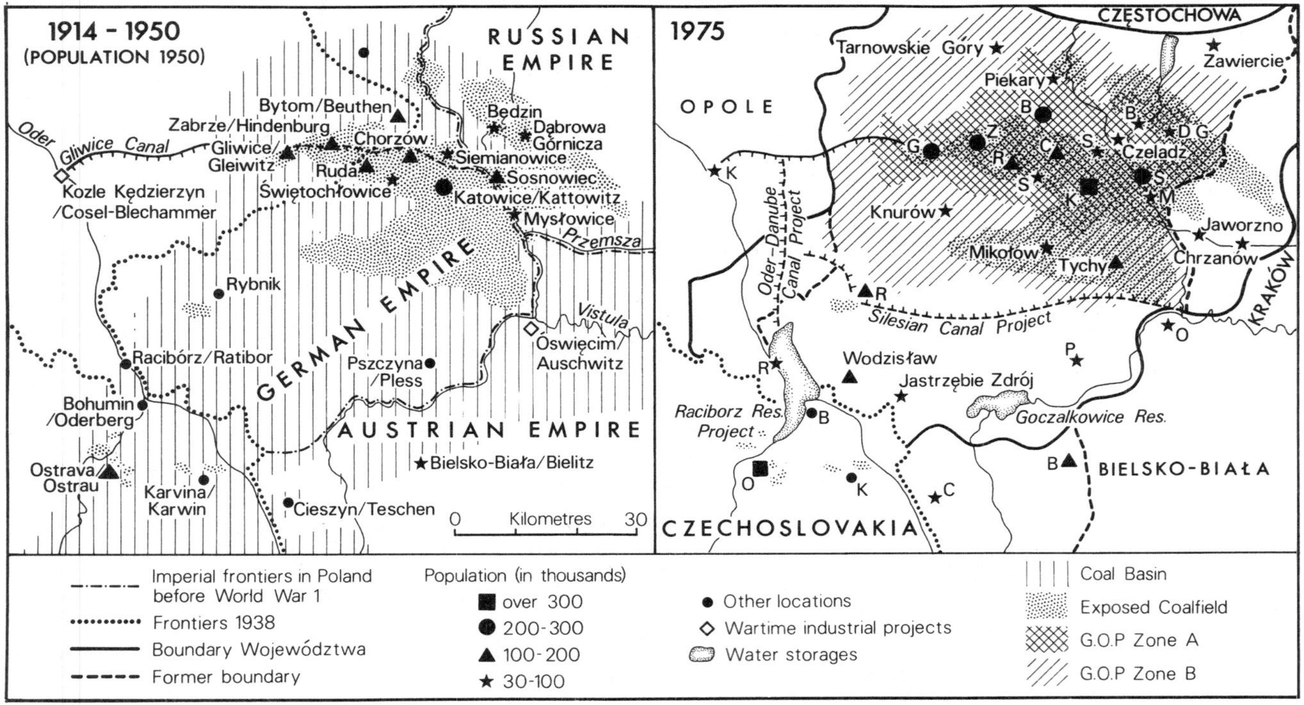

Source: Turnock 1978: 211.

the centre (from 87.3 per cent of all employment in industry in 1960 to 78.5 in 1976) but increased in the fringe area (59.5 per cent to 68.6), leaving the high level of specialization in the core region as a whole little changed. In 1976 the basic industries accounted for 78.5 per cent of all industrial employment, compared with only 56.0 for the whole of Poland.

Post-war investment in metallurgy has been made first at Czestochowa, where a large increase in domestic iron ore production was anticipated. When it became clear that heavy dependence on Soviet ores would be inevitable, further investment was put into a new suburb of Krakow (Nova Huta). A location close to the Soviet border was rejected in preference for the eastern edge of the Upper Silesian industrial region. The extensive riverside site finally selected was close to the main-line railway but the main interest in the Krakow area was to boost the influence of the proletariat in a city embracing traditional bourgeois values. Still more recently, political support for Upper Silesia has been seen subsequently in the decision to build the new Katowice metallurgical complex at Dabrowa Gornicza, as already noted. It appears from the decision to locate on the edge of Upper Silesia resulted from the personal associations of the minister with Dabrowa Gornicza. No account was apparently taken of the cost of transport of iron ore (eventually requiring a specially-built broad-gauge railway) from the Soviet frontier or the expenses of supplying clean industrial water, or the risks of pollution to the nearby Ojcow National Park. Furthermore, the very site of the new works, allegedly the minister's childhood playground, was an attractive area of woodland with a varied flora and fauna much appreciated for hunting and general recreation as part of Upper Silesia's green belt. Decentralization is more evident in Poland's non-ferrous metallurgical industry. The long-standing involvement in the production of lead and zinc (located principally at Bukowno, Miasteczko Slaskie, and Szopien in Upper Silesia) has been complemented by recent exploitation of copper ores in the Legnica-Glogow area. Work began on a new mine (Sieroszewice) in 1977 to supplement the output from Lubin, Polkowice, and Rudna but like other development projects of the 1970s this plan to increase the output of electrolytic copper to 500,000 tonnes in 1985 has proved over-ambitious. Moreover, the aluminium smelter opened at Skawina near Krakow in 1960 (using electric power generated on the

217

coalfield) has recently been closed as a result of strong pressure by environmentalists during the Solidarity era: like Nova Huta, the smelter was a major source of pollution.

Metallurgical industries and regional development: Yugoslavia

Poland has done little to relocate her metallurgical industries in the interest of regional development. By contrast Yugoslavia has implemented a policy of dispersal in the context of very serious inherited inequalities between the constituent republics. The country is of course unique in having an effective federal system which enables each republic to seek its own stake in the basic industries. Ever since the first Five Year Plan was formulated the avoidance of uneven development has been emphasized, and federal funds have been pumped into the underdeveloped regions. The Soviet blockade of 1948-54 had a significant short-term impact through the avoidance of locations in Slovenia, Croatia and Vojvodina (and large cities in general) in preference to dispersal among smaller towns situated on the railway system well away from the Bulgarian, Hungarian, and Romanian frontiers. The Belgrade-Bor and Karlovac-Sarajevo-Dubrovnik axes allowed metals (copper and steel) and components to be shuttled between numerous separate manufacturers located according to suitable infrastructure. A range of industries has been established in Montenegro including steel (Niksic), aluminium (Titograd), engineering (Titograd), paper and cellulose (Ivangrad), woollen textiles (Bijelo Polje), cement (Pljevlja) and lead-zinc flotation (Mojkovac).

The modern metallurgical industry in Yugoslavia began with the late nineteenth century development of steel works in Slovenia at Jesenice and Ravne because fuel was available at certain locations on the railways between the Styrian iron ore field and the shipyards of Trieste. There was also an iron industry at Vares in Bosnia in 1891 which developed as a result of the Habsburg occupation (later annexation) of that province. During the inter-war years there was some expansion at Jesenice (blast furnaces and steel works), Ravne (rolling mill), and Store (rolling mill and steel works). However, the Slovenian plant was supplemented by steel and rolling capacity at Smederevo on the Danube near Belgrade in 1937. Steel produced from pig iron and scrap was forwarded to engineering works at Kragujevac, Krusevac, and Smederevska Palanca. Then, in 1938, with growing instability in Eastern Europe and a need to support munitions industries with additional iron and steel output from secure locations, Zenica in Bosnia was equipped with steel furnaces and a rolling mill while blast furnaces were erected at Majdanpek in Serbia and at Sisak and Topusko Beslinac in Croatia. Production advanced from the 1918 levels of 0.04 million tonnes of pig iron and 0.15 million tonnes of steel to 0.10 and 0.31 respectively in 1939. Positive plans envisaged the continued operation of existing works, for despite their peripheral position the Slovenian works produced high-quality goods and had their fuel and power supply problems eased by delivery of bituminous coal from Rasa in Istria, supplementing the Trbovlje brown coal and Velenje lignite, and the production of hydroelectricity which encouraged the installation of electric steel furnaces in the area (also at Sibenik in 1947). Rasa coal was also being delivered to the country's other metallurgical centres in the mid-1950s. However, it was also decided that Bosnia should have a new integrated plant at Doboj: only limestone was available in the immediate vicinity but with the completion of new railways (Banja Luka-Doboj-Tuzla) iron ore could be supplied from Ljubija and coke from Lukavac in the Kreka/Tuzla coalfield. Additional coal and iron ore could be supplied from Zenica and Vares respectively. The location was also convenient for the supply of finished products to markets in central and southern Yugoslavia.

The expulsion of Yugoslavia from the Cominform in 1948 created a new situation. Soviet assistance was withdrawn, requiring consideration of less costly ways of increasing production, and external pressure on the country (to generate conflict between the constituent republics of Yugoslavia) suggested a strategy of dispersal to give each part of the federation a stake in the industry. Zenica became an integrated plant for Bosnia while the supply of fuel from the adjacent oil refinery gave further rationality to the Sisak plant in Croatia, using Lukavac and imported coke and Ljubija/Vares ore. Installation of a steel works and a tube mill at Sisak was related to demand for pipes in the Croatian natural gas field. Meanwhile, the harnessing of hydroelectricity created a basis for electric steel-making at Niksic in Montenegro (1956), converting pig and scrap railed in from Bosnia: the transport and production costs were extremely high but the steel mill has contributed to the growth of engineering in the area. The need to depend on domestic fuel and power suggested a considerable expansion of electric steel-making - at Smederevo (Serbia) Ilijas (Bosnia) and Skopje (Macedonia), as well as the other locations already mentioned. Further development at Skopje was related to the low-grade Macedonian ore and coke manufactured in Kosovo. Although exploitation of low-grade resources is costly, there is some reduction of pressure on the iron ore of Bosnia and on the national railway system. Finally, Smederevo has become an integrated unit with the installation of blast furnaces in which natural gas from Banat could be used to supplement coke.

Such was the fifteen-year plan for the iron and steel industry launched in 1958 (with the terminal year brought forward from 1973 to 1969 in 1964). Dispersal has some political and strategic advantages, but it also encourages the development of engineering industries, as in Montenegro where factories have appeared in Bileca, Cetinje, and Trebinje, as well as the republic's capital of Titograd, since the Niksic steel works opened. However, most works are too small to enjoy economies of scale. Some small units have closed: the Ilijas electric furnace opened in 1956 but was closed in 1968, while the late inter-war units at Majdanpek and Topusko Beslinac did not apparently re-open after the Second World War. There are still, however, too many units of production in relation to the total output of steel of 2.0 million tonnes, which could all come from a single plant. However, pig iron and steel production has been brought quite closely into line, thus avoiding the anomalous state of affairs in the inter-war period when iron ore was exported and pig iron imported. The supply of furnace fuel has been a problem: indeed, the Yugoslav industry is gravely weakened by lack of coking coal. Even the Rasa coal is unsuitable for coking without the removal of ash and some mixing with imported coal. Still less satisfactory has been the coking of domestic coal Lukavac (Tuzla) in 1952 and Zenica in 1954. Imported fuel is again needed with high transport costs involved in the journey to Lukavac and thence (as coke) to Jesenice and Sisak.

The significance of the federal system of government for industrial location is seen in the aluminium industry with alumina/aluminium works located at Mostar (Bosnia and Hercegovina), Kidricevo (Slovenia), Sibenik (Croatia), and Titograd (Montenegro). Sibenik was functioning before the revolution, drawing bauxite from Drnis and hydroelectricity from the Krka River scheme. However, immediate post-war planning identified Strnisce near Ptuj in Slovenia as a second location for there were premises available at a German wartime plant, while Hungary could supply bauxite and power would come from the nearby Drava River stations. The result would be an increased supply of metal to the rolling mills in Sibenik, where capacity was double the local smelter output, yet where smelting could not be increased at the time because of an electricity shortage which was not overcome until the grid was extended in 1955. The plan was however upset by the blockade and the need to switch to bauxite from Istria, some 270 kilometres away. However, in the present context of a national electricity supply system, the Slovenian industry is of course less rational. It is not without significance that the chief federal planner at the time was B. Kidric and that Strnisce was renamed Kidricevo!

The industrial location policy has not been a great success, however. All three regions with above average incomes in 1947 (the republics of Croatia and Slovenia and the autonomous region of Vojvodina) have made further progress against the national average, and the regions below the average in 1947 have fallen further back except for Macedonia and Serbia. Rates of GNP per capita have actually widened progressively during the post-war period. The value for the backward areas as a whole (Bosnia-Hercegovina, Kosovo, Macedonia, and Montenegro) was 77.2 per cent of the national figure in 1947, but 66.3 in 1960, 63.1 in 1970, and 59.5 in 1980. In the rest of the country the values rose from 109.9 to 116.5, 119.6, and 123.5. The extremes can be seen in Slovenia with a rise from 163.3 to 203.6 and in Kosovo with a decline from 50.4 to 29.1, despite the political pressures to soften Albanian protest through economic development. All that can be said of the regional policy is that without it contrasts might be greater still. (20)

Plainly there are major variations (through transport costs and labour productivity) in the efficiency of different locations for industry, and a government that wishes to maximize national growth rates cannot easily solve deep-seated regional problems simultaneously. In some respects, perhaps federalism in Yugoslavia has been economically unhelpful, reflecting merely a shift in the Party's domination from the centre to the regions. Autarkic prestige projects have left the country with many new factories running at below full capacity and as each republic struggles to protect its own regional economy the national market is virtually fragmented into eight competitive units. Nevertheless, further progress must be made in the backward areas of Yugoslavia to extend industrialization to a larger number of centres (in such a way as to retain economies of scale) along with the expansion of the tertiary sector. However, an important complementary effort is needed in agriculture: credit is available to purchase equipment suitable for small family farms but strict control of farm size frustrates any great increase in efficiency. These restrictions 'seem to satisfy ideological and psychological needs rather than rational economic purposes.' (21) Morever, presentation by the Yugoslav media of a more balanced view of the relative advantages of rural and urban life might reduce some of the pressures of rural-urban migration in future. (22)

Chapter Seven

SOCIALIST AGRICULTURE AND THE DRIVE FOR SELF-SUFFICIENCY

Despite substantial improvements in output, agriculture remains a serious problem in Eastern Europe (Table 7.1) (1). Production has increased by around 3 per cent per annum between 1952 and 1982 (actually 3.4 in Bulgaria, 2.8 in Hungary, 2.9 in Romania, and 2.7 in Yugoslavia) and per capita increases have also been significant (2.7, 2.4, 1.7 and 2.0 respectively for the four countries already referred to). However, such has been the growth of demand that a food surplus has been converted into a deficit. Eastern Europe has a long history as an agricultural exporter and over the period 1934-8 net exports were equivalent to the production from 3.74 million ha (6.4 per cent of the total area of 58.30). By 1962-6, however, there was a net import, equivalent to the output from 2.97 million ha (5.9 per cent of the total land area of 50.56 million ha). (2) Production has kept pace with the growth of population over the post-war decades but it has not fully satisfied rising demand and expectations. Communist governments try to maintain credibility at home and abroad, and when radical reforms are constrained by Soviet strategic requirements there remains the easy option of raising real wages so that a sense of prosperity can then strengthen the government's legitimacy. However, given existing living standards and restrictions on personal spending (East Europeans cannot usually own real estate and home ownership must respect the official standards regulating per capita living space which prevents extensions to houses or the merging of apartments), most of the increased spending power is directed to consumer goods and foodstuffs. Agriculture cannot respond immediately and significant increases in

Table 7.1 Production of major crops, 1961-85

Country	Yield (quintals per hectare) and production (million tonnes) for:							
	Cereals				Potatoes			
	1961-5		1981-5		1961-5		1981-5	
Albania	10.6	0.29	28.6	1.02	73.1	0.03	83.9	0.13
Bulgaria	19.0	4.86	41.4	8.55	86.0	0.40	106.3	0.42
Czechoslovakia	21.8	5.66	43.2	10.90	114.0	5.63	185.7	3.59
GDR	25.3	5.97	41.4	10.37	166.0	12.07	205.9	9.95
Hungary	20.3	6.90	49.5	14.41	79.0	2.00	182.1	1.44
Poland	17.0	15.43	27.4	22.23	154.0	43.68	167.0	36.59
Romania	15.9	11.10	34.4	21.70	85.0	2.60	192.3	5.75
Yugoslavia	17.3	3.80	39.0	16.77	87.0	2.71	92.5	2.57
Eastern Europe	23.7	54.01	36.5	105.95	139.6	69.12	166.9	60.44

	Sugar beet				Sunflowers			
	1961-5		1981-5		1961-5		1981-5	
Albania	172.1	0.08	371.2	0.32	10.3	*	15.1	0.04
Bulgaria	205.0	1.44	220.9	1.11	13.4	0.34	17.9	0.46
Czechoslovakia	270.0	6.28	244.6	7.30			17.4	0.04
GDR	243.0	5.37	287.1	7.09				
Hungary	246.0	3.09	382.2	4.45	9.6	0.11	20.2	0.61
Poland	268.0	11.44	330.3	15.61				
Romania	149.0	2.64	217.1	6.07	11.1	0.50	16.0	0.79
Yugoslavia	279.0	2.34	426.6	6.12	16.5	0.21	18.3	0.21
Eastern Europe	244.3	32.68	324.6	48.07	12.2	1.16	18.4	2.15

Source: FAO yearbooks.

Note: * denotes a total less than 0.01.

Table 7.2 Agricultural output, employment, and investment 1960-80

Country	1960 A	B	C	D	1970 A	B	C	D	1980 A	B	C	D
Albania	44.4	71.3	1.6	0.3	34.5	62.0	1.8	0.5	n.a.	55.9	n.a.	n.a.
Bulgaria	32.2	55.5	1.7	1.2	22.6	35.7	1.6	0.9	16.5	18.1	1.1	0.9
Czechoslovakia	14.7	25.9	1.8	1.5	10.1	18.3	1.8	1.5	7.3	13.1	1.8	1.6
GDR	16.4	17.3	1.1	0.9	11.6	13.0	1.1	1.3	8.5	10.6	1.2	1.1
Hungary	30.8	38.9	1.1	0.6	17.7	26.4	1.5	1.5	15.8	18.2	1.2	0.5
Poland	30.3	44.2	1.5	0.6	17.5	34.7	2.0	1.3	15.3	28.5	1.9	1.1
Romania	34.9	65.6	1.9	0.7	19.1	49.3	2.6	1.1	14.5	30.5	2.1	0.7
Yugoslavia	25.0	56.2	2.2	0.9	18.3	49.8	2.7	0.7	14.8	32.3	2.2	0.4

Sources: Wadekin, 1977 (note 1) and statistical yearbooks.

Notes: A - Contribution of agriculture and forestry to national income (per cent);
B - Ditto, employment;
C - B divided by A;
D - Agriculture and forestry's share of state investment divided by A;
n.a. - not available.

output may not be possible if they are going to depend on imported cereals and fodder. Problems in Poland in the 1970s arose out of a food supply system which was inadequate to cope with rising urban incomes. Only in Hungary has agriculture done particularly well, accounting for a quarter of all exports (one-third for convertible currency trade). The domestic food supply situation frequently astonishes visitors from other socialist countries: it is not usually necessary to queue for meat and supplies are available in shops right up to closing time.

Because of the emphasis placed on economies of scale, in contrast to the stimulation of initiative and innovation by dedicated workers, agriculture has been severely embarrassed by the political imperative of Party control over the means of production. Also in so far as Marxist theory has been relevant to the decision to create collective/co-operative and state farms, then it has plainly been suspect through exaggerated expectations of productivity gains to follow simply from the abolition of private ownership, overlooking the problem of dependence of agriculture on the residual labour force which has lacked the ability or motivation to migrate to the towns, to say nothing of the difficulty of supervising a spatially scattered work-force (Table 7.2). (3) Yields on state farms in Poland are only a quarter higher than those on private farms, although the margin should be approximately 40 per cent when allowance is made for the better quality of land and the disproportionately high levels of investment in fertilizers and machinery. (4) Reorganization of state farms into smaller units could be helpful and would make a great difference in the northern and western territories where at least a quarter of all agricultural land falls to such farms. The private sector also requires some reorganization, especially in areas where the density of the agricultural population is high and investment levels low, yet where good soils offer considerable potential given further rural-urban migration.

Many of the farm workers have few qualifications and only limited motivation. Agriculture should be seen as a worthwhile career but talented young people are easily prejudiced against farm employment partly by the experience of 'patriotic work', with minimal pay and poor working conditions, to secure the harvest, and partly by the attitudes of parents and teachers. Peasant parents often feel ashamed if their children choose to stay on the land: by

Table 7.3 Socialist agriculture, 1950-80

Country	Year	State Farms		Collective farms		National Farm land involved (per cent)
		A	B	A	B	
Bulgaria	1950	90	0.77	2,501	0.23	11.4
	1960	67	5.62	932	4.86	99.0
	1970	156	6.00	744	5.50	99.6
	1980	283	16.87	19	n.a.	n.a.
Czecho-slovakia	1950	182	0.49	3,138	0.31	27.1
	1960	365	0.31	10,816	0.45	87.2
	1970	336	4.26	6,270	0.68	90.0
	1980	200	10.50	1,722	2.50	92.7
GDR	1950	559	0.32	1,906	0.11	5.7
	1960	669	0.59	19,313	0.28	92.4
	1970	511	0.87	9,009	0.60	93.5
	1980	469	0.87	3,946	1.28	94.5
Hungary	1950	454	1.48	2,185	0.20	30.6
	1960	333	2.91	4,265	0.86	79.2
	1970	180	5.55	2,441	1.98	94.3
	1980	131	7.59	1,338	3.48	n.a.
Poland	1950	5,679	0.25	635	0.30	10.4
	1960	5,734	0.38	1,668	0.14	13.1
	1970	5,356	0.52	1,071	0.26	16.1
	1980	2,096	1.67	2,286	0.37	25.1
Romania	1950	363	2.07	1,027	0.28	23.6
	1960	560	3.07	13,685	0.56	81.9
	1970	370	5.64	4,626	1.96	90.8
	1980	407	5.00	4,011	2.26	90.6
Yugo-slavia	1950	858	0.43	15,605	0.13	31.6
	1960	475	0.63	4,233	0.17	24.1
	1970	270	1.32	1,102	0.56	30.1
	1980	n.a	n.a.	4,853	0.34	16.8

Table 7.3 continued

Sources: C.E. Miller and others (1973) Agricultural Statistics
of Eastern Europe and the Soviet Union, Washington, DC: US
Department of Agriculture; H. Trend (1974) Agriculture in
Eastern Europe: A Comparative Study, Munich: Radio Free
Europe; FAO yearbooks.

Notes: A - Number of units; B - Average size '000 ha; n.a. -
not available. The nearest available figures have been used
for 1950 in the cases of Czechoslovakia, GDR, and Hungary.
The 1980 figures for Yugoslavia cover both categories of
farm.

contrast professional careers carry the all-important seal of
approval; and schoolteachers may try and stimulate
backward pupils by asserting that a poor scholastic
performance leaves little choice of employment other than
the co-operative farm. The GDR has probably been most
successful in expanding agricultural output within the
confines of the socialist system. Farm workers seem better
integrated into the collectives and state farms than their
Soviet counterparts. They may keep a few chickens in their
gardens but they purchase most of their food requirements
and do not spend long hours cultivating private plots. They
appear satisfied with production incentives which
effectively tie personal ambitions to the success of the
collective in meeting or exceeding plan targets. Yet even
here there are problems in raising production to meet rising
demand. Should more incentives be offered to farm workers
or should there be sharp price rises to reduce demand?
Neither course would be palatable to a regime which prides
itself on the purity of its socialist system and the stability
of prices.

FARM ORGANIZATION

Current organizational trends can be seen in two very
different ways (Table 7.3). First there is a tendency to
amalgamate co-operative and state farms to create very
large enterprises. 'Gigantism' was a characteristic of the
1970s, seeking economies of scale, easier supervision from
the centre (given a smaller number of units), and economic
viability (combining stronger and weaker co-operatives). (5)

There is no consensus on optimum farm size, any more than there is with optimum populations for towns, but most farms would fall into the range 4,000-25,000 ha. Thus, in the Nitra area of Czechoslovakia there is now an Agrokomplex comprising eight large enterprises operating over 45,000 ha. It has an important research function developing new technology, combatting crop diseases, and looking at ways of using manure to replace chemical fertilizers. Practical training is provided for students from the Third World who enroll at the agricultural college in Nitra. However, large-scale organization is also developing for normal production purposes and developments in Bulgaria and the GDR may be noted. On the other hand it is necessary to stimulate individual enterprise so that farming on small peasant holdings (still very numerous in Poland and Yugoslavia) and on co-operative-farm household plots can be as intensive as possible. The smallholding system may also be extended to areas which are inaccessible to heavy farm-machinery: 200,000 ha of such land in Slovakia is worked as small fruit and vegetable farms. Most of the information on small farms is, however, drawn from Hungary and Poland.

Large farms: Bulgaria and the GDR

Bulgaria's New Economic Mechanism has some relevance to agriculture through the aim of greater efficiency in planning coupled with some increase in the independence of the individual farms, without however permitting the same scope for price-fixing allowed under the Hungarian system. However, Bulgaria has pressed ahead with very large farming organizations known as Agricultural-Industrial Complexes (Agro-Promishleni Kompleksi). The idea is to achieve horizontal integration, bringing together farms with the same soil climatic and terrain conditions. This is expected to lead to a general increase in yield and more efficient use of land, given advanced technology in agriculture which made it feasible to undertake large-scale production of various commodities: irrigation systems, new milking equipment and poultry farming complexes were all part of the new agriculture. (6) Indeed, the significance of industry in the title of the new enterprise would appear to relate generally to modern technology with its industrial character rather than the inclusion of manufacturing units within the organization, although the latter is not ruled out.

The AICs follow a consolidation of co-operatives from 3,290 (almost one for each town and village in the country) in 1958 to 972 by the end of 1959, with an increase in average size from 1,153 to 4,186 ha. By 1969 there was a further reduction to 795 with 5,118 ha of arable land each on average (compared with 6,000 ha for state farms, which numbered 156). Increased specialization developed spontaneously during the late 1960s and then the first official recommendation for 'combines' came in 1968 by which time one complex had been set up at Ivaylovgrad consisting of five state farms with a total of 18,425 ha of arable. By the end of 1969 there were two further complexes in Targovishte and a combine near Plovdiv associated with the <u>Vitamina</u> canning factory. The Party approved the AIC concept in 1970 and by the end of that year 170 AICs had been set up averaging 28,000 ha of land and 6,200 workers. A national AIC was set up in 1977 and is the largest economic management complex in the country, producing 27 per cent of GNP, 32 per cent of all exports, and 45 per cent of all goods supplied to the home market. The national complex had already existed for some years <u>de facto</u> but even so there must still be some doubts about its capacity to operate efficiently. At the national level the AIC links producer with consumer through connections with the food and tobacco industries. Industrial links are also maintained through the supply of chemicals and machinery.

It is not the intention to restrict each AIC to a single enterprise but rather to consolidate different enterprises within each farm. The AIC at Slivo Poe near Ruse has 18,700 ha of arable land with chernozem soil suitable for cereals, fodder, sugar beet and vegetables. Other land is devoted to herds of 2,500 cows and 16,000 sheep, with new buildings provided for milking and for the fattening of young animals. Greenhouses supply tomatoes and cucumbers to the fresh market and also provide the raw material for two canning factories which are part of the complex. With twelve villages distributed over its territory the complex has to deploy labour carefully and has motor transport at its disposal. Meanwhile, very large complexes may develop close links with manufacturing. The first Industrial-Agricultural Complex (IAC), named <u>Dimitur Blahoev</u>, was formed in 1973 and combined Ruse sugar refinery and two AICs: 40,000 ha of land and refinery capacity of 400,000 tonnes per annum. The entire production cycle is covered. The year 1977 then saw the creation of an IAC at Harmanli for the production of silk. The enterprise manages some 800 ha of mulberry plantations and produces silkworm seed at Berkovitsa, Plovdiv, and Vratsa, as well as Harmanli. Continuous growth of cocoon production has been secured amounting to some 200 tonnes per annum. Mulberry plantations are being extended to 1,400 ha in 1985 and old trees are being replaced on the original plantations while the breeding of silkworms makes use of an automated Japanese process.

Amalgamations have in some cases become quite remarkable. The Silistra project of 1974 consolidated six AICs into one AIC and one IAC for grain/livestock and fruit/vegetable enterprises respectively, and two years later the two units merged into a single AIC which brought almost the entire territory of one administrative region into a single farm, more than six times larger than the average AIC. Irrigation systems have been installed since 1977 and western firms have been approached to help modernize the complex in other ways. However, farm amalgamation can be counter-productive where activities are dispersed and incapable of efficient co-ordination by managers. Attempts at concentrating work may involve the construction of new buildings, at considerable expense, leaving some of the existing accommodation unused. At Botevgrad near Sofia it has been found that the specialists and managers have been placed at the centre of the complex while only limited leadership and supervision is provided in the villages, which previously acted as farm centres with their own directors. Moreover, the complex has been organized according to enterprises and several of these may be carried out in any one locality, but without any co-ordination that might allow labour to be transferred between them when special needs arise. To avoid the problems of overconcentration the number of AICs increased to some 280 by 1981, when the average arable holding was 13.2 thousand ha employing 2,850 people.

For the GDR, Freeman has described the situation around Berlstedt, where there is close co-operation between the local collective (LPG), two adjacent collectives (Hottelstedt and Vippachedelhausen), and a state farm (VEG) at Neumark. The four units have taken responsibility for a specific area of specialized production and certain enterprises have been given up altogether. (7) While Vippachedelhausen concentrates on cropping (including sugar beet and vegetables on irrigated land) Berlstedt specializes in dairy cattle, Hottelstedt in poultry and Neumark in pigs. In this way modern machinery can be used efficiently and the most suitable livestock units can be provided. Such arrangements are now quite typical in the GDR. Some combine collectives with state farms, as at Berlstedt, and this results in an 'Inter-Enterprise Institution' (Zwischenbetriebliche Einrichtung or ZBE), while others involve a group of collectives only, resulting in an 'Inter-Collective Institution' (Zwischengenossenschaftliche Einrichtung or ZGE). In the process it has been possible for small collectives to be absorbed into stronger units. Thus, a small LPG at Neumark has become attached to the VEG in the same village and another small collective at Stedten has joined the larger LPG at Berlstedt. Further co-operation can be arranged through a link between farm production and food processing when the output of a particular product (say, milk or sugar beet) is sufficiently large. Such an arrangement constitutes a 'Co-operative Association' (Kooperationsverband or KOV). The specialized LPG at Berlstedt receives heifers in calf from a state breeding station in the Harz Mountains (VEG Nordhausen) and supplies calves in return. Fresh milk is supplied to the dairy in Erfurt and by-products from this factory go to a fodder plant which in turn supplies the Berlstedt farm. Pigs from Neumark go to the abattoir in Weimar and grain from Vippachedelhausen goes to the local flour mill. Specialization may go too far in some cases and create diseconomies through ecological problems. Specialization also seems to have led to some serious problems of labour scarcity at times of peak demand now that the agricultural work-force has been reduced to less than 0.60 million. There is less scope than there used to be for workers to be transferred from one enterprise to another to meet seasonal fluctuations in demand. Because of these difficulties there are plans to give more prominence to mixed arable and pastoral farming.

The small-farm problem

In Romania the remaining private smallholders are now obliged to sell all their animals, in a live condition, to the state at prices set by the authorities. This amounts to a return to the system of compulsory deliveries, introduced when the communists first came to power, but abandoned by

Table 7.4 Agricultural population of Yugoslavia, 1953–81

Year	A	B	Agricultural population					Active population in agriculture			
			C	D	E	F	G	H	J	K	L
1953	10.32	154.1	2.9	-16.3	-0.3	-203.8	-3.9	5.36	57.7	n.a.	68.4
1961	9.20	121.0	1.6	-17.7	-0.2	-243.0	-3.1	4.69	57.0	41.6	56.2
1971	7.25	54.3	0.7	-8.0	-0.1	-241.1	-2.9	3.90	56.7	52.5	43.5
1981	4.55	-5.3	-0.1	-1.3	*	-264.6	-4.5	2.62	53.7	70.0	26.2

Source: Statistical yearbooks.

A – Total (millions);
B – Average annual natural increase (thousands);
C – Ditto per thousand of the population;
D – Average annual net migration (thousands);
E – Ditto per thousand of the population;
F – Average annual transfer of employment (thousands);
G – Ditto per thousand of the population;
H – Total (millions);
J – Percentage male;
K – Percentage aged over 40;
L – Percentage of the total active population of the country;
* – denotes a total less than 0.1;

the 1960s. Illegal dealings in livestock are minimized by heavy penalties for illicit sale or slaughter and by a strict system of registration for newly born animals. With the present regime of state contracts some peasants prefer to concentrate on the production of hay (which can be sold to large farms in the lowlands when they face a fodder shortage) rather than rear livestock that is well adapted to local conditions. Although local authorities are supposed to encourage the individual farmer the constraints on effective stimulation are such as to minimize their integration into the councils which often co-ordinate the activities of state and co-operative farms within particular areas.

Even in Yugoslavia the situation is unsatisfactory. The socialist sector is small, covering only 1.5 million ha in contrast with 10.01 for private farms. However while 58.9 per cent of the land in socialist farms involves units larger than 50,000 ha holdings smaller than 5 ha (74.7 per cent of all private farms) cover 40.5 per cent of all non-socialist land. The average size of private farms, which fell from 5.5 ha in 1931 and 4.6 ha in 1949 to 4.2 ha in 1960 (after the reduction of the maximum holding to 10 ha in 1953) has continued to decline to 3.9 in 1969 and 3.5 in 1981. There is little incentive for young people, so the proportion of illiterates is relatively high and the general educational standard is low since parents send the more successful children to schools which provide training for non-farm occupations (Table 7.4). All this hinders the introduction of new agricultural technologies, which require a certain level of education. Since 1975 Slovenia has allowed private farmers to work as much as 20 ha of land in areas higher than 200 metres provided that two-thirds of it was placed under wheat; and where the farm is in the mountains and concerned with livestock breeding, holdings up to 45 ha are permitted. Similar changes have been contemplated in Croatia and Serbia but problems will remain over the hiring of non-family labour, which is presently forbidden in the interest of supressing 'capitalist relationships'. Meanwhile, the flight from the land continues, with almost universal rural populations decline. Much land is wasted on the Adriatic coast as terraces deteriorate and fields revert to juniper scrub. (8)

Encouraging the small producer in Hungary and Poland

Although almost all the land in Hungary is in the hands of co-operatives and state farms, the government has encouraged individual enterprise on private plots which can be used in conjunction with various collective projects. At the same time The New Economic Mechanism in Hungarian agriculture reduces the role of the state in fixing prices, thus allowing the prices of seasonal products to follow market trends. Farms will have much more scope for independent action so as to maximize their potential to meet consumer demand and at the same time to raise living standards in the countryside. (9) Some 40 per cent of all Hungarian families now work household plots, assisted by the improved supply of machinery suitable for small farms. In some areas private farmers have the opportunity to loan equipment from state farms where there is spare capacity. One co-operative (Ocsa near Budapest) allocates private plots on the basis of the number of cows each member agrees to look after (0.75 ha per animal), while another (Pastzo in Nograd county) leases vineyards to individuals in units of 1,500 square metres as part of a scheme which could enable the total area of vineyards to increase over the steep hill slopes of Badacsony and Tokaj.

In a number of villages in north-eastern Hungary (Szabolcs-Szatmar), co-operatives have planted orchards and arranged for routine spraying while contracting out the everyday tending of the trees and the picking of the fruit to private farmers who can work in the knowledge that there is a guaranteed outlet for the produce at the end of the day. Further, in several wine-growing areas, co-operative farms have rejuvenated old vineyards on private plots. On the Nagyrede co-operative in the Eger wine district, more than 200 ha of private-plot vineyards suitable for large-scale production technology are tended by more than a thousand co-operative members. A similar approach may be taken to irrigated vegetable growing and pig farming. A co-operative near Sopron in Hungary has made arrangements with several hundred gardeners and smallholders (with their main employment in the secondary and tertiary sectors) for the supply of grapes, vegetables, and poultry. Business is particularly brisk on account of proximity to the Austrian border and the existence of a local border traffic association which expedites limited international trade on a relatively informal basis. State farms in Hungary have made similar arrangements with small producers. The Mezotur farm near Szolnok has started to lease out buildings and pastures on remote parts of the farm so that would-be part-time farmers can engage in useful work. Further co-operation can take the form of fodder deliveries to the smallholder and this form of assistance has enabled the Kiskoros state farm to recruit more than a thousand part-time workers for fattening livestock.

Despite the disappearance of the old Stalinist prejudice against private-plot farming, typical of the Rakosi era, there is still some attitude of ambivalence. The urban population is pleased that the food supply has improved, but when people see the new houses and consumer goods which successful farmers can now afford there is a belief that private plots must be 'gold mines': hence the need for 'education' to establish the legitimacy of the materialist ambitions of the rural dwellers and to encourage the latter to direct their affluence along socially acceptable channels. Higher taxes on the peasants, like those imposed in 1974, can easily sap incentive and result in a reduced output of fruit, pig meat, and vegetables.

In Poland, where the individual peasant farmer has an important stake, the policies of the state are again generally stimulative. The authorities claim that the old ideological distinction between socialized and private agriculture is no longer important: the most relevant factor is the standard of farming, which can only improve with adequate attention to the rural infrastructure. It is therefore acknowledged that family farms make more effective use of inputs than state farms. The increase in harvest resulting from the application of fertilizer has been reckoned at nearly four times greater on private family farms than on state farms. (10) However, there are social costs incurred through long hours of work. The number of family farms in Poland is falling (3.2 million in 1970, but 2.8 in 1985) and the land occupied has also fallen from 15.8 to 14.4 million ha, mainly because of transfer of ownership to the state (in exchange for old-age and disability pensions) and partly because of non-agricultural developments. The average size of the farm has increased slightly from 4.9 to 5.1 ha. Farms larger than 10 ha now account for 16 per cent of all farms (and 44 per cent of the land) compared with 13 per cent in 1970, while very small farms with less than 2 ha account for 30 per cent of all farms compared with 27 per cent in 1970. There would appear to be some polarization into full-time holdings and small units which can be properly tended on a part-time basis. The government has now increased commodity prices as an incentive to farmers and incomes have risen considerably, helped also by the reduction in the farm population and gains in efficiency. Incomes for peasant farmers have risen from 24,800 zloti in 1970 to 30,000 in 1970 and 59,400 in 1979, respectively 79.5, 77.3 and 94.0 per cent of non-agricultural incomes.

There are always good opportunities for fruit and vegetable growers in the vicinity of the cities and ready markets for milk and dairy products. The demand for flowers is very considerable and a recent study of flower production in Poland reveals a massive output of carnations in the immediate surroundings of Warsaw and especially in Jablonna, where many farmers have successfully transferred from mixed-crop and livestock farming to the specialized production of flowers, grown under glass with the aid of carefully prepared manures and composts and a pure water supply which can be obtained at depths of less than 20 metres. (11) The area is close to Warsaw without being too vulnerable to suburban expansion, and an efficient local organization ensures regular supplies of coal, fertilizers, and pesticides which further encourage local specialization. There is also wide experience in marketing and many young farmers have been attracted into the area (borrowing money from the banks and from family members). With 11,800 square metres of glass per hundred hectares of farmland, Jablonna exceeds the rate for Warsaw as a whole by more than ten times (while Warsaw exceeds the national average by the same margin). Although the market in Warsaw is buoyant enough to support the heavy investment in glasshouses and the various inputs (of which coal is the most important), the concentration in Jablonna may be limited by labour supply problems (500 square metres of glass can employ two people through the year) and risks of disease which have already stimulated some diversification from carnations and chrysanthemums to alstromeria and gerberas. However, it is significant that in Poland such enterprise is possible, with private farmers employing four or five workers in addition to members of the family: this would not be possible in the Romanian context, for example, where private enterprises are restricted to the family circle. In Poland the state takes a pragmatic attitude on this ideological issues and benefits financially from high land taxes.

THE GRAIN PROBLEM: CONSTRAINTS ON PRODUCTION

The range of attitudes and approaches indicated by the previous discussion reflects a degree of pragmatism in the context of fundamental vested interests in socialist organization. The aim of the exercise is increased production, especially in cereals, which occupy a focal position. Failure to meet rising demand in this department has been a major shortcoming. While the area devoted to cereals was allowed to fall from 33.6 million ha in 1950 to 29.6 in 1980, the increase in yield, from 12.1 quintals per ha to 32.9 was not sufficient to compensate for this and to keep pace with rising demand. Hence, we see an increased dependence on imports: 9.5 per cent of total consumption of 71.3 million tonnes in 1965 but 14.2 per cent of the 1980 consumption of 113.5 (Table 7.5). Eastern Europe tended to rely initially on the Soviet Union to meet any grain deficiencies. In 1947, when the Gottwald government in Czechoslovakia tried to ease the grain shortage (caused by a poor harvest badly affected by drought) by soliciting US aid under the Marshall Plan, Stalin intervened and promised to supply grain as an act of 'selfless fraternal aid'. During the 1950s and 1960s the Soviet Union was therefore regarded as the Canada of the socialist camp, although the cost of grain from the USSR was about a quarter more expensive than grain produced at home. Over the years, however, the grain imports have increased, but difficulties with Soviet harvests forced Eastern Europe to buy from North America as well. (12) As the GDR's cereal consumption rose from 38.6 million tonnes in 1960-4 to 43.6, 56.5, and 62.0 during the three subsequent five-year periods, the percentage of imports rose from 25.1 (1960-4) to 28.2 (1975-9), while the Soviet contribution to imports fell from 94 per cent in 1963 to 11 per cent in 1979. Dependence on the west has involved much higher costs, more than double the cost of home production (2.7 being the estimate in Czechoslovakia, for instance). The need to find hard currency to pay for the bulk of the imports has imposed strains at a time when western borrowing is being more carefully controlled. Thus, a concerted effort has been made during the 1980s to reduce the level of imports.

Table 7.5 Cereal yields production and trade, 1965–85

Country	1965 A	1965 B	1965 C	1970 A	1970 B	1970 C	1975 A	1975 B	1975 C
Albania	0.32	0.3	+0.1	0.31	0.5	–	0.34	0.6	–
Bulgaria	2.30	5.2	+0.3	2.17	6.8	-0.3	2.26	7.1	+0.5
Czechoslovakia	2.46	5.3	+1.8	2.62	7.2	+1.4	2.72	9.3	+1.0
GDR	2.30	6.7	+1.7	2.29	6.5	+3.4	2.51	8.9	+3.2
Hungary	3.21	7.5	+0.5	2.99	7.6	-0.6	3.12	12.1	-1.1
Poland	8.64	16.2	+2.7	8.41	16.4	+2.4	7.86	19.8	+4.0
Romania	6.77	12.6	-0.8	5.90	10.6	-0.3	6.25	15.2	+0.2
Yugoslavia	5.15	10.6	+0.4	4.90	11.6	-0.2	4.72	15.0	–
Eastern Europe	31.15	64.5	+6.7	29.59	67.3	+5.8	29.78	88.1	+7.8
USSR	121.09	114.4	+2.3	114.18	179.2	-4.1	122.25	134.6	+12.3
USA	60.31	183.7	-41.8	72.75	186.6	-40.0	72.28	284.1	-80.2
Western Europe	24.51	57.5	+5.5	24.14	65.2	+1.0	23.75	74.0	-1.2
Japan	4.30	18.9	+19.1	3.45	17.7	+14.9	2.98	17.6	+18.8

Table 7.5 continued

| | | 1980 | | | 1985 | |
	A	B	C	A	B	C
Albania	0.40	0.87	-0.01	0.36	1.05	*
Bulgaria	2.33	8.68	+0.04	1.83	7.13	+0.45
Czechoslovakia	2.60	10.74	+2.05	2.51	11.77	+0.39
GDR	2.52	9.64	+4.01	2.51	11.54	+1.72
Hungary	3.02	13.61	+0.06	2.87	14.78	-2.14
Poland	7.86	18.34	+7.77	8.20	23.79	+2.32
Romania	6.55	20.23	+1.09	6.11	23.05	-0.12
Yugoslavia	4.28	15.27	+1.11	4.23	15.84	-0.77
Eastern Europe	29.56	97.38	+16.12	28.62	108.95	+1.85
USSR	123.97	182.81	+28.95	112.54	180.61	+41.40
USA	71.52	269.98	-110.98	72.75	346.88	-19.91
Western Europe	24.09	108.24	-6.95	23.43	121.44	-21.42
Japan	2.72	13.20	+23.65	2.71	15.86	+26.45

Source: FAO yearbooks.

Notes: A - Area sown (million hectares); B - production (million tonnes); C - Net trade (million tonnes).

The complication of livestock farming

Expanding the herds means increased cereal consumption. A better supply of meat and dairy products is needed for the consumer while the livestock sector also sustains a leather industry with outlets in western markets for high-quality footwear, gloves, and other leather goods. The Hungarian leather industry employs some 60,000 workers in approximately 100 different enterprises. Livestock farming also provides good opportunities for export, especially if processing units can satisfy the stringent hygiene regulations imposed on those exporting to the USA. Hungary has therefore modified its factories at Kapuvar and Papa to meet US requirements and the trade in ham, salami, and other high-quality pork delicacies is now buoyant. Modernization of the Kaposvar factory with western assistance will lead to a significant increase in meat exports to the USA which exceeded $20 million in 1980. There is an international dimension in animal breeding which involves not only the socialist bloc but western countries too. Co-operation in agriculture between Bulgaria and the Soviet Union has involved the crossing of Bulgarian sheep breeds with the Soviet 'Romanov' breed, the use of dairy-farming methods perfected in Soviet Estonia on Bulgarian farms (and also the use of Bulgarian seeds and seedlings in orchards and vineyards in the southern parts of the USSR). Under an agreement reached between Hungary and the Soviet Union in 1978 the Babolna poultry farm has set up four large poultry farms in the Soviet Union using its up-to-date 'Tetra' technology. Breeding cattle from North America and Western Europe have led to the genetic improvement of the Hungarian dappled cow to ensure higher milk and meat yields. French dairying methods have also been employed by several state farms in western Hungary (Devecser, Palpiszta, and Sarvar) to achieve more efficient milk production. Mention may also be made of horse breeding in Czechoslovakia, an appropriate interest for the country which holds its famous steeplechase at Pardubice. International auctions are held annually at Pisek in Bohemia and Topolcianky in Slovakia, with most interest shown by Czecholsovakia's immediate socialist neighbours including the USSR. The farms existed before the revolution. That at Topolcianky dates to 1921 and its stock includes the Hutzul breed, native to the Carpathians. However, as livestock farming has developed, the area of meadow and pasture land has been crucial and a considerable proportion of the cereal harvest has been required as animal fodder. (13)

There is of course plenty of grain in Eastern Europe to feed the population: only about a third of the harvest is required for human consumption and in this connection only a few special cereal products like macaroni need be imported. The problem arises with the livestock sector, which has been able to develop very largely on the basis of increased use of grain as animal feed. There is always a danger that progress in stock rearing will be lost through the need for excessive slaughter due to sudden cut-backs in grain consumption. In Czechoslovak agriculture, crop production lags behind livestock production, for which 80 per cent of the arable output is needed in support. The pressure to increase meat production and to meet government promises of higher living standards, coupled with unrealistic targets for domestic cereal production, have led to growing deficits. Thus, in 1976 the country imported 11.6 million tonnes of grain and protein concentrates and this supported a quarter of the total meat production (more than a third in the case of pork and poultry meat). However, greater restraint in 1981 led to a decline in the pig population in Czechoslovakia of 0.59 million in 1981 following a grain deficit of 1.5 million tonnes and this duly affected meat production the following year: reduced supplies and higher prices in 1982 reduced per capita meat consumption to 79.1 kg compared with 85.6 in 1980. There have been similar experiences in Poland. In the late 1960s the government tried to achieve self-sufficiency in grain production by increasing supplies of fertilizer and by raising procurement prices so that farmers would sell more of their own produce. The manipulation of prices had the effect of discouraging meat production. Furthermore, centralized production of fodder (involving the mixing of cereals with other feedstuffs) turned out to be much less efficient than expected: this led to higher fodder prices and, at the end of the day, to higher procurement prices for livestock. The strategy also failed to provide resources to meet harvest shortfalls: without reserves in the form of cash or raw materials (coal, timber, and so on) to allow for imports, the long-term repercussions of a poor harvest can be serious on account of the damage to animal stocks, which must be reduced in sympathy with the fodder shortage. Then, in 1982 an incentive scheme was launched to induce farmers to deliver grain that would tide the country over until the harvest, but on this occasion the stocks seem to have remained on the farms because of shortages of alternative animal fodder and also of seed grain needed for sowing.

Such short-term solutions are undesirable and what is needed is greater emphasis on those branches of livestock rearing that can be best sustained from domestic output, with fullest use of the grazings in hill and mountain country. The logic of linking livestock rearing with cereal production in the lowlands has been carried to extremes in Romania. The more prosperous co-operatives in the lowlands have made substantial investments in buildings to house animals reared on locally grown fodder. However, there are many deficiencies arising from poor building, unsatisfactory fodder preparation, and negligence by workers tending the animals. By contrast, in the hill country, with ample grazing land and a tradition in stock rearing, the best returns are obtained by selling fodder to the lowland stock farms when the best prices are obtainable. A more restrained expansion in the lowlands, balanced by intensification in the hills, would have been a more rational policy. The fodder shortage could be eased somewhat by better processing of slaughter-house refuse, more than 80 per cent of which was found going to waste in Hungary in the mid-1970s. Waste vegetables and kitchen waste could also be turned into protein and used in livestock rearing. Further economies could arise from the fullest use of soy meals, forage cake, and fish meal. Thanks to such measures in part, Poland now claims that its livestock production is based exclusively on the domestic fodder base.

Reallocation of cereal lands

The problems with cereals have been aggravated by other factors. First of all there has been a transfer of land to other farm enterprises (both agricultural and non-agricultural). Crops for industrial use have become more important and this category includes not only textile plants, sunflowers, and sugar beets but also a number of relatively localized enterprises like the production oils and tobacco in Bulgaria. The cultivation of some crops, like oleaginous roses in the Kazanlik valley of Bulgaria, is long-established, but the land area has often increased substantially over the years. Rose oil (attar of roses) was being made by the end of the seventeeth century and in 1860 enterprising merchants started to export what is now a central ingredient of the western perfume industry. Some 250 varieties of roses are now grown for processing in the factories of the Bulgarska Roza combine. Bulgarian peppermint oil, with an intense aroma and an agreeably cool taste, is widely used in the foods and medicines (for flavouring mixtures and toothpastes) as well as perfumes. Lavender oil is produced in various parts of the country and is much in demand on account of its capacity to blend with other aromatic products. Bulgaria's tobacco industry is also of national importance, with an emphasis on continuing innovation in various parts of the country. Machinery is being assimilated to harvest the small leaves of plants where ripening takes place in stages and to handle broad-leaved American tobacco which needs to be kept moist to avoid brittleness. The Bulgarians are also working on new methods of sun-drying and on the development of high-quality Oriental tobacco.

The production of fruits and vines has required more land in the post-war period. Statistics for the Kiskoros region of Hungary reveal that gardens, orchards, and vineyards have increased their share of the land from 7.5 per cent in 1897 and 19.1 in 1935 to 32.9 in 1965. (14) Non-agricultural uses have increased from 6.1 per cent and 8.2 to 12.6, while a commensurate decline is evident in arable, pasture, and woodland (86.4 per cent in 1987 to 54.5 in 1965). Of course wherever possible the new enterprises are developed on poorer, sandy land and research is continuing on the better use of such marginal land through irrigation or the mixing with loessic material which is sometimes intercalated between beds of sand. (15) Moreover, wherever there is an emphasis on local self-sufficiency, as is now the case in Romania with its policy of self-finance for the regions and communes, there is a threat to crops which are best suited to local conditions. Close to the cities vegetable production is very important and considerable effort now goes into storage (involving the latest cooling/air-regulating technology) and distribution. Further, when luxuries like chocolates are frequently scarce and expensive, flowers can be purchased at reasonable cost to meet a range of social and religious needs. Florist's shops are not particularly numerous but street stalls are very prominent and flower sellers often frequent places of evening entertainment. Large socialist organizations are involved in some areas, like Prague, where gardening at Velka Chuchle dates back the last century. The state farm has 19 ha under glass and combines flower growing with fruit and vegetable production. There is a significant export business in potted plants.

Pressure to reduce the cereal area has also come from non-agricultural uses. With urbanization some considerable transfers of land have been inevitable but it is clear that too much land has been wasted in the process because it has not been given a sufficiently high value. In the case of Romania, a typical case, the

> encroachment by builders upon agricultural land, and more particularly arable land, was facilitated by the government's policy, pursued until 1968, of treating land as a free good and assigning no value to it in calculating the cost of industrial and housing investment projects. (16)

Construction projects are now much more carefully assessed and protection measures (which date back to c. 1960 in some of the northern countries) are more rigorously imposed. In Hungary a land protection act in 1961 laid down principles for rational land use but the conversion of land from agriculture to urban-industrial uses was not carefully controlled until after the Party's declaration in 1975 that all land represents national wealth. (17) Agricultural output is also threatened in some areas by polluted air and water, and by large opencast mineral workings like the Turoszow lignite field in Poland, which covers 20 square kilometres.

Inefficiency in grain production

Another set of problems involves inefficiency in the cultivation, harvesting, and consumption of cereals. Low-yielding strains have been used for too long but now improved Soviet varieties, especially for winter wheat, have become available. 'Bezostaya-1' has been widely used in Bulgaria as a basis for new low-stalk varieties (like Ogosta, Rubin, Trakia, and Vratsa) which have contributed to higher yields. Bulgaria's Institute of Genetics has also produced a successful wheat-rye hybrid named 'Peroun', an early-ripening disease-resistant variety which also has the merit of high yield. In Hungary 'Jubilee' has resulted from the hybridization of the Hungarian 'Flyman' with the Soviet

'Bezostaya-l'. US technology has also been used in Hungary since the 1970s, at Babolna and Mezohegyes state farms for maize and sugar-beet production respectively. In 1972, just one year after the initiative was taken, workers from Babolna were recruited to carry out commission work in Czechoslovakia and the Soviet Union. Yugoslavia introduced high-yielding French and Italian wheat varieties in the 1950s and 1960s and went on to produce new domestic varieties like 'Osjecanka' and 'Zlatna Dolina', which can yield up to 10 tonnes per hectare. American maize varieties were used in the 1950s and domestic hybrids emerged in the following decade.

Reference may also be made to the failure to gain adequate returns from irrigation, frequently advocated as a solution to the problems of drought in the Balkans. (18) Initially, Bulgaria made the greatest progress and the irrigated area increased from 0.13 million ha in 1950 to 0.72 in 1960 and virtually a million in 1968. However, this was well short of the target of two million to be achieved by 1965 (according to a decree of 1959) and the present area of 1.20 million ha is way below the target of 2.90 which was set for 1980 by the Party congress in 1962 (Table 7.6). Romania has now exceeded the Bulgarian level and parts of the relatively dry south-east have been transformed (Figure 7.1). Even here, however, plans have not been fulfilled entirely. It seems that the economics of irrigation have not been fully considered. Two harvests are necessary to justify the capital investment and compensate for the loss of land arising from the irrigation installations themselves, but recent evidence suggests that output has been increased by only a fifth. Bulgaria and the Soviet Union are co-operating over irrigation work, notably through research to establish optimum watering rates for different crops and install computers to design and operate irrigation systems. A related problem is the failure to realise the full genetic potential for higher yields because the increasing fertilizer inputs have to some extent become counter-productive. Too much nitrate has been applied and soil has been compacted by excessive use of heavy-weight machinery. There have also been some quality deficiencies through excessive fertilizer applications. Thus, increases in the unwanted protein content in barley have made it unsuitable for export for brewing purposes. Rodents and diseases also affect yields. Production of oil crops in Yugoslavia was hit badly in the 1970s through disease (phomosis) for which no

Figure 7.1 Land improvement on the Lower Danube: the Bucharest area of Romania

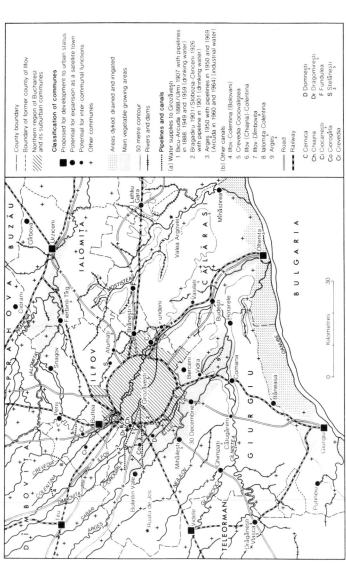

Source: Topographical maps.

immediate remedy was available: the annual average area, which reached 0.43 million ha in 1976-80, fell to 0.20 in 1981-4.

Harvesting and storage losses may account for between a third and a half of the total yield. They arise from the poor quality Soviet SK 4 harvesters constructed for low-yielding grain lands in the Soviet Union (their capacity is limited to 4 kg of grain per second). Inability to buy the best farm machinery tends to thrust Comecon members into each others' arms, with various machines produced under specialization agreements. Thus, the factory producing sugar-beet harvesters in the Ukrainian town of Ternopol draws components from five Comecon member states. There have been contributions from Czechoslovakia and Hungary involving both design and components, but the major suppliers are Bulgaria (electronic signalling and hydraulic transmission), the GDR (cab, conveyer belts, and steering) and the Soviet Union (chassis, engine, and transmission equipment). Combine harvesters, first the E512 and since 1977 the E516, are a product of co-operation between the GDR, Hungary, and the Soviet Union. (19) However, these standard machines do not always suit the requirements of individual countries, for great flexibility is needed: hence the importance of recent developments like the special farming truck produced at Trnava in Czechoslovakia, including a trailer and various fittings to deal with liquid or solid fertilizers, snow clearance, and so on. The situation should also improve as more experts from Eastern Europe assimilate western technology. Hungary has shown a particular willingness to buy the best agricultural equipment available since the growth of hard currency earning through the export of food justifies this. An important breakthrough in farm mechanization was achieved in 1974 when the Babolna state farm successfully persuaded the Gyor wagon and machine factory to take out a licence for the production of the American Steiger tractor. Hungary has also found that Claas combine harvesters from the FRG have made an important contribution to efficient harvesting during the 1970s. Further, the cost in hard currency has been reduced by a co-operation deal under which Hungary produces spare parts for the company.

Table 7.6 Fertilizer application and irrigation, 1965-84

Country	1965 (a)					A	B	1975		
	A	B	C	D	E			C	D	E
Albania	1	+5	6	4.9	205	61	+2	63	59.1	240
Bulgaria	220	+3	223	39.0	945	849	-170	679	113.0	1,128
Czecho-slovakia	381	+323	704	98.6	72	975	+709	1,684	241.2	92
GDR	2,255	-1,145	1,110	171.5	124	3,940	-2,114	1,826	290.2	160
Hungary	144	+154	298	42.6	100	712	+806	1,518	225.2	130
Poland	647	+395	1,042	52.7	275	2,434	+1,237	3,671	192.1	231
Romania	157	+10	167	11.4	230	1,674	-477	1,197	81.1	1,474
Yugoslavia	185	+204	389	26.2	118	555	+165	720	51.1	133
Eastern Europe	3,990	-51	3,939	51.2	2,069	11,200	+158	11,358	149.9	3,588

	A	B	C	1984 (b) D	E
Albania	93	+1	94	84.5	382
Bulgaria	1,047	+12	1,059	171.2	1,185
Czecho-slovakia	1,056	+774	1,830	268.1	189
GDR	4,733	-2,971	1,762	282.4	165
Hungary	924	+622	1,546	236.4	155
Poland	2,238	+1,163	3,401	180.2	100
Romania	2,977	-1,149	1,828	120.2	2,390
Yugoslavia	900	+310	1,210	85.6	160
Eastern Europe	13,968	-1,238	12,730	170.0	4,726

Source: FAO yearbooks.

Notes: A – Fertilizer production (thousand tonnes);
B – Ditto trade;
C – Ditto consumption;
D – Fertilizer application (tonnes per thousand ha);
E – Irrigated land (thousand ha);

a. Fertilizer figures are averages for 1961–5;
b. Irrigation figures for 1982.

The role of fishing

The reference to fish meal draws attention to the expanding fishing industry of Eastern Europe. In the 1960s a protein supply of 92,900 tonnes was derived from a catch of 38,500 and net imports of 53,400. This figure compares with one of just 6,600 for the catch in the 1930s. In terms of protein production from agriculture this is equivalent to 5.96 million ha land, an increase of 11.8 per cent on the land actually available. In the 1930s this 'fish area' would have been very small, certainly less than 1 per cent. Over the last two decades the fish supply has increased considerably and the agricultural land equivalent will now be much greater. Fish is available for human consumption, usually in tins (because high-quality fresh fish is very difficult to find), and also for animal feed, all the net imports consisting of fish meal.

Substantial quantities of fish are caught in lakes and ponds. Many of these have been created artificially, especially for fishing, like most of 500 ponds managed by the Trebon branch of Czechoslovakia's national fisheries enterprise, covering some 7,500 ha in all. The system at Trebon is largely the result of work by Jakub Krcin of Jelcany who constructed an ingenious system of ponds in the late sixteenth century. Krcin's projects included the 721-ha Rozmberk fish-pond, the biggest in Europe. Another Medieval engineer Stephanek Netolicky built some remarkable canals in order to provide an adequate water supply. Some 2,000 tonnes of fish are produced annually at Trebon (mainly carp) and output is maximized by modern breeding and feeding technology which also ensures that hygiene regulations do not constrain export possibilities. The ponds are emptied twice a year with labour which comes from Agricultural-Technical schools in Trebon and Vodnany, where strong emphasis is placed on the needs of the fishing industry. The fish ponds contribute to the tourist resources of upland Bohemia, where the landscape is frequently compared with Canada and Finland. Fish ponds exist in other East European countries, and Hungary in particular has increased her investments in fish farming with an important new installation at Szazhalombatta, which opened in 1974 with FAO financial support. Romania has rich fishing grounds in the Danube delta, where a number of canals have been cut in order to improve the circulation of water.

However, sea fishing has been all-important in the post-war increase in the domestic fish supply: 0.25 million tonnes in 1953, 1.39 in 1974, and 1.48 in 1983. Bulgaria's catch varied between 4,500 and 6,000 tonnes during the early post-war years, but reached 17,000 in 1965, 118,700 in 1974, and 121,100 in 1983. Deep-sea fishing was launched in 1964 through an agreement with the USSR which provided for the delivery of Soviet trawlers and refrigerating vessels in the period up to 1970. By 1975 total tonnage of the fleet, built largely in Poland, had reached 100,000. Illegal fishing incidents reported from the coasts of Argentina and the USA indicate the wide scope of Bulgarian operations at the present time. Under a recent agreement Bulgarian trawlers are operating in Indian waters. Growth has occurred in other maritime states of Eastern Europe. The GDR has built up a fishing industry based at Rostock and Sassnitz while Romanian trawlers operate out of Tulcea. Poland is not only an important fishing nation but a prominent builder of fishing vessels. It was agreed in 1972 that Polish factory trawlers would operate in Peruvian waters as part of a co-operation arrangement which would involve Polish assistance to Peru for the training of fishermen, and the processing and sale of fish. Interest also extends to seaweed (in the Black Sea for example) which has been found suitable for the production of certain medicines and for alginic acid.

Conclusion

Self-sufficiency in grain is becoming a high priority. Some countries will have the greatest difficulty eliminating imports altogether and the GDR's investment in the Rostock grain terminal suggests that substantial imports will continue even if the planned increase in the harvest to 10.4 million tonnes in 1985 (compared with 9.6 in 1980) is realized. It will be necessary to increase yields to almost 40 quintals/ha (compared with levels of 36.2 in 1971-5 and 35.8 in 1976-80 after the poor years of 1976 and 1979), and this will require attention to various deficiencies already noted. It will also be necessary to increase the area sown and here it is noticeable that throughout Eastern Europe the contraction of the arable area is now relatively small. Considerable progress has been made. In 1983 Yugoslavia was not obliged to import wheat, the first time for many years that domestic output has been adequate (due to an increase in the area cultivated as well as the increased use of fertilizers and other inputs made possible by the financial assistance of the World Bank). A small amount (0.27 million tonnes) was nevertheless imported under an agreement reached before the results of the harvest were known. On the other hand the much improved yields have enabled Hungary as well as Romania to go into surplus and help to alleviate shortages persisting elsewhere in the bloc. Better yields in Czechoslovakia then reduced imports to only 0.6 million tonnes in 1985 as the domestic output passed the elusive target of 11.0. It appears that further plant breeding has made it possible to derive new varieties well adjusted to prevailing climatic conditions and disease hazards, and capable of making efficient use of the fertilizers applied. Soviet winter wheats like 'Mironovskaya' have provided the basic material for breeding new Czech varieties.

Chapter Eight

TOURISM AND THE IMPORTANCE OF FOREIGN VISITORS

Tourism has an important role in socialist countries for various reasons. First there is the need for the work-force to enjoy some form of recreation. As a Yugoslav ideologist put it, travel and tourism constitute a form of leisure which has 'a positive feedback on the work itself, diminishing its monotony and routine'. (1) Creative leisure helps to integrate work and culture; so throughout Eastern Europe enterprises and unions offer facilities. In Hungary the trade unions run 160 hotels which can accommodate 390,000 workers each year, while individual enterprises and institutions can provide for 670,000 people in 1,400 holiday homes, and co-operatives receive 75,000 people annually in some 220 separate homes. Workers pay only a nominal fee for heavily subsidized holidays. The pioneer and youth camps receive about 450,000 young holiday-makers each year. Individuals may provide for themselves through construction of weekend villas, of which there are now some 300,000, and through membership of camping and caravanning clubs, which number around 100,000. There are also co-operative schemes whereby families can buy an interest in blocks of holiday flats with the right to use the accommodation for a specified number of weeks each year. In Poland all major employers organize vacations for their workers and many run their own holiday centres. These heavily-subsidized wczasy (workers' holidays) can, however, result in the takeover of tourist facilities and frustrate the individual family, which has to make its own arrangements. The problem is increased by the pressure on tourist organizations to meet their plan targets (so block bookings from major enterprises are particularly welcome) and by the lack of an

Table 8.1 Tourism: numbers of visitors and total income, 1956-83

Country	Visitors (millions)							Income (billion US dollars)				
	1956	1960	1965	1970	1975	1980	1983	1965	1970	1975	1980	1983
Bulgaria	0.01	0.20	1.08	2.54	4.05	5.49	5.77	0.04	0.08	0.23	0.26	0.27
Czechoslovakia	n.a.	n.a.	2.95	3.54	n.a.	5.05	4.58	0.04	0.04	n.a.	0.34	0.30
GDR	n.a.	n.a.	n.a.	n.a.	1.08	1.52	1.50	n.a.	n.a.	n.a.	n.a.	n.a.
Hungary	n.a.	n.a.	1.32	4.04	4.95	9.41	6.76	0.03	0.07	0.24	0.50	0.43
Poland	0.08	0.18	1.16	1.89	n.a.	5.66	1.92	0.01	0.03	0.15	0.28	0.08
Romania	n.a.	0.10	0.29	2.29	3.21	6.74	5.80	n.a.	0.06	0.13	0.32	0.20
Yugoslavia	0.39	0.87	2.66	4.75	5.83	6.41	5.95	0.08	0.28	0.77	1.11	0.93

Source: United Nations yearbooks.

Note: n.a. – not available.

Table 8.2 Tourism: countries of origin, 1960-80

Country	1960			1970			1980		
	A	B	C	A	B	C	A	B	C
Bulgaria	9.8	51.1	16.4	6.1	51.7	38.1	6.0	38.4	50.3
Czechoslovakia	n.a.	n.a.	n.a.	1.9	75.0	16.6	4.4	77.3	15.9
Hungary	7.2	51.2	17.2	3.7	81.4	14.5	4.0	82.9	10.6
Poland	12.4	37.1	14.8	17.8	69.2	8.3	10.1	77.4	9.0
Romania	9.2	69.1	4.9	7.1	76.2	16.0	8.0	77.6	10.0
Yugoslavia	0.6	5.5	85.1	1.6	6.6	80.6	3.2	10.2	78.7

Source: United Nations yearbooks.

A - Soviet Union; B - Eastern Europe; C - Western Europe; n.a. - not available.
Figures represent the percentage distribution for the total numbers of visitors indicated in Table 8.1. The balance is made up by visitors from other parts of the world and others whose country of origin is not specified (this means that the Western Europe shares may be understated in some cases).

efficient central tourist information pool. The basic problem, however, is the limited amount of accommodation: just two places per thousand of the population in Poland (though six in Czechoslovakia and twelve in Bulgaria), compared with thirty-one in France. It seems that large families with low incomes, and peasant households generally, are most underprivileged where tourism is concerned. Improved petrol supplies will be needed if people are to have better access to the countryside. The stringent economies in public transport and the various prohibitions affecting weekend use of private cars in Romania greatly restrict the opportunities for city dwellers at present.

Another motive for tourism is concerned with the encouragement of foreign visitors, but this has not always been a high priority. (2) A promising expansion of tourism during the 1930s was undermined by the war years and the immediate aftermath, when communist leaders sought an overwhelming commitment to work, and equated leisure and recreation with idleness. Although there were some strong reactions to these attitudes, seen in the 1956 events in Hungary for example, they nevertheless encouraged a cloistered mentality which was not conducive to tourism. Visitors did arrive, but only to encounter complex frontier formalities, a limited selection of generally sub-standard accommodation, along with poor roads and motoring services, and limited tourist information (Table 8.1). Eastern Europe had virtually nothing to offer at a time when the package-holiday business was gathering momentum in the west. Although facilities improved during the 1960s the main effort went into domestic tourism. Furthermore, a significant amount of international tourism involved groups from one Comecon country visiting another: such traffic accounted for about 80 per cent of foreign tourists in the six Comecon states in Eastern Europe in 1970 (Table 8.2). There were differences between countries in the attitude to western visitors at this time. Albania's frontiers were virtually closed (in both directions) while Yugoslavia's welcoming attitude resulted in a particularly rapid growth of western tourism during the 1960s, all the more so in view of massive investment in hotel building and road construction along the Adriatic coast. (3)

REGULATION OF TRAVEL

Travel has become much more straightforward in terms of financial cost and administrative complexities, especially for westerners visiting Eastern Europe. Governments have become confident enough to accept the modest security risks in return for substantial amounts of hard currency. Police posts checking internal traffic have largely disappeared and such movement is now relatively free. From 1967 travellers from virtually any country have been allowed into Bulgaria without a visa for any period up to two months, and ten years later the compulsory currency exchange requirement was waived. The bilateral agreement between Austria and Hungary in 1978 resulted in the abolition of visas and led to a great increase in the number of Austrians visiting Hungary - a total of 0.9 million in 1979. A $300 million credit from an Austrian banking consortium is assisting Hungarian developments in tourism, including hotels in Budapest which Austrian firms are building. This is seen as a very positive expression of the spirit of the Helsinki Final Act. The other Comecon countries generally require visas and currency exchanges and in some countries there are controls on accommodation: visitors to the GDR must usually make their accommodation arrangements beforehand, while travellers in Romania, although they can move around on an impromptu basis, must stay in accommodation managed by the state or by co-operatives. In the early 1970s formalities in Romania were minimal, with visas obtainable on demand at frontier crossing-points, no currency exchange requirements and no controls on accommodation. Visas are still easy to obtain, though the cost has risen sharply, but compulsory currency exchanges were required in 1974 and a year later foreigners were forbidden to stay in private houses (or more precisely, Romanian householders were forbidden to accommodate foreigners except very close relatives).

Albania has adopted a most cautious approach, however. Sandwiched between Greece and Yugoslavia, the country has good potential for tourism, with attractive coastal and mountain scenery, historic towns (especially the 'museum towns' of Berat, Gjirokaster, and Kruje), and archaeological sites. Yet as Hall points out, 'with successively ruptured relations the Albanian leadership has been obsessed with the xenophobic fear of contagion from foreigners pursuing very different life styles under markedly contrasting ideological conditions to those obtaining in fortress Albania'. (4) In order to enter the country, visitors must undergo, through their visa applications, a selection procedure which rejects citizens of certain countries, especially the USA and USSR, and they must meet the state's sartorial requirements, sometimes with the benefit of attention from the barber and tailor present at the international airport. Inside the country visitors must travel in groups following an itinerary arranged by the Albturist organization which leaves the individual with virtually no opportunity to travel alone, on foot, or by public transport. The insistence on the use of state hotels where foreigners are strictly segregated means that contact with Albanians is non-existent apart from a few state employees who dispense the Party line on various aspects of Albanian life. Since individuals must carry their own luggage in an egalitarian socialist society there is not even an opportunity for conversation with the hotel porter! Albania is also the only country in Eastern Europe where the visitor is restricted to a small number of approved routes and centres. Until the opening of routes to Peshkopi and Kukes in 1982 the whole of the north-eastern part of the country was closed to visitors. Durres was the most prominent centre for tourism in the Soviet period, when a hotel was built there, and it remains most prominent with a beach complex and five hotels (totalling some 1,500 beds). Tirana has two hotels (one of them dating back to 1940) with a total of some 500 beds, while four other centres offer some 200 beds each: Elbasan, Korce, Sarande, and Shkoder, where hotels were built in the 1970s. It is likely that some liberalization will be possible in future with the change in leadership, wider trade contacts, and an international railway link with Yugoslavia, in addition to scheduled air flights from Greece, Hungary, and Romania. However, access will remain relatively difficult. A railway link with Yugoslavia by Lake Ohrid has been discussed (though not agreed) but there is no prospect of a continuous coast road through Albania from Yugoslavia into Greece.

For East Europeans travelling to other socialist countries there are rather more protracted formalities in leaving their own countries and some complications can arise while they are abroad. In 1979, for example, Romania unilaterally demanded payment in hard currency for all petrol sales to foreigners (previously this had only been necessary for western visitors). The Romanians argued that their oil imports were paid for in hard currency and therefore sales of oil products to foreigners should be charged in the same way. However, the other Comecon states have gradually followed suit and while the problem can be overcome by the issue of vouchers, it nevertheless creates an interest in balanced exchanges and further constrains freedom to travel. Sensitivities have also increased over excessive purchases of foodstuffs by foreigners and 'shopping tourism' has been restricted in some cases. The greatest difficulties arise when East Europeans wish to travel to the west, but even here there have been improvements. In the past it has been virtually impossible for citizens of the GDR below retirement age to travel to the west, but there is now a significant number of family celebrations, anniversaries, and crises which will attract official approval for a visit to close relatives in the FRG. Thus, each country can now point to a complex pattern of comings and goings. Foreign visitors to Hungary (including transit passengers) numbered 6.3 million in 1970, 9.4 in 1975, and 15.1 in 1985, of which 3.8 million were from hard currency countries (mainly Austria with 2.0 million, and the FRG). In the other direction there were 5.5 million Hungarians travelling abroad in 1981. The great majority of them visited other socialist countries of Eastern Europe (Czechoslovakia, 2.52 million; Romania, 0.65; GDR, 0.61; Yugoslavia, 0.45; Bulgaria, 0.44; and Poland, 0.18), but 0.48 million visited capitalist countries, more than twice the number travelling to the Soviet Union (0.22), with Austria, the FRG and Italy the most popular choices. In 1982 the Hungarian government conceded that every citizen had the right to travel to a hard-currency country once each year, with the right to purchase foreign currency for a visit once every three years (the discrepancy arising from anticipation that family vists would account for the majority of such travels).

TOURISM: THE INVESTMENT STRATEGY

Foreign tourism should be valuable for political and ideological reasons, contributing to international understanding and demonstrating the merits of the socialist system while at the same time bringing hard currency into the country and inducing various improvements to the nation's infrastructure without undue risks with regard to ecological damage, alienation, or subversion. However, interest is overwhelmingly economic and the importance of hard currency has resulted in a barely disguised exploitative attitude to western tourists, with compulsory currency exchange regulations ensuring a basic minimum expenditure (usually $10 for each day for which the visitor's visa is valid). Western tourists are also assisted by special shops. The equivalent of the Torgsin shops founded in the Soviet Union in the 1930s are to be seen in all East European countries except Yugoslavia. Known as Corecom in Bulgaria, Tuzex in Czechoslovakia, Intershop in the GDR, Intertourist in Hungary, Pewex in Poland, and Comturist in Romania, these chains offer a wide range of goods available only to those with hard currency. Such shops provide a useful service to the tourist, who would not normally find a selection of western goods in East European shops, and they bring in hard currency to East European treasuries; but they are at the same time heavily criticized for ideological subversion: emphasizing the desirability of western goods and fostering a petit-bourgeois fetishism, all the more so because the shops may be used by favoured members of the Party and government.

The danger of subversion is minimized by hotel-building programmes which provide quite a high standard of accommodation and, at the same time, inhibit the close contact with local people that would arise if the use of private accommodation were encouraged. In each country the basic hotel network and tourist information service is provided by the state tourist agency: Albtourist (Albania), Balkantourist (Bulgaria), Cedok (Czechoslovakia), Interhotel (GDR), Ibusz (Hungary), Orbis (Poland), Carpati (Romania), and Progress (Yugoslavia). Generally there are separate organizations for young people like the youth and student travel agency in Hungary but they do not always deal with foreign visitors. Accommodation is often provided by co-operatives and local authorities: even private management of boarding houses and campsites is encouraged in Hungary and Yugoslavia. Yugoslavs returning from a spell of work in Western Europe may invest in tourism by building large houses with bedrooms which can be rented to tourists, by setting up a restaurant or perhaps by running a boat on excursions to offshore islands.

There is also scope for foreign investment in hotel building. Many new hotels in Hungary have been built primarily with Austrian visitors in mind and some of them have been financed by Austria, with Austrian firms involved in planning and construction. The Novotel in Budapest is linked to a French network and there is American involvement in the luxury hotel (Atrium Hyatt) opened on the Danube embankment in Budapest in 1982. Two new spa hotels are to be built in Budapest. The Danubius company, in co-operation with Finnish firms, is building a thermal hotel in Pest; while another project in Buda will involve assistance from Switzerland. The Club Tihany holiday village, situated on the Tihany peninsula of Lake Balaton, was built with the help of Austrian and Danish capital. The complex was opened in 1986 and can accommodate 1,400 people in a hotel and luxury bungalows. Guests are provided with a full range of services and varied entertainments. In Poland ten new hotels are being built for Orbis by the Austrian company Warimpex: some of them will be in the major cities and others at the seaside resorts (like Miedzyzdroje) and the touring centres (like Jelenia Gora, which is a base for the Sudety).

Tourist centres (Figure 8.1)

Seaside developments came first on the Baltic coast at places like Kuhlungsborn. The Balkan beaches were too remote and interest was restricted until after the First World War. Cruises along the Dalmatian coast could be taken from Trieste and Rijeka (then Fiume) to Dubrovnik and Kotor (with excursions into Montenegro available from the latter place). However, the entire Yugoslav coast has come into its own since 1945, especially as the coastal shipping-route has been complemented by the Adriatic Highway and improved access from the interior by road and rail. Romania has developed a chain of resorts on the Black Sea coast, expanding the complexes of Eforie and Mamaia (respectively south and north of Constanta, which date to the inter-war period) and initiating new developments between Eforie and Mangalia. The same scale of growth has occurred on the Bulgarian Black Sea coast where the number of tourist beds has increased from less than a thousand in 1950 to around 90,000 in 1970 and a quarter of a million by 1985. There is a group of three resorts near Varna (Albena, Druzhba, and Zlatni Pyassatsi/Golden Sands), all of which have the benefit of local mineral springs, complemented by Slunchev Bryag/Sunny Beach and Dyuni Primorsko (with its

Figure 8.1 Natural resources and tourist centres

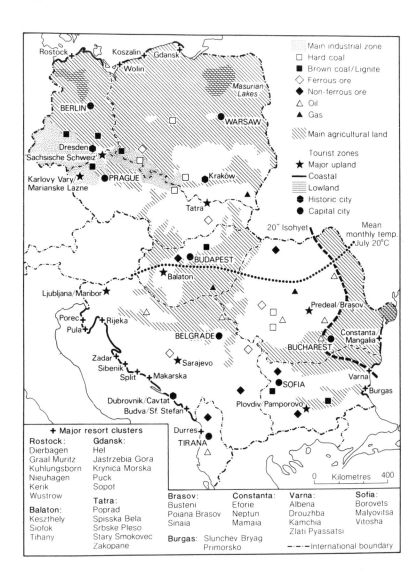

Source: Compiled from topographical maps.

Georgi Dimitrov youth centre) in the Burgas area, where the curative muds of nearby Pomorie are an additional attraction. Development dates back to the late 1950s when building began at Zlatni Pyassatsi (1956) and Slunchev Bryag (1958). There are also some tourist developments around the old towns of Balchik, Nesebur Primorsko, and Sozopol. In all these coastal areas it is necessary to maintain strict controls against pollution. Bulgaria has restricted the growth of industries with pollution hazards throughout a 30-kilometres-broad coastal belt and have given priority to service industries in this zone. A rich vegetation, maintained through further afforestation, the creation of a national park with special botanical interest near the Ropotamo River, and harmonious architecture are other priorities in Bulgarian planning.

The watering places remain important. After post-war conversion to cater almost exclusively for domestic tourists with medical needs, supported by state or trade union funds, there has been some effort to attract the wealthy clientele which supplied the original aristocratic connotations back in the last century. New hotels in the resorts best placed with regard to mineral water supplies, scenic resources, and transport services cater for wealthy foreigners in need of 'Der Kur'. Spa treatment is available in most countries, with the resorts of Czechoslovakia probably the best known. They include Frantiskovy Lazne, Jachymov, Karlovy Vary, and Marianske Lazne in Bohemia, as well as Piestany and Trencianske Teplice in Slovakia. Piestany's waters were known in Medieval times but both here and elsewhere it was the nineteenth century that saw the construction of magnificent spa houses. The isolation of radium from Jachymov pitchblende in 1898 directed attention to the radioactive waters of the town and the world's first radioactive spa was set up in 1906 with the construction of the Radium Palace (now the Marie Curie-Sklodowska sanatorium). State control of the spas was introduced in 1948 when the government became the sole owner of all spas and mineral springs. The primary function of some fifty spas and climatic resorts became the care of the health of working people. Only in the late 1950s was it possible for foreigners to return and for Czechoslovak citizens to use the facilities on a paying basis. This followed the decision of 1957 to place all spas under the Ministry of Health, which possessed the resources to undertake reconstruction. Notable new investments include the new sanatorium at

Jachymov (named after the Czech radiologist Frantisek Behounek), the Fucik sanatorium at Teplice v Cechach the Balneocentrum at Piestany, and other projects at Karlovy Vary and Trebon in Bohemia and at Darkov and Luhacovice in Moravia. Cures can be provided for problems concerned with circulation, digestion, and the respiratory system. Treatment is also available for serious diseases and heart attacks, while treatment for childrens' diseases and geriatric disorders is also developing. Moreover, some international events have been held at Marianske Lazne, including meetings of Comecon commissioners. Thus, foreign visitors are returning, but they account for no more than 10 per cent of the total number of patients.

Hungary's spas include Hajduszoboszlo, whose iodic and bromic waters have given rise to an international reputation for people with rheumatic complaints, and Parad in the forested Matra where aluminous, arsenic, and sulphurous waters are a consequence of post-volcanic activity. However, in spite of some revival in Hungary only about 15 per cent of thermal waters serve medical purposes. There are ample resources for further development and recent hotel projects linked with bathing in thermal waters concern Budapest and two places in the provinces: Harkany and Heviz. In the Balkans there are some spas well known in classical times (Baile Herculane in Romania, Sandiski, and Velingrad in Bulgaria). Many others have developed in modern times with further post-war expansion: Hissar, Kyustendil, and Vurshets in Bulgaria; Calimanesti/Olanesti, Felix, and Singeorz Bai in Romania. The mineral water from various spas is bottled in large quantities and widely distributed, the water of Borsec in Romania having an international reputation.

Winter sports facilities have attracted many foreigners. The first developments occurred in the north in the Erzgebirge/Ore Mountains and Krkonose Hory/Giant Mountains, where more than a hundred ski tows and lifts were available by the 1970s. However, the most notable resorts are those in the Tatra Mountains: Poprad, Srbske Pleso, and Stary Smokovec on the Czechoslovak side and Zakopane in Poland. Hungary has the beginnings of a winter sports complex around the sanatorium on the Kekes plateau in the Matra Mountains but most recent investment has been made in the Balkans: at Brasov, Predeal, and Sinaia in Romania; and at Bled, Iablanica, Ohrid, Plitvice, and Sarajevo in Yugoslavia (the last-mentioned location having been used for the winter olympics of 1984). (5) Progress in Bulgaria has also been impressive. Aleka is a small resort in the Vitosha Mountains at 1,810 metres below the peak of Cherni Vruh (2,290 metres). The accommodation can be used for winter sports between November and May and at other times to appreciate mountain scenery and other local attractions, including the flora (safeguarded at the Torfeno Branishte and Bistrisko Branisht reserves), culture (reflected in both the Dragalevtsi monastery and the Shoppe folk traditions demonstrated in the taverns - mehana), and health treatment available at the 'Vitality Centre'. Bansko, a new resort opened in 1981 in the Pirin Mountains, offers winter sports over a similar six- to seven-month period, but there is also interest in landforms, fauna (wild goats), and above all vegetation, with a national park containing such reserves as Bayuvi Doupki (black fir and edelweiss) and Malka Djindiritsa (white fir). By contrast, Borovets at 1,300 metres in the Rila Mountains is a rather larger resort close to Sofia, which first developed a tourist industry when facilities were provided for the Bulgarian royal family in the late nineteenth century. The largest resort is Pamporovo near Smolyan with some 1,500 beds. The site is 1,650 metres up in the Rhodope below the peaks of Mourgavets and Snezhanka. Winter sports are available between December and April.

Rambling and walking in the hills and mountains of Eastern Europe has considerable potential. Many footpaths are available, in regular use by the local population, and considerable chalet or hostel accommodation is provided in the most scenically attractive areas like the Fagaras Mountains of Romania. However, a better information system is required to attract foreign visitors. A 500-kilometre section of the European Wanderway was inaugurated in 1986: the route extends through Austria and enters Hungary at Koszeg, running to the northern shore of Lake Balaton by way of Sarvar and Sumeg.

Sporting and cultural attractions

Other tourist attractions may be summarized briefly. Hunting and fishing attract western visitors. Hunting is very expensive and is definitely a minority interest, with little scope for further development. However, it is a highly profitable business. About 7,000 visitors from Western

Europe (mainly from Austria, the FRG, France, and Italy) hunt each year in Hungary alone. On the other hand, fishing offers considerable potential and could be promoted as a means of extending the short summer season at Lake Balaton, for example. However, the fish stocks in the lake have been neglected and restocking on a generous scale is required. Sporting events have some significance and even the occasional events can be worthwhile. Among the more unusual events is the great Pardubice steeplechase of 6.9 kilometres over a mixed terrain comprising grassland, sands, and ploughed fields with more than thirty obstacles, including the challenging Taxis ditch. Again, following construction of a circuit at Mogyorod near Budapest in 1985, Hungary staged its first Formula One motor race in 1986. Educational and cultural programmes have made some headway. Hungary offers study programmes at a number of provincial centres as well as at Budapest. This represents an extension of the 'Summer University' programme which began in Debrecen in the 1920s. Students are attracted by the educational opportunities and the pleasant cultural and recreational diversions. Courses are available at places like Eger (Museum Studies), Esztergom (Music), Szarvas (Agriculture), Szekesfehervar (Computing), and Veszprem (Natural Sciences).

There is tremendous scope for holidays with a historical interest related to the prehistoric and classical monuments (like the Roman remains at Cavtat and the fortified villa of Narona in the Neretva valley of Yugoslavia). The Medieval legacy comprises historic settlements like Dubrovnik (with its elaborate fortification system including Ston at the neck of the Peljesac peninsula) and Pliska near Shumen (the first capital of Bulgaria); not to mention the churches (like the early Croatian churches on the offshore islands of Yugoslavia and the Moldavian Orthodox churches with their exterior frescoes) and monasteries like Rila (the largest in the Balkans) and others in Bulgaria (Bachkovo, Rozhen and Troyan). The Turkish influence has touristic value as in Mostar with its restored tekke (religious house of the dervishes), as do the monuments recalling heroic struggles and revolutions like the town of Koprivshtitsa in Bulgaria and Kruje in Albania: even the Dracula legend in Romania has been carefully exploited! (6) Then there is the wealth of modern history which can be appreciated in the capital cities through the great public buildings and culture houses, and some potential in unusual economic activities such as the cultivation of roses between Sofia and Kazanlik in Bulgaria. Of course there is always the danger of resources being undermined through modernization and pollution. This requires the protection of some entire settlements and hence the museum status given to various places in Bulgaria: Arbanassy, Bozhentsy, Koprivshtitsa, Kotel, Melnik, Nesebur, Sozopol, Veliko Turnovo, and Zheravna, as well as the old part of Plovdiv.

It is desirable that folk customs should be maintained, like the music, costume, and dance of the Chodsko (descendants of privileged Medieval frontier guards) which are still demonstrated at the Chodsko hyjta (festival) at Domazlice in Czechoslovakia. Where this is not possible, however, then the museums become indispensible. Some of these were founded before the First World War, like the ethnographic museum at Prerov nad Labem in Bohemia which opened in 1900 after the local estate owner, the traveller and ethnographer L.S. Toskansky, purchased an old Bohemian cottage in 1896. This has become an important regional museum with an open-air section opened in 1967. The national technical museum at Prague-Letna dates to 1908. However, the rapid pace of modernization has meant the disappearence of many traditional costumes and work methods, requiring a continual effort in preservation everywhere. The threat of pollution affects historic buildings but also important natural monuments, like the stone columns of Pobititi Kamun (petrified forests) near Varna-Devnya and the rocks of Belogradtchik, and both the flora and fauna. There are now nature reserves in the Danube delta, although it is widely felt that the protection of this unique area is inadequate, and in southern Hungary protected areas like Devavanya, Kardoskut, and Szegedi-feherto have a rich bird population, including the native bustards and migratory cranes which circulate between the Baltic and Sahara.

SPREADING THE BUSINESS

So tourism is now big business and Hungary at present has a net annual convertible currency income approaching $300 million, with an increase to $850 million expected by 1990. Growth cannot be taken for granted in all parts of Eastern Europe, however. The tourist industry in Romania has been adversely affected by the economic crisis and the number of foreign visitors dropped by a million from 7.0 to 6.0 million between 1981 and 1982. Food shortages along with poor accommodation and service seems to be mainly responsible for the decline in interest from western countries. The problems continue, with early closure of bars and night clubs (to save electricity) a particularly frequent source of complaint. Undoubtedly better facilities and professional retraining of staff can help, but a promising strategy for the future would appear to be further decentralization of tourism from the ministry to local co-operatives, following experiments carried out in the Iasi area in the early 1980s. Agricultural co-operatives could take on responsibilities for tourist services and care of historical monuments putting their local knowledge to good use.

Related to this is the danger of over-concentration. Some three-quarters of all tourist accommodation in Bulgaria and Yugoslavia is located in coastal resorts. Although only Albania has sought to close large parts of the country to foreign visitors and restrict them to a limited network of approved routes, it is nevertheless true that the central planning system results in a clear establishment of priorities over the provision of facilities and the supply of information, an approach which can easily be reconciled with the requirements of foreign package-tour companies. Individuals and small groups find their way to many remote places as the perceived dangers of western tourists projecting their consumer affluence have dwindled. However, limited information along with poor roads and public transport provision tends to discourage the majority of independent travellers from moving far from the major towns and lines of communication. Domestic tourists tend to be relatively more prominent in the smaller towns and the inland scenic regions generally. Greater decentralization could help to bring about a wider spread of foreign tourism and reduce congestion in the main centres. New roads and motorways can help, while co-operative and private management of facilities might be encouraged, as in Hungary in connection with catering and the administration of campsites and guest houses. There may be scope for establishing rural recreation facilities in depopulated mountain villages: at Beli Osam near Troyan in Bulgaria there are nearly a hundred empty houses and half the village income could come from tourism in future (plus 35 per cent from industry, leaving agriculture with only 15 per cent).

The Romanian case

International tourism has so far impinged only slightly on the rural areas. Figure 8.2 demonstrates the importance of the accommodation provided in the principal towns and, above all, the resorts of the Black Sea coast. However, there is a large potential elsewhere which rural planning is beginning to harness, thanks in part to the economic reform movement and the scope for local self-management. The present situation is summarized in Figure 8.3, which shows a number of small health resorts and a large number of communes which have some involvement in tourism: through historical monuments, museums, and other permanent displays, nature reserves and various forms of accommodation (hotels, motels, hostels, or camp sites). The summary of results in Table 8.3 shows that while rural tourism is rather weak overall, the mountain districts are in a relatively strong position. The contrast with the lowlands is widened further by consideration of the scenic attractions of the mountains and their considerable ethnographic interest: architecture and folk-life as well as traditional organization in agriculture and industry. The imbalance is likely to increase in future: for in the lowlands there is a strong emphasis on intensive farming, and some increase in pollution is taking place as the completion of the electricity grid draws industry away from the old fuel and raw material bases. By contrast, the broad rhythm of economic development in the Carpathians can be more easily reconciled with a strategy of conservation conducive to the development of tourism.

In several cases investment is allocated with benefits to tourism in mind. Hydroelectricity projects have multiplied, given the great increase in demand for power at a time when oil and gas were being reserved for petrochemistry and coal production could not increase rapidly enough. Although the large hydro potential had long been known it was only in the 1950s that Romania developed an adequate manufacturing base to undertake projects on the principal rivers. The water storages were seen as being important for tourism (such as Cincis for Hunedoara and Strimtori for Baia Mare) and several new hotels have been opened on lakeside sites, like the motel on Lake Bicaz. However, the more recent schemes have been integrated with tourism more closely through the siting of camps for construction workers in such a way as to permit continued use of the

271

Figure 8.2 Main tourist routes and hotel accommodation in Romania

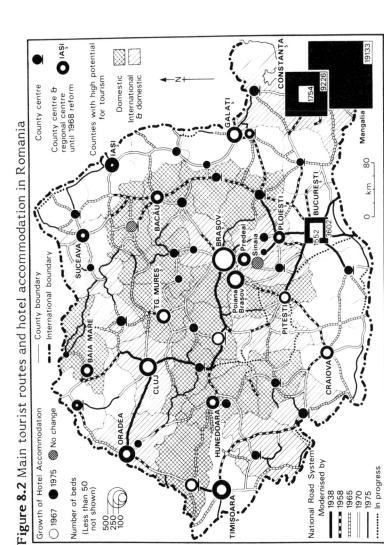

Source: Compiled from the national atlas and tourist literature.

Figure 8.3 Tourism in the rural areas of Romania

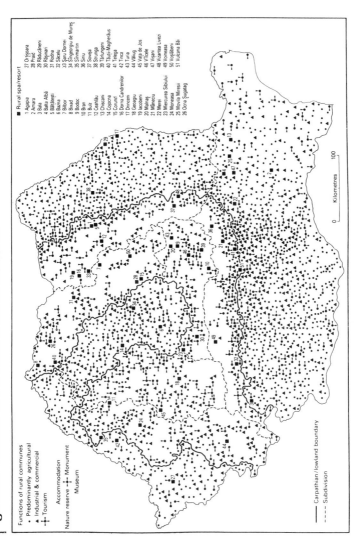

Functions of rural communes
- Predominantly agricultural
- ▲ Industrial & commercial
- ✛ Tourism

Accommodation
Nature reserve ✛ Monument
⊕ Museum

■ Rural spa/resort

1 Agapia	27 Ortișoara
2 Amara	28 Praid
3 Bala	29 Răbucăñeni
4 Baia Albă	30 Răspan
5 Bălilești	31 Rodna
6 Bazna	32 Săcelu
7 Bibor	33 Saru Dornei
8 Bixad	34 Singeorgiu de Mures
9 Bodoc	35 Sinmarnin
10 Bran	36 Siriu
11 Buiz	37 Soveja
12 Ceahlău	38 Sirunga
13 Chiscani	39 Tărluñgeni
14 Coparoa	40 Tiush-Magherilus
15 Corund	41 Telega
16 Dorna Candrenilor	42 Tinca
17 Drincorm	43 Turia
18 Geoagiu	44 Vălisug
19 Iacobeni	45 Vata de Jos
20 Mălnaș	46 Vîboăle
21 Mănecru	47 Vișani
22 Merei	48 Vizantea Liveni
23 Mercurea Sibiului	49 Voneasa
24 Moneasa	50 Vojăbem
25 Movila Miresii	51 Vulcana Bâi
26 Ocna Șugatag	

—— Carpathian / lowland boundary

---- Subdivision

0 _____ 100
        Kilometres

Sources: See Table 8.3.

Table 8.3 Functional classification of Romanian communes

Region	Number of communes in category:					Index	
	A	B	C	D	Total	E	F
East-Inner	8	33	67	39	147	118	146
East-Outer	8	39	57	25	129	154	196
South-Inner	8	45	14	28	95	235	282
South-Outer	6	58	42	53	159	170	182
West-Inner	2	66	32	50	150	191	189
West-Outer	4	37	73	59	173	100	98
Carpathians	36	278	285	254	853	155	173
Centre	3	56	56	146	261	96	80
East	3	79	57	301	440	78	72
South	7	148	224	601	980	67	60
West	2	29	35	105	171	76	67
Lowlands	15	312	372	1,153	1,852	75	66
Romania	51	590	657	1,407	2,705	100	100

Source: Calculated from M. Maciu and others (1986) <u>Mic dictionar enciclopedic</u>, Bucharest: Editura Stiintifica si Enciclopedica, and other sources.

Notes: A - Holiday resorts;
 B - Scores in at least one tourism indicator;
 C - Industrial functions;
 D - Predominantly agricultural functions;
 E - Proportion of communes in categories A and B related to the national average;
 F - Number of tourism indicators for category B communes related to the national average.

accommodation for tourist purposes, as at Belis on the Somes River near Cluj-Napoca. The 1973 law on the protection of the environment envisaged a 25-30-year programme to increase the number of water storages to 1,400 with a total capacity of 34.0 milliard cubic metres, so there will be further scope for this practice.

Forestry has also developed in a manner conducive to the development of tourism. The silvicultural authorities control hunting and fishing, with considerable emphasis on fish farming. While woodcutting has increased, each lumber enterprise must respect the protective function of woodlands in the vicinity of reservoirs so that the local environment has usually escaped damage in such cases. However, the extension of woodcutting into areas that were previously ignored, partly because of inadequate capacities for the processing of beechwood and partly because of valley profiles too steep for forest railway construction, has made it easier for tourists to penetrate deep into the mountains by means of vehicular transport. The forest railways were certainly important for tourism and various lodges were built (some of them specifically geared to the hunting of wild animals) where such transport was available. Now, however, the road network is much more comprehensive and unlike railways, where tourists are restricted to the services which the operator provides, they are available at all times to private motorists. Although the roads are unsurfaced the standard of construction is improving as larger timber lorries are introduced and cars can usually proceed without difficulty. The great majority of roads follow rivers and terminate at the head of the valley but there are some through roads which greatly increase the tourist potential.

Forest road developments must be seen in the context of other improvements relating to the national road network. Vehicular routes across the mountains are still limited but they are far more numerous than they were before 1918 when the international frontier along the main watershed was in force. Between 1936 and 1938 a new road was driven through the Bicaz Gorges and this is now an important tourist route linking Piatra Neamt in Moldavia with Gheorgheni in Transylvania by way of Lacu Rosu, a lake (created by a landslide) displaying petrified tree stumps. This small resort has been developed to capacity as a result of the new transport artery and given the restricted site and sensitive environment little further expansion is desirable. Then in the late 1960s the village of Soveja acquired a significant tourist function on the strength of the improved road links not only with Focsani but also with Tirgu Secuiesc in Transylvania, the latter now accessible by a new road across the mountains from Lepsa. Although Soveja has a history as a trading centre between Vrancea and Tara Birsei only rough tracks and pathways across the main watershed were available until the 1960s.

The most important new road is the 91.5 kilometre Transfagaras Highway built between 1970 and 1974 to link Cumpana at the head of the Arges valley in Wallachia and Cirtisoara in Transylvania. The road climbs to just beyond 2,000 metres and passes under Paltin Mountain in a tunnel 882 metres long. There is close co-ordination with other elements of rural planning in the sense that forest roads integrate with the new highway, and woodlands have an important protective function where there is a danger of avalanches and soil erosion. Particularly hardy species have been planted on road talus and ground where vegetation has been damaged by stone fragments. The link with hydroelectricity is brought out by the Arges dam and the Vidraru reservoir, which mark the southern terminus on the new road. The greatly improved accessibility and the enhanced tourist resources have already led to a substantial increase in accommodation in new hotels on the Vidaru lake shore and also at Bilea just north of the main watershed. Here the original hostel built by a local travel society in 1884 (and replaced after fire damage in 1905 and again in 1924) has been complemented by a modern hotel and linked by cable car with a cluster of hostels beside Bilea Lac where development dates to 1894.

Environmental protection was much discussed in the inter-war years with a powerful lead supplied by academics at Cluj University who were interested in botany and speleology. There was widespread support for the protection of monuments of nature from naturalists and scientists but landowners were less enthusiastic. The first law (1930) was not very effective but it did provide for a commission on natural monuments, organized within the Romanian Academy, and gave momentum for the designation of reserves until a new phase was initiated by further legislation in 1950 and 1954. The first reserves, such as Domogled near Baile Herculane (1931), Zimbru near Arad (1938), and Beusnita Forest (1943) have been supplemented by some 250 other places of botanical and geological interest. The botanical interest comes out in the remarkably varied flora of the Bucegi Mountains (213 species within just 8,000 ha) and individual phenomena like the water lily at the 1 Mai spa, preserved from the Tertiary period because warm waters compensated for the falling temperatures of the Quaternary. Geological interest emerges in the marble of Ruschita, the volcanic muds of Berca, and the volcanic lake of Sf. Ana near Tusnad. The touristic value of these sites is often enhanced by special regimes in the surrounding areas, a point which also applies to historic buildings like the monastery of Tismana near Tirgu Jiu.

The Lotru Mountains

With these trends in mind it may be appropriate to consider the Lotru and Retezat Mountains as examples of recent developments in rural tourism. The Lotru Mountains are a part of a massive block of the Carpathians between the Jiu and Olt Rivers, sometimes labelled the Paring although this range comprises only a small proportion of the total area. The area lies adjacent to the Olt but north of the tributary river the Lotru, although it also comprises the whole of the territory drained by its headwaters (Figure 8.4). There have been radical changes in spatial relationships. Historically the lowland depression around the Olt-Lotru confluence, Tara Lovistei, was linked with the core area of Wallachia (Curtea de Arges/Tirgoviste) by means of a north-west-south-east routeway from Hateg in Transylvania following the Lotru valley to a crossing of the Olt near Brezoi; thence by Perisani to the Topolog valley into the Arges district. Lovistea was a cuib (nest) within the mountains and sheltered from the danger of penetration by Dark Age and Medieval invaders. Although arable farming was restricted there was an ample basis for subsistence. The forests provided nuts and fruit as well as timber while the high mountain surfaces, indicated by the element plai, were important for pastoral farming.

The Olt valley, although it forms a deep trench through the mountains, was difficult to penetrate in its natural condition. The Romans built a road through the gorges but otherwise, sustained use of the valley as a through route dates back only to the road built during the Austrian occupation in the eighteenth century and the railway which followed in the nineteenth. However, these modern lines of communication interrupted the traditional orientation, which continued to be important only for pastoralism. The new alignment was formalized by the administrative linkage of Lovistea with Rimnicu Vilcea (further south along the Olt valley) rather than Curtea de Arges. Today, Lovistea, along with the Lotru Mountains, remains part of the judet of Vilcea. The Lotru Mountains became a remote backwater seldom explored by the tourists who visited the spa of

Figure 8.4 The Lotru Mountains

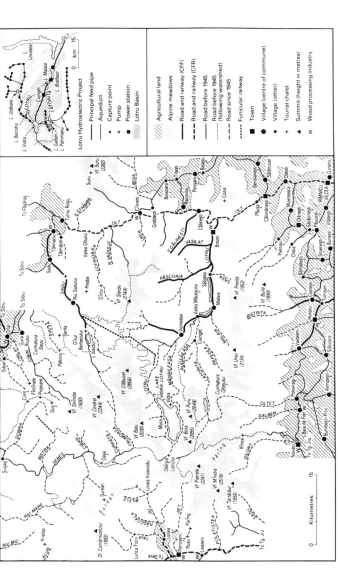

Source: Compiled from topographical maps.

Calimanesti or the monastery of Cozia. Yet in the post-war period the historical importance of the district has been rediscovered and it is now a leading district for mountain tourism with a regular bus service along the Lotru valley connecting with main line trains at Lotru station near Brezoi.

The transformation has arisen in the first place from the commercial exploitation of the forests from a base at Brezoi where a steam-powered sawmill was built in 1873. Timber was floated down the Latorita and Lotru valleys, while other valleys in the system like the Pascoaia and Vasilat were reached by a narrow-gauge railway from Brezoi, which also had a standard-gauge connection with the main-line railway at Lotru. After the Second World War the forest railway was extended in 1949 up the Lotru valley to the lumber centre of Voineasa and on to the Voinesita. The floating of timber (which involved substantial losses) then declined. However, the steep profile of the upper Lotru valley, above Voineasa, prevented further extension of the railway and timber continued to be taken out by means of a funicular over the watershed into the Sadu valley where a forest railway ran to a sawmill at Talmacel. However, in the inter-war period strategic considerations led to the construction of an alpine highway from Sebes in Translyvania to Novaci in Oltenia in 1935, crossing the Lotru close to its source (Obirsia Lotrului). Branch roads, often crossing the high surfaces, ran eastwards to Lovistea and westwards to Petrosani; and in connection with the partial opening up of the area, tourist interest increased and several mountain hostels were built.

The further development of tourism arose from the modernization of the timber industry with the building of forest roads. Because lorries can cope with steeper gradients than a railway all the valleys in the Lotru basin have now been penetrated, including the Latorita where the floating of timber continued until the 1960s. There is now a comprehensive road system in the Lotru basin including connections across the watershed not only with Petrosani via Obirsia Lotrului but also with Polovragi in Gorj, by means of a road from the Latorita valley over Curmatura Oltetului into the Oltet valley, and with the Sadu valley and Talmacel via Poiana Arsa. These roads are unsurfaced apart from the main road from Lotru station through Brezoi to Voineasa, but most are satisfactory for cars as well as more robust vehicles.

Figure 8.5 The Retezat Mountains

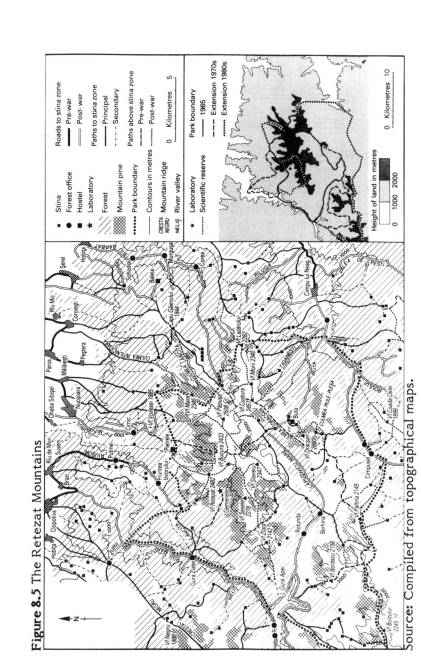

Source: Compiled from topographical maps.

A further element is provided by hydroelectricity for the Lotru has been dammed at Vidra and the storage lake is fed not only by the Lotru but by other streams diverted by means of aqueducts. A reservoir on the Latorita is linked with Vidra by means of a pipeline through which water is pumped using off-peak power. From Vidra the water runs to a power station at Ciunget. Further power is generated downstream at Malaia and Bradisor where other water storages have been constructed and the developments continue beyond the Olt-Lotru confluence towards Rimnicu Vilcea. The hydroelectric works provided a further stimulus for road improvements and are also helpful to tourism through the creation of lakes, especially Vidra which lies in an excellent situation. Tourist complexes at Alba for winter sports, Mura for health care and Vidra for water-based recreation, now supplement the older hostel of Obirsia Lotrului. However, the links between hydroelectricity and tourism are particularly close becaues of the planned takeover of construction workers' accommodation by the tourist industry. There is a large hotel at Voineasa (670 metres) run by the Romanian trade union movement as a rest-house (<u>casa de odihna si tratament</u>) since 1981. The hotel is supplemented by several large boarding-houses so Voineasa now accommodates some 3,000 people and the thriving resort, in a Swiss architectural style, is being developed as a future town. The capacity of the resorts around Vidra reservoir at altitudes of some 1,850 metres is around 5,000.

The Lotru Mountains constitute an outstanding example of co-ordinated development of tourism. The unspoilt mountain landscape with a rich cultural heritage and great potential for winter sports (and for medical care in a pure and stimulating environment) has been harnessed within a very short period of time through several related investment programmes, increasing the potential through construction of lakes. However, careful management will be needed to maintain the quality of landscape. Heavy grazing as well as tourist pressure leads to erosion and it seems that co-operative farms have been sending excessively large flocks into the mountains. Some areas are also disfigured by serious storm damage to woodlands.

The Retezat Mountains

This range also forms part of the Southern Carpathians. It lies between the Jiu valley and the Timis corridor in an area where the Carpathians are relatively high and wide so there are extensive areas of high ground with glacial landforms very much in evidence. These features are especially characteristic of the Retezat lying between the Upper Jiu/Strei and Riul Mare/Lapusnicul Mare in the county of Hunedoara (Figure 8.5). There are excellent possibilities for mountain tourism given the fine scenery developed on granite and limestone and a network of paths used by shepherds taking flocks to the high grazings for the summer. The main ridge runs for more than 10 kilometres from Retezat (2,482 metres) to Bucura (2,433 m), Peleaga (2,509 m), Papusa (2,508m), Custura (2,457m), Marin (2,340m), Gruniu (2,294 m), and Lazarul (2,282m). However, the area has for long been remote and until forest roads were pushed up the valleys in the post-war period climbers faced a long walk from places like Cimpu lui Neag (above Uricani in the Jiu valley) Hobita on the Riul Barbat, Nucsoara on the river of that name, and Riu de Mori on the Riu Mare. The pressure from ramblers, hunters, and fishermen remained light until the inter-war period when the potential of the cetatea alpina (alpine fortress) was widely appreciated as a museum of natural history (Popescu 1986).

Botanists at the University of Cluj appreciated the varied flora, including not only the massive stands of beech (to 1,200m) and spruce to 1,700-1,800m) but also interesting pinewoods. These include pinus cembra (zimbru) of an age and size exceeding the norm for the Carpathians and also the mountain pine pinus mugo (jneapan), a bush growth found in the alpine zone well abve the normal forest limit. While zimbru fades out above 1,900m, jneapan, with the occasional zimbru, exists up to around 2,000m. The fauna includes wild boar and wild cats, as well as the bear, lynx, and mountain goat, not to mention the fish of the rivers and such alpine lakes as Bucura, Gemenele, and Zanoaga. Bucura is the largest (some 9 ha) and Zanoaga the deepest (29m). The area merited a sustained research effort and the fragile ecosystems required protection at a time when recreational interest was being added to the traditional pastoral economy and the continuing deforestation associated with it. There was also commercial tree felling in progress and the Italian company Feltrinelli constructed a series of timber dams (opusturi) on the Lapusnicu Mare (a headwater of the Riul Mare) so that spruce wood could be floated towards the railway line at Hateg.

The movement in favour of national park status developed contemporaneously with the interest in conservation already outlined. In 1923 the director of the botanic garden at Cluj University, A. Borza, asked the authorities responsible for implementing the agrarian reform programme to reserve land in the Retezat for a national park. This initiative was not successful, given the prevailing emphasis on peasant proprietorship, but Romanian naturalists repeated the call during their first congress at Cluj in 1928. The national park was set up in 1935, just five years after the first legislation for the protection of nature. The aim was to regulate pastoralism, woodcutting, hunting, and fishing in the park itself and in the perimeter zone. However, powers were inadequate until 1955, when a scientific zone was created and when grazing was restricted in the whole of the 13,000-ha park.

Over the years control has become gradually more effective. In order to encourage the regeneration of zimbru, grazing was restricted to just two months of the year and in 1973 all grazing was forbidden in the great glacial caldarea of Bucura and the Stinisoara valley. Activity in the 1,840-ha scientific reserve is most stringently controlled, with only a number of clearly marked paths available for visitors. Scientific work has been expedited by the construction of the Gemenele laboratory (1961-4) close to the lake at 1,780m and three observation points at Gura Zlata in the Riu Mare valley (where the park administration is located) and higher up at Rotunda (1,100m) and Pietrele (1,480m). A Carpathian herbarium has been created at Gemenele, with some 4,000 species, and research has identified some 1,200 plants in the Retezat documented in a major monograph on flora and vegetation. Commercial forestry operations continued on the park margins, with particular emphasis on the spruce wood. The dams on the Lapusnicu Mare were maintained until the 1950s, by which time road building was under way. One forest road advanced from Riu de Mori to the Casa Verde (a river gauging station) in the 1950s, to Gura Zlata and Gura Apei in the 1960s and continued along the Lapusnicu Mare in the 1970s. Forest roads were also built from the Upper Jiu (Buta and Pilugu valleys) and from the Strei valley villages of Hobita, Nucsoara, and Suseni. The programme helped to open up the Retezat to visitors

283

with hostels on the fringes. Some on the main routeways like Cimpu lui Neag (850m) in the Jiu valley and Gura Zlata (775m) on the Riu Mare; and others on the higher ground: Baleia (1,410m), Buta (1,580m), and Pietrele (1,480m), along with the refuge of Gentiana (1,670m). The total accommodation is some 500. However, heavy cutting on the park margins has now ceased. Clear felling over extensive surfaces was stopped in 1976 and then all clearance, including small pockets, was renounced in 1985. This is in addition to the decision to extend the park itself to include the Lapusnicu catchment (previously the river itself formed the southern limit of the park) and the upper part of the Valereasca catchment. Thus, there is now a park of some 20,000 ha and an outer pre-park or protection zone amounting to some 30,000 ha. Grazing continues in this outer zone, but since all communal grazing land has been placed under the management of the silvicultural authorities since 1985 there is a new policy in force which allows for periodical resting of individual surfaces so that a more varied flora can emerge.

Thus, the Retezat is now safeguarded for the future. No rapid increase in tourism can be anticipated because the area remains relatively remote and the authorities do not wish to encourage mass penetration. For many years the construction of a through road from Cimpu lui Neag to the Cerna valley, to facilitate forest exploitation and tourism, was opposed even though the road would only touch the park boundary. It is evident that naturalists and conservationists have been particularly effective in working for improved management of the area and many of those concerned with administration are both dedicated and well-qualified. For the present the ethos of the Retezat is one of wilderness, offering scope for those who appreciate the unique qualities of the district. In this context the Retezat complements the Tara Hategului with its archaeological/historical monuments and considerable enthographical interest. The hostels in the mountains (and a proposed hotel at Gura Bucurei which would follow from road modernization) are therefore outposts of more substantial complexes in towns like Hateg and Petrosani and villages like Sintamarea Orlea and Sarmizegetusa. It is likely that a larger scale of tourism may emerge in the Riu Mare where the Riu Mare-Retezat hydroelectric scheme is presently under way. A large lake is being formed at Gura Apei and a chain of water storages will also emerge between Hateg and Riu de Mori.

DISCUSSION

Tourism, geared to the needs of each country's nationals but increasingly to foreign visitors as well, is gaining greater prominence as an important facet of environmental management. The change in approach is a very gradual process because for so long planning has been geared to maximizing the output of raw materials and ensuring the adequate provision of other essential inputs: conservation has been related primarily to the protection of water catchments and main lines of communication. The result of relatively unsophisticated central planning has been a concentration of investment on major tourist projects providing mass recreation facilities without adequate consideration for integration with other facets of the relevant local economy and environment. Development of facilities for winter sports at Borovets in Bulgaria has paid insufficient attention to preserving the tree cover (sacrificed to provide more ski runs) and ensuring adequate medical services in the immediate vicinity. Black Sea resorts in Bulgaria and Romania are compromised by pollution hazards associated with industrial complexes emerging in Burgas, Constanta/Navodari, and Varna. The Romanian spa of Baile Herculane has been threatened by the Cerna-Motru-Tismana water diversion scheme (providing industrial water for Oltenia) and a further diversion (taking water from the Bela Rece to the Cerna) has been needed to protect the internationally famous resort. As the dangers of large-scale developments became apparent the economic reform process may be particularly important in stimulating local investment initiatives which could help to diversify the geography of tourism and achieve a better balance between over-used and under-used resources. The issues are however extremely complex and the companion volume will provide further discussion of related problems: conserving the environment and extending tourist accommodation through the building of dachas or second homes in the remoter and more heavily depopulated rural areas.

CONCLUSION

Eastern Europe has experienced a radical reorganization in the post-war period affecting its political and economic structures. A new territorial structure arose out of the Second World War with particularly radical changes in the northern part of the region. On the other hand there has been absolute stability in boundaries since 1945 and while the strains arising from former political geographies, and from continuing ethnic minority problems in several countries, have not disappeared, they are nevertheless contained by the discipline imposed by monopoly communist governments and by the strong powers of co-ordination imposed on the majority of governments by the USSR. While Russian influence over parts of Eastern Europe has been evident in the past (a large part of present-day Poland was included in the Russian Empire for more than a century before 1918), it has never applied to the whole of the region under review in this book. Now the influence is spatially more extensive and, being Marxist-Leninist in inspiration, involves not only the idealizing of a monopoly party system but equal priority for state ownership of the means of production and central planning of the economy in relation to each country's own resources: involvement in an integrated economy for the bloc, and even more so the global pattern of specialization, has carried only limited priority until recently. The result has been a remarkable change from an agricultural to an industrial emphasis backed up by intensive working of domestic raw materials and fuels (especially low-grade coal), by changes in settlement patterns as young people have left the land and migrated, often on a permanent basis, to the towns, and by the harnessing of domestic, Soviet, and, increasingly, western technology. Differences between countries remain, given the prime emphasis on the nation state, but very high rates of growth have been achieved throughout the region.

Such great changes in their wake naturally give rise to curiosity about the essential ingredients for such revolutionary upheavals. The political and economic elements of Eastern European Socialism are complementary but they are not inseparable and it cannot be assumed that rapid economic development would not have occurred irrespective of political arrangements. It has yet to be convincingly demonstrated that the broad rationale of economic development departs significantly from western practice. Certainly, geographers have recognized the same basic problems throughout the continent: while the ecologists express concern over the threat to the environment the spatial scientists find that centre-periphery antagonisms are by no means restricted to western 'capitalist' countries. Regional variations have been held in check by improvements in infrastructure (transport and power) but imbalances in raw materials and skilled labour must be recognized by central planners who seek a high rate of growth nationally. Changes in the system of administrative regions have helped planners to direct capital to compelling resources in areas previously obscured by the demands of large cities under whose authority the backward areas were subordinated. However, the large scale of modern factory working, the efficiency involved in developing an integrated industrial estate, and the feasibility of assembling a large labour force by permanent rural-urban migration and daily/weekly commuting all continue to conspire against the expansionist ambitions of many small towns and key villages. Geographers in Eastern Europe have taken considerable interest in the regional problem and try to discharge their professional responsibility by competing with economists for access to the leading decision-makers in Party and government.

Eastern Europe shows dramatic centralizing tendencies, perhaps arising inevitably from central planning related to very large agricultural and industrial organizations and an infrastructure which is better organized nationally (integrating the major cities) than it is regionally and locally. Arguably, therefore, to a greater extent than in the west there is a reluctance to establish industries in small towns and to farm marginal areas given the distance from the centre of administration and the additional problems arising from poor transport and power supply. At the same time the system of central planning, typically involving major choices over sector and regional allocations relevant to resources and market requirements (nationally and internationally) for periods of five years or more, creates an element of rigidity in the economy which makes for complicated day-to-day operation as well as inability to adjust. The situation is all the more complex because the vested political interests in the decision-making process make it very difficult to alter course. Eastern Europe therefore displays abundant evidence of economically irrational decision-making which could not be found in the west to the same extent. The enormous costs of centralization and inefficient decision-making is borne by the population in terms of long working hours, low wages, and shortages of everyday requirements. Compared with the west the service sector is poorly developed, given similar levels of agricultural and industrial output. Inevitably, 'the traditional system has been challenged for its failure to live up to ideals of socialism and for the dehumanizing effect of the industrialization rush'. (1) However, the situation is exacerbated by an ambivalent attitude by governments towards their people: prosperity can result in greater legitimacy for governments, yet propaganda demands for self-sacrifice in the construction of socialism remain important in recruiting an ideologically motivated community of Party members who are essential, along with the military and security organizations, for maintaining the system.

The problem is complicated by the early post-war experience with excessive and premature expansion of manufacturing related to Soviet needs and Soviet fuels and raw materials. This strategy produced rapid structural change in the 1950s and 1960s but it is now difficult to exploit the potential for co-operation with firms in the west and specialization within Eastern Europe. During the 1970s and 1980s there has been less structural change in Eastern Europe than in the west. However, changes in the future will arguably bring Eastern and Western Europe closer together. It is no longer possible to maintain a high rate of growth by heavy investment working up to as much as 40 per cent of GNP. To maintain growth the socialist economies must become more efficient and this in turn requires a better use of resources, better management, and planning; and a work-force motivated by a clear link between efforts and rewards. All this suggests higher living standards and further economic reform. However, when one contemplates the recasting of the central planning system or the break-up of collective farms, there are enormous political problems involving vested interests and also Soviet sensibilities. Thus, for example, greater efficiency and productivity have serious implications for job security, a socialist principle which governments have been reluctant to ignore (perhaps in part because it helps to maintain the integrity of central planning despite falling growth rates). Major structural changes are needed in the economies of Eastern Europe but these changes cannot really be accomplished without some radical change in the system itself. Economic reform became the slogan of the decade in the 1960s yet even when the changes were superficial the mere allusions to reform constituted a significant gesture by the traditionalists to the economic realities: (2) for despite the propaganda emphasis on revolution the East European system is highly conservative and reforms have been tentative in the extreme. 'We have yet to see a welfare-oriented, consistent, and coherent reform, accompanied by a revision of the growth strategy and by a system of checks and balances to curb the omnipotence of the system's directors'. (3)

THE WAY AHEAD

As Eastern Europe has lost its competitiveness in international trade, the search for effective solutions is heavily constrained by the Soviet Union's cautious attitude to reform. All the socialist countries of Eastern Europe (except Yugoslavia) now perceive a sharp conflict between the desire for closer links with western industrialized nations and the need for Soviet economic assistance which is of more immediate value to them. Eastern Europe is almost certainly an economic liability to the Soviet Union at the present time but since the Soviet interest in the region is essentially political there is a willingness to pay an economic price even though it sustains higher living standards than are available to most citizens of the USSR. (4) However, if the Soviet Union wishes, at the same time, to reduce tension in the world and to improve access to western technology, then it must observe certain conventions of civilized behaviour in dealing with its allies.

Here it is evident that 'normalization' in Czechoslovakia, for all its bitter disappointments in the eyes of many Czechoslovaks, did not involve the violent arbitrary actions characteristic of Stalinist repression. Thus, a balance was struck and the opposition to radical reform in Czechoslovakia was not so insensitive as to prevent the formulation of an Ostpolitik by the Brandt government in the FRG in 1969, a move which the Soviets encouraged its allies to reciprocate at a meeting of Warsaw Pact leaders in Moscow at the end of that year. Thus, it may be that the challenge over human rights can be absorbed. There is certainly a democratic tradition, especially in the north, and given the effective parliamentary activity in Eastern Europe (and the scope for individual initiative in business, literature, and religion) before the communist revolution, it is inappropriate to claim that the early post-war experience precludes the development of democratic institutions indefinitely. For many people, however, the limited progress already made (resulting in greater freedom of speech in Eastern Europe than the Soviet Union) and limited change promised for the future (involving, for example, a revitalization of parliamentary life in Hungary and Poland) may be acceptable.

However, while greater democracy could lead to more pronounced 'differentiation' between the policies of the Soviet Union and those of the East European states, it could also result in more strained relations within the region. Nationalism is becoming stronger. Hungary, for example, has been swept by a wave of 'Habsburg nostalgia' with people openly expressing positive romantic feelings about the 'time of peace' between 1871 and 1914, when war was averted without potentially dangerous nuclear strategies. Yet nationalism can easily sharpen territorial disputes with four most sensitive issues (Kosovo, Macedonia, the Baltic coast, and Transylvania) involving all eight East European states except for Czechoslovakia. In addition there is the problem of the Soviet Union's western frontier; a sensitive issue in Poland and Romania especially. More open discussion could also be dangerous in the context of domestic affairs since the East European states are still not truly homogeneous. The migration process, operating through history, has given rise to ethnic and religious divisions, while the development of modern national movements in a largely agrarian context creates the possibility that free expression could take counter-modernizing forms with support for the traditional life-styles which presently come most strongly from Moslem peoples like the Albanians of Kosovo. It may therefore be in the interest of all communist governments in the bloc to retain a large measure of control.

Despite the progress made in superpower negotiations in the late 1980s it would be premature to suppose that greater western penetration of Eastern Europe (through an enhanced economic contribution by the FRG or a more powerful cultural presence by the USA) will alter the reality of the rival military systems. It is distinctly fanciful for right-wing analysts to postulate popular support for nationalist anti-communist movements in Comecon countries and in the constituent republics of Yugoslavia to the point where a new state system, guaranteed by the US, would stand as a barrier to Soviet expansionism. Equally academic are the critical thinkers in Eastern Europe who do not seek a restoration of capitalism but rather a genuinely democratic framework for socialism which could embrace both Eastern and Western Europe. Very important here is the peace movement, which looks forward to a dismantling military alliances, the dissipation of great power influences, and the creation of an environment in which the reunification of Germany as a non-aligned state could then take place. Needless to say, such sentiments are regarded with mixed feelings by the authorities in Eastern Europe. Peace movements are to be supported in the west but they must be regarded as subversive at home. Yet containment must be restrained otherwise the authorities place themselves in the untenable position of failing to discriminate between those 'enemies of socialism' who seek return to western-style capitalism and those activists who advocate a more democratic socialism as provided for by the Constitutions of the East European states at the present time. A policy of restraint is required in the hope that political activities can be brought under the control of Party organizations or churches which have established good working relations with the authorities.

Economic problems may be more serious. Since East Europeans greatly value the modest improvements to their living standards which they have secured since the early years of communist rule, any moves to reduce food consumption through smaller deliveries and higher prices have been highly unpopular. It is evident that the reform movement in Czechoslovakia arose in no small measure as a result of economic stagnation and it is evident that lack of material progress is a critical factor in creating instability to the point when people become impatiently resentful of the need to compromise national interests to suit Soviet security requirements. The one major event in Eastern Europe since 1968, the rise of the reform movement in Poland, was triggered off by economic failures in 1970 when proposed price rises led to rioting and the downfall of the Gomulka regime. Attempts by the government of E. Gierek to increase prices were also frustrated: opposition in 1976 led to the withdrawal of the proposed increases and in 1980 more determined action led to Gierek's removal from power and the formation of a free trade union Solidarity. In 1981 a state of martial law was imposed, the trade union was suppressed, and increases in food prices of up to 400 per cent were imposed. (5)

Disillusionment in Romania is becoming profound on account of the economic difficulties combined with an ideological drive for self-sacrifice which has lost much of its credibility. The country remains hard at work and major public works minimize unemployment but with high investment the economy cannot provide an improvement in living standards necessary to maintain a strong sense of regime legitimacy. (6) In assessing the performance of Romania, N. Burakow concedes that there has been rapid economic growth and attention to basic human needs, organized on a basis of self-reliance. However, 'without proper limits and controls restrictions on human rights and personal freedom can easily extend beyond any temporary measures which could be justified' and furthermore, once basic human needs have been satisfied, 'the model has not exhibited the ability or the necessary flexibility to provide further significant improvements in the standard of living'. (7) The problems are most acute in Poland and Romania with absolute declines in consumption in the early 1980s but they are symptomatic of the East European system which, despite its promises, finds great difficulty in meeting even the more modest consumer demands over housing, food, and transport.

Writing in 1988 during a period of reform in the Soviet Union, it is evident that feelings in Eastern Europe indicate caution and uncertainty rather than euphoria. Even if there are none of the miscalculations which have in the past destroyed radical movements in Eastern Europe overestimating Moscow's capacity for accommodation (the

'Prague Spring' of 1968 being the clearest example), there are profound uncertainties. Economic reform in the Soviet Union will almost certainly result in greater pressure on Eastern Europe to produce better quality goods. The heavy dependence that was conditioned by Soviet military supremacy at the end of the Second World War (and expressed through sweeping institutional changes and the formation of joint companies) is maintained by the co-ordinating role of Comecon and also by the rising cost of Soviet oil (from 1981) which has increased Eastern Europe's exports to the Soviet Union and reduced the scope for trade with the west and with the Third World at a time when political conditions might appear conducive to development. Hard currency debts have become more acutely embarrassing and the dramatic reappraisal of western trading links (converting a $3.1 billion trade deficit in 1980 into a $5.1 billion surplus two years later) has been a major component of the crises already described. Western sanctions (against Poland in retaliation for the suppression of the Solidarity union) have merely served to heighten dependency on the Soviet Union. Western technology will certainly remain very much in demand but perhaps the lessons of the 1970s point to Eastern Europe's capacity for no more than gradual assimilation in sympathy with a hesitant reform process. (8) For even the pace-setting Hungarians face the acute danger of becoming overwhelmed by debts as the propensity to borrow runs ahead of the readiness to compromise such basic tenets of socialism as full employment. The mood is thus one of acute uncertainty and it remains to be seen how far glasnost in the Soviet Union can raise spirits in Eastern Europe. Maximizing economic growth in association with western technology while having proper regard for the constraints of the socio-economic system which the Soviets seem likely to insist on retaining remains the key problem for the years ahead.

NOTES

INTRODUCTION

1. D. Kideckel (ed.) (1983) 'Political rituals and symbolism in socialist Eastern Europe', Anthropological Quarterly 56: 52-104; L. Kolakowski (1982) 'Ideology in Eastern Europe', in M. Drachkovitch (ed.), pp. 43-53; C.K. Wilber & K.P. Jameson (eds) (1982) Socialist Models of Development, Oxford: Pergamon.
2. Rugg 1985: 119. See also D.S. Rugg (1971) 'Aspects of change in the landscape of East Central and Southeast Europe', in G.W. Hoffman (ed.), pp.83-126.
3. I. Berend (1960) 'The historical evolution of Eastern Europe as a region', International Organization 40: 329-46; D.W. Paul (1979) The Cultural Limits of Revolutionary Politics, Boulder, Col.: East European Monographs.

CHAPTER 1: COMMUNIST POWER IN EASTERN EUROPE

1. Wolff 1974: 249.
2. W.S. Churchill (1951) The Second World War, Boston, Mass.: Houghton Mifflin, V, p. 286.
3. Wolff 1974:250.
4. L.E. Davis (1974) The Cold War Begins: Soviet-American Conflict over Eastern Europe, Princeton, NJ: Princeton University Press; J.L. Gaddis (1988) The Long Peace: Aspects of the Cold War, Oxford: Oxford University Press; G.V. Kacewicz (1978) Great Britain the Soviet Union and the Polish Government in Exile

1939-1945, The Hague: Nijhoff; S.D. Kertesz (ed.) (1956) The Fate of East Central Europe: Hopes and Failures of American Foreign Policy, Notre Dame, Ind.: University of Notre Dame Press; C.S. Maier (ed.) (1978) The Origins of the Cold War and Contemporary Europe, Leamington Spa: Berg; J. Wheeler-Bennett and A. Nicholls (1972) The Semblance of Peace, London: Macmillan.

5.   M.J. Hogan (1987) The Marshall Plan: American Britain and the Reconstruction of Western Europe 1947-1952, Cambridge: Cambridge University Press.

6.   J. Lovenduski and J. Woodall (1987) Politics and Society in Eastern Europe, London: Macmillan.

7.   A. Clark (1985) Barbarossa: The Russian-German Conflict 1941-5, London: Macmillan.

8.   I. Ceausescu and others (1985) A turning point in World War Two: 23 August 1944 in Romania, Boulder, Col.: East European Monographs; V. Georgescu (1985) Romania: Forty Years 1944-1984, New York: Praeger; P.D. Quinlan (1977) Clash over Romania: British and American Policies Towards Romania 1938-1947, Los Angeles, Calif.: American-Romanian Academy of Arts and Science; H.C. Reese (1961) 'Soviet Policy Toward Rumania 1944-1947', unpublished PhD thesis, New York University.

9.   P.A. Toma (1987) Socialist Authority: The Hungarian Experience, New York: Praeger; I. Szent-Miklosy (1987) The Hungarian Independence Movement, New York: Praeger.

10. J. Coutorvides and J. Reynolds (1988) Poland 1939-1945, Leicester: Leicester University Press; J. Garlinski (1985) Poland in the Second World War, London: Macmillan; R.F. Leslie (1981) 'The Polish underground and the origins of communist rule 1939-1945', European Studies Review 11: 397-407; J.M. Shotwell and M.M. Laserson (1945) Poland and Russia 1919-1945; New York: Carnegie Trust for International Peace.

11. K. Kaplan (1987) The Communist Party in Power: A Profile of Party Politics in Czechoslovakia, Boulder, Col.: Westview.

12. Pounds 1969: 193.

13. M. Blacksell and M. Brown (1983) 'Ten years of Ostpolitik', Geography 68: 260-2; R. Bleimann (1972) 'Détente and the GDR', World Today 28: 289-95; L.J.

Whetten (1971) Germany's Ostpolitik, Oxford: Oxford University Press.

14. M.M. Boll (1984) Cold War in the Balkans: American Foreign Policy and the Emergence of Communist Bulgaria 1943-1947, Lexington, Ky.: University Press of Kentucky; F. Larrabee (1972) 'Bulgaria's politics of conformity', Problems of Communism 21 (4): 42-52; M.L. Miller (1975) Bulgaria During the Second World War, Stanford, Calif.: Stanford University Press; N. Oren (1971) Bulgarian Communism: The Road to Power 1934-1944, New York: Columbia University Press.

15. J.R. Adelman (ed.) (1983) Terror and Communist Systems: The Role of the Secret Police in Communist States, Boulder, Col.: Westview; R.K. Carlton (1954) The Economics of Forced Labour in Eastern Europe, New York: Mid-European Studies Center; D. Warriner (1950) Revolution in Eastern Europe, London: Turnstile Press.

16. George and Scanlon 1976; P. Mojzes (1987) Church and State in Post-war Eastern Europe, London: Greenwood Press.

17. S. Alexander (1979) Church and State in Yugoslavia Since 1945, Cambridge: Cambridge University Press.

18. George and Scanlon 1976.

19. Lewis 1982. See also J. Ericson (1971) Soviet Military Power, London: Royal United Services Institute for Defence Studies; J. Eyal (1988) The Warsaw Pact and the Balkans, London: Macmillan; D.C. Herspring (1980) 'The Warsaw Pact at twenty five', Problems of Communism 29(5): 1-15; R.L. Hutchings (1980) '25 years of the Warsaw Pact', Radio Free Europe Background Report 105; F.S. Larrabee (1977) 'Balkan security', Adelphi Papers 135; J. Simon (1984) Warsaw Pact Forces: Problems of Command and Control, Boulder, Col.: Westview.

20. D.A. MacGregor (1986) 'Uncertain allies: East European forces in the Warsaw Pact', Soviet Studies 38: 227-47; C. Rice (1984) The Soviet Union and the Czechoslovak Army 1948-1983: Uncertain Allegiance, Princeton, N.J.: Princeton University Press.

21. Nelson 1984: 265. See also T.M. Forster (1980) The East German Army, London: George Allen & Unwin; D.R. Herspring (1984) 'GDR naval build-up', Problems of Communism 33(1): 54-62.

22. M. Checiuski (1983) 'Poland's military burden', Problems

of Communism 32(3): 31-44.
23. A. Braun (1987) The Warsaw Pact: Change and Modernization in the Gorbachev Era, Boulder, Col.: Westview; R. Kolkowicz (1969) 'The Warsaw Pact: entangling alliance', Survey: Journal of Soviet & East European Studies 70(1): 86-101.
24. A. Alexeiev (1981) 'Romania and the Warsaw Pact: the defence policy of a reluctant ally', Strategic Studies 1; R. Weiner (1984) Romanian foreign policy and the United Nations, New York: Praeger.
25. Narkiewicz 1986:1. See also C.J. Bukowski and M.A. Cichock (1987) Prospects for Change in Communist Systems, New York: Praeger; R. Davy (1972) 'The European Security Conference and the politics of Eastern Europe', World Today 28: 289-95; K. Dawisha (1986) 'State and politics in developed socialism: recent developments in Soviet theory', in J.A. Hall (ed.) States in History, Oxford: Blackwell, pp. 211-27; K. Dawisha (1988) Eastern Europe, Gorbachev and Reform, Cambridge: Cambridge University Press; C. Gati (1974) 'East Central Europe: touchstone for détente', Journal of International Affairs 28: 158-74; R.B. King and R.W. Dean (eds) (1974) East European Perspectives on European Security and Cooperation, New York: Praeger; H.G. Skilling (1988) Samizdat and an Independent Society in Eastern Europe, London: Macmillan; L. Spencer (1988) 'Elites, nationalism and regime legitimacy: Czechoslovakia and Yugoslavia', Slovo: Journal of Contemporary Soviet and East European Affairs 1(1): 25-39; R.L. Tokes (ed.) (1978) Eurocommunism and Détente, New York: New York University Press; R.L. Tokes (1979) Opposition in Eastern Europe, London: Macmillan; R. Wesson (1982) 'Eurocommunism and Eastern Europe', in Drachkovitch (ed.), pp. 55-79.
26. R.D. Asmus (1980) 'The search for historical roots in the GDR', Radio Free Europe Background Report 193; P. Sugar and others (1985) 'Eastern Europe: a question of identity', East European Program, Wilson Center Occasional Paper 2. For Romanian examples see G. Cioranescu (1976) 'Michael the Brave: evaluation and revaluation of the Wallachian prince', Radio Free Europe Background Report 191; G. Cioranescu (1977) 'Vlad the Impaler: current parallels with a Medieval Romanian prince', Radio Free Europe Background

Report 23; D. Deletant (1988) 'The past in contemporary Romania: some reflections on current Romanian historiography', Slovo: Journal of Contemporary Soviet and East European Affairs 1 (2): 77-91.

27. A. Dorpalen (1986) German History in Marxist Perspective: The East German Approach, London: Tauris; N.M. Naimark (1983) 'Writing the GDR's history', Problems of Communism 32(4): 51-6; D. Smith (1988) 'GDR policies on German national identity in the age of Perestroika', Slovo: Journal of Contemporary Soviet and East European Affairs 1(2): 1-8.

28. R. Bleimann (1973) 'Détente and the GDR; the internal implications', World Today 29: 289-95; G.H. Quester (1984) 'Transborder television' Problems of Communism 33(5); 76-87.

29. B.K. Kiraly and P. Jones (eds.) (1978) The Hungarian Revolution of 1956 in Retrospect, Boulder, Col.: East European Monographs; F.A. Vali (1961) Rift and Revolt in Hungary: Nationalism Versus Communism, Cambridge, Mass.: Harvard University Press; P.E. Zinner (1962) Revolution in Hungary, New York: Columbia University Press.

30. R.K. Evanson (1985) 'Regime and working class in Czechoslovakia 1948-1968', Soviet Studies 37:248-68; I. Gadourek (1953) The Political Control of Czechoslovakia: A Study in Social Control of a Soviet Satellite State, Leiden: Stenfert Kroese; Z. Gitelman (1970) 'Power and authority in Eastern Europe', in Johnson (ed.), pp. 255-63; J. Krejci (1972) Social Change and Stratification in Post-war Czechoslovakia, London: Macmillan; M. Myant (1981) Socialism and Democracy in Czechoslovakia 1945-1948, Cambridge: Cambridge University Press; E. Taborsky (1961) Communism in Czechoslovakia 1948-1960, Princeton, NJ: Princeton University Press; P.E. Zinner (1963) Communist Strategy and Tactics in Czechoslovakia 1918-1948, London: Pall Mall.

31. P. Brock and H.G. Skilling (eds.) (1970) The Czech Renaissance, Toronto: Toronto University Press; J. Bugaiski (1987) Czechoslovakia: Charter 77's Decade of Dissent, New York: Praeger; F. Eidlin (1980) The Logic of Normalization: The Soviet Intervention in Czechoslovakia and the Czechoslovak Response, Boulder, Col.: East European Monographs; K. Dawisha

(1984) The Kremlin and the Prague Spring, Berkeley: University of California Press; P. Windsor and A. Roberts (1969) Czechoslovakia 1968: Reform Repression Resistance, New York: Columbia University Press.

32. N.G. Andrews (1985) Poland 1980-1: Solidarity Versus the Party, Washington, DC: National Defense University Press; L.S. Graham and M.K. Ciechocinska (1987) The Polish Dilemma: Views from Within, Boulder, Col.: Westview; D. Lane and G. Kolankiewicz (1973) Social Groups in Polish Society, London: Macmillan; G.C. Malcher (1984) Poland's Politicized Army: Communists in Uniform, New York: Praeger; D.S. Mason (1985) Public Opinion and Political Change in Poland 1980-1982, Cambridge: Cambridge University Press; W. Majkowski (1985) People's Poland: Patterns of Social Inequality and Conflict, London: Greenwood Press; P. Ralna (1985) Poland 1981: Towards Socialist Renewal, London: George Allen & Unwin; W.F. Robinson (ed.) (1980), August 1980: The Strikes in Poland, Munich: Radio Free Europe Research; R. Taras (1986) 'Official etiologies of Polish crises', Soviet Studies 38: 53-68.

33. I.M. Pascu (1983) 'The Balkans: a Romanian perspective', in Carlton and Schaerf (eds) pp. 136-51. See also Drewnowski 1982.

34. G. Cioranescu (1980) '40th anniversary of the annexation of Bessarabia and Northern Bucovina', Radio Free Europe Background Report 183; G. Cioranescu (1981) 'The problem of Bessarabia and Northern Bucovina during World War Two', 61 and 136; N. Dima (1982) Bessarabia and Bukovina: The Soviet-Romanian Territorial Dispute, Boulder, Col.: East European Monographs.

35. S. Sampson (1983) 'Bureaucracy and corruption as anthropological problems: a case study from Romania', Folk 25: 63-97; S. Sampson (1984) 'Muddling through in Romania: why the mamaliga doesn't explode', International Journal of Romanian Studies 3: 165-85; S. Sampson (1985) 'Rumours in socialist Romania', Survey 28: 142-64.

36. Pavlowitch 1971: 205.

37. Wolff 1974: 328.

38. Ibid.: 332.

39. Pavlowitch 1971: 206.

40. Wolff 1974: 367. See also D. Carlton (1983) 'Great power spheres of influence in the Balkans', in Carlton and Schaerf (eds) pp. 51-68; S. Clissold (ed.) (1975) Yugoslavia and the Soviet Union 1939-1973: A Documentary Survey, London: Royal Institute for International Affairs; A.N. Dragich (1954) Tito's Promised Land, New Brunswick, NJ: Rutgers University Press; M. Milivojevic and others (eds) (1988) Yugoslavia's Security Dilemmas, Leamington Spa: Berg; S.K. Pavlowitch (1980) 'The grey zone on NATO's Balkan flank', Survey: Journal of East-West Studies 25: 20-42; D. Rusinow (1976) The Yugoslav Experiment Under Tito 1948-1974, London: Royal Institute for International Affairs; J. Sallnow and A. John (1978) 'Tito's foundations for Yugoslavia's future: independence in the communist bloc', Geographical Magazine 50: 240-2; A.B. Ulam (1952) Tito and the Cominform, Cambridge, Mass.: Harvard University Press; D. Wilson (1979) Tito's Yugoslavia, Cambridge: Cambridge University Press.
41. Pavlowitch 1971: 379. See also Adizes 1971; W.J. Bartlett (1979) 'Economic Development, Institutional Reform and Unemployment in Yugoslavia 1945-1975', unpublished PhD thesis, University of Liverpool; Bicanic 1973; J. Milenkovitch (1971) Plan and Market in Yugoslav Economic Thought, New Haven, Conn.: Yale University Press; Moore 1980; L. Sirc (1979) The Yugoslav Economy Under Self-Management, London: Macmillan.
42. Wolff 1974:429.
43. Pavlowitch 1971: 388.
44. ibid.: 398.
45. J. Krejci and V. Velimsky (1981) Ethnic and Political Nations in Europe, London: Croom Helm, pp. 139-54. See also Burg 1983; S.L. Burg (1986) 'Elite conflict in post-Tito Yugoslavia', Soviet Studies 38: 170-93; Carlton and Schaerf 1983.
46. H. Hamm (1963) China's Bridgehead in Europe, New York: Praeger; A. Schnytzer (1977) 'Economic Planning and Industrialization Policy in the PRA', unpublished D.Phil. thesis, Oxford University.
47. N.C. Pano (1974) 'The Albanian cultural revolution', Problems of Communism 23(4): 44-57; P.E. Peifti (1972) 'Albania's expanding horizons', Problems of Communism 21(1): 30-9.

48. K. Kolsti (1981) 'Albanianism: from humanists to Hoxha', in C. Klein and M.J. Reban (eds.) The Politics of Ethnicity in Eastern Europe, New York: Columbia University Press, pp. 15-44. See also M.A. Beqiraj (1963) 'From Village to Nation: A Study of Albanian Society', unpublished PhD thesis, Cornell University.
49. G. Reti (1983) 'The foreign policy of Albania after the break with China', in Carlton and Schaerf (eds) pp. 189-99.
50. Kolsti, 'Albanianism', op. cit., p. 23.
51. M. Alder (1986) 'A state apart', Geographical Magazine 58: 132-7; M. Biber (1980) 'Albania alone against the world', National Geographic Magazine 158:530-57; E. Biberaj (1985) 'Albania after Hoxha: dilemmas of change', Problems of Communism 34(6): 32-47; F.B. Singleton (1975) 'Albania and her neighbours: the end of isolation', World Today 31: 383-90.

CHAPTER 2: POST-WAR CHANGES IN STATE BOUNDARIES

1. D.J. Nelson 1978; A. L. Philipps 1975. See also G. Kolko (1969) The Politics of War: Allied Diplomacy and the World Crisis of 1943-1945, London: Weidenfeld & Nicolson; T. Sharp (1975) The Wartime Alliance and the Zonal Division of Germany, Oxford: Clarendon Press; G. Wettig (1975) Community and Conflict in the Socialist Camp: The Soviet Union East Germany and the German Question 1965-1972, London: Hurst.
2. E. Wiskemann 1956: 71. See also A. Kruszewski (1972) The Oder-Neisse Boundary and Poland's Modernization, New York: Praeger; B.N. Stein (1969) 'The Boundaries of Eastern Europe with Emphasis on the Oder-Neisse Boundary', unpublished PhD thesis, New York University; S.M. Terry (1983) Poland's Place in Europe: General Sikorksi and the Origin of the Oder-Neisse Line 1939-1943, Princeton, NJ: Princeton University Press; Wagner 1957.
3. Moodie 1945. See also B. Navak (1970) Trieste 1941-1954: The Ethnic Political and Ideological Struggle, Chicago: University of Chicago Press.
4. Wolff 1974: 313-14.
5. Francisco and Merritt 1985; F. Friedensburg (1967) 'The geographical elements of the Berlin situation',

Geographical Journal 133: 137-47; C.B. Robson (1960) Berlin: Pivot of German Destiny, Chapel Hill: University of North Carolina Press.

6. Davison 1958.
7. R. Slusser (1973) The Berlin Crisis of 1961, Baltimore, Maryland: Johns Hopkins University Press, p. 129.
8. McAdams 1985.
9. Freund 1972; Plock 1985. See also D.L. Bark (1974) Agreement in Berlin: A Study of 1970-1977 Quadripartite Negotiations, Washington, DC: American Enterprise Institute; M. Blacksell and M. Brown (1983) 'Ten years of Ostpolitik', Geography 68: 260-2; S.R. Bowers (1975) 'The West Berlin Issue in the Era of Superpower Détente: East Germany and the Politics of West Berlin 1968-1974', unpublished PhD Thesis, University of Tennessee. G. Langguth (1988) Berlin and the German Question: The Berlin Policy of the German Democratic Republic, Boulder, Col: Westview.
10. D.M. Kelly (1986) Breakthrough in Ostpolitik: The 1971 Quadripartite Agreement Boulder, Col.: Westview.
11 R.L. Merritt (1973) 'Infrastucture change in Berlin', Annals, Association of American Geographers, 63: 58-70.
12. T.H. Elkins and B. Hofmeister (1988) Berlin: The Spatial Structure of a Divided City, London: Routledge; H. Heineberg (1979) 'Service centres in East and West Berlin', in French and Hamilton (eds), pp. 305-34.
13. Heineberg 'Service centres', op. cit. p. 327.

CHAPTER 3: THE REGIONAL DIMENSION

1. Pecsi (ed.) 1964; Pounds and Spulber 1957. See also S. Kozlowski (1972) 'Regional prognoses in the management of natural resources', Przeglad Geograficzny 44: 233-46; B. Malisz (1975) 'Research work as an input in the construction of the national plan', Geographia Polonica 32: 113-19; B. Sarfalvi (ed.) (1969) Research Problems in Hungarian Applied Geography, Budapest: Hungarian Academy of Sciences.
2. Connor 1979; Kende and Strmiska 1987; I.S. Koropeckyj (1972) 'Equalization of regional development in socialist countries: an empirical study', Economic Development & Cultural Change 21: 68-85.
3. L. Lacko (1984) 'An assessment of regional policies and

progress in Eastern Europe', in Demko (ed.) pp. 134-56.
4. G.S. Demko and R.J. Fuchs (1984) 'A comparison of regional development policy instruments and measures in Eastern and Western Europe', in Demko (ed.), pp. 83-98.
5. L. Niznansky & W.F. Robinson (1979) 'Slovakia after a decade of federation', Radio Free Europe Background Report 5: 19.
6. F.E.I. Hamilton (1975). See also G. Labuda (1975) 'Poland's return to the Baltic and Odra-Nysa in 1945: historical and current conditions', Polish Western Affairs 16:3-36; M. Orzechowski (1972) 'Wroclaw in the recent history of the Polish state and nation', Polish Western Affairs 13: 305-33; E. Rosset (1970) 'Demographic factors concerning repolonisation of the western and northern territories', Polish Western Affairs 11: 67-88; A.W. Walczak (1972) 'The source of West Germany's eastern policy', Polish Western Affairs, 13: 274-304.
7. H. Rechowicz (1972) Western and Northern Poland, Warsaw: Interpress.
8. Z. Rykiel (1985) 'Regional consciousness in the Katowice region, Poland', Area 17: 285-93; Z. Rykiel (1985) 'Regional integration and the boundary effect in the Katowice region', Geographia Polonica 51: 323-32.
9. R. Kolaczkowski (1974) 'Interport: a new solution to the long tug of war over Szczecin?', Radio Free Europe Research Report 9.
10. S. Pribichevich (1982) Macedonia: Its History and People, University Park: Pennsylvania State University; Wilkinson 1951.
11. J. Bajec (1983) 'Regional disparities in Yugoslavia', in D. Seers and K. Ostrom (eds) The Crisis of the European Regions, London: Macmillan; M.B. Gregory (1973) 'Regional economic development in Yugoslavia', Soviet Studies 25: 213-28; J. Halpern (1969) 'Yugoslavia: modernization in an ethnically diverse state', in W. Vucinich (ed.) Contemporary Yugoslavia: Twenty Years of Socialist Experiment, Berkeley Calif.: University of California Press, pp. 321-9; M.I. Logan (1968) 'Regional economic development in Yugoslavia 1953-1964', Tijdschrift voor Economische en Sociale Geografie 59: 42-52.
12. A.N. Dragich and S. Todorovich (1985) The Sage of Kosovo: Focus of Serbian-Albanian Relations, Boulder,

Col.: East European Monographs.

13. R.F.R. Artisien (1984) 'A note on Kosovo and the future of Yugoslav-Albanian relations: a Balkan perspective', Soviet Studies 36: 267-76; R.F.R. Artisien and R.A. Howells (1981) 'Yugoslavia Albania and the Kosovo riots', World Today 37: 419-27; M. Baskin (1983) 'Crisis in Kosovo' Problems of Communism 32(2): 61-74; W.B. Bland (1981) The Question of the Albanians in Yugoslavia, Ilford: Albanian Society.

14. Cadzow and Luganyi 1983. See also S. Beck and J.W. Cole (1981) 'Ethnicity and nationalism in Southeastern Europe', University of Amsterdam Papers on European & Mediterranean Societies 14; T. Gilberg (1974) 'Ethnic minorities in Romania under socialism', East European Quarterly 7: 435-58; E. Illyes (1982) National Minorities in Romania: Change in Transylvania, Boulder, Col.: East European Monographs; A. Ludenyi (1971) 'Hungarians in Romania and Yugoslavia', unpublished PhD thesis, Louisiana State University; M. MacArthur (1976) 'The Saxon Germans: political fate of an ethnic minority', Dialectical Anthropology 1: 349-64; J. Pataki and others (1985) 'Hungarian minorities in Romania and Czechoslovakia', in V. Mastny (ed.) Soviet/East European survey 1983-1984, Durham, NC: Duke University Press; P.D. Quinlan (1982) 'The US and the problems of Transylvania', in Fischer-Galati and others (eds) pp. 369-83; G. Schopflin (1978) The Hungarians of Romania, London: Minority Rights Group.

15. T. Morariu (1969) 'The position of Transylvania within the unitary territory of Romania', Revue Roumaine: Geographie 13: 13-23.

16. R. Zaharia (ed.) (1978) Hungarians and Germans in Romania Today, Bucharest: Meridiane.

17. ibid.: 185.

18. C. Thomas (1979) 'Population mobility in frontier communities: examples from the Julian March 1931-1945', Transactions, Institute of British Geographers 4: 44-61.

19. J.B. Borchert (1975) 'Economic development and population distribution in Albania', Geoforum 6: 177-86.

CHAPTER 4: POPULATION PROBLEMS

1. G. Demko and R. Fuchs (1970) 'Population distribution

policies in developed socialist and western nations', Population & Development Review 5: 439-70; R. Fuchs and G. Demko (1977) 'Spatial population policies in the socialist countries of Eastern Europe', Social Science Quarterly 58: 60-73; Kosinski 1974.

2. J. Berent (1970) 'Causes of fertility decline in Eastern Europe and the Soviet Union', Population Studies 24: 53-8; H.P. David and R.J. McIntyre (1981) Reproduction Behaviour: Central and Eastern European Experience, New York: Springer; K. Dziewonski and others (1975) 'Population potential of Poland between 1950 and 1970', Geographia Polonica 31: 5-28; M.R. Jackson (1985) 'Comparing the Balkan demographic experience 1860 to 1970', Journal of European Economic History 14: 223-72; R.J. McIntyre (1980) 'The Bulgarian anomaly: demographic transition and current fertility', Southeastern Europe 7(2): 47-70.

3. Besemeres 1980. See also R.J. McIntyre (1975) 'Pronatalist programmes in Eastern Europe', Soviet Studies 27: 366-80; A. Macura (1974) 'Population policies in the socialist countries of Europe', Population Studies 28: 369-72; K.-H. Mehlen (1965) 'The socialist countries of Eastern Europe', in B. Berelson (ed.) Family Planning and Population Programmes, Chicago: Chicago University Press, pp. 207-26.

4. J. Adam (1984) Employment and Wage Policies in Poland Czechoslovakia and Hungary since 1950, London: Macmillan; J. Adam (1984) 'Regulation of labour supply in Poland Czechoslovakia and Hungary', Soviet Studies 36: 69-86.

5. W. Moskoff (1980) 'Pronatalist policies in Romania', Economic Development & Cultural Change 28: 597-614; I. Stefanescu (1981) 'Active population in the urban area of the SRR', Revue Roumaine: Geographie 25: 121-7; I. Stefanescu & N. Baranovsky (1978) 'Romania's population dynamics over the 1966-1977 period', Revue Roumaine: Geographie 22: 265-74.

6. T. Bauer (1983) 'A note on money and the consumer in Eastern Europe', Soviet Studies 35: 376-84; M. Ciochocinska (1977) 'Regional sociology in Poland against a world background', in A. Kuklinski (ed.) Regional Studies in Poland, Warsaw: Polish Academy of Sciences Committee for Space Economy & Regional Planning; B.L. Faber (ed.) (1976) The Social Structure of Eastern Europe, New York: Praeger; P. Kende and Z.

Strmiska (1987) Equality and Inequality in Eastern Europe, Leamington Spa: Berg; J.F. Triska and C. Gati (eds) (1981) Blue Collar Workers in Eastern Europe, London: George Allen & Unwin; P.J.D. Wiles (1974) Distribution of Incomes: East and West, Amsterdam: North Holland.

7. I. Kemeny (1979) 'Poverty in Hungary', Social Science Information 18: 247-67.

8. Welsh 1981: 496.

9. ibid.: 495.

10. J. Rezler (1974) 'The rebirth of sociology in Hungary', East European Quarterly 8: 223-9; G. Schopflin (1977) 'Hungary: an uneasy stability', in A. Brown and J. Gray (eds) Political Culture and Political Change in Communist States, London: Macmillan, pp. 131-58.

11. Welsh 1981: 502.

12. J. Krejci (1972) Social Change and Stratification in Post-War Czechoslovakia, New York: Columbia University Press; M. Simek and J. Dewetter (1986) Cultural Policy in Czechoslovakia, Paris: Unesco.

13. Bromke 1985. See also W.D. Connor (1977) 'Social change and stability in Eastern Europe', Problems of Communism 26: 16-32; W.D. Connor (1980) 'Dissent in Eastern Europe: a new coalition', Problems of Communism 29(1): 1-17; V. Havel and others (1985) The Power of the Powerless: Citizens Against the State in Central and Eastern Europe, London: Hutchinson; D.N. Nelson (1981) 'Worker-party conflict in Romania', Problems of Communism 30(5): 40-9; A. Pravda (1982) 'Poland 1980: from "premature consumerism" to labour solidarity', Soviet Studies 34: 167-99; P. Raina (1981) Independent Social Awareness in Poland, London: London School of Economics; H.G. Skilling (1981) Charter 77 and Human Rights in Czechoslovakia, London: George Allen & Unwin; J. Staniszkis (1981) 'The evolution of forms of working class protest in Poland', Soviet Studies 33: 204-31.

14. B.R. Bociurkiw (1985) 'Factors shaping communist religious policies in Eastern Europe', in G.W. Hoffman and others, Eastern Europe: religion and nationalism', Smithsonian Institution, Wilson Center, East European Program Occasional Paper 3: 3-29 (quotation, p. 6).

15. Beeson 1982; Bociurkiw and Strong 1975; de George and Scanlan 1976.

16. D.I. Dunn (1979) Détente and Papal-Communist

relations 1962-1978, Boulder, Col.: Westview.

17. P. Remet (ed.) (1984) Religion and Nationalism in Soviet and East European Politics, Durham, NC: Duke University Press.

18. P. Ramet (1985) 'Patterns of religio-national symbiosis in Eastern Europe: Poland, Czechoslovakia, Hungary', in G.W. Hoffman and others, 'Eastern Europe', pp. 42-58; E. Weingaertner (ed.) (1976) Church Within Socialism: Church and State in East European Socialist Republics, Rome: IDOC.

19. B. Szajkowski (1983) Next to God ... Poland: Politics and Religion in Contemporary Poland, New York: St Martin's Press.

20. S.L. Kegerreis (1980) 'A church within socialism: religion in the GDR today', Radio Free Europe Background Report 240; P. Ramet (1984) 'Church and peace in the GDR', Problems of Communism 33(4): 44-57.

21. A. Kratochvil (1982) 'The church in Czechoslovakia', Radio Free Europe Background Report 78; J.M. Lochman (1970) The Church in Marxist Society: The Czechoslovak View, London: SCM.

22. P.A. Compton (1973) 'Population trends and differentials in Hungary between 1960 and 1970', Transactions, Institute of British Geographers 53: 59-84; J. Halpern (1975) 'Some perspectives in Balkan migration patterns', in B.M. du Toit and H.I. Safa (eds) Migration and Urbanization: Models and Adaptive Strategies, The Hague: Mouton, pp. 77-115; L. Kosinski and A. Zurek (1967) 'Concentration of population in East Central Europe', Geographia Polonica 11: 121-8; D.R. Vining and R. Pallone (1982) 'Migration between core and peripheral regions', Geoforum 13: 339-410.

23. E.A. Hammel (1969) 'Economic change social mobility and kinship in Serbia', Southwestern Journal of Anthropology 25: 188-97; E.A. Hammel (1977) 'The influence of social and geographical mobility on the stability of kinship systems: the Serbian case', in A.A. Brown and E. Neuberger (eds) Internal Migration: A Comparative Perspective, New York: Academic Press, pp. 401-15; G.W. Hoffman (1973) 'Currents in Yugoslavia: migration and social change', Problems of Communism 22(6): 16-31.

24. Kostanick 1977.

25. Schoenberg 1970.

26. H.L. Kostanick (1957) 'Turkish resettlement of Bulgarian Turks 1950-1953', University of California, Publications in Geography 8(2): 65-146; S. Monnesland (1987) 'The Turkish minority in Bulgaria', Nordic Journal of Soviet & East European Studies 4(3): 53-63.

27. J.L. Kerr (1975) 'Gastarbeiter in Eastern Europe', Radio Free Europe Research Background Report 169.

28. H. Trend (1975) 'The Orenburg gas project', Radio Free Europe Background Report 165.

29. W. Zimmerman (1977) 'National-international linkages in Yugoslavia: the political consequences of openness', in Triska and Cocks (eds), pp. 334-64.

30. King 1973. See also R. Gerner (1987) 'Nationalities and minorities in the Soviet Union and Eastern Europe', Nordic Journal of Soviet & East European Studies 4(2): 5-30; M. Horak and others (1985) East European National Minorities 1919-1980: A Handbook, Littleton: Libraries Unlimited; L.A. Kosinski (1969) 'Changes in the ethnic structure of East-Central Europe 1930-1960', Geographical Review 59: 388-402.

31. G. Stone (1972) The Smallest Slavonic Nation: The Sorbs of Lusatia, London: Athlone Press.

32. Burg 1983. See also G.W. Hoffman (1977) 'The evolution of the ethnographic map of Yugoslavia', in Carter (ed.) pp. 437-99; W. Meier (1983) 'Yugoslavia's national question', Problems of Communism 32(3): 47-60; G. Schopflin (1980) 'Nationality in Yugoslav politics Survey', Journal of East & West Affairs 25: 1-19; P. Shoup (1963) 'Yugoslavia's national minorities under communism', Slavic Review 22: 64-81; P. Shoup (1968) Communism and the Yugoslav National Question, New York: Columbia University Press; P. Shoup (1972) 'The national question in Yugoslavia', Problems of Communism 21(1): 18-29; F. Singleton (1972) 'The roots of discord in Yugoslavia', World Today 28: 170-80.

33. C.N.O. Bartlett (1980) 'The Turkish minority in Yugoslavia', Bradford Studies on Yugoslavia 3.

34. Welsh 1981: 503.

35. Mayer et al. 1953. See also P. Lendvai (1971) Anti-semitism in Eastern Europe, London: Macdonald; A. Polonsky and others (eds) (1986) The Jews in Poland, Oxford: Blackwell.

36. D. Denrick and G. Puxon (1972) The Destiny of Europe's Gypsies, New York: Basic Books.

37. O. Ulc (1968-9), 'Communist national minority policy:

the case of the gypsies in Czechoslovakia', Soviet
Studies 20: 421-43.
38. K. Magnusson (1987) 'The Serbian reaction: Kosovo and
ethnic mobilization among the Serbs', Nordic Journal of
Soviet & East European Studies 4(3): 3-30; K. Nystrom
(1987) 'The Serbs in Croatia: a dual identity', Nordic
Journal of Soviet & East European Studies 4(3): 31-52.

CHAPTER 5: ECONOMIC GROWTH AND CENTRAL PLANNING

1. P. Bairoch (1976) 'Europe's gross national product 1800-
   1975', Journal of European Economic History 5: 273-
   340. See also J. Marer (1985) Dollar GNPs of the USSR
   and Eastern Europe, Baltimore: Johns Hopkins
   University Press.
2. Gati 1974; Fallenbuchl 1975. See also J. Debardeleben
   (1983) 'Marxism-Leninism and economic policy: natural
   resource pricing in the USSR and the GDR', Soviet
   Studies 35: 36-52; P. Marer (1979) 'East European
   economies: achievements problems prospects', in
   Rakowska-Harmstone and Gyorgy (eds), pp. 244-89; A.
   Zwass (1984) Economies of Eastern Europe in a Time of
   Change, Armonk, NY: Sharpe; G. Schopflin (1988)
   'Reform in Eastern Europe: some methodological
   considerations', Slovo: Journal of Contemporary Soviet
   and East European Affairs 1(1): 1-6.
3. Kaser 1968; Kaser and Zielinski 1970; Montias 1962;
   Spulber 1957.
4. S.R. Sacks (1983) Self-management and Efficiency:
   Large Corporations in Yugoslavia, London: George
   Allen & Unwin.
5. Z. Antic (1982) 'What's wrong with Yugoslavia's
   economic system?', Radio Free Europe Background
   Report 237; S. Estrin (1982) 'The effects of self-
   management on Yugoslav industrial growth', Soviet
   Studies 34: 69-85; S. Estrin (1983) Self-management
   Economic Theory and Yugoslav Practice, Cambridge:
   Cambridge University Press; Lydall 1984; Moore 1980;
   F. Singleton (1973) 'Yugoslavia: democratic centralism
   and market socialism', World Today 29: 160-8; C. Zebot
   (1982) 'Yugoslavia's self-management on trial',
   Problems of Communism 31: 42-9.
6. P. Boot (1983) 'Continuity and change in the planning

system of the GDR', Soviet Studies 35: 331-42; P. Gregory and G. Leptin (1977) 'Similar societies under different economic systems: the case of the two Germanys', Soviet Studies 29: 519-42; G. Leptin and M. Melzer (1978) Economic Reform in East German Industry, Oxford: Oxford University Press; M. Melzer (1981) 'Combine formation in the GDR', Soviet Studies 33: 88-106.

7. J. Vanous (1982) 'East European economic slowdown', Problems of Communism 31(4): 1-19; J. Winiecki (1986) 'Are Soviet type economies entering an era of long-term decline?', Soviet Studies 38: 325-48.

8. Hohmann et al. 1975. See also W. Brus (1972) The Market in a Socialist Economy, London: Routledge & Kegan Paul;. W. Brus (1973) The Economics and Politics of Socialism, London: Routledge & Kegan Paul; W. Brus (1975) Socialist Ownership and Political Systems, Routledge & Kegan Paul.

9. Balassa 1969; Hare et al. 1981. See also J. Adam (1974) 'The system of wage regulation in Hungary', Canadian Journal of Economics 3: 578-93; J. Adam (1987) 'The Hungarian economic reform in the 1980s', Soviet Studies 39: 610-27; B. Balassa (1973) 'The firm in the NEM in Hungary', in M. Bronstein (ed.) Plan and Market, New Haven, Conn.: Yale University Press, pp. 347-72; G. Barta (1986) 'Spatial impacts of organizational change in Hungarian industrial enterprises', in F.E.I. Hamilton (ed.) Industrial Change in Advanced Economies: Spatial Perspectives, London: Croom Helm, pp. 197-207; H. Flakierski (1979) 'Economic reform and income distribution in Hungary', Cambridge Journal of Economics 3: 15-32; P. Galasi and G. Sziraczki (1985) 'State regulation enterprise behaviour and the labour market in Hungary 1968-1983', Contemporary Journal of Economics 9: 203-19; A. Gollner (1978) 'The Politics of the Hungarian NEM', unpublished PhD thesis, London School of Economics; P.G. Hare (1981) 'The investment system in Hungary', P.G. Hare et al., (eds) Hungary: a decade of economic reform, London: George Allen & Unwin, pp. 83-109; P.G. Hare (1983) 'The beginnings of institutional reform in Hungary', Soviet Studies 35: 313-30; J. Kornai (1983) 'Comments on the present state and prospects of the Hungarian economic reform', Journal of Contemporary Economics 7: 225-52; R. Nyers (1971) 'Hungarian economic policy in practice', Acta

Oeconomica 7: 255-74; B.A. Racz (1984) 'Recent developments in Hungarian enterprise democracy', Soviet Studies 36: 544-59; R.L. Tokes (1981) 'Hungarian reform imperatives', Problems of Communism 33(5): 1-23.

10. I. Jefferies (1981) 'Introduction and summary', in I. Jefferies (ed.) The Industrial Enterprise in Eastern Europe, New York: Praeger, pp. 1-28; N. Watts (1983) 'inflation in the USSR and Eastern Europe', in S.F. Frowen (ed.) Controlling Industrial Economies, London: Macmillan, pp. 127-56.

11. J. Eronen (1988) 'Economic development and economic thought in Czechoslovakia', Nordic Journal of Soviet and East European Studies 5: 33-41; W.F. Foster (1974) 'A Comparison of Soviet Reaction to Change in Rumania and Czechoslovakia in the 1960s', unpublished PhD thesis, American University, Washington, DC; K. Ivanicka (1986) 'The need for a new evolutionary theory of time and space - contemporary Czechoslovak industrial change', in Hamilton (ed.) Industrial Change, pp. 13-22.

12. Feiwel 1971; Touraine 1983; Zielinski 1973. See also G. Blazyca (1983) 'Polish economic management 1970-1981', in Frowen (ed.) Controlling Industrial Economies, pp. 157-73; S. Gomulka and J. Rostowski (1984) 'The reformed Polish economic system', Soviet Studies 36: 386-405; Z.M. Fallenbuchl (1984) 'The Polish economy under martial law', Soviet Studies 36: 513-27; P.G. Hare and P.T. Wanless (1981) 'Polish and Hungarian reforms: a comparison', Soviet Studies 33: 491-517; G. Sanford (1984) 'The Polish communist leadership and the onset of the state of war', Soviet Studies 36: 494-512; P.T. Wanless (1980) 'Economic reform in Poland', Soviet Studies 32: 28-57; J. Woodall (1982) The Socialist Corporation and Technocratic Power: The PUWP Industrial Organisation and Workforce Control 1958-1980, Cambridge: Cambridge University Press; J.G. Zielinski (1978) 'On system remodelling in Poland: a pragmatic approach', Soviet Studies 30: 3-37.

13. Feiwel 1977. See also M.R. Jackson (1983) 'Recent economic performance and policy in Bulgaria', Arizona State University, College of Business Administration, Faculty Working Papers 17.

14. Keefe et al. 1972: 229. See also Dobrescu and Blaga 1973; Spigler 1973.

15. D. Nelson (1981) 'Romania - participatory dynamics in "developed socialism"', in J.F. Trisk and C. Gati (eds) Blue Collar Workers in Eastern Europe, London: George Allen & Uwin, pp. 236-52.
16. J.P. Hardt and C.H. McMillan (eds) (1988) Planned Economies: Confronting the Challenges of the 1980s, Cambridge: Cambridge University Press; V.V. Kusin (1986) 'Gorbachev and Eastern Europe', Problems of Communism 35(1): 39-53; O. Norgaard and S. Sampson (1984) 'Poland's crisis and East European socialism', Theory & Society 13: 773-96.
17. Triska and Gati (eds) Blue Collar Workers, p. xli.
18. Drewnowski 1982. See also A. Arato (1981) 'Civil society against the state: Poland 1980-1981', Teleos 47: 23-47; E. Freund (1983) 'Nascent dissent in Romania', in J. Curry (ed.) Dissent in Eastern Europe, New York: Praeger, pp. 60-8; D.S. Mason (1983) 'Solidarity, the regime and the public', Soviet Studies 35: 533-56; J. Montias (1980) 'Economic conditions and political instability in communist countries: observations on strikes riots and other disturbances', Studies in Comparative Communism 13: 285-305; G. Schopflin (1984) 'Corruption informalism and irregularity in Eastern Europe: a political analysis', Sudosteuropa, pp. 389-403.
19. B. Kortus (1985) 'Towards a more humanistic social approach to Polish industrial geography', Geographia Polonica 51: 207-11.
20. M. MacQueen (1980) 'Butcher baker candlestickmaker: private artisans in the GDR', Radio Free Europe Background Report 211.
21. B. Gervai (1968) 'The role and situation of private artisans in Hungary', Acta Oeconomica 3: 441-8.
22. A. Aslund (1984) 'The functioning of private enterprise in Poland', Soviet Studies 36: 427-44; H. Brezinski (1987) The Second Economy in the GDR: Pragmatism is Gaining Ground, Paderborn: Universitat, Gesamthochschule Arbeitspapiere des Fachbereichs Wirtschaftwissenschaft; H. Brezinski and P. Petrescu (1986) The Second Economy in Romania: A Dynamic Sector, Paderborn: Universitat-Gesamthochschule Arbeitspapiere des Fachbereichs Wirtschaftwissenschaft; J.A. Dellenbrandt (1988) 'The cooperative renaissance: reflections on new cooperatives and economic reforms in Eastern Europe', Nordic Journal of Soviet and East

European Studies 5: 43-53; E. Hankiss (1985) The Second Society: The Reduplication of the Social Paradigm in Contemporary Society - The Case of Hungary, Budapest: Institute of Sociology; F. Haslinger (1985) 'Reciprocity loyalty and the growth of the underground economy: a theoretical note', Europaische Zeitschrift fur Politische Okonomie 3: 309-23; T.R. Gabor (1979) 'The second economy', Acta Oeconomica 22: 291-311; I. Kemeny (1982) 'The unregistered economy in Hungary', Soviet Studies 34: 349-66; J. Kenedi (1981) Do it Yourself: Hungary's Hidden Economy, London: Pluto Press; S.L. Sampson (1983) 'Rich families and poor collectives: an anthropological approach to Romania's second economy', Bidrag til Oststatsforskning 2: 44-77; S.L. Sampson (1986) 'The informal sector in Eastern Europe', Teleos 66: 44-66.

23. M. Pecsi (1984) 'Geographical studies of the environment in Hungary', in P.A. Compton and M. Pecsi (eds) Environmental Management: British and Hungarian Case Studies, Budapest: Hungarian Academy of Sciences, pp. 5-23.

24. P. Gastescu and others (1972) 'Romania's waters and their potential', Revue Roumaine: Geographie 16: 65-74; R. Stoian (1971) 'The meteorological occurences which contributed to the May 1970 floods', Revue Roumaine: Geographie 15: 33-50; D. Turnock (1979) 'Water resource management problems in Romania', GeoJournal 3: 609-22.

25. L. Constantinescu (1978) 'An extreme Romanian earthquake and its wider geonomical setting', Revue Roumaine: Geographie 22: 179-206.

26. M.R. Jackson (1983-4) 'Romania's debt crisis: its causes and consequences', Arizona State University, Bureau of Business & Economic Research, College of Business Administration, Faculty Working Paper 13.

CHAPTER 6: INDUSTRY: PLANNING TECHNOLOGY AND REGIONAL DEVELOPMENT

1. Z.M. Fallenbuchl (1970) 'The communist pattern of industrialization', Soviet Studies 21: 458-84.

2. Feiwel 1968; Lane 1976; Stolper 1960; Zauberman 1964. See also G.R. Feiwel (1971) Poland's Industrialization Policy: A Current Analysis, New York: Praeger; C.

Herbst and I. Letea (1976) 'Regional structural modifications in the industry of socialist Romania', Revue Roumaine: Geographie 20: 211-15; B. Kortus (1976) 'Changes in industrial structure: the case of the Upper Silesian industrial district', Geographia Polonica 33: 183-90; P.S. Lee (1968) 'Structural change in Romanian industry 1938-1963', Soviet Studies 20: 219-28; I. Velcea (1969) 'Change in the geography of the economic branches of the SRR', Revue Roumaine: Geographie 13: 111-27.

3. R. Hayter (1987) Forest Products in the Global Economy, London: Croom Helm.

4. A. The main land use zones showing: (1) The predominantly forested zone (A - Eastern Carpathians; B - Curvature Carpathians; C - Southern Carpathians; D - Banat Mountains; E - Apuseni Mountains; F - North Dobrogea) (2) The mixed zone (A - Moldavian Plateau; B - Moldavian Hills; C - Southwest Dobrogea; D - Western Hills; E - Transylvanian Plateau) (3) The predominantly agricultural zone (A - North-east Moldavia; B - South Moldavia-Baragan; C - Dobrogea; D - Southern Oltenia; E - Western Plains; F - Central Transylvania) (4) Danube delta and floodplain. B. Some aspects of the plan to alter the balance of species.

5. F.E.I. Hamilton (1970) 'Changes in the industrial geography of Eastern Europe since 1940', Tijdschrift voor Economische en Sociale Geografie 61: 300-5. Case studies include W.H. Berensten (1981) 'Regional change in the GDR', Annals, Association of American Geographers 71: 50-66; H. Kohl (1978) 'Complex territorial change in old industrial areas of the GDR', in F.E.I. Hamilton (ed.) Industrial Change, London: Longman, pp. 65-72; S. Leszczycki (1969) 'Spatial structure of Poland's economy', Geographia Polonica 11: 77-96; S. Leszczycki and others (1975) 'Spatial structure of the national economy of Poland', Geographica Polonica 30: 29-40; E. Tajti (1971) 'Industrialization and population change on the Great Hungarian Plain', in Sarfalvi (ed.), pp. 133-44.

6. G. Enyedi (1984) 'Quality and quantity of regional development indicators in Eastern and Western Europe', in Demko (ed.) pp. 49-56; R. Fuchs and G. Demko (1979) 'Geographic inequality under socialism', Annals, Association of American Geographers 69: 301-18; I.S. Koropeckyj (1972) 'Equalization of regional

development in socialist countries: an empirical study',
Economic Development & Cultural Change 21: 68-86.
7. F.E.I. Hamilton (1970) 'Aspects of spatial behaviour in
planned economies', Papers of the Regional Science
Association 25: 85-105; F.E.I. Hamilton (1971) 'Decision
making and industrial location in Eastern Europe',
Transactions, Institute of British Geographers 52: 77-
84.
8. T.M. Poulsen (1971) 'Administrative and regional
structure in East Central and Southeast Europe', in
Hoffman (ed.) pp. 225-70.
9. B. Kortus (1985) 'Toward a more humanistic-social
approach to Polish industrial geography', Geographia
Polonica 51: 207-11.
10. T. Stryjakiewicz (1985) 'The relationships between the
location of the agricultural processing industry and the
agricultural produce base in the Poznan region',
Geographia Polonica 51: 189-98.
11. Turnock 1974, 1986. See also C. Herbst and others
(1975) 'The structure and territorial distribution of
industry in Romania', Geoforum 6: 49-55; D. Turnock
(1970) 'The pattern of industrialisation in Romania',
Annals, Association of American Geographers 60: 548-
59; D. Turnock (1979) 'Spatial aspects of modernisation:
the Romanian case', Contact: Journal of Urban &
Environmental Studies 11(2): 113-42. For the
administrative reform see R.A. Helin (1967) 'The
volatile administrative map of Rumania', Annals,
Association of American Geographers 57: 481-502; V.
Tufescu and C. Herbst (1969) 'The new administrative
map of Romania', Revue Roumaine: Geographie 13: 25-
37.
12. H. Gabor (1986) 'Recent East European regional
development experience', in F.E.I. Hamilton (ed.)
Industrialization in Developing and Peripheral Regions,
London: Croom Helm, pp. 85-113; I. Jefferies (ed.)
(1981) The Industrial Enterprise in Eastern Europe, New
York: Praeger.
13. M. Dobrowolska (1976) 'The growth pole concept and
the socioeconomic development of regions undergoing
industrialization', Geographia Polonica 33(2): 83-101 K.
Dziewonski (1977) 'Population problems in Polish
regional planning', in Kostanick (ed.) pp. 81-97; Z.M.
Fallenbuchl (1975) 'The development of the less
developed regions of Poland 1950-1970', in Burghardt

(ed.), pp. 14-42; G. Karaska (1975) 'Perspectives on the less developed regions of Poland', in Burghardt (ed.) pp. 43-64; I.S. Koropeckyj (1977) 'Regional development in Poland', Soviet Studies 29: 108-27; J.S. Kowalski (1986) 'Regional conflicts in Poland: spatial polarization in a centrally planned economy', Environment & Planning A 18: 599-617; J. Loboda (1974) 'The diffusion of television in Poland', Economic Geography 50: 70-82; K. Podoski (1975) 'A preliminary concept of the distribution of social infrastructure in Poland', Geographia Polonica 33(2): 75-84; H. Zimon (1979) 'Regional inequalities in Poland 1960-1975', Economic Geography 55: 242-52.

14. T. Lijewski (1976) 'Tendencies in the location of new industrial plants in Poland 1945-1970', Geographia Polonica 33(2): 157-69; T. Lijewski (1985) 'The spread of industry as a consequence of the location of new factories in Poland 1945-1982', Geographica Polonica 51: 199-206. See also A.H. Dawson (1969) 'The changing distribution of Polish industry 1949-1965', Transactions, Institute of British Geographers 50: 177-98; A.H. Dawson (1969) 'The changing pattern of the wool textile industry in the Polish western territories', Scottish Geographical Magazine 85: 47-63; L.W. Murray (1973) 'The Spatial Structure of Polish Industry 1950-1970', unpublished PhD thesis, Clark University; L.W. Murray and G.J. Karaska (1975) 'An econometric model of industrial development in Poland 1950-1970', Geographia Polonica 31: 29-39; R. Wilczewski and others (1978) 'Spatial industrial changes in Poland since 1945', in Hamilton (ed.) Industrial Change, pp. 80-98; M.J. Woodall (1979) 'The Policy of Industrial Concentration and Amalgamation in Poland Since 1958', unpublished PhD thesis, Manchester University.

15. A. Wrobel (1980) 'Industrialization as a factor of regional development in Poland', Geographia Polonica 43: 187-97; A. Wrobel (1984) 'Regional development issues in Poland', in Demko (ed.) pp. 214-29. See also S. Rog (1972) 'An attempt to determine the degree of industrialization of voivodships and powiats', Geographia Polonica 20: 85-98.

16. F.E.I. Hamilton (1982) 'Regional policy for Poland: a search for equity', Geoforum 13: 121-32.

17. C.G. Alvstam and others (1986) 'The transport sector in Polish economic planning and Polish-Soviet traffic

capacity problems', in J. Ambler and others (eds) Soviet and East European Transport Problems, London: Croom Helm, pp. 221-54 (quotation p. 224).

18. K. Dramowicz (1985) 'Some problems of disparities in Poland's regional development', Geographia Polonica 51: 313-22.

19. L. Pakula (1980) 'The Upper Silesian core region', Geographia Polonica 43: 223-30. See also Z. Ziolo (1976) 'The development of optimum territorial forms of industrial concentration', Geographica Polonica, 33(2); 171-81.

20. M. Connock (1982) 'A note on industrial efficiency in Yugoslav regions', Soviet Studies 34: 86-95; D. Flaherty (1988) 'Plan market and unequal regional development (Yugoslavia)', Soviet Studies 40: 100-24; M.B. Gregory (1973) 'Regional economic development in Yugoslavia', Soviet Studies, 25: 213-28; S. Ilesic (1977) 'The regions of Slovenia', Geographia Polonica 36: 73-82; F.B. Singleton (1979) 'Regional economic inequalities: migration and community response with special reference to Yugoslavia', Bradford Studies on Yugoslavia 1.

21. Hoffman 1972: 31. See also G.W. Hoffman (1980) 'Variations on centre-periphery relations in Southeast Europe', in J. Gottman (ed.) Centre and Periphery: Spatial Variations in Politics, London: Sage Publications, pp. 111-33.

22. J. Halpern (1967) 'Farming as a way of life: Yugoslav peasant attitudes', in J.F. Karcz (ed.) Soviet and East European Agriculture, Berkeley: University of California Press, pp. 356-81.

CHAPTER 7: SOCIALIST AGRICULTURE AND THE DRIVE FOR SELF-SUFFICIENCY

1. R. Deutsch (1986) The Food Revolution in the Soviet Union and Eastern Europe, Boulder, Col.: Westview; W.A.D. Jackson (ed.) (1971) Agrarian Policies and Problems in Communist and Non-communist Countries, Seattle: University of Washington Press. K.-E. Wadekin (1977) 'The place of agriculture in the European communist countries', Soviet Studies 29: 238-54; K.-E. Wadekin (1982) Agrarian Policies in Communist Europe: A Critical Introduction, The Hague: Nijhoff.

2. G. Borgstrom and F. Annegers (1971) 'Eastern Europe:

an appraisal of food and agriculture in the thirties compared with the sixties', Tijdschrift voor Economische en Sociale geografie 62: 114-25; G.S. Brown and others (1970) Eastern Europe's Agricultural Development and Trade: Patterns and Perspectives, Washington, DC: US Department of Agriculture, Economic Research Service; C.E. Miller and others (1973) Agriculture Statistics of Eastern Europe and the Soviet Union, Washington, DC: US Department of Agriculture, Economic Research Service; H. Trend (1974) Agriculture in Eastern Europe: A Comparative Study, Munich: Radio Free Europe.

3. M. Ellman (1982) 'Agricultural productivity under socialism,' in C.K. Wilber and K.P. Jameson (eds) Socialist Models of Development, Oxford: Pergamon, pp. 979-89.

4. S. Chelstowski (1974) 'A regional plan for the future', Polish Perspectives 17: 5-13; E. Cook (1984) 'Agricultural reform in Poland: background and prospects', Soviet Studies 36: 406-26; A.H. Dawson (1982) 'An assessment of Poland agricultural resources', Geography 67: 297-309; B. Galeski (1982) 'The solving of the agrarian question in Poland', Sociologia Ruralis 22: 149-66; J. Kostrowicki (1975) 'Transformation trends in the spatial organization of agriculture in Poland 1960-1990', Geographia Polonica 32: 27-41; W. Quaisser (1986) 'Agricultural price policy in Poland', Soviet Studies 38: 562-85.

5. J.C. Brada and K.-E. Wadekin (eds) (1987) Socialist Agriculture in Transition: Organisation Response and Failing Performance, Boulder, Col.: Westview; J. Kostrowicki and W. Tyszkiewicz (eds) (1970) 'Essays on agricultural typology and land use', Geographia Polonica 19: 1-290; W. Tyszkiewicz (1979) 'Agricultural typology of the Thracian basin, Bulgaria', Geographica Polonica 40: 171-86; W. Tyszkiewicz (1980) 'Types of agriculture in Macedonia as a sample of the typology of world agriculture', Geographica Polonica, 43: 163-85.

6. E.W. Entwistle (1972) 'Agrarian-industrial complexes in Bulgaria', Geography 57: 246-8; P. Wiedemann (1980) 'The origins and development of agro-industrial development in Bulgaria', in Francisco et al. (eds), pp. 97-135; M.L. Wyzan (1988) 'The Bulgarian experience with centrally planned agriculture', in K.R. Gray (ed.) Contemporary Soviet Agriculture: Comparative

Perspectives, Ames: Iowa State University Press.
7. V.D. Freeman (1983) 'Agricultural reorganization in the GDR 1965-1980', GeoJournal 7: 59-66; R.P. Sinclair (1979) 'Bureaucratic agriculture: planned social change in the GDR', Sociologia Ruralis 19: 211-26. See also V. Bajaja (1980) 'Concentration and specialization in Czechoslovak and East German farming', in Francisco et al. (eds) pp. 263-94.
8. J.B. Allcock (1980) 'The socialist transformation of the village: Yugoslav agricultural policy since 1945', in Francisco et al. (eds), pp. 199-216. R. First-Dilic (1978) 'The production roles of farm women in Yugoslavia', Sociologia Ruralis 18: 125-39; C. Thomas (1978) 'Decay and development in Mediterranean Yugoslavia', Geography 63: 179-87.
9. P.D. Bell (1984) Peasants in Socialist Transition: Life in a Collectivised Hungarian Village, Berkeley: University of California Press; P.S. Elek (1980) 'The Hungarian experiment in search of profitability', in Francisco et al. (eds), pp. 165-84; L.A. Fisher and P.E. Uren (1973) The New Hungarian Agriculture, Montreal: McGill-Queen's University Press; A. Gyenes (1976) 'Some aspects of stratification in Hungarian cooperative farms', Sociologia Ruralis 16: 161-76; M. Hollos and B.C. Maday (eds) (1983) New Hungarian Peasants: An East Central European Experience with Collectivisation, Boulder, Col.: East European Monographs; I. Lazar (1976) 'The collective farm and the household plot', New Hungarian Quarterly 63: 61-77; C.H. Rosenfeld (1979) 'Hungarian agriculture: a symbiosis of collective and individual enterprises', Wye College Miscellaneous Study 6; N. Swain (1985) Collective Farms Which Work?, Cambridge: Cambridge University Press; N. Swain (1987) 'Hungarian agriculture in the early 1980s: retrenchment followed by reform', Soviet Studies 39: 24-39.
10. W. Biegajlo and W. Jankowski (1972) 'Land use mapping in Poland', Geographia Polonica 22: 105-12; W. Jankowski (1982) 'Polish experience in land use mapping', Geographica Polonica, 48: 59-69; J. Kostrowicki (1970) 'Some methods of determining land use and agricultural orientations as used in Polish land utilization and typological studies', Geographica Polonica 18: 93-120; J.A. Pielkiewicz (1979) 'Kulak-ization of Polish agriculture', in Francisco et al. (eds),

pp. 86-107; H. Szulc (1972) 'The development of the agricultural landscape of Poland', Geographia Polonica 22: 85-103.

11. W.B. Morgan (1985) 'Cut flowers in Warsaw', GeoJournal 11: 339-48.
12. W.A. Dando (1974) 'Wheat in Romania', Annals, Association of American Geographers 64: 241-57; G. Jaehne (1980) Problems of agricultural integration within the CMEA', in Francisco et al. (eds), pp. 221-35.
13. I. Stefanescu (1973) 'Regional types of animal breeding in the SRR', Revue Roumaine: Geographie 17: 53-65.
14. I. Berenyi (1971) 'Development of the agricultural structure around Kiskoros', in Sarfalvi (ed.) pp. 123-32. See also I. Bencze (1971) 'Fruit and vegetable canning in the Great Hungarian Plain', in Sarfalvi (ed.), pp. 89-105.
15. G. Iacob (1968) 'The rational use of sandy soils in Romania', Revue Roumaine: Geographie 12: 171-4; I. Iordan (1977) 'Works of land melioration in the SRR', Revue Roumaine: Geographie, 21: 42-50; I. Stefanescu (1972) 'Fruit growing in Romania', Revue Roumaine: Geographie 16: 125-32; I. Stefanescu (1977) 'Changes occurring in the agriculture of Dobrogea during the last hundred years', Revue Roumaine: Geographie, 21: 87-101.
16. Keefe et al. 1972: 256.
17. E. Daroczi (1984) 'The protection of agricultural land on the urban fringe: the case of Veszprem city', in P.A. Compton & M. Pecsi (eds) Environmental Management: British and Hungarian Case Studies, Budapest: Hungarian Academy of Sciences, pp. 51-74.
18. S. Marosi and S. Papp (1978) 'Landscape factors modified by agricultural activity', Geographia Polonica 41: 73-80.
19. H. Trend (1973) 'Agricultural mechanization in Hungary: some successes and problems', Radio Free Europe, Research Report, Hungary 7. See also J. Hajda (1980) 'The impact of current policies on modernizing agriculture in Eastern Europe', in Francisco et al. (eds), pp. 295-310.

CHAPTER 8: TOURISM AND THE IMPORTANCE OF FOREIGN VISITORS

1. M. Dragicevic (1980) 'The Yugoslav experience:

socialist development and participation: answers to socio-economic and leisure-related questions', in G. Cherry and I. Travis (eds) Leisure in the 1980s: Alternative Futures, London: Leisure Studies Association, pp. 46-55.

2. S. Dragomirescu and I. Nicolae (1980) 'International tourism of Balkan countries', Revue Roumaine: Geographie 24: 175-83.

3. T.M. Poulsen (1977) 'Migration on the Adriatic coast: some processes associated with the development of tourism' in Kostanick (ed.), pp. 197-215; F. Violich (1972) 'An urban development policy for Dalmatia', Town Planning Review 43: 151-65, 243-53.

4. D.R. Hall (1984) 'Foreign tourism under socialism: the Albanian "Stalinist" model', Annals of Tourism Research 11: 539-55 (quotation, p. 547).

5. R.S. Ciobanu (1979) 'The population of the upper Prahova valley with special consideration on the town of Sinaia', Revue Roumaine: Geographie 23: 131-42; D. Turnock (1974) 'Tourism in the Romanian Carpathians', Town & Country Planning 41: 268-71; D. Turnock (1977) 'Romania and the geography of tourism', Geoforum 8: 51-6.

6. H.A. Senn (1982) Were-Wolf and Vampire in Romania, New York: Columbia University Press.

CONCLUSION

1. G.R. Feiwel (1982) 'A socialist model for economic development: the Polish and Bulgarian experience', in C.K. Wilber and K.P. Jameson (eds) Socialist Models of Development, Oxford: Pergamon pp. 929-50 (quotation, p. 947).

2. G. Grossman (ed.) (1970) Essays in Socialism and Planning in Honour of Carl Landauer, Englewood Cliffs, NJ: Prentice-Hall.

3. Feiwel, 'A socialist model for economic development', p. 947.

4. P. Marer (1976) 'Has Eastern Europe become a liability to the Soviet Union?', in C. Gati (ed.) The International Politics of Eastern Europe, New York: Praeger, pp. 59-80.

5. P. Summerscale (1982) The East European Predicament: Changing Patterns in Poland, Czechoslovakia and

Romania, Aldershot: Gower. See also R. Bahro (1978) The Alternative in Eastern Europe, London: New Left Books; J.F. Brown (1977) Eastern Europe's Uncertain Future, New York: Praeger; T. Gilberg (1985) 'Eastern Europe at the crossroads: contradictory tendencies of subservience and autonomy', in S. Bethlen and I. Volgyes (eds) Europe and the Superpowers: Political Economic and Military Policies in the 1980s, Boulder, Col.: Westview; P. Lewis (ed.) (1984) Eastern Europe: Political Crisis and Legitimation, London: Croom Helm; M.J. Sodaro and S.L. Wolchik (eds) (1983) Foreign and Domestic Policy in Eastern Europe in the 1980s: Trends and Prospects, London: Macmillan; A.B. Ulam (1974) 'The destiny of Eastern Europe', Problems of Communism 23(1); 1-12.

6. M.E. Fischer (1977) 'Participatory reforms and political development in Romania', in J.F. Triska and P.M. Cocks (eds) Political Developments in Eastern Europe, New York: Praeger, 217-37.

7. N. Burakow (1982) 'Romania and Greece: socialism versus capitalism', in Wilbur and Jameson (eds) Socialist Models, pp. 907-28 (quotation, p. 924).

8. T.W. Simons (1988) 'Approaching relations with Eastern Europe in the late 1980s', Wilson Center, East European Program, Occasional Paper 12. See also J.P. Hardt and C.H. McMillan (1988) Planned Economies: Confronting the Challenge of the 1980s, Cambridge: Cambridge University Press.

BIBLIOGRAPHY

References on East European trade, transport, energy and settlement patterns will be found in the companion volume. The attention of readers is drawn to two German atlases: the work of T. Kraus and others (1959) Atlas Ostliches Mitteleuropa (Bielefeld: Velhagen & Klasing) is excellent for the GDR, Poland, and northern Czechoslovakia, while the remaining parts of Eastern Europe feature in Atlas der Donaulander by J. Breu (Vienna: Osterreichisches Ost- und Sudosteuropa Institut, 1970). National atlases are available for Bulgaria (1973), Czechoslovakia (1966), and Romania (1979).

Adizes, N. (1971) Industrial Democracy Yugoslav Style: The Effect of Decentralization on Organizational Behaviour, New York: Free Press.
Alton, T.P. (1955) Polish Post-war Economy, New York: Columbia University Press.
Bairam, E. (1988) Technical Progress and Industrial Growth in the USSR and Eastern Europe: An Empirical Study 1961-75, Aldershot: Gower.
Balassa, A.A. (1969) The Hungarian Experience in Economic Planning, New Haven, Conn.: Yale University Press.
Banac, I. (1984) The National Question in Yugoslavia, Ithaca, NY: Cornell University Press.
Beeson, T. (1982) Discretion and Valour: Religious Conditions in Russia and Eastern Europe, Philadelphia: Fortess Press.
Bell, J.D. (1986) The Bulgarian Communist Party from Blagoev to Zhivkov, Oxford: Clio.
Beloff, N. (1987) Tito's Flawed Legacy: Yugoslavia and the

West Since 1939, Boulder, Col.: Westview.

Benes, V.L. and Pounds, N.J.G. (1970) Poland, London: Benn.

Bentley, R. (1984) Technological Change in the GDR, Boulder, Col.: Westview.

Berxholi, A. and Qiriasz, P. (1986) Albania: a Geographical View, Tirana: 8 Nentori Publishing House.

Besemeres, J.F. (1980) Socialist Population Politics: The Political Implications of Demographic Trends in the USSR and Eastern Europe, White Plains, NY: Sharpe.

Betts, R.R. (ed.) (1950) Central and Southeastern Europe 1945-1948, London: RIIA.

Bialecki, I. and others (eds) (1987) Crisis and Transition: Polish Society in the 1980s, Leamington Spa: Berg.

Biberaj, E. (1986) Albania and China: A Study of an Unequal Alliance, Boulder, Col.: Westview.

---- (1989) Albania: a Nation in Transition, Boulder, Col.: Westview

Bicanic, R. (1973) Economic Policy in Socialist Yugoslavia, Cambridge: Cambridge University Press.

Bielasiak, J. and others (eds) (1984) Polish Politics: Edge of an Abyss, New York: Praeger.

Bland, W.B. (1988) World Bibliographical Series: Albania, Oxford: Clio.

Bociurkiw, B.R. and Strong, J.W. (eds) (1975) Religion and Atheism in the USSR and Eastern Europe, London: Macmillan.

Bombelles, J. (1968) The Economic Development of Communist Yugoslavia 1947-1964, Stanford, Calif.: Hoover Institution.

Bornstein, M. and others (eds) (1981) East-West Relations and the Future of Eastern Europe, London: George Allen & Unwin.

Bracewell, B. (1976) Economic Integration: East and West, London: Croom Helm.

Bradley, J.F.H. (1981) Politics in Czechoslovakia 1945-1971, Washington, DC: University Press of America.

Bromke, A. (1985) Eastern Europe in the Aftermath of Solidarity, Boulder, Col.: East European Monographs.

Brown, J.F. (1966) The New Eastern Europe, London: Pall Mall.

---- (1970) Bulgaria Under Communist Rule, London: Pall Mall.

Bryson, P.J. (1984) The Consumer Under Socialist Planning: The East German Case, New York: Praeger.

Burg, S.L. (1983) Conflict and Cohesion in Socialist Yugoslavia: Political Decision Making Since 1966, Princeton, NJ: Princeton University Press.

Burghardt, A.F. (ed.) (1975) Development Regions in the Soviet Union, Eastern Europe and Canada, New York: Praeger.

Burks, R.V. (1961) The Dynamism of Communism in Eastern Europe, Princeton, NJ: Princeton University Press.

Busek,V. and Spulber, N. (eds) (1957) East Central Europe Under the Communists: Czechoslovakia, New York: Praeger.

Butler, T. (ed.) (1976) Bulgaria Past and Present, Columbus, Ohio: American Association for the Advancement of Slavic Studies.

Byrnes, R.F. (ed.) (1957) East Central Europe Under the Communists: Yugoslavia, New York: Praeger.

Cadzow, J.F. and Ludanyi, A. (eds) (1983) Transylvania: The Roots of Ethnic Conflict, Kent, Ohio: Kent State University Press.

Carlton, D. and Schaerf, C. (eds) (1983) Southeastern Europe after Tito: A Powder Keg for the 1980s?, London: Macmillan.

Carter, F.W. (ed.) (1977) Historical Geography of the Balkans, London: Academic Press.

Checinski, M. (1982) Poland: Communism, Nationalism, Anti-Semitism, New York: Kanz-Cohl.

Childs, D. (1983a) Germany Since 1918, London: Batsford.

---- (1983) The GDR: Moscow's German Ally, London: Allen & Unwin.

---- and others (1989) East Germany in Comparative Perspectives, London: Routledge.

Ciechocinska, M.K. and Graham, L.S. (eds) (1986) The Polish Dilemma: Views from Within, Boulder, Col.: Westview.

Cohen, L.J. (1987) Yugoslavia: Tradition and Change in a Multi-ethnic State, Boulder, Col.: Westview.

---- and Warwick, P. (1983) Political Cohesion in a Fragile Mosaic: The Yugoslav Experience, Boulder, Col.: Westview.

Connor, W.D. (1979) Socialism, Politics and Equality, New York: Columbia University Press.

Curry, J.L. (ed.) (1983) Dissent in Eastern Europe, New York: Praeger.

Davies, N. (1986) Heart of Europe: A Short History of Poland, Oxford: Oxford University Press.

Davison, W.P. (1958) The Berlin Blockade: A Study of Cold

War Politics, Princeton, NJ: Princeton University Press.

Dawisha, K. and Hanson, P. (eds) (1981) Soviet-East European Dilemmas, London: Holmes & Meier.

Dawson, A.H. (ed.) (1986) Planning in Eastern Europe, New York: Praeger.

Deletant, A. and Deletant, D. (1985) World Bibliographical Series: Romania, Oxford: Clio.

Dellin, L.A.D. (ed.) (1957) East Central Europe Under the Communists: Bulgaria, New York: Praeger.

Demek, J. and others (1971) Geography of Czechosolvakia, Prague: Academia.

Demko, G. (ed.) (1984) Regional development: Problems and Policies in Eastern and Western Europe, London: Croom Helm.

Dickinson, R.E. (1953) Germany: A General and Regional Geography, London: Methuen.

Dobbs, M. (1970) Socialist Planning: Some Problems, London: Lawrence & Wishart.

---- (1981) Poland Solidarity Walesa, Oxford: Pergamon.

Dobrescu, E. and Blaga, I. (1973) Structural Patterns of Romanian Economy, Bucharest: Meridiane.

Drachkovitch, M. (ed.) (1982) East Central Europe Yesterday, Today, and Tomorrow, Stanford, Calif.: Hoover Institution Press.

Drewnowski, J. (ed.) (1982) Crisis in the East European Economy: The Spread of the Polish Disease, London: Croom Helm.

Dubey, V. and others (1975) Yugoslavia: Development with Decentralization, Baltimore: Johns Hopkins University Press.

Dunn, D.J. (ed.) (1987) Religion and Nationalism in Eastern Europe and the Soviet Union, London: Lynne Rienner.

Elkins, T.H. (1969) Germany, London: Chatto & Windus.

Elkins, T.H. and Hofmeister, B. (1988) Berlin: The Spatial Structure of a Divided City, London: Methuen.

Ellman, M. (1989) Socialist Planning, Cambridge: Cambridge University Press.

Enyedi, G. (1976) Hungary: An Economic Geography, Boulder, Col.: Westview.

Fallenbuchl, Z.M. (ed.) (1975) Economic Development in the Soviet Union and Eastern Europe, New York: Praeger.

Feis, H. (1967) Churchill Roosevelt Stalin: The War They Waged and the Peace They Sought, Princeton, NJ: Princeton University Press.

Feiwel, G.R. (1968) New Economic Patterns in

Czechoslovakia, New York: Praeger.
---- (1971) Problems in Polish Economic Planning, New York: Praeger.
---- (1977) Growth and Reforms in Centrally Planned Economies: The Lessons of The Bulgarian Experience, New York: Praeger.
Fischer-Galati, S. (ed.) (1956) Rumania, New York: Mid-European Studies Center.
---- (ed.) (1957) East Central Europe Under the Communists: Rumania, New York: Praeger.
---- (1963) Eastern Europe in the Sixties, New York: Praeger.
---- (1965) Twentieth Century Rumania, New York: Columbia University Press.
---- (1967) Romania: From People's Democracy to Socialist Republic, Cambridge, Mass.: MIT Press.
---- (1969) The Socialist Republic of Romania, Baltimore: Johns Hopkins University Press.
---- (1970) Twentieth Century Romania, New York: Columbia University Press.
---- (1981) Eastern Europe in the 1980s, Boulder, Col.: Westview.
---- and others (eds) (1982) Romania Between East and West, Boulder, Col.: East European Monographs.
Fisher, J.C. (1966) Yugoslavia: A Multinational State, San Francisco, Calif.: Chandler House.
Fisher, M.E. (1989) Nicolae Ceausescu: a political biography, London: Lynne Rienner.
Floyd, D. (1965) Rumania: Russia's Dissident Ally, London: Pall Mall.
Francisco, R.A. and others (eds) (1979) The Political Economy of Collectivised Agriculture, New York: Pergamon.
---- (1980) Agricultural Policies in the USSR and Eastern Europe, Boulder, Col.: Westview.
Francisco, R.A. and Merritt, R.L. (eds) (1985) Berlin Between Two Worlds, Boulder, Col.: Westview.
French, R.A. and Hamilton, F.E.I. (eds) (1979) The Socialist City: Spatial Structure and Urban Policy, Chichester: Wiley.
Freund, M. (1972) From Cold War to Ostpolitik: Germany and the New Europe, London: Wolff.
Gamarnikov, M. (1968) Economic Reforms in Eastern Europe, Detroit: Wayne State University Press.
Gati, C. (ed.) (1974) The Politics of Modernization in

Eastern Europe, New York: Praeger.

---- (1976) The International Politics of Eastern Europe, New York: Praeger.

de George, R.T. and Scanlan, J.P. (eds) (1976) Marxism and Religion in Eastern Europe, Dordrecht: Reidel.

Georgescu, V. (ed.) (1985) Romania: Forty Years 1944-1984, New York: Praeger.

Gerner, K. (1985) Soviet Union and Central Europe in the Post-War Era, Aldershot: Gower.

Gething, M.J. (1982) Warsaw Pact Air Power in the 1980s, London: Arms and Armour Press.

Gianaris, N.V. (1982) The Economies of the Balkan Countries, New York: Praeger.

---- (1984) Greece and Yugoslavia: An Economic Comparison, New York: Praeger.

Gilberg, T. (1975) Modernization in Romania Since World War Two, New York: Praeger.

Golan, C. (1973) Reform Rule in Czechoslovakia: The Dubcek Era 1968-1969, Cambridge: Cambridge University Press.

Graham, L.S. (1982) Romania: A Developing Socialist State, Boulder, Col.: Westview.

Griffiths, W.E. (1962) Albania and Sino-Soviet Rift, Cambridge, Mass.: MIT Press.

Hakovirta, H. (1988) East-West Conflict and European Neutrality, Oxford: Clarendon Press.

Hamilton, F.E.I. (1975) Poland's Western and Northern Territories, Oxford: Oxford University Press.

Hammond, Y.T. (ed.) (1975) The Anatomy of Communist Takeovers, New Haven, Conn.: Yale University Press.

Hanhardt, A.M. (1986) German Democratic Republic, London: Frances Pinter.

Hardt, J.P. and McMillan, C.H. (eds) (1988) Planned Economies: Confronting the Challenges of the 1980s, Cambridge: Cambridge University Press.

Hare, P.G. and others (eds) (1981) Hungary: A Decade of Economic Reform, London: Allen & Unwin.

Heinrich, H.-G. (1986) Hungary: Politics, Economics and Society, London: Frances Pinter.

Helmrich, E. (ed.) (1957) East Central Europe Under the Communists: Hungary, New York: Praeger.

Heuser, D.B.G. (1989) Western Containment Policies Towards Yugoslavia 1948-53, London: Routledge.

Hills, D. (1988) Return to Poland, London: Bodley Head.

Hoensch, J.K. (1988) A History of Modern Hungary, London:

Longman.

Hoffman, G.W. (1972) Regional Development Strategies in Southeastern Europe, New York: Praeger.

Hoffman, G.W. (ed.) (1971) Eastern Europe: Essays in Geographical Problems, London: Methuen.

Hoffman, G.W. and Neal, F.W. (1962) Yugoslavia: The New Communism, New York: Twentieth Century Fund.

Hohmann, H.-H. and others (1975) The New Economic Systems of Eastern Europe, London: Hurst.

Horvat, B. (1976) The Yugoslav Economic System: The First Labor-managed Economy in the Making, New York: Sharpe.

Hutchings, R.L. (1983) Soviet-East European Relations: Consolidation and Conflict 1968-1980, Madison: University of Wisconsin Press.

Ignotus, P. (1972) Hungary, London: Benn.

Ionescu, G. (1964) Communism in Rumania 1944-1962, Oxford: Oxford University Press.

James, R.R. (ed.) (1969) The Czechoslovak Crisis 1968, London: Weidenfeld & Nicholson.

Jankovic, B.M. (1988) The Balkans in International Relations, London: Macmillan.

Johnson, C. (ed.) (1970) Change in Communist Systems, Stanford, Calif.: Stanford University Press.

Jones, C.R. (1981) Soviet Influence in Eastern Europe: Political Autonomy and the Warsaw Pact, New York: Praeger.

Jowitt, K. (1971) Revolutionary Breakthrough and National Development: The Case of Romania 1944-1965, Berkeley: University of California Press.

Kabdebo, T. (1980) World Bibliographical Series: Hungary, Oxford: Clio.

Kadar, J. (1974) For a Socialist Hungary, Budapest: Corvina.

Kanet, R.E. (ed.) (1988) The Soviet Union Eastern Europe and the Third World, Cambridge: Cambridge University Press.

Kaplan, K. (1986) The Communist Party in Power: A Profile of Party Politics in Czechoslovakia, Boulder, Col.: Westview.

Kaser, M. (ed.) (1968) Economic Development for Eastern Europe, London: Macmillan.

Kaser, M. and Zielinski, J.G. (1970) Planning in East Europe, London: Bodley Head.

Keefe, E.K. and others (1972) Area Handbook for Romania,

Washington, DC: American University.

Kende, P. and Strmiska, Z. (1987) Equality and Inequality in Eastern Europe, Leamington Spa: Berg.

Kerner, R.J. (ed.) (1949) Yugoslavia, Berkeley: University of California Press.

Kertesz, S.D. (1962) East Central Europe and the World: Developments in the Post-Stalin Era, Notre Dame, Ind.: University of Notre Dame Press.

King, R.B. (1973) Minorities Under Communism, Cambridge, Mass.: Harvard University Press.

---- (1980) History of the Romanian Communist Party, Stanford, Calif.: Hoover Institution Press.

Kintner, W.R. and Klaiber, W. (1971) Eastern Europe and European Security, New York: Dunellan.

Kohler, H. (1965) Economic Integration in the Soviet Bloc with an East German Case Study, New York: Praeger.

Kolankiewicz, G. (1986) Poland, London: Frances Pinter.

Kosinski, L.A. (ed.) (1974) Demographic Developments in Eastern Europe, New York: Praeger.

Kostanick, H.L. (ed.) (1977) Population and Migration Trends in Eastern Europe, Boulder, Col.: Westview.

Kovrig, B. (1979) Communism in Hungary from Kun to Kadar, Stanford, Calif.: Hoover Institution Press.

Krisch, H. (1981) The GDR: A Profile, Boulder, Col.: Westview.

---- (1985) The GDR: The Search for Identity, Boulder, Col: Westview.

Kruszewski, A. (1972) The Oder-Neisse Boundary and Poland's Modernization, New York: Praeger.

Krystufek, Z. (1981) The Soviet Regime in Czechoslovakia, Boulder, Col.: East European Monographs.

Kuhlman, J.A. (ed.) (1978) The Foreign Policies of Eastern Europe, Leiden: Sijthoff.

Lampe, J.R. (1986) The Bulgarian Economy in the Twentieth Century, London: Croom Helm.

Lane, D. (1976) The Socialist Industrial State, London: George Allen & Unwin.

Lavigne, M. (1974) The Socialist Economies of the Soviet Union and Europe, London: Martin Robertson.

Lendvai, P. (1968) Eagles in Cobwebs: Nationalism and Communism in the Balkans, London: Macdonald.

Lewanski, R.C. (1984) World Bibliographical Series: Poland, Oxford: Clio.

Lewis, P.G. (1984) Eastern Europe: Political Crisis and Legitimation, London: Routledge.

Lewis, W.J. (1982) The Warsaw Pact: Arms Doctrine and Strategy, Cambridge, Mass.: Institute for Foreign Policy Analysis.

Lichtenberger, E. and Pecsi, M. (eds) (1988) Contemporary Essays in Austrian and Hungarian Geography, Budapest: Hungarian Academy of Sciences.

Linden, R.H. (1979) Bear and Foxes: The International Relations of the East European States 1965-1969, Boulder, Col.: East European Monographs.

Loczy, D. (ed.) (1988) Land Evaluation Studies in Hungary, Budapest: Hungarian Academy of Sciences.

London, K. (ed.) (1967) Eastern Europe in Transition, Baltimore, Johns Hopkins University Press.

Loth, W. (1988) The Division of the World 1941-1955, London: Routledge.

Ludz, P.C. (1984) 'The GDR from the sixties to the seventies: a sociopolitical analysis', University Press of America, Occasional Papers in International Affairs 26.

Lydall, H. (1984) Yugoslav Socialism in Theory and Practice, London: Oxford University Press.

McAdams, J.A. (1985) East Germany and Détente: Building Authority After the Wall, Cambridge: Cambridge University Press.

McCauley, M. (1983) The GDR Since 1945, London: Macmillan.

McCauley, M. (ed.) (1977) Communist Power in Europe 1944-1949, London: Macmillan.

McFarlane, B. (1988) Marxist Regimes: Yugoslavia - Politics, Economics, Society, London: Pinter.

McGregor, D.A. (1989) The Soviet-East German Military Alliance, Cambridge: Cambridge University Press.

McIntyre, R.J. (1988) Bulgaria, London: Frances Pinter.

Mackenzie, A. (1983) Romanian Journey, London: Hale.

Markham, R-H. (1949) Rumania Under the Soviet Yoke, Boston, Mass.: Meador.

Marmallaku, R. (1975) Albania and the Albanians, London: Hurst.

Mastny, V. (1987) Soviet-East European Survey 1986-1987, Boulder, Col.: Westview.

Matejko, A.J. (1986) Comparative Work Systems: Ideologies and Reality in Eastern Europe, New York: Praeger.

Matley, I.M. (1970) Romania: A Profile, London: Pall Mall.

Mayer, P. and others (1953) The Jews in the Soviet Satellites, Syracuse: Syracuse University Press.

Meinecke, F. (1950) The German Catastrophe, Cambridge,

Mass.: Harvard University Press.

Mellor, R.E.H. (1975) Eastern Europe: A Geography of the Comecon Countries, London: Macmillan.

---- (1978) The Two Germanies: A Modern Geography, London: Harper & Row.

Menderhausen, H. (1955) The Postwar Recoveries in the German Economy, Amsterdam: North Holland Publishing Company.

Mihailovic, K. (1972) Regional Development: Experiences and Prospects in Eastern Europe, The Hague: Mouton.

Mikolajczyk, S. (1948) The Rape of Poland: Pattern of Soviet Aggression, New York: Whittlesey House.

Montias, J.M. (1962) Central Planning in Poland, New Haven, Conn.: Yale University Press.

---- (1967) Economic Development in Communist Rumania, Cambridge, Mass.: MIT Press.

Moodie, A.E.F. (1945) The Italo-Yugoslav Boundary, London: Philip.

Moore, J.H. (1980) Growth with Self-Management: Yugoslav Industrialization 1952-1975, Stanford, Calif.: Hoover Institution Press.

Moreton, E. (1987) Germany between East and West, Cambridge: Cambridge University Press.

Myant, M. (1989) The Czechoslovak Economy 1948-1988: The Battle for Economic Reform, Cambridge: Cambridge University Press.

Narkiewicz, O.A. (1981) Marxism and the Reality of Power 1919-1980, London: Croom Helm.

---- (1986) Eastern Europe 1968-1984, London: Croom Helm.

Nelson, D.J. (1978) Wartime Origins of the Berlin Dilemma, University of Alabama Press.

Nelson, D.N. (1980) Democratic Centralism in Romania, Boulder, Col.: East European Monographs.

---- (1986) Alliance Behaviour in the Warsaw Pact, Boulder, Col.: Westview.

Nelson, D.N. (ed.) (1981) Romania in the 1980s, Boulder, Col.: Westview.

---- (1983) Communism and the Politics of Inequality, Lexington, Mass.: Lexington Books.

---- (1984) Soviet Allies: The Warsaw Pact and the Issue of Reliability, Boulder, Col.: Westview.

Osborne, R.H. (1967) East Central Europe, London: Chatto & Windus.

Overy, R. (1982) The German Economic Recovery, London:

Macmillan.

Pano, N.C. (1968) The People's Republic of Albania, Baltimore: Johns Hopkins University Press.

---- (1986) Albania, London: Frances Pinter.

Paul, D.W. (1981) Czechoslovakia: Profile of a Socialist Republic at the Crossroads of Europe, Boulder, Col.: Westview.

Pavlowitch, S.K. (1971) Yugoslavia, London: Benn.

---- (1988) The Improbable Survivor: Yugoslavia and its Problems 1918-1988, London: Hurst.

Pecsi, M. (ed.) (1964) Applied Geography in Hungary, Budapest: Hungarian Academy of Sciences.

Pecsi, M. and Sarfalvi, B. (1964) The Geography of Hungary, London: Collets.

Phillips, A.L. (1975) Soviet Policy Towards East Germany Reconsidered: The Postwar Decade, London: Greenwood.

---- (1986) Soviet Policy Towards East Germany Reconsidered: The Post-war Decade, London: Greenwood Press.

Plock, E.D. (1985) The Basic Treaty and the Evolution of East-West German Relations, Boulder, Col.: Westview.

Ploss, S.I. (1986) Moscow and the Polish Crises: An Interpretation of Soviet Policies and Intentions, Boulder, Col.: Westview.

Polonsky, A. and Drukier, B. (1980) The Beginning of Communist Rule in Poland, London: Routledge & Kegan Paul.

Portes, R. (1981) The Polish Crisis: Western Economic Policy Options, London: Routledge.

Pounds, N.J.G. (1964) Poland Between East and West, Princeton, NJ: Princeton University Press.

---- (1969) Eastern Europe, London: Longman.

---- and Spulber, N. (1957) Resources and Planning in Eastern Europe, Bloomington: Indiana University Press.

Prifti, P.R. (1978) Socialist Albania Since 1944: Domestic and Foreign Developments, Cambridge, Mass.: MIT Press.

Rachwald, A.R. (1983) Poland Between the Superpowers: Security Versus Economic Recovery, Boulder, Col.: Westview.

Radulovic, M. (1948) Tito's Republic, London: Coldharbour Press.

Raina, P. (1981) Independent Social Movements in Poland, London: London School of Economics.

Rakowska-Harmstone, T. and Gyorgy, A. (eds) (1979) Communism in Eastern Europe, Bloomington: Indiana University Press.

Ramet, P. (ed.) (1985) Yugoslavia in the 1980s, Boulder, Col.: Westview.

Reti, T. (1988) Soviet Economic Impact on Czechoslovakia and Romania in the Early Postwar Period 1944-56, Washington, DC: Wilson Center, Smithsonian Institution.

Richet, X. (1989) The Hungarian Model: Planning and the Market in a Socialist Economy, Cambridge: Cambridge University Press.

Ritter, G. (1965) The German Problem, Columbus: Ohio State University Press.

Robinson, W.F. (1973) The Pattern of Reform in Hungary, New York: Praeger.

Rugg, D.S. (1985) The World's Landscapes: Eastern Europe, London: Longman.

Rupnik, J. (1986) Czechoslovakia, London: Frances Pinter.

Sanford, G. (1983) Poland: Communism in Crisis, London: Croom Helm.

---- (1986) Military Rule in Poland: The Rebuilding of Communist Power 1981-1983, London: Croom Helm.

Sarfalvi, B. (ed.) (1970) Recent Population Movements in East European Countries, Budapest: Hungarian Academy of Sciences.

---- (1971) The Changing Face of the Great Hungarian Plain, Budapest: Hungarian Academy of Sciences.

Scharf, B. (1984) Politics and Change in East Germany: An Evaluation of Socialist Democracy, London: Frances Pinter.

Schoenberg, H.W. (1970) Germans from the East: A Study of Their Migration Resettlement and Subsequent Group History Since 1945, The Hague: Nijhoff.

Schopflin, G. (ed.) (1970) The Soviet Union and Eastern Europe: A Handbook, London: Blond.

Schwarze, H.W. (1970) The GDR Today: Life in the Other Germany, London: Wolff.

---- (1973) Eastern Europe in the Soviet Shadow, New York: Day.

Shafir, M. (1985) Romania: Politics, Economics and Society, London: Frances Pinter.

Sharman, T. (1988) Poland, London: Columbus Books.

Short, D. (1986) World Bibliographical Series: Czechoslovakia, Oxford: Clio.

Silnitsky, F. and others (1979) Communism in Eastern Europe, Brighton: Harvester Press.

Simecka, M. (1984) The Restoration of Order: The Normalization of Czechoslovakia, London: Verso.

Simmonds, G.D. (ed.) (1977) The USSR and Eastern Europe in the Era of Brezhnev and Kosygin, Detroit: University of Detroit Press.

Simon, J. and Gilberg, T. (eds) (1985) Security Implications of Nationalism in Eastern Europe, Boulder, Col.: Westview.

Sinanian, S. and others (eds) (1972) Eastern Europe in the 1970s, New York: Praeger.

Singleton, F.B. (1970) Yugoslavia: The Country and its People, London: Queen Anne Press.

---- (ed.) (1987) Environmental Problems in the Soviet Union and Eastern Europe, London: Lynne Rienner.

---- and Carter, B. (1982) The Economy of Yugoslavia, London: Croom Helm.

Sirc, L. (1969) Economic Devolution in Eastern Europe, London: Longman.

Skendi, S. (1958) East Central Europe Under the Communists: Albania, New York: Praeger.

Skilling, H.G. (1976) Czechoslovakia's Interrupted Revolution, Princeton, NJ: Princeton University Press.

Smith, A.H. (1983) The Planned Economies of Eastern Europe, London: Croom Helm.

Snyder, L. (1952) German Nationalism: The Tragedy of a People, Harrisburg, Pa.: Stackpole.

Spigler, I. (1973) Economic Reform in Rumanian Industry, Oxford: Oxford University Press.

Spulber, N. (1957) The Economics of Communist Eastern Europe, Cambridge, Mass.: MIT Press.

Staar, R.F. (1962) Poland 1944-1962: The Sovietisation of a Captive People, Baton Rouge: Louisiana State University Press.

---- (1967) The Communist Regimes of Eastern Europe, Stanford, Calif.: Hoover Institution Press.

Steion, S. (1982) The Poles, London: Collins.

Stevens, J.N. (1985) Czechoslovakia at the Crossroads: The Economic Dilemmas of Communism in Post-War Czechoslovakia, Boulder, Col.: East European Monographs.

Stolper, W. (1960) The Structure of the East German Economy, Cambridge, Mass.: MIT Press.

Sugar, P.F. (ed.) (1980) Ethnic Diversity and Conflict in

Eastern Europe, Santa Barbara, Calif.: ABC Clio.

Sugar, P.F. and Lederer, I.V. (eds) (1969) Nationalism in Eastern Europe, Seattle: University of Washington Press.

Sugar, P. and others (1988) The Problems of Nationalism in Eastern Europe Past and Present, Washington, DC: Wilson Center, Smithsonian Institution.

Syrop, K. (1982) Poland in Perspective, London: Hale.

Szczypiorski, A. (1981) The Polish Ordeal: The View from Within, London: Routledge.

Szymanski, A. (1984) Class Struggle in Socialist Poland, New York: Praeger.

Tamke, J. (1983) The People's Republics of Eastern Europe, London: Croom Helm.

Taras, R. (1986) Poland: Socialist State Rebellious Nation, Boulder, Col.: Westview.

Teichova, A. (1988) The Czechoslovak Economy 1918-1980, London: Routledge.

Terry, S.M. (ed.) (1984) Soviet Policy in Eastern Europe, New Haven, Conn.: Yale University Press.

Tismaneanu, V. (1988) The Crisis of Marxist Ideology in Eastern Europe: The Poverty of Utopia, London: Routledge.

Toma, P. (ed.) (1970) The Changing Face of Communism in Eastern Europe, Tucson: University of Arizona Press.

Touraine, A. (1983) Solidarity: The Analysis of a Social Movement - Poland 1980-1981, Cambridge: Cambridge University Press.

Trebici, V. (1976) Romania's Population and Demographic Trends, Bucharest: Meridiane.

Triska, J.F. (1969) Communist Party States: Comparative and International Studies, Indianapolis, Ind.: Bobbs Merrill.

---- and Cocks, P.M. (eds) (1977) Political Development in Eastern Europe, New York: Praeger.

Tsantis, A. and Pepper, R. (1979) Romania: The Industrialization of an Agrarian Economy under Socialist Planning, Washington, DC: World Bank.

Turner, R.A. (1987) The Two Germanies since 1945, New Haven, Conn.: Yale.

Turnock, D. (1974) An Economic Geography of Romania, London: Bell.

---- (1978) Studies in Industrial Geography: Eastern Europe, Folkestone: Dawson.

---- (1986) The Romanian Economy in the Twentieth

Century, London: Croom Helm.
---- (1988) The Historical Geography of Eastern Europe, London: Routledge (2 vols).
Vale, M. (ed.) (1981) Poland: The State of the Republic, London: Pluto Press.
Vali, F. (1961) Rift and Revolt in Hungary, Cambridge, Mass: Harvard University Press.
Vanek, J. (1972) The Economics of Workers' Management: A Yugoslav Case Study, London: George Allen & Unwin.
Van Ness, P. (ed.) (1988) Market Reform in Socialist Societies, London: Lynne Rienner.
Vine, R.D. (ed.) (1987) Soviet-East European Reforms as a Problem for Western Policy, London: Croom Helm.
Volgyes, I. (1981) Hungary: A Profile, Boulder, Col.: Westview.
---- (1982) Hungary: A Nation of Contradictions, Boulder, Col.: Westview.
Volgyes, I. (ed.) (1978) Soviet Deviance in Eastern Europe, Boulder, Col.: Westview.
Wachtel, H.M. (1973) Workers' Management and Workers' Wages in Yugoslavia: The Theory and Practice of Participatory Socialism, Ithaca, NY: Cornell University Press.
Wagner, W. (1957) The Genesis of the Oder-Neisse Line: A Study in the Diplomatic Negotiations of World War Two, Stuttgart: Brentano.
Wallace, I. (1987) World Bibliographical Series: East Germany, Oxford: Clio.
Wallace, W.W. (1977) Czechoslovakia, London: Benn.
Wanklyn, H.G. (1954) Czechoslovakia: A Geographical and Historical Study, London: Philip.
Wanless, P.T. (1985) Taxation in Centrally Planned Economies, London: Croom Helm.
Wedel, J. (1986) The Private Poland: An Anthropologist's Look at Everyday Life, New York: Facts on File Publications.
Weiner, R. (1984) Romanian Foreign Policy and the United Nations, New York: Praeger.
Welsh, W.A. (1988) Bulgaria, Boulder, Col.: Westview.
Welsh, W.A. (ed.) (1981) Survey Research and Public Attitudes in Eastern Europe and the Soviet Union, New York: Pergamon.
Wilczynski, J. (1972) Socialist Economic Development and Reform, London: Macmillan.
Wilkinson, H.R. (1951) A Review of the Ethnographic

Cartography of Macedonia, Liverpool: Liverpool University Press.

Wiskemann, F. (1956) Czechs and Germans: Problems Relating to the Oder-Neisse Line and the Czech Frontier Region, Oxford: Oxford University Press.

Wolfe, T.W. (1970) Soviet Power and Europe 1945-1970, Baltimore: Johns Hopkins University Press.

Wolff, R.L. (1974) The Balkans in our Time, Cambridge, Mass.: Harvard University Press.

Woodall, J. (ed.) (1982) Policy and Politics in Contemporary Poland, London: Frances Pinter.

Woodward, S. (1987) Yugoslavia, London: Frances Pinter.

Yergin, A.S. (1980) East-West Technology Transfer: European Perspectives, Beverly Hills: Sage Publications.

Zauberman, A. (1964) Industrial Progress in Poland, Czechoslovakia and East Germany 1937-1962, Oxford: Oxford University Press.

Zielinski, J.G. (1973) Economic Reform in Polish Industry, Oxford: Oxford University Press.

Zonoviev, A. (1984) The Reality of Communism, London: Gollancz.

INDEX